Fundamentals of
Patent Drafting

Written and compiled
by Paul Cole

Papers by:
E.W.E Micklethwait
M.J. Daley
R.P. Hickman and M.J. Roos

[signature]

JA Kemp, London
November 2012

CIPA
The Chartered Institute of Patent Attorneys

2006

Published and placed on sale by:

The Chartered Institute of Patent Attorneys
95 Chancery Lane
London WC2A 1DT

Tel: 020 7405 9450
Fax: 020 7430 0471
Website: www.cipa.org.uk

© 2006 The Chartered Institute of Patent Attorneys

Printed and bound by: Latimer Trend & Company Ltd, Plymouth

First printed in July 2006. Reprinted in October 2006

ISBN: 0 903932 23 7

Fundamentals of Patent Drafting

CONTENTS

CHEMICAL DRAFTING SKILLS

XIV – Empirical research inventions – allowable generic claim scope

XV – Can "Reach-through" claims be enforced? The US Federal Court decision in *University of Rochester v G. D. Searle & Co., Inc et al.*

SUCCESSFUL INVENTIONS

XVI – WORKMATE – Ronald P. Hickman (inventor) and Michael J. Roos (patent agent)

XVII – The Anywayup Cup

Preface

From the very beginning of the patents systems operated by Governments around the world, there has been a requirement for a written description to be provided showing how to put the invention into practice.

From the early days of the patent attorney profession in the UK, skilled engineers were used by many entrepreneurs and inventors to help them put their inventions into practice and became adept at understanding the vagaries of the patents system and of obtaining grant of Letters Patent from the authorities. In time these skilled engineers also became adept at describing, in words and pictures how to put an invention into practice and the profession of patent attorney (or formerly patent agent) was born.

Fundamental to the patent attorney is a knowledge of drafting, skilful construction and framing of a patent specification which will stand up to the rigours of time, close examination by other attorneys and the courts of the land, and initially at least, to scrutiny by patent examiners in this and other countries.

UK patent attorneys have always been renowned for their ability to draft forthright and accurate specifications and to frame claims defining the protected area while excluding the non-protectable area. Drafting a specification which is sufficient to support the claims while avoiding the impractical or indeed overdosing the word count is a skill much appreciated by clients and colleagues alike.

Consider the major problem facing us – the claims bring together three unlikely companions: plain language, technology and the law. Technology in this day and age moves extremely fast, the law changes with almost equal speed and yet the basic tool of the patent attorney remains the same – the language and the skill to put it together.

In this book, Paul Cole, with the assistance of colleagues within our profession has collected together some of the best-known published papers on patent drafting and interpretation and on the experience of UK inventors, and has combined them with much additional material. The resulting book should provide students and qualified practitioners with a guide which will serve us well in our ambitions to be better draftsmen of patent specifications which complete the bargain of teaching an invention in exchange for a monopoly granted by the state. Thus whichever country's laws under which you are practising and whichever date of Patents Act you are currently running with, the fundamental skill of *drafting* which underpins our professional reputation can only be enhanced by the lessons taught herein.

The Chartered Institute of Patent Attorneys is grateful to Paul Cole and his colleagues and to the families of Eric Micklethwait and Michael Daley for their permission to republish their historic papers here. It is proud to publish and commend this work for the benefit of present and future patent attorneys throughout the world.

Dave Bradley
Chairman, Textbooks and Publications Committee
The Chartered Institute of Patent Attorneys
June 2006.

About this book

The papers collected here bring together advice on patent drafting from authors spanning three generations of patent attorneys, and it is hoped that they will be helpful to students preparing for the CIPA finals examinations and the EPO qualifying examinations, as well as to the profession in general.

Although a number of legal concepts relevant to specification drafting are introduced, general background knowledge of patent law is assumed. A reasonable command of language is also assumed. Many textbooks on drafting focus on language problems, but in the author's view selection of language is not at the root of the difficulties that students face. The meaning of *consisting of*, *comprising*, *at least one*, and similar expressions commonly found in claims is available in dictionaries and is rapidly learned during daily work. What has received less attention in the past are the principles of systematic technical analysis which enable the concepts to be developed which are then expressed in words in the description and claims. When an effective technical analysis has been made and a draftsman knows and clearly understands the subject-matter that needs to be described and claimed, the selection of appropriate words becomes relatively easy and in any event is a matter of reading and practice.

The first paper provides a brief introduction to the patent system. It uses as a starting point the submission of a manuscript to a peer-reviewed scientific journal and introduces concepts of novelty, inventive step, qualifying subject-matter, enablement and utility which are considered in more detail in subsequent papers that appear in the LEGAL BACKGROUND section. A following paper deals with the interpretation of claims in view of the importance of that topic, especially in the US under the so-called *Markman* practice. Functional claim language creates particular problems in the US and many European practitioners are insufficiently aware of the profound differences in the treatment of means-plus-function or step-plus-function claim language in the US and Europe and of the implications of those differences. The LEGAL BACKGROUND section therefore concludes with a paper considering functional claims. Readers should bear in mind that the purpose of these papers is *not* to give a comprehensive guide to the law, which is more fully explained in already available textbooks, but to introduce the fundamental principles and to explain the kinds of problem that can arise when specifications are examined by patent offices or attempted to be enforced through the courts.

Classic papers by Micklethwait and Daley make up the next section entitled DRAFTING SKILLS – HISTORIC PAPERS, and it is hoped that these will be readily understood by students even at the beginning of their professional training. Drafting is an iterative process requiring repeated checking, as Micklethwait points out: it would be wonderful if we could devise automatic checking software for our patent specifications comparable to the pneumatic checking machine that he describes. Attention is particularly drawn to Mr Micklethwait's checklist at pages 167-168.

A further section entitled DRAFTING SKILLS – MORE DETAILED PAPERS contains papers aiming at developing algorithmic drafting skills and includes papers on the definition of technical field, the background section, definition of the invention, and a case study based on the *Windsurfer* invention which though in an apparently simple field of technology highlights problems that are encountered with depressing frequency covering specifications in a surprising diversity of technologies. The paper ends with a further checklist (page 245) summarizing as bullet points some of the issues previously discussed. Readers should realize that with rapid developments in law and in technology such checklists should not be static: they should be used as starting points for development of a personal checklist that serves a student or practicing attorney in his working environment and should be continuously updated.

Professional examinations generally concentrate on drafting skills related to the mechanical arts, but a CHEMICAL SKILLS section has been included that contains papers on inventions resulting from empirical research and on reach-through claims as considered by the US courts in the *University of Rochester* case.

Inventors' experiences of the patent system are of relevance. Therefore a final SUCCESSFUL INVENTIONS section includes papers describing the *Hickman* and *Haberman* inventions, *Hickman* being a classic paper marking the centenary of the Chartered Institute.

The most dangerous journey any invention makes is from the brain of the inventor to his mouth, pen or keyboard. Much insight can be gained by regarding a patent specification as the answer to an examination paper with the importance and formality of a university finals paper and containing just two questions: firstly describe your invention in its several known or predictable embodiments in sufficient detail that it can be understood and reproduced by others, and secondly provide definitions of your invention both in its broadest and in its preferred and more specific aspects. As teachers know, parents routinely complain that their children had learned the syllabus but somehow failed to get their knowledge into their examination answer and therefore did not get the marks that they deserved. Many of the more controversial patent cases that have been litigated are similar: the inventor had the necessary knowledge, but somehow his knowledge did not find its way into the specification and as a result the patent could not be enforced because it was invalid or not infringed. The most positive thing that we can do to minimize the risk when we encounter something we do not understand is to have the confidence to say: "Could we just stop and go over this point again?" Sometimes the technical facts stated by the inventor are wrong and need correction. On other occasions the technical facts are correct, but have been explained incompletely or in a way that does not effectively convey the facts to the reader. In either case, lack of understanding is a signal that something is wrong and needs to be further investigated.

Our specifications are aimed not just at the skilled scientist or engineer but also at managers, patent office examiners and judges, and we need to be able to present the invention to this wider readership. It is hoped that the papers collected here will provide the tools needed.

In accordance with current educational practice, many of the papers in this volume are prefaced by a *coverage* section briefly indicating the contents of the paper, which is followed by an *outcome statement* indicating the skills and knowledge that readers should have gained, or started to gain, by reading the paper and studying the key materials specified. It will be noted that many of the footnotes refer to cases of particular importance or educational value, identified as **required reading** and students should aim to read all of the references in this category and as many as possible of the others.

Students will note that much US case law is included as well as case law of the UK Patent Office and courts and the EPO Appeal Boards, and may be tempted to ask why it is necessary to study so much US law if they are working in the UK or Europe. One answer is that much US case law is interesting and instructive in its own right, and even if the case is not citable in the UK or at the EPO as persuasive authority, it may include arguments that can be adopted and presented in Europe. A second reason is that many of the cases we first file in the UK or Europe will in due course have US counterparts, and if we draft in ignorance of US legal requirements we may make damaging mistakes or omissions. A third reason is that many of us represent US clients or clients from countries such as Japan where practitioners are on the whole more familiar with the US patent system than those in Europe. In order to give effective advice, we need to be aware of the issues that our non-European colleagues face in their daily work and the sensitivities that arise from the decisions of the US courts, especially concerning issues of claim construction and file-wrapper estoppel.

Students will also note that at a number of points in this book, litigation is considered from an "accident investigation" standpoint, e.g. in the discussion of the *Windsurfer* patent. The intention is to highlight shortcomings in documents, not people, and the observations made are with hindsight of litigation and of its outcome. However, explanation of effective drafting is facilitated by the identification of mistakes discernible from published court decisions – we learn from mistakes and it is less painful to learn from the past mistakes of others than from future mistakes of our own. In a sense nearly every patent that is litigated is the result of an error in drafting because the granted specification contains shortcomings that create sufficient doubt to justify litigation. Whenever litigation takes place, our objectives as patent drafters should be to review the judgment not just in order to learn the principles of law that it teaches but also to find out what went wrong with the drafting of this patent that triggered the ensuing litigation and how can we adjust our practice to avoid this kind of problem in the future. As reflective practitioners we know we cannot achieve perfection in the patents that we draft, but adoption of a structured approach to drafting based on the lessons of past case law and with the objective of a steady improvement in the quality of the specifications that we write is a realistic and achievable aim. The points raised in this book are *not* intended or believed to be of mere academic interest – they highlight ways in which important information can be missed and important legal requirements overlooked, and are therefore a survival guide.

Most of the materials referred to in this book, including statutes and case law are now available on-line. Opinions of the US Supreme Court since 1983 are available online from *FindLaw*,[1] and those of the Court of Appeal for the Federal Circuit are available from Georgetown Law Library.[2] Decisions of the EPO Appeal Boards are available from the website of the EPO.[3] Many UK High Court decisions are available from the BAILII website[4] and the UK Patent Office website[5] has databases of decisions of the Comptroller, the decisions being identified by British Library accession references. Very often the process of searching a specific database can be short-cut by simply typing the name of the case or in the case of an EPO decision the T or G number into a search engine such as Google.

Except where other authors are specifically attributed, the writer is the author of the papers in this book. Relevant decisions up to December 2005 have been taken into account, plus a few decisions in early 2006.

Thanks are due especially to Alan White, Tibor Gold and Paul Casbon, and also for helpful discussions and advice to Brian Lucas, Keith Beresford and Mr Yoshiyuki Osuga of Osuga & Associates. Further thanks should be given to the staff of the Chartered Institute of Patent Attorneys and especially Iain Ross and Nicola Diss for their help and encouragement in the preparation of the book. Thanks also to my wife Deirdre for reviewing and proofreading the book in draft and for her patience and support over many evenings and weekends when this book was being compiled and written.

Paul Cole
June 2006

---

1. www.findlaw.com/casecode/supreme.html

2. www.ll.georgetown.edu/federal/judicial/cafed.cfm

3. www.european-patent-office.org/index.en.php. Selecting the link "Search engines and site index" leads to a page with links to the EPO Boards of Appeal Decisions and also to the EPO Enlarged Board of Appeal decisions which are indexed separately.

4. www.bailii.org

5. www.patent.gov.uk/ Select Patents, then Patent Law and Legal Decisions and then either patent Legal Decisions or Patent Decisions – Case Summaries.

LEGAL BACKGROUND

Introduction

Coverage

The patent system is introduced by comparing the procedure for submission of scientific papers to peer-reviewed journals with the corresponding procedure under the provisions of the Patents Cooperation Treaty.

After you have read this paper, you should be aware of:

1. **The similarities between submitting a paper to a peer-reviewed journal and submitting an application to a Patent Office.**

2. **The principal requirements for patentability: novelty, inventive step, qualifying subject-matter and enabling disclosure and their similarities to corresponding requirements for publication in a peer-reviewed journal.**

3. **Credit given not to the inventor's knowledge but to the subject-matter that finds its way into the specification; there is a close analogy between an answer to an examination question and the disclosure in a patent specification.**

Scientific publications

Publication of a scientific work in a peer-reviewed journal closely resembles publication of an invention in a patent specification.

Learned societies, for example the American Physical Society, the American Institute of Physics and the American Chemical Society, act as publishing houses for peer-reviewed journals in which scientific results are reported. Authors are encouraged to submit papers to the editors of such journals, who have the responsibility and authority to accept or reject papers submitted to them, but normally act with the advice of one or more independent scientists acting as peer reviewers.

---

6. Mark Twain, *A Connecticut Yankee in King Arthur's Court*, first published in 1889.

Peer-reviewed journals usually conform to a system of scientific priority. The date when a manuscript was first received, together sometimes with dates of receipt of amended versions and/or the date of acceptance for publication often appear in the published paper.

Ethical guidelines govern the credited authorship of a paper. All those who have made significant scientific contribution to the work reported and who share responsibility and accountability for the results should be mentioned as authors.

Peer-reviewed journals are for the publication of new and original results.[7] An author is under an obligation to perform a literature search to find, and then cite earlier publications that describe closely related work. He should also cite those publications that have been influential in determining the nature of the reported work and that will guide the reader quickly to earlier work that is essential for understanding the results being reported. However, authors should minimize citation of earlier work that is not relevant to the results being reported and should keep review material to a minimum. The tasks of the reviewer include checking for novelty, drawing the attention of the author(s) to any observation, derivation or argument that has previously been reported, and supplying relevant citations in support of any objections raised.

Manuscripts are not published merely on the basis that what they report is novel. The research has to make a sufficiently significant contribution to justify publication in the journal in question.[8] For that purpose a reviewer of a manuscript is asked to judge objectively the quality of the manuscript, of the experimental and theoretical work reported, and of its interpretations and expositions with due regard for the maintenance of high scientific and literary standards.

In order to be acceptable, a scientific paper has to relate to subject-matter in which the journal in question specializes and in which its readers are likely to be interested.[9] For example the *Journal of Physics A: Mathematical and General*, published by the Institute of Physics, publishes mathematical papers only if they are clearly motivated by actual or potential application to physical phenomena. The editor would be unlikely to publish a paper, however meritorious, if it concerned pure mathematics and had no relevance to any physical phenomenon.

As regards contents, an author's central obligation is to present an accurate account of the research carried out as well as an objective discussion of its significance. Repetition of the experiments of others is an essential part of scientific research.[10] A research report

---

7. Compare the requirement for novelty in patent law: see the paper on *Novelty* beginning at page 9, and the further paper *The background section and the closest prior art* beginning at page 193.

8. Compare the requirement for inventive step in patent law: see the paper *Inventive step-recognizing invention* beginning at page 21.

9. Compare the requirement industrial applicability in patent law: see the paper *Qualifying subject-matter* beginning at page 39.

10. See "*Cargo—Cult Science*" in "*Surely You are Joking Mr Feynman*", Edward Hutchings (Ed.), Vintage, 1992 (This paper, insofar as it explains and emphasises scientific integrity and the need for repeatable experiments, is **required reading**).

should therefore contain sufficient detail and reference to public sources of information to permit the author's peers to repeat the work.[11] Papers that describe proposed experiments are considered as falling into a special category. For such papers to be acceptable, the experiments must be demonstrated to be novel and feasible, and the author must show that their proposal is likely to stimulate research that might not otherwise be undertaken. Fabrication of data or selective reporting of data with the intent to mislead or deceive is "an egregious departure" from the expected norms of scientific conduct, as is the theft of data or research results from others.

The patent system

Granted patents give legal rights in claimed inventions, and it is not surprising that the "publishing houses" which receive and examine patent applications, and publish specifications of pending applications and granted patents are government organizations.

Until recently patent applications were received and patents were granted only under the domestic laws of nation states. Patent offices were established by the governments of individual countries, and patents in countries of interest could only be obtained by application for a national patent to the patent office of the country required, together with submission of a patent specification in an official language of that country.

As an example of a national patent office, the US Patent and Trademark Office (USPTO) was established in its current form in 1836. The UK Patent Office was established by the *Patent Law Amendment Act, 1852.* By the 1970s virtually every country in the world had a national patent office for receiving applications and granting patents, in some countries with a detailed examination as to technical merits, and in others with consideration of formal matters only.

Considerations of duplication and cost brought about the establishment of regional patent offices, of which the European Patent Office (1978) established under the EPC is perhaps the best known. It operates alongside the national patent systems of the EPC contracting states, e.g. UK, France, Germany and Italy, and provides an alternative route for receiving and examining patent applications and granting patents.

---

11. Compare the requirement for enablement in patent law: see the paper *Clarity, enablement and* utility beginning at page 79. As an example where necessary information is often withheld, peer-reviewed journals in the field of optics regularly publish articles by scientists working for micro-lithographic equipment manufacturers. Such articles report the ability to obtain closely spaced and finely resolved lines in optically sensitive films on the surface of semiconductor substrates. Such fine resolution is necessary for the production of semiconductor chips having increasingly fine features in accordance with Moore's Law. The articles are routinely accompanied by micrographs that enable the reader to see the quality of the optical resolution that has been achieved. But almost nothing is said about the equipment used, which remains a closely-guarded trade secret, so that peer-repetition of the original experiment is impossible. It is submitted that such articles are mere advertisements posing as scientific papers and make little real contribution to human knowledge.

An international patent filing system was established by the *Patents Cooperation Treaty* (PCT), administered by the World Intellectual Property Organization (WIPO) established in 1970 and since 1974 a specialized agency of the United Nations. It provides a framework for internationally filing and searching patent applications and for conducting a preliminary examination thereof. However, after the so-called "International Phase" ends at 30 months from the filing or earliest priority date, the application has to be brought into effect in the desired national or regional patent offices which have the power of grant or refusal.

Like peer-reviewed papers, patents are subject to a system of priority, which has to be applied even more strictly than in the case of peer-reviewed papers since patents give positive legal rights that are enforceable against third parties. In the simplest case, a national or regional application has only its date of filing, in which case novelty and inventive step are considered having regard to the state of the art as it existed before that date. But where there has been a prior national or regional application not more than 12 months before the date of filing, the applicant can claim priority under the Paris Convention, a further treaty administered by WIPO. The effect of claiming priority is that for most situations the filing date of the priority application can count as the filing date of a subsequent national or regional application. Within the first 12 months an applicant can file abroad for the invention he disclosed in his first filed application and is entitled to his original filing date. The importance of the priority system is that it enables an applicant to establish priority for what he has invented by a single filing in a single Paris Convention contracting state, and then file elsewhere in an orderly manner provided that he does so within the 12-month priority period.

Like editors of peer-reviewed journals, many patent offices including the USPTO, the EPO, the Chinese and Japanese Patent Offices and the authorities designated by WIPO for International applications[12] study applications submitted to them and decide whether they qualify for grant. Instead of the part-time reviewers used by peer-reviewed journals, such patent offices have a legally and scientifically trained examining staff who work full time and whose members consider and report on the merits of the patent applications received, the applicant having opportunities to respond to objections raised by examiners until either the application reaches a form where it is grantable or the possibilities for amendment and argument have been exhausted and the application must be refused.

In order to explain how most examining patent offices operate, we may use the PCT as a model since its provisions represent the highest common factor amongst the patent laws of most countries and regions.

International (PCT) applications are required to contain an application form (request), a description, one or more claims, drawings if required, and an abstract.

Echoing the requirement for peer-reviewed papers that what is described should be repeatable, the description of a patent application is required to disclose the

---

12. Called the *International Search Authority* and the *International Preliminary Examining Authority*; in practice these are national or regional patent offices approved by WIPO.

invention in a manner that is sufficiently clear and complete that the invention can be carried out by a person skilled in the art,[13] and is required to be accompanied by drawings when these are necessary for understanding the invention.

According to the *PCT Regulations*, it shall first state the title of the invention and shall:

(1) Specify the technical field to which the invention relates.[14]

(2) Indicate the background art which, as far as known to the applicant, can be regarded as useful for the understanding, searching and examination of the invention, and, preferably, cite the documents reflecting such art.[15]

(3) Disclose the invention, as claimed, in such terms that the technical problem (even if not expressly stated as such) and its solution can be understood, and state the advantageous effects, if any, of the invention with reference to the background art.

(4) Briefly describe the figures in the drawings, if any.

(5) Set forth at lest one mode for carrying out the invention claimed. This shall be done in terms of examples, where appropriate, and with reference to the drawings, if any. Where required by law, the disclosed mode(s) shall include the best mode contemplated by the applicant.[16]

(6) Indicate explicitly, when it is not obvious from the description or nature of the invention, the way in which the invention is capable of exploitation in industry and the way in which it can be made and used, or, if it can only be used, the way in which it can be used. The term "industry" is to be understood in its broadest sense as in the *Paris Convention for the Protection of Industrial Property*.

Fabrication or misreporting of data or representing experiments as having been conducted when in truth this has not happened are no less misconduct in a patent specification. In the US, representing an experiment as having been carried out when this is not the case amounts to "inequitable conduct", making the resulting patent unenforceable.[17] Examples that have been carried out may be written in the past tense. Predictive examples are permissible but *must* be written in the present or future tense. If there is litigation and the issue is raised, the original research records will be required to be produced, and the true position will become apparent. Failure

---

13. See the above-mentioned paper entitled *Clarity, enablement and utility* beginning at page 79.

14. See the paper entitled *Technical field* beginning at page 185.

15. See the paper entitled *The Background section and the closest prior art beginning at page 193.*

16. Best mode is a requirement of US law but is not a requirement in the UK, Europe or most other countries. Since many of the applications we draft in Europe will eventually have US counterparts, asking about best mode and including the best mode in the specification should be routine irrespective of the country of origin of the invention.

17. For a recent example, see *Euroceltique S.A. v Endo-Pharmaceuticals Inc.,* Fed Cir., 1 Feb 2006, where the patentees had alleged that they had produced a controlled release formulation for the compound oxycodone which controlled pain in 90% of patients using a relatively narrow dosage range, whereas in truth this was an insight based on differences between oxycodone and other opioids, and had not been established by clinical tests. The test for inequitable conduct required a material misrepresentation coupled with intent and the Federal Circuit remitted the case to the District Court for consideration of evidence of intent based on a finding that there had been misrepresentation, but at a low level of materiality.

to abide by this rule is therefore eventually discoverable by third parties and may have disastrous consequences.

Claims are required to be clear and concise and to define the subject-matter for which protection is sought. According to the *PCT Regulations*, the definition of the matter for which protection is sought should be in terms of the technical features of the invention. Whenever appropriate, claims should contain:

(i) a statement indicating those technical features of the invention which are necessary for the definition of the claimed subject-matter but which, in combination, are part of the prior art, and

(ii) a characterizing portion – "the improvement comprises", or any other words to the same effect – stating concisely the technical features which, in combination with the features stated under (i), it is desired to protect.

The *PCT Regulations* also provide for dependent claims which are construed as including all the limitations contained in the claim to which they refer or, if the dependent claims are multiple dependent claims, all the limitations contained in the particular claims in relation to which they are considered. The Regulations also provide that dependent claims should be grouped together.

The application is subject to a search by an *International Searching Authority* – e.g. the US Patent Office, the European Patent Office, or the Chinese or Japanese patent offices – who are required to discover as much of the relevant prior art as their facilities permit. The International Searching Authority may additionally decide that subject-matter contained in the application does not qualify for a search or that the application relates to more than one invention, in which case the applicant may be asked to pay additional search fees. The application is then published promptly after the expiration of 18 months from the earliest priority date and it and the search report are transmitted to the "designated" national or regional patent offices.

An international search is made on the basis of the claims, with due regard to the description and the drawings (if any) and with particular emphasis on the inventive concept towards which the claims are directed. In so far as possible and reasonable, it covers the entire subject-matter to which the claims are directed or to which they might reasonably be expected to be directed after they have been amended. The minimum documentation that has to be searched is defined by PCT Rule 34 and includes the published patents of the US and most other major countries.

Everything that has been made available to the public anywhere in the world by means of written disclosure (including drawings and other illustrations) and that can be of assistance in determining whether or not the claimed invention is new and whether or not it involves an inventive step (i.e., that it is or is not obvious) is relevant prior art as defined in the *PCT regulations*, provided that the making available to the public occurred prior to the international filing date. When any written disclosure refers to an oral disclosure, use, exhibition, or other means by which the contents of the written disclosure were made available to the public, and such making available to the public occurred on a date prior to the international filing date, the international search report is required to mention separately that fact and the date on which it occurred, although in practice this is rare. Furthermore, the international search report is required to mention any published application or any patent whose publication date is the same as, or later than, but whose filing date, or, where applicable, claimed priority date, is earlier than the international filing date of the international application searched, and which would constitute relevant prior art for the purposes of *Article 15(2)* had it been published prior to the international filing date.

According to *PCT Rule 43bis* at the same time as the International Searching Authority issues its search report, it must issue a written opinion as to whether the claimed invention appears to be *novel*, to involve an *inventive step* and to *be industrially applicable*. If dissatisfied with the contents of that written opinion, the applicant may respond to that opinion by amendment of the description, claims and drawings provided that such amendments do not go beyond what had been disclosed in the international application as filed. He may then apply for international preliminary examination, the objective of which is to formulate a preliminary and non-binding opinion as to novelty, inventive step and industrially applicability. Thereafter an International Preliminary Examination Report is established stating in relation to each claim whether the criteria of novelty, inventive step and industrial applicability are satisfied, and that report is transmitted to the "elected" national or regional patent offices. The International Preliminary Examining Authority may also consider whether the application relates to more than one invention.

The law governing the granting of patents by national or regional patent offices coincides with or approximates to the provisions of the PCT as regards the core requirements of novelty, inventive step, qualifying subject-matter and enablement (with significant additional requirements in the US for "written description" and utility), and details of national or regional procedure, except so far as are relevant to patent drafting, are outside the scope of this book. The powers of a patent office include:

1. Document receipt, processing and publication.

2. Novelty searching.

3. Examination for patentability.

4. Grant or refusal.

The search and examination authorities working under the PCT have the first three of these powers. However, subject to any provisions for appeal, only national or regional patent offices have the power of grant or refusal.

Novelty

" ... there could never again be a beginning "[18]

Coverage

This paper provides a brief introduction to the laws of novelty in the UK, the US and under the EPC.

Early in your career, you will mainly be concerned with drafting and prosecution, where the prior art that you are likely to have to consider takes the form of earlier published patent specifications, journal articles, and other documents found in a pre-filing search or cited by an examiner during prosecution. The date of publication of such documents and their availability are almost always beyond serious dispute. An overwhelming majority of the disclosures which patent attorneys have to consider during their professional career fall within this category.

A main concern of this paper is therefore to explain the legal tests that apply to the interpretation of such documents.

Ability to justify selection of a species within a known genus is important, especially for chemical, biotechnological and medical inventions, and this topic is briefly considered.

You will less frequently have to consider other forms of disclosure, e.g. oral disclosure, disclosure at an exhibition or prior use, especially when you start to work on EPO opposition proceedings and or proceedings before a court for enforcing or declaring invalid a granted patent. Main points to be considered when dealing with these more difficult forms of disclosure are briefly outlined.

After studying this paper and the "must read" materials you should:

1. Understand the structured sequence of enquiries that have to be made when considering under UK law, the EPC and US law whether the disclosure of a document is potentially detrimental to the novelty of subsequently claimed subject-matter.

---

18. L. T. C. Rolt, *George and Robert Stephenson*, Penguin, 1960 at page 335 (quoting from an obituary of George Stephenson, pioneer of the steam locomotive).

2. Understand the "clear and unmistakeable directions" test of UK law and its counterparts under the EPC and under US patent law and be aware of the principle that what would infringe if later than the patent anticipates if earlier.

3. Be aware of special situations, e.g. selection inventions and inventions based on unexpected new uses.

4. Understand the importance of an accurate assessment of prior disclosures for the patent drafting and prosecution process.

Clear and unmistakeable directions – UK test

A number of decisions concerning the objection of lack of novelty handed down prior to the *Patents Act, 1977* remain of enduring significance in UK patent law.

The simplest situation is where an alleged anticipation is an earlier patent specification, journal article, textbook reference or other printed publication which has clearly been made available to the public prior to the priority or filing date of the application or patent in issue, and bears a date stamp or other marking that puts the date of publication beyond reasonable doubt. It is not necessary to prove that an alleged publication was actually read by any member of the public; merely that it can be inspected as of right by members of the public.[19] That situation is the most common in our profession because the official searches of patent offices are document-based.

An early, and much quoted, judgment concerning earlier publication in a printed document is that of Lord Westbury in *Hill v Evans*:[20]

> The question then is, what must be the nature of the antecedent statement? I apprehend that the principle is correctly thus expressed: the antecedent statement must be such that a person of ordinary knowledge of the subject would at once perceive, understand, and be able practically to apply the discovery without the necessity of making further experiments and gaining further information before the invention can be made useful. If something remains to be ascertained which is necessary for the useful application of the discovery, that affords sufficient room for another valid patent...
>
> The invention must be shewn to have been before made known. Whatever, therefore, is essential to the invention must be read out of the prior publication. If specific details are necessary for the practical working and real utility of the alleged invention, they must be found substantially in the prior publication. Apparent generality, or a proposition not true to its full extent, will not prejudice a subsequent statement which is limited and accurate, and gives a specific rule

19. *Patents Act, 1977*, s.130(1).
20. (1862) 4 De G F & J 288; 44 E.R. 1195

of practical application. The reason is manifest, because much further information, and therefore much further discovery, are required before the real truth can be extricated and embodied in a form to serve the use of mankind. It is the difference between the ore and the refined and pure metal which is extracted from it. Again, it is not, in my opinion, true in these cases to say, that knowledge, and the means of obtaining knowledge, are the same. There is a great difference between them. To carry me to the place at which I wish to arrive is very different from merely putting me on the road that leads to it. There may be a latent truth in the words of a former writer, not known even to the writer himself; and it would be unreasonable to say that there is no merit in discovering and unfolding it to the world. Upon principle, therefore, I conclude that the prior knowledge of an invention to avoid a patent must be knowledge equal to that required to be given by a specification, namely, such knowledge as will enable the public to perceive the very discovery and to carry the invention into practical use.

The subsequent case of *Flour Oxidising Co Ltd v Carr & Co Ltd*[21] concerned a claim for a process of conditioning flour by passing it *"through an atmosphere containing a gaseous oxide of nitrogen or chlorine or bromine oxidising agent in the gaseous or vapourised state."* Objection of anticipation was made based on two prior specifications: one for treating flour in a somewhat different atmosphere, the other for treating substances such as flour by *"subjecting the substances to be treated to the action of electricity whether in the form of rays from lamps, currents or sparks"*, and illustrating apparatus said to be appropriate for performing that operation. Parker J found that the apparatus illustrated in each of the prior specifications might be used for the purpose of treating flour by the method claimed in the patent in suit but that neither prior specification amounted to anticipation. He summarised his reasons as follows:

> But where the question is solely a question of prior publication, it is not, in my opinion, enough to prove that an apparatus described in an earlier Specification could have been used to produce this or that result. It must also be shown that the Specification contains clear and unmistakable directions so to use it.

The above reasoning was adopted and applied in *The General Tire & Rubber Co v The Firestone Tyre and Rubber Co Ltd*[22] which continues to be the leading authority on prior documentary publication and formed the basis of the test for lack of novelty written into the EPO Examination Guidelines. The principles were explained by the Court of Appeal as follows:

> If the earlier publication... discloses the same device as the device which the patentee by his claim, so construed, asserts that he has invented, the patentee's claim has been anticipated, but not otherwise... If the prior inventor's publication contains a clear description of, or clear instructions to do or make,

---

21. (1908) 25 RPC 428
22. [1972] RPC 457

something that would infringe the patentee's claim if carried out after the grant of the patentee's patent, the patentee's claim will have been shown to lack the necessary novelty, that is to say, it will have been anticipated... If, on the other hand, the prior publication contains a direction which is capable of being carried out in a manner which would infringe the patentee's claim, but would be at least as likely to be carried out in a way which would not do so, the patentee's claim will not have been anticipated, although it may fail on the ground of obviousness. To anticipate the patentee's claim the prior publication must contain clear and unmistakable directions to do what the patentee claims to have invented... A signpost, however clear, upon the road to the patentee's invention will not suffice. The prior inventor must be clearly shown to have planted his flag at the precise destination before the patentee.

The above criterion was further explained by the EPO Appeal Board in *High Tear Strength Polymers/UNION CARBIDE*[23] as follows:

It may be easy, given a knowledge of a later invention, to select from the general teachings of a prior art document certain conditions, and apply them to an example in that document, so as to produce an end result having all the features of the later claim. However, success in so doing does not prove that the result was inevitable. All that it demonstrates is that, given knowledge of the later invention, the earlier teaching is capable of being adapted to give the same result. Such an adaptation cannot be used to attack the novelty of a later patent.

The above decisions were recently reviewed by the Federal Court of Australia in *Bristol-Myers Squibb Co v F H Faulding & Co Ltd*[24] where the invention concerned a particular dose regime for administering the anti-cancer drug taxol without giving rise to adverse patient reactions. A number of publications were put forward as allegedly anticipating the claimed invention, but only one of them succeeded. In the context of finding a practical method of administering a drug which was difficult to administer on account of its low water-solubility and side-effects, what mattered was not merely what had been described but what had been taught in the sense of *directing, recommending or suggesting* the claimed method.

Enablement under UK patent law as a condition for lack of novelty

A further condition for a finding of lack of novelty is that the earlier disclosure must be enabling.[25] As recently explained by the House of Lords in *Synthon BV v Smithkline Beecham plc*[26] there is a distinction between what has been disclosed in a

23. T 0396/89; [1992] EPOR 312.
24. [2000]FCA 316 (22 March 2000) (This case is down-loadable from the Internet and is **required reading**). There was a parallel UK decision in *Bristol-Myers Squibb Co v Baker Norton Pharmaceuticals Inc*, [1999] RPC 253.
25. *Asahi Kasei Kogyo KK's Application* [1991] RPC 485 (House of Lords).
26. [2005] UKHL 59, 20 October 2005.

prior document and what has been enabled. In the case of a written description, the skilled person is taken to be trying to understand what the author of that description meant, his background knowledge being relevant to the achievement of that understanding. But once the meanings of the prior disclosure and of the patent have been determined, the skilled person is assumed to be trying to make what is in the prior disclosure work. He is then expected to apply ordinary methods of trial and error to achieve the previously disclosed result and to try obvious modifications.

For example, in *Synthon* the specification of the patent in issue disclosed a compound in crystalline form but specified in the example a solvent which was in fact unsuitable for making the crystalline form of the compound. The House of Lords held that once the existence of a crystalline form had been disclosed, a negative result with that solvent would not have lead the skilled person to loose his belief in the existence of and possibility of obtaining the disclosed crystalline form, and that he would have tried another solvent from the range of solvents disclosed in the specification or from his common general knowledge and would have been able to make the compound in crystalline form within a reasonable time.

Although non-enablement is an important issue when considering lack of novelty, and is considered in more detail in the subsequent *Clarity, enablement and utility* paper,[27] a non-enabling disclosure does not wholly lack significance, especially when considering inventive step. For example, a novel by H. G. Wells, *The First Men in the Moon,* discloses a fictional voyage from the earth to the moon made possible by the material "*Cavorite*" which acted as a gravity shield. A material with such properties is as yet undiscovered. However, Wells, Jules Verne and other science fiction authors had undoubtedly disclosed the *idea* of going to the moon, and the history of space exploration shows that their work played a significant part in persuading the public to make a decision in favour of developing the necessary technology. By the 1960s when the goal was about to be achieved it would have been impossible for anyone to patent traveling from the earth to the moon, although patents for particular ways of traveling to the moon might in principle have been possible. A commentator familiar with the European approach to inventive step would say that H.G. Wells, amongst others, had disclosed the problem of devising technical means by which people could travel from the earth to the moon, although he had not disclosed a technically feasible solution. Similarly the idea of producing *Cavorite* and its postulated properties have been disclosed. The implementation of that idea requires an act of empirical discovery that has not yet taken place and according to modern concepts of physics is unlikely ever to take place.

Novelty before the EPO

Under the EPC, subject-matter that has entered the state of the art is citable against the novelty of a later application or patent. The state of the art comprises everything that has been made available to the public. Anything that has lawfully entered the public domain anywhere in the world is therefore citable.

---

27. Page 79

For a disclosure to be relevant to the novelty or inventive character of claimed subject-matter, it must have:

(1) happened before the priority or filing date;
(2) been disclosed in public, not privately; and
(3) provided an enabling disclosure.[28]

To establish lack of novelty, the disclosure must further have:

(4) clearly and unmistakeably disclosed the subject-matter of the subsequent claim;
(5) not fallen within the exception for selection patents; and
(6) not fallen within the exception for newly discovered medical indications and other technical effects.[29]

During examination, objections will almost invariably be based on published documents because examiners have ready access to such documents but have no resources to investigate what may have been disclosed orally or by prior use but which has not been recorded in a document.

Any document to which the public can have access qualifies as published, irrespective of whether any member of the public knew of its existence or location. For example, a document placed in the official file of a published patent application is a published document.[30] However, events that are not validly citable include placing an un-indexed thesis in the archives (as opposed to the open shelves) of a library, sending a manuscript to the editor of a journal for publication (the editor is normally under an obligation to keep the manuscript confidential until publication), and addressing a copy of a magazine to a member of the public and placing it in a post-box (it is the date of receipt that matters).[31]

In opposition proceedings, allegations of prior use may arise. The EPO practice is to require proof of these allegations[32] beyond reasonable doubt where the prior use comes from an opponent or a third party, but proof to the lesser standard of balance of probabilities where the alleged prior use is by the patentee. In order to decide whether an alleged prior use is comprised in the state of the art it is necessary to establish:

(1) the date on which the alleged prior use occurred;
(2) exactly what was used; and
(3) the circumstances relating to the use by which it was made available to the public e.g. place of use; possible conditions of secrecy.

---

28. Subject to the comments at page 13 above as regards disclosure of the *idea*.
29. *Second medical indication/EISAI* G 0005/83, and *Friction Reducing Additive/Mobil II* T 0059/87 [1988] OJEPO 347, *Friction Reducing Additive/Mobil III* G 0002/88, [1990] OJEPO 9, and *Friction Reducing Additive/Mobil IV* T 0059/87 [1991] OJEPO 561. All of these decisions are **required reading** irrespective of the technical field in which you practice.
30. T 0444/88 *Japan Styrene Resin.*
31. T0381/87 *Publication/ RESEARCH ASSOCIATION.*
32. T 0194/86/ *Shower fitting/ALBANY*

In the case of a product demonstrated at an exhibition, it is necessary to prove that a skilled person would have derived the necessary teaching from the demonstration.[33] In the case of a chemical product, proof of one or more instances of prior use may not be sufficient if the product varies from batch to batch.[34] In the case of products supplied in small quantities, the EPO will readily infer that this was a non-commercial transaction for purposes of evaluation and therefore subject to confidentiality. A secrecy agreement may not be needed for a disclosure to be considered non-public since the EPO can infer confidentiality from the circumstances.[35] Technical discussions between suppliers and customers and between manufacturers and subcontractors are often treated as being secret (letters, drawings, reports, etc).

However, issues of confidentiality before the EPO may be complex because the EPC does not contain its own law of confidentiality. It arises under national law which varies from country to country (in the US from state to state). An opinion from a local practitioner about the relevant law and its application to a particular transaction may need to be supplied to the EPO. Without a written agreement specifying applicable law, it is submitted that it is the law where the recipient is domiciled that is relevant because it is the courts where the recipient is located that have the task of enforcing any obligation of confidentiality. For example with both sending and recipient companies located in Japan, it is Japanese law that decides whether there is an obligation of confidentiality. If the sender is in Japan and the recipient is in California, then in absence of contrary agreement it is submitted that the relevant law is the state law of California. In the US it may be difficult to assert an obligation of confidentiality without a written secrecy agreement. For a recent example, see *Eolas Technologies v Microsoft Corporation*[36] where demonstration of a web browser called Viola to two Sun Microsystems engineers without any obligation of secrecy was held to be public use. Letters and documents sent from one country to another can therefore raise issues concerning the courts which have jurisdiction and the national or state law which applies, and detailed specialist advice may be necessary to determine which is the applicable law, and then to determine how that applicable law applies to a particular factual situation under investigation.

As regards the disclosure of product characteristics, according to the opinion of the Enlarged Board of Appeal,[37] the intrinsic characteristics e.g. chemical composition of a product become part of the state of the art when the product is available to the public and can be analysed and reproduced by a skilled person. That happens irrespective of whether the skilled person has reasons for analysing the product and determining its characteristics. If direct access to the information is possible, that information is in the public domain irrespective of whether there was a reason for

---

33. T 0326/93 *Thermal limiter/THORN EMI.*

34. T 0600/90/ *Detergent powder/UNILEVER.*

35. T 0782/92 *Dual-type damper device/TOKAI RUBBER.*

36. Fed. Cir. 2 March 2005, citing *Netscape Communications Corp. v Konrad* 295 F. 3d 1315 at 1318 (Fed. Cir. 2002) where the circumstances were similar.

37. G 0001/92 *President's reference*

looking for it. However, extrinsic characteristics of the product which depend on choice and on interaction with outside conditions e.g. materials that can be reacted with the product to produce particular technical effects do not enter the state of the art. For example, in *Green Glass/AVIR*,[38] the invention concerned low sulphide green glass of high UV absorption for making *inter alia* champagne bottles. 182,000 bottles of this type had been sold by opponents before the priority date. The patentees argued that it was not known at the time that high UV absorption could be obtained with low sulphide and the skilled person would not have analysed the bottles for sulphide, whose concentration remained hidden. The Appeal Board rejected this argument on the basis that composition and UV absorption were intrinsic characteristics. *G 0001/92 President's Reference* only required analysability and reproducibility, and not that the skilled person should know in advance what characteristics he needed to investigate. The claimed composition of the glass was therefore not new, and the patent in issue was revoked.

For an oral disclosure to be citable, the content of the disclosure must be proved beyond reasonable doubt. What matters is evidence from the person who received the disclosure, not evidence from the person who made it. *Immunoglobulin preparations/GENENTECH*[39] provides a practical illustration and shows how complete the evidence has to be in order to prove the contents of an oral disclosure, and how closely that evidence will be scrutinized by the EPO. In 1983, Dr Köhler, a discoverer of monoclonal antibodies was scheduled to give the *Mallincrodt Award Lecture* and to receive a prize. He was unable to attend and Dr Schulman took his place. He gave evidence during EPO opposition proceedings that during the lecture he had disclosed work on recombinant chimeric immunoglobulins and that he had illustrated his disclosure with slides. This work had subsequently been published in *Nature* in 1984, but if it had been first disclosed in 1983 at the lecture then the subject-matter of the patent in issue would not be novel. The opponents supported their allegations that recombinant chimeric immunoglobins had been disclosed at the lecture with a declaration from the lecturer (Dr Schulman), a declaration from the organiser of the meeting (Dr Hamilton), and evidence from a technician who had ordered the slides before the date of the lecture. The opponents averred that Dr Schulman was a skilled lecturer, and that what he had disclosed could be reconstructed from his notes and slides. The patentees responded that the *Mallincrodt* lecture was an unlikely forum for an announcement of this new discovery, Dr Schulman had neither informed nor obtained consent from his colleagues for the disclosure: his colleagues were co-authors of the paper in *Nature*, no notes or copies of slides had been given to members of the audience, there was no written record (e.g. instructions to a technician) confirming that the slides had been shown, and a witness on their behalf, Dr Lyle, had attended the lecture as a member of the audience, and his evidence was that Dr Schulman had said nothing new.

The Board's decision was that the contents of the lecture had not been proved. The mere evidence of the lecturer did not prove safely and with certainty what had been disclosed. Evidence was needed from the audience. The contemporary written notes

---

38. T 0301/94

39. T 1212/97

of at least two members of the audience could prove what had been disclosed. The notes of a single individual would be less reliable as they might reflect his thoughts and not the content of the lecture. If the disclosure had been as alleged, it was surprising that there was no positive evidence from members of the audience. A typescript or manuscript for the lecture would have been helpful but not conclusive; in this case no typescript was available. Dr Hamilton's evidence was unreliable because he could have confused the content of the lecture with his subsequent knowledge. There had been ten years between the date of the lecture and when he gave his evidence. Furthermore, he had read Dr Schulman's declaration, and there was no explanation of what was his independent recollection. Disclosure so far in advance of the paper in *Nature* was improbable.

Selection patents

Recognition of selection inventions originated in UK law, and has been adopted and developed by the EPO Appeal Boards.[40] A generic disclosure does not anticipate a species contained within the genus and found to have newly discovered advantages or effects, see *Beecham Group's (Amoxycillin) application*[41] and *Du Pont's (Witseipe's) application*[42] both of which concern selection from a group or list. Although selection situations most commonly occur in the fields of chemistry, biochemistry and biotechnology, they can occur in the fields of engineering or electronics e.g. in the selection of a particular material for an engineering purpose[43] on account of its unexpectedly good properties.

The EPO recognition of selection patents applies, particularly, to circumstances where the selection is made from two or more lists.[44] If two classes of starting substances are required to prepare an end product, and examples of individual entities in each class are given in two lists of some length, the substance resulting from the reaction of a specific pair from the two lists can be regarded for patent purposes as a selection and hence as novel. The EPO also recognises selection of parameters within a range. The criteria applied by the boards of appeal were developed in *Thiochloroformates/HOECHST*[45] and are subsequently summarised in *Polyurethane elastomers/TEXACO*[46] as follows. A selection of a sub-range of numerical values from a broader range is novel when each of the following criteria is satisfied:

40. It is notable that the first ever published decision of an EPO Appeal Board, *Carbonless copying paper/BAYER*, T 0001/80, [1982] RPC 321 approved the principle that patents can be granted on the basis of selection.

41. [1980] RPC 261 (**required reading**)

42. [1982] FSR 303 (**required reading**)

43. For example, at the time of writing carbon fibre composites are coming into increasing use for the manufacture of large structural members such as wing panels for civil airliners.

44. See e.g *Diastereoisomers/BAYER*, T 0012/81 and *Enantiomers/HOECHST*

45. T 0198/84

46. T 0279/89 – 3.3.3

(1) the selected sub-range is narrow;
(2) it is sufficiently far removed from the preferred part of the known range; and
(3) it is not arbitrarily chosen specimen and instead provides a new invention (purposive selection).

The jurisprudence of the EPO concerning selection inventions has developed extensively, and detailed investigations into relevant case law may be required to deal adequately with particular difficult situations.[47]

The fact that selection plus advantage is a positive indicator of patentability should not come as a surprise because selection plus advantage is a force of nature. In biology it drives the process of evolution and has given rise to the diversity of plants and animals that populates our world. Technology can be regarded as a human "meme"[48] which evolves or develops with time and is subject to the same type of selection pressure because good and workable concepts and artifacts are selected and developed, whereas erroneous concepts and unworkable artifacts become rejected and abandoned.

US – novelty

In order to be patentable, an invention must be novel.[49] The statute prohibits patenting of subject-matter that before its alleged *invention* by an applicant for a patent had been patented or described in a printed publication in the US or in another country (an absolute standard for documentary publications), or that had been known or used by others in the US (a local standard for other forms of disclosure). Therefore, in contrast to most other countries, novelty is determined at the date of invention, not at the date of filing an application at the Patent Office, which may be significantly later. However, there is a cut-off period or so-called "statutory bar" on the patenting of inventions that had been patented or described in a printed publication in the US or any other country, or that had been in public use or on sale in the US more than one year prior to the date of application in the US. Grant of a foreign patent for the invention by an applicant before the filing of an application in the US is also prohibited. There is also provision for another inventor to establish priority if he can establish in so-called "interference" proceedings that he had made the invention before the alleged invention by the applicant and had not thereafter abandoned, suppressed or concealed his invention.[50]

UK practitioners will mostly be dealing with applications before the USPTO, and will therefore mostly be facing allegedly prior published documents for which

---

47. See e.g. the *Case law of the Boards of Appeal of the European Patent Office*, and the *CIPA Guide to the Patents Acts* where selection patents are reviewed.

48. The term *meme* first came into popular use with the publication of the book *The Selfish Gene* by Richard Dawkins in 1976. Dawkins defined the meme as "*a unit of cultural transmission, or a unit of imitation*". See Susan Blackmore, *The Meme Machine*, Oxford, 1999.

49. 35 USC §102

50. Interference proceedings will become obsolete if the US adopts a first-to-file system like that of Europe and of most other national and regional patent systems. For details of interference procedure, readers should consult one of the standard textbooks on US patent law.

neither the fact of publication not the date of publication is controversial. According to the US *Manual of Patent Examining Procedure*, a claim is anticipated only if each and every element as set forth in the claim is found, either expressly or inherently described, in a single prior art reference. When a claim covers several structures or compositions, either generically or as alternatives, the claim is deemed anticipated if any of the structures or compositions within the scope of the claim is known in the prior art. The identical invention must be shown in as complete detail as is contained in the claim.[51] Generally speaking the reasoning as regards alleged lack of novelty with which UK practitioners are familiar is also applicable in the US.

A generic claim cannot be allowed to an applicant if the prior art discloses a species falling within the claimed genus. The species in that case will anticipate the genus.[52] Conversely a previously disclosed genus does not always anticipate a subsequent claim to a species within the genus. There may therefore be scope for the type of "selection" arguments with which UK practitioners are familiar. However, when the species is clearly named in the prior art, a subsequent claim covering that species is anticipated no matter how many other species are additionally named. Where a preferred structural formula in a prior reference discloses only a limited number of compounds, and the number of possible substituents at each possible site on an unchanging nucleus is low, it may be found that the reference sufficiently described *"each of the various permutations here involved as fully as if he had drawn each structural formula or had written each name."*[53]

---

51. *Richardson v Suzuki Motor Co.*, 868 F.2d 1226, 1236, 9 USPQ2d 1913, 1920 (Fed. Cir. 1989).

52. *In re Slayter*, 276 F.2d 408, 411, 125 USPQ 345, 347 (CCPA 1960); *In re Gosteli*, 872 F.2d 1008, 10 USPQ2d 1614 (Fed. Cir. 1989).

53. *In re Petering*, 301 F.2d 676, 133 USPQ 275 (CCPA 1962).

Inventive step – recognising invention

"The greatest challenge to any thinker is stating the problem in a way that will allow a solution "[54]

Coverage

This paper provides a brief introduction to the law of inventive step in the UK, the US and under the EPC.

There is an abundance of journal literature and jurisprudence concerning inventive step from the UK, the US and the EPO Appeal Boards, and a number of tests have been propounded. Relatively few of these are of help at the drafting stage. Three tests which it is submitted can provide useful insight are the collocation test (US, UK, EPC), the "motivation-to-combine" test which has become a standard in the US and the technical-problem test which has become standard in the EPO. Tests which provide less assistance at the drafting stage include the "right-to-work" test (UK, Germany), the *Windsurfer* test (UK), and the very similar *Graham v John Deere* test (US).

After studying this paper and
the "must-read" materials you should understand:

1. The main details of the tests for inventive step used by the EPO, the USPTO, US courts and the UK courts and the significance for patent drafting of the various tests that they use.

2. The critical role of features for which an unexpected new function, result or advantage can be identified, and the importance of identifying and claiming all such features.

3. The relative credibility of features identified as being inventive in the application as filed vis-à-vis features whose inventive contribution is only subsequently identified.

---

54. Bertrand Russell (1872-1970, English logician and philosopher, co-author of *Principia Mathematica*)

Introduction

The *EPC*, like the *UK Patents Act 1977* and like *35 USC* bolts together concepts of inventiveness and obviousness that are not synonymous. Article 52(1) EPC requires an invention to involve an inventive step. Article 56 explains that an invention should be considered as involving an inventive step if it is not obvious to a person skilled in the art. But if "inventive step" makes no significant addition to the Convention, why did not Article 52(1) simply specify un-obviousness as its third criterion?

On one view what matters is whether there is a step beyond the prior art. If not then there is no novelty. If there is such a step, the size of the step is irrelevant. What matters is whether the step was inventive in the sense of not having been obvious at the priority date of the claim in issue to a person skilled in the art.

The word "invention" comes from the Latin noun *invenium* from the verb *invenire* meaning to find or to come upon. On that basis, the Convention requires an invention to have the positive attribute of an underlying discovery by the inventor. That requirement fits the structure of patent claims, which specify a set of integers, relationships between the integers and a function or result that flows from providing those integers and establishing those relationships. The new function or result, if unexpected, provides the required positive attribute and can be identified with the *invenium* or finding upon which the concept of "invention" is based. That formulation is consistent with the expectations of most scientists and engineers who it is submitted expect a patentee to have achieved something positive before he can apply for a patent. It is also consistent with the views of those who drafted the US Constitution, who were working in the common law tradition and in the light of some 160 years experience since the passing of the *Statute of Monopolies*.[55] They included in the Constitution a provision authorizing Congress "To promote the progress of useful arts by securing for limited times to inventors the exclusive right to their *discoveries*."

Before the introduction of obviousness as a statutory requirement into UK[56] and US[57] law, the courts focused on the requirement of inventiveness, and older UK and US decisions should be read with this in mind. For example, in the UK the courts held that a scintilla of invention was needed to support the subject-matter of a claim.[58] In the US, the Supreme Court held that patentability required the involvement of more ingenuity than the work of a mechanic skilled in the art[59] and in 1941 controversially went on to say that an invention should reveal the flash of creative genius.[60]

---

55. 21 Jac 1, c. 3 (1623): a patent could be granted to the true and first inventors of any manner of new manufacture. That could include a person who imported the invention into England, see the quotation by T.A. Blanco White, Patents for Inventions, 4th Ed at 5-105 from *Edgeberry v Stevens* (1691) 1 WPC 35: "Whether learned by travel or study it is the same thing." But it should be borne in mind that a man who made a sea voyage at that time put his life in jeopardy.

56. in 1932, Patents and Designs Act, 1932.

57. in 1952, see 35 USC 103

58. *Parkes v Cocker* (1929) 46 RPC 241 at p. 248.

59. *Hotchkiss v Greenwood* 52 U.S. (11 How.) 248 (1850).

Obviousness comes from the Latin *ob* + *via*, meaning by the wayside.[61] So the emphasis is not on discovery but on accessibility, and what is being looked for is a negative attribute i.e. that the skilled person would have come upon the claimed subject-matter sooner or later and without having to display ingenuity. When introduced into statute law, an obviousness test tends to become substituted for an enquiry into inventive character. Indeed, Judge Giles S. Rich argued that the introduction of obviousness standard into US law removed any separate requirement for inventive character, which he described as a rough-hewn stopgap with which the courts had filled in a void in the patent law, but which had now been replaced by a carefully worked-out statutory substitute of non-obviousness.[62]

Unfortunately life is not that simple. Many things are not obvious in the sense of readily accessible but do not involve ingenuity. A familiar example is the set of winning numbers for the next draw in the National Lottery.[63] It mildly entertaining and very easy to devise groupings of familiar objects that would be difficult to trace collectively to the prior art[64] but which do not achieve any unexpected effect or solve any technical problem.

It is arguable that the point raised by Judge Rich had already been answered by the US Supreme Court in *Graham v John Deere*[65] where it was held that the requirement for invention or patentable novelty had existed in US law since at least 1850, and that the new law had merely codified existing judicial precedents and introduced an enquiry as to the obviousness of the subject-matter claimed as a prerequisite to patentability. In

---

60. *Cuno Engineering Corp. v Automatic Devices Corp.*, 314 U.S. 84, 91; 51 U.S.P.Q. 272, 275 (1941) per Douglas J, see the discussion of this case in *Graham v John Deere Co.*, 383 US 1, 148 U.S.P.Q. 459 (1966). Between school and university the writer used a crystal of sodium iodide and a photomultiplier to detect the flashes of light given off on the radioactive decay of individual atoms of a radioactive isotope of sulphur, and is therefore more disposed than most to believe that the existence or absence of a scintilla of invention is a binary event and should be readily and reliably detectable.

61. For an example of the word used in precisely this sense in literature, see an account of the travel of a party of knights along a path towards a dragon's cave in J.R.R. Tolkien, *Farmer Giles of Ham*, Unwin Paperbacks, 1975 at p. 57: "*The knights were discussing points of precedence and etiquette and their attention was distracted. Otherwise they would have observed that the dragon marks were now obvious and numerous.*"

62. "*Escaping the tyranny of words ... is evolution in legal thinking impossible*" (1978) 60 Journal of the Patent Office Society 271.

63. The whole point of a lottery is that firstly the winning number or combination of numbers should *not* be obvious in advance, and secondly that no more skill or ingenuity should be associated with the winning entry than with any other entry, so that all entries are alike. Much skill and effort is spent in trying to predict in advance what numbers are likely to come up at the next draw, or what will be the winning entry in Football Pools, or how to win at roulette. If the competition works properly, such effort should be vain, and the outcome should be random. It is not apparent that the EPC, the national laws of the EPC contracting states or 35 USC 103 sanctions the granting of alleged inventions arrived at merely by chance: typical inventions in empirical research fields (e.g. the finding of antibiotic-producing organisms by the systematic screening of soil samples) are the outcome of deliberate, prolonged, painstaking and skilled investigation.

64. For example a table having a built-in baby bath and an attached can-opener; the more objects you specify the harder it is to find a reference specifying that the specified objects should be assembled or grouped together.

65. 383 US 1, 148 USPQ 459 (1966) (**required reading**); see US-A-2627798.

other words, to be patentable an invention must have patentable novelty *and* be free from objection on the ground of obviousness. Essentially the same point arose before the EPO Appeal Board[66] where applicants argued that the significant question in relation to the obviousness of a claimed class of compounds was whether it was obvious to prepare any compound within the class, and not whether all the compounds within the class solved a technical problem. The Appeal Board rejected this argument on the basis that the extent of the patent monopoly should correspond to and be justified by the technical contribution to the art: it follows that there must be a positive technical contribution to justify a patent. Both discovery and accessibility can be important and both of them are habitually considered by the EPO and by national courts under the heading of "obviousness". From the standpoint of the patents draftsman, however, it is usually the ability to identify features that make a positive technical contribution that offers the more valuable indicators for potentially inventive features.

The "right-to-work" test (UK)

The objection of anticipation prohibits the re-patenting of subject-matter that was known, and has a logical extension, on the *de minimis* principle, to cover trivial extensions of known subject-matter which it would naturally occur to the skilled person to make. It has been described in a paper by Brian Reid[67] as "the right to work".

The most celebrated statement of the principle is in *Gillette Safety Razor Co v Anglo-American Trading Co,*[68] where Lord Moulton held that it was a defence to proceedings for patent infringement that the alleged infringement was not patentable over the pleaded prior art and commented:

> In practical life it is often the only safeguard to the manufacturer. It is impossible for an ordinary member of the public to keep watch on all the numerous patents which are taken out and to ascertain the validity and scope of all their claims. But he is entitled to feel secure if he knows that what he is doing differs from that which has been done of old only in non-patentable variations, such as the substitution of mechanical equivalents or changes of material, shape or size.

A danger inherent in the test is failure to appreciate that small differences often produce significant effects, and the warning of Lord Herschell in *Siddell v Vickers*[69] about how easy things can look in hindsight should be kept in mind:

> If the apparatus be valuable by reason of its simplicity, there is a danger of being mislead by that very simplicity into the belief that no invention was needed to produce it. But experience has shown that not a few inventions ... have been of so simple a character that even when once they were made known it was difficult ... not to believe that they must have been obvious to everyone.

---

66. T 939/92 *AGREVO/Triazoles* (**required reading**)
67. [1982] EIPR 6.
68. (1913) 30 RPC. 465 at 470
69. (1890) 7 RPC 292 at p. 304

In particular, the test is not applicable where the changes solve a problem or provide a new result. For example, in *Fichera v Flogates*,[70] the invention concerned a ladle for molten steel having a bottom discharge outlet closed by a sliding gate valve. The improvement involved providing a ring of refractory material in the bottom of the ladle, a bush with a vertical hole for tapping metal mounted in the ring, and a stationary refractory plate having an upper surface on which the bush rested and a lower surface along which the valve slid. The bush was well known in a different form of bottom discharge outlet, and the defendants objected that the provision of this well-known bush in a known form of outlet was within the range of variants which a skilled person would make without any invention. However, the effect of the change was to move the seat of erosion by the molten steel from the sliding parts of the valve to the top of the bush, where it is less damaging, and to enable the outlet to be used to pour many charges of molten steel instead of only a single charge as in the prior art. Both the Patents Court and the Court of Appeal held on the basis of the evidence given that the patent was valid and warned against treating dismissively apparently small changes seemingly simple structures. It is apparent that what persuaded both courts that the patent was valid was the technical effect of moving the place where erosion took place and the associated advantage of greatly increased working life.

It is submitted that the value of the right-to-work test is post-grant when the test can be applied to restrain unduly wide interpretation of granted patents. It is less valuable and often dangerous to apply at the drafting stage because it leads too easily to the fallacy that because a change is small or simple it must therefore have been obvious.

The *Graham* and the *Windsurfer* tests (US, UK)

Courts in the US and in the UK have found it advantageous to conduct their investigations within a structured approach. That put forward by the US Supreme Court in *Graham v John Deere*[71] involves the following steps:

(1) Determining the scope and content of the prior art.

(2) Ascertaining the differences between the prior art and the claims at issue.

(3) Resolving the level of ordinary skill in the pertinent art.

(4) Against this background, determining the obviousness or non-obviousness of the subject-matter claimed.

The *Graham* test also allows for evaluating secondary considerations that provide *indicia* of obviousness or non-obviousness, e.g. commercial success, long-felt but unresolved needs, failure of others. On this authority, much effort has been expended during US infringement trials on investigation of surrounding circumstances and, for example, whether alleged commercial success is the result of the merits of the

---

70. [1984] RPC 257

71. 383 US 1, 148 USPQ 459 (1966), see US-A-2627798 (**required reading**)

invention or has unrelated causes e.g. good marketing. Study of the *Graham* decision and two related cases decided on the same day, *Calmar v Cook Chemical*[72] and the *United States v Adams*[73] *(the Adams Battery case)*, reveals that each was decided simply on the technical relationship between the claimed subject-matter and the prior art, and circumstantial evidence played no part in any of the three decisions. In the *Calmar* case, the court acknowledged that such economic or motivational considerations were easier for judges than the highly technical facts often presented in patent litigation, but that they did not tip the scales of patentability in the particular case before the court since the alleged invention was based on exceedingly small and non-technical mechanical differences in a device which was old. The famous "*trilogy*" is therefore not good authority for the proposition that investigation of circumstantial evidence is likely to be profitable.

One of the major features of the *Adams Battery* case was that the inventor had disclosed the first battery that could be made and distributed in a dry state and could be activated by mere addition of seawater. The US Supreme Court explained that reliance on water-activation was not "*the afterthought of an astute trial lawyer*", that the battery was set apart from the prior art by this feature, and that the operating characteristics of the Adams battery far surpassed those of other batteries. In contrast, the *Graham* case turned on the ability of a plough shank to flex in a particular region along its length, but the patent specification was entirely silent about the importance or effects of that feature. In the *Cook Chemical* case, which concerned a pump sprayer for a bottle, the alleged invention concerned the way that a protective over-cap fitted to the sprayer, it being arranged firstly with an internal rib seal to prevent leakage of contents accidentally dispensed during transit, and secondly so that the over-cap could not be screwed down so tightly as to contact the container cap. The patent specification gave no hint that either of these features or the combination of them led to anything unexpected or advantageous.

Two subsequent Supreme Court decisions gave rise to controversy at the time that they were handed down but concerned features which the specification as filed treated in a similarly insignificant manner.

Anderson's-Black Rock v Pavement Co[74] concerned the problem of "cold joint" between strips of bituminous pavement, which it aimed to solve by combining on one chassis a radiant heat burner for heating the exposed edge of a cold strip of pavement, a spreader for placing bituminous material against that strip, and a tamper and screed for shaping the newly placed material. In effect, it combined a known radiant-heat burner with known equipment for spreading and shaping asphalt. Although the patent in issue said much about the advantages of radiant energy (which turned out to be known), it did not disclose or suggest that providing these elements on a single chassis produced any surprising or unexpected advantage. Uncontested evidence showed that the provision of the burner and the other elements in the same machine was not essential to the elimination of cold joints, and for

---

72. Appears in the same report as *Graham*, see US-A-2870943
73. 383 US 39 (1966) **(required reading)**
74. 396 US 57; 163 USPQ 673 (1969); US-A-3055280 **(required reading)**

transverse cold joints in pavement it was normal to use that a separate heater in combination with a standard paving machine. Unsurprisingly the patent was held to lack inventive character.

In *Sakraida v Ag Pro Inc*,[75] the invention concerned keeping cows in barns, and the allegedly novel feature was the provision of a tank that abruptly released a large volume of water. The testimony at trial was that a sheet of water has a rolling action that gives better cleaning than a hose. Nothing about this was stated in the patent in issue, where the tank was disclosed in a matter-of-fact manner without any suggestion that it was important or lead to unexpected advantage.[76] It is apparent that judges, and especially non-specialist judges such as those in the US District Courts and the Supreme Court, are markedly unimpressed with features whose ingenuity is not mentioned in the patent specification.

The framework suggested by the Court of Appeal in *Windsurfer v Tabur Marine*[77] is of comparable status in the UK to *Graham* in the US and is strikingly similar. It involves the following steps:

(1) identifying the inventive concept embodied in the patent in suit;

(2) assuming the mantle of the normally skilled but unimaginative addressee in the art at the priority date and imputing to him what was, at that date, common general knowledge in the art in question;

(3) identifying what, if any, differences exist between the matter cited as being "known or used" and the alleged invention; and

(4) asking whether, viewed without any knowledge of the alleged invention, those differences constitute steps which would have been obvious to the skilled person or whether they require any degree of invention.

UK courts have in the past been prepared to investigate commercial success and other circumstantial evidence with the same enthusiasm as their US counterparts, but more recently have come to realise that[78]

> Secondary evidence of this type has its place, and the importance or weight to be attached to it will vary from case to case. However, such evidence must be kept firmly in its place. It must not be permitted, by reason of its volume and complexity, to obscure the fact that it is no more than an aid in assessing the primary evidence.

---

75. 425 US 273, 189 USPQ 449 (1976); see US-A-3223070 (**required reading**).

76. The Court referred *inter alia* to the fifth labour of Heracles which was to cleanse in a single day the stables of King Augeas. This he achieved by diverting a mighty stream so that the water flowed in one end of the stables and flowed out of the other. According to legend, Heracles took on the task in return for a tithe of the cattle King Augeas owned, but when the work had been completed, Augeas refused to pay.

77. [1985] RPC 59 at 73-74.

78. [1997] RPC 1; see also the observations of Laddie J in *Hoechst Celanese v B.P. Chemicals* [1997] RPC 547.

The test for inventive step has recently been restated by the Patents Court in *GE Healthcare Limited v Perkinelmer Life Sciences (UK) Limited*[79] as follows:

> First, it is convenient to address the question using the structured approach explained by the Court of Appeal in *Windsurfing International Inc. v Tabur Marine (Great Britain) Ltd* [1985] RPC 59...
>
> Secondly, the primary evidence is that of the expert witnesses. All other evidence is secondary to that primary evidence. Secondary evidence has its place and the weight to be attached to it will vary from case to case. However, such evidence must be kept firmly in its place: *Mölnlycke v Procter & Gamble Ltd* (No 5) [1994] RPC 49 at 113.
>
> Thirdly, a decision on obviousness does not require a conclusion as to whether or not the skilled person would be slightly, moderately or particularly interested in any document. Any prior document relied on must be deemed to be read properly and in that sense with interest: *Asahi Medical Co Ltd v Macopharma (UK) Ltd* [2002] EWCA Civ 466 at [21]-[25].
>
> Fourthly, what matters is whether the inventive concept is technically obvious over the prior art, not whether it is commercially obvious to take that step: *Hallen Co v Brabantia UK Ltd* [1991] RPC 195.
>
> Fifthly, if a particular route is an obvious one to take, it is not rendered any less obvious from a technical point of view merely because there are a number, and perhaps a large number, of other obvious routes as well: *Brugger v Medic-Aid Ltd* [1996] RPC 635 at 661.
>
> Further, I was cautioned ... to be wary of any submission that the invention in the present case was one which was obvious to try. The "obvious to try"doctrine needs to be applied with caution. As Jacob LJ said in *St Gobain v Fusion Provida* [2005] EWCA Civ 177 at [35]: *"Mere possible inclusion of something within a research programme on the basis you will find out more and something might not turn up is not enough. If it were otherwise there would be few inventions that were patentable. The only research which would be worthwhile (because of the prospect of protection) would be into areas totally devoid of prospect. The 'obvious to try' test really only works where it is more-or-less self-evident that what is being tested ought to work".*

Experience shows that UK judges are usually equally unimpressed with features picked out of an otherwise pedestrian specification by trial lawyer hindsight, and whose importance appears late in the proceedings. An example is provided by the Court of Appeal decision in *Windsurfer*.[80] No emphasis had been placed up to the hearing of the appeal that inventive character could be added by the selection of a surfboard hull, and at this late stage and in the absence of any indication in the

---

79. Kitchen J, 17 February 2006, [2006] EWHC 214 (Pat).

80. See page 273

specification itself that this feature contributed to inventiveness or any claim requiring a surfboard hull, the Court of Appeal was not prepared to take any notice of it.

The positive indications that we can derive from the *Graham* and the *Windsurfer* tests as applied in practice are that judges are much more impressed with the underlying technical facts than they are with the surrounding circumstances, that they are looking for real advantages of an unexpected character, and that alleged advantages unsupported in the patent application as filed and only identified by hindsight lack persuasive power.

Motivation to combine (US)

Motivation to combine has become a practical standard for the US Patent Office and for the US Courts supplementing that in *Graham v John Deere*.

The basic requirements of a *prima facie* case of obviousness are explained in the USPTO Manual of Patent Examining Practice.[81] There must be:

(1) a suggestion or motivation, either in the references themselves or in the knowledge generally available to one of ordinary skill in the art, to modify the reference or to combine reference teachings;

(2) a reasonable expectation of success to be found in the prior art and not with hindsight in the applicant's disclosure; and

(3) A teaching or suggestion of all the claim limitations in the prior art reference (or references) when combined.

There are three possible sources for a motivation to combine references: the nature of the problem to be solved, the teachings of the prior art and the knowledge of persons of ordinary skill in the art.[82] The rationale to modify or combine the prior art does not have to be expressly stated in the prior art. It may be expressly or implicitly contained in the prior art or it may be reasoned from knowledge generally available to one of ordinary skill in the art, established scientific principles, or legal precedent established by prior case law.[83] The strongest rationale for combining references is a recognition, expressly or implicitly in the prior art or drawn from a convincing line of reasoning based on established scientific principles or legal precedent, that some advantage or expected beneficial result would have been produced by their combination.[84] However, as in the jurisprudence of the EPO Appeal Boards, the reason or motivation to modify the reference may often suggest what the inventor has done, but for a different purpose or to solve a different problem. It is not

81. At 2143
82. *In re Rouffet*, 149 F.3d 1350, 1357, 47 USPQ2d 1453, 1457-58 (Fed. Cir. 1998)
83. *In re Fine*, 837 F.2d 1071, 5 USPQ2d 1596 (Fed. Cir. 1988); *In re Jones*, 958 F.2d 347, 21 USPQ2d 1941 (Fed. Cir. 1992).
84. *In re Sernaker*, 702 F.2d 989, 994-95, 217 USPQ 1, 5-6 (Fed. Cir. 1983).

necessary that the prior art suggest the combination to achieve the same advantage or result discovered by the applicant.[85]

Guidelines in the USPTO Manual of Patent Examining Procedure[86] deal with selection (genus/species) situations. Factors which are relevant include:

(1) the size of the genus from which selection is made;

(2) the motivation which can be derived from the prior art to make the subsequently claimed selection;

(3) any structural similarity, based on the reasonable expectation that structurally similar species usually have similar properties;

(4) the known useful properties of the prior art;

(5) the predictability of the technology; and

(6) any other teaching to support the selection of the subgenus or species.

However, the suggestion to combine references cannot be found merely in the level of skill in the art,[87] not is the fact that modification of the prior art to produce the claimed invention was within the ordinary skill in the art.[88] Furthermore there must be a reasonable expectation of success.[89]

Arguments against an obviousness rejection based on a combination of references typically allege

(1) impermissible hindsight;

(2) an improper "obvious to try" rationale;

(3) lack of suggestion to combine the references;

(4) that the prior art teaches away from the invention, or the proposed modification of the prior art renders it unsatisfactory for its intended purpose or changes its principles of operation; and/or

---

85. *In re Linter*, 458 F.2d 1013, 173 USPQ 560 (CCPA 1972); *In re Dillon*, 919 F.2d 688, 16 USPQ2d 1897 (Fed. Cir. 1990), cert. denied, 500 U.S. 904 (1991)

86. At 2144.08 onwards

87. *Al-Site Corp. v VSI Int'l Inc.,* 174 F.3d 1308, 50 USPQ2d 1161 (Fed. Cir. 1999).

88. *Ex parte Levengood*, 28 USPQ2d 1300 (Bd. Pat. App. & Inter. 1993); *In re Kotzab*, 217 F.3d 1365, 1371, 55 USPQ2d 1313, 1318 (Fed. Cir. 2000)

89. *In re Merck & Co., Inc.*, 800 F.2d 1091, 231 USPQ 375 (Fed. Cir. 1986); *In re Rinehart*, 531 F.2d 1048, 189 USPQ 143 (CCPA 1976); *Amgen, Inc. v Chugai Pharmaceutical Co.*, 927 F.2d 1200, 1207-08, 18 USPQ2d 1016, 1022-23 (Fed. Cir.), cert. denied, 502 U.S. 856 (1991); In re O'Farrell, 853 F.2d 894, 903, 7 USPQ2d 1673, 1681 (Fed. Cir. 1988)

(5) making the invention required the inventor to do something that was contrary to accepted wisdom.

The collocation test (US, UK and EPC)

If, as explained above, new function or result created or discovered by the inventor is the *invenium* that supports patentability, we can adopt as a working hypothesis that the existence or non-existence of such new function or result is a good indicator for inventive step. There is ample jurisprudence to support the above hypothesis.

An early explanation by the US Supreme Court appears in *Pickering v McCulloch*:[90]

> In a patentable combination of old elements, all the constituents must so enter into it so that each qualifies every other: to draw an illustration from another branch of the law, they must be joint tenants of the domain of the invention, seized of every part *per my et per tout*, and not mere tenants in common with separate interests and estates. It must form either a new machine of a distinct character and function or produce a result due to the joint and cooperating action of all the elements, and which is not the mere adding together of the separate contributions. Otherwise it is only a mechanical juxtaposition and not a vital union.

The same point was made positively in *Carnegie Steel v Cambria Iron Company*[91] where the US Supreme Court affirmed that:

> It may be laid down as a general rule, though perhaps not an invariable one, that if a new combination and arrangement of known elements produce a new and beneficial result, never attained before, it is evidence of invention.

Despite its simplicity and self-evident utility the collocation test has at least since the 1980s been highly unpopular with US courts and is currently almost never used as the basis of decision. The reason is that it has in the past been perceived to have been applied in an unjust way, see the controversial opinions of the US Supreme Court in *Funk Bros. Seed Co. v Kalo Inocculant Co.*[92] and infamously in *Great A. & P. Tea Co v Supermarket Corp*[93] which brought it into prolonged disrepute. It was applied in the *Andersons-Black Rock* and *Sakraida* decisions discussed above, but arguably with insufficient discussion as to why the alleged new functions were not credible (significance not disclosed in the specification; no surprising new function on the facts before the court).

---

90. 104 US (14 Otto) 310, 318.

91. 185 US 403 (1901)

92. 333 US 127, 76 U.S.P.Q. 280 (1947) **(required reading)**

93. 340 US 147, 87 U.S.P.Q. 305 (1950) **(required reading)**, see Paul Cole, *Supermarket Check-outs Revisited,* Patent World, March 1988, pp. 12-17.

There has been a new proposal to revive the collocation test since the decision of the Court of Appeals for the Federal Circuit in *KSR v Teleflex*.[94] The invention in that case concerned an adjustable pedal assembly for use with an automobile which combined (a) a particular pedal structure and (b) an electronic control. The patentees averred that the particular structure solved the problem of saving space, economy of parts and mechanical simplicity. The Federal Circuit found for the patentees *inter alia* on the ground that there was a conflict of expert testimony about inventiveness which could not be resolved at the summary judgment stage. In a currently pending petition to the US Supreme Court for leave to appeal (*certiorari*) KSR argued that this was a straightforward combination of a pre-existing type of adjustable pedal with a pre-existing electronic control, and that what was being claimed was a combination of pre-existing off-the-shelf components in which each component performed precisely the function that it was designed to perform. In their answer, the patentees averred that the defendants had over-simplified the problem, that theirs was the only adjustable pedal system in which the electronic throttle system remained fixed, that as a result of their design the pedal arm could be made more compact and moved in a narrower space, and that the system left more foot-well space free for other vehicle components. The defendants replied that the "teaching-suggestion-motivation" test applied by the Federal Circuit was too lenient, and that the standard of legal review ought to be aligned with that in *Andersons-Black Rock* and *Sakraida v Ag Pro*. The defendants are supported by reply briefs from University-based *amici* and by a recent amicus brief filed on behalf of Microsoft and others which argues that current patentability standards are too lax, and that there are too many trivial patents. For example, Microsoft pointed out that 200 patents issued in 2004 for golf balls. A similar petition for *certiorari* is expected in *GroupOne, Ltd. v Hallmark Cards, Inc.*[95] It is not yet apparent whether the Supreme Court will decide to hear these cases, but either way the controversy is significant for future inventive step determination in the US.

To support the hypothesis that unexpected new function or result is a predictor of success, the following are examples of recent US cases where new function or result can be identified and the patents concerned have been upheld. These examples are not exhaustive, but are believed typical of the kind of cases that currently come before the CAFC:

(1) In *Chiuminatta Concrete Concepts, Inc v Cardinal Industries, Inc*,[96] the invention related to the cutting of concrete while it was still soft by means of a saw with an up-cutting rotary movement. These conditions surprisingly produced an acceptable cut where a conventional cutter in hard concrete produced unacceptable chipping and cracking.

(2) In *Kolmes v World Fibers Corp*,[97] the invention concerned a non-metallic composite cut-resistant yarn for use in making strong flexible cut-resistant products. It comprised (a) non-metallic core including at least one strand of

---

94. (Fed. Cir. 2005), see US-A-6237565.
95. Fed. Cir. 16 May 2005.
96. *Infra;* see the illustration at page 150
97. 107 F.3d 1534, 1539, 41 USPQ2d 1829, 1832 (Fed. Cir. 1997).

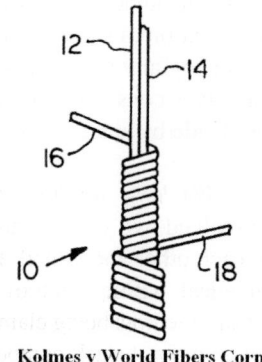

Kolmes v World Fibers Corp

fiberglass and (b) a non-metallic covering wrapped on said core, said covering including at least two un-braided strands spirally wrapped in opposite directions around the core. The inventors had discovered that the new composite yarn did not need to incorporate wire but still had substantially the same cut resistance and slash resistance as a conventional wire-containing yarn and could be formed into fabric on conventional machinery.

(3) In *Embrex, Inc v Service Engineering Corp*,[98] the invention concerned the immunization of un-hatched chicks against viral disease, and claimed injecting vaccine (which was an attenuated virus) into the amnion or yolk-sack of an egg during the final quarter of the incubation period. The inventor's discovery was that this set of conditions enabled the chick to produce an immune response without being killed by the vaccine, and that a hatch rate similar to that of untreated eggs could be achieved.

As to collocations or aggregations, the EPO *Guidelines for Examination* explain:[99]

> The invention claimed must normally be considered as a whole. When a claim consists of a "combination of features", it is not correct to argue that the separate features of the combination taken by themselves are known or obvious and that "therefore" the whole subject-matter claimed is obvious. However, where the claim is merely an "aggregation or juxtaposition of features" and not a true combination, it is enough to show that the individual features are obvious to prove that the aggregation of features does not involve an inventive step. A set of technical features is regarded as a combination of features if the functional interaction between the features achieves a combined technical effect which is different from, e.g. greater than, the sum of the technical effects of the individual features. In other words, the interactions of the individual features must produce a synergistic effect. If no such synergistic effect exists, there is no more than a mere aggregation of features...

---

98. 216 F.3d 1343, 55 U.S.P.Q.2D 1161, (Fed. Cir. 2000)
99. Chapter IV, para 9.5

The *Guidelines* go on to explain that objection arises where an invention consists merely in the juxtaposition or association of known devices or processes functioning in their normal way and not producing any non-obvious working inter-relationship, e.g. a machine for producing sausages consisting of a known mincing machine and a known filling machine disposed side by side.[100]

A recent example appears in *Washing methods/PROCTOR AND GAMBLE COMPANY*[101] where the claim involved two washing methods (for culinary utensils) having no technical bearing on each other and which were held not to form a single multi-step process (i.e. a "technical whole") though being linguistically linked together in a claim. If one of these methods already formed part of the state of the art, the subject-matter of this claim did not satisfy the requirements of Articles 52(1) and 54 EPC.

In the UK, the House of Lords in *Sabaf SpA v MFI Furniture Centres Limited*[102] approved the explanation of combination versus juxtaposition or aggregation in the *EPO Guidelines for Examination* (above) and reaffirmed the statement of Lord Tomlin in *British Celanese Ltd v Courtaulds Ltd*[103] that:

> A mere placing side by side of old integers so that each performs its own proper function independently of any of the others is not a patentable combination, but that where the old integers when placed together have some working inter-relation producing a new or improved result then there is patentable subject-matter in the idea of a working interrelation brought about by the collocation of the integers.

Lord Hoffmann giving the opinion in *Sabaf* went on to explain that there was no conflict between the law of collocations and the test for inventive step set out in *Windsurfing International Inc v Tabur Marine (Great Britain) Ltd*[104] and that:

> I quite agree that there is no law of collocation in the sense of a qualification of, or gloss upon, or exception to, the test for obviousness stated in section 3 of the [Patents Act, 1977]. But before you can apply section 3 and ask whether the invention involves an inventive step, you first have to decide what the invention is. In particular, you have to decide whether you are dealing with one invention or two or more inventions. Two inventions do not become one invention because they are included in the same hardware. A compact motor car may contain many inventions, each operating independently of each other but all designed to contribute to the overall goal of having a compact car. That does not make the car a single invention.

---

100. This example is clearly derived from the UK Court of Appeal decision in *Williams v Nye* (1890) 7 RPC 62 and is strikingly similar to the factual situation in *Anderson's-Black Rock* (above).

101. T 0380/01 – 3.3.6

102. [2005] RPC 208 (**required reading**)

103. (1935) 52 RPC 171, 193

104. [1985] RPC 59, 73-74

If we follow the reasoning of Lord Hoffmann, we recognize the ability of a set of elements and relationships between them defined by a patent claim to satisfy the collocation test as simply a property of those elements. If there is a new function or improved result that flows from the claimed elements and relationships, there is a true combination, and nothing can alter the fact. If the claimed elements and relationships provide no such new function or improved result, we are dealing with a collocation, and again nothing can alter that fact. One may, in obedience to the dictates of judicial fashion omit to ask whether the claimed subject-matter is a true combination or a collocation, but the answer is always there for anyone who decides to look for it.

Simplification

It should be noted that both the inclusion of a known integer in a known combination and the omission of a known integer from a known combination may give rise to patentable subject-matter.[105] In particular, simplification and reduction of component inventory are important aspects of product design, and achieving a previously known technical result with a smaller set of integers, making a single component do the work that two components previously did, has long been recognized as an indicator of patentability. The same is in principle true under the EPC. For example in *American National Can Company*[106] the invention concerned an oriented multiple layer polymeric film that differed from prior art film in the omission of an adhesive layer. The problem with which the invention was concerned was held to be the provision of alternative food packaging films of simpler structure in which the desirable combination of properties possessed by the film was not impaired. Inventive step was affirmed. However, simplification is a known *desideratum*, and it is also possible to find EPO Appeal Board decisions that point in the opposite direction.

The "effect-based" technical problem
test applied by the European Patent Office

Under the *European Patent Convention* the criterion of existence or non-existence of an unexpected new function or result arises positively through an effect-based approach to evaluation of inventive step during problem/solution analysis. Although European technical analysis is conducted within the formal framework of problem/solution, the outcome principally determined by whether the claimed subject-matter leads to a new effect, some new function or advantage that cannot be predicted from the teachings of the prior art references considered collectively.[107]

---

105. *Raleigh v Miller* (1948) 65 RPC 141 at p. 152 (HL).

106. T 0741/95

107. The existence of an unexpected new effect may be a *necessary* condition for patentability but it is not a *sufficient* condition. If the prior art when considered collectively suggests some other advantageous new effect, then arguments concerning mere *"bonus effect"* or *"one-way street"* become relevant, and inventive step may be denied.

Szabo made that clear, for the chemical field for which he was an Appeal Board member, when he said[108] that:

> The practice of the Board of Appeal (Chemistry) has been relying on an effect-centreed problem and solution approach to the question of inventive step. It seems that the principles of this approach have been applied to ordinary cases as well as to other kinds which have not been satisfactorily resolved in the past in a manner which is consistent through all fields of technology.

The EPO *Guidelines for Examination* now make the same point:

> In the context of the problem-and-solution approach, the technical problem means the aim and task of modifying or adapting the closest prior art to provide the *technical effects* that the invention provides over the closest prior art. [emphasis added]

This approach is also explained in the jurisprudence of the EPO Appeal Boards, see e.g. Triazoles/ AGREVO,[109] where the Appeal Board said:

> ...the notional "person skilled in the art" is not to be assumed to seek to perform a particular act without some concrete technical reason: he must be assumed to act not out of idle curiosity but with some specific technical purpose in mind.

> For this reason the Boards of Appeal consistently decide the issue of obviousness on the basis of an objective assessment of the results achieved by the claimed subject-matter, compared with the results achieved according to the state of the art. It is then assumed that the inventor did in fact seek to achieve these results and therefore these results are taken to be the basis for defining the technical problem...

In the EPO, problem and solution analysis determines the citations which an examiner is likely to select when he puts forward an objection as to lack of inventive step, and the arguments which are most advantageously put forward in response to that objection. As those who study EPO Appeal Board decisions rapidly realise, EPO staff, including both examiners and appeal board members, are trained to ask themselves the following sequence of questions:

(1) What is the field of the invention?

(2) What is the most relevant prior art in that field?

(3) Starting from that prior art, what was the technical problem to be solved?

(4) Does the invention as claimed in fact provide a solution of the technical problem?

---

108. G.S.A. Szabo, *"The Problem and Solution Approach to the Inventive Step"*, [1986] 10 EIPR 293-303.
109. T 0939/92 (**required reading**)

(5) Was it inventive to identify the technical problem? If not:

(6) Was it inventive to find the particular solution provided by the claimed subject-matter?

(7) Especially in biotechnology:
   (a) Was the alleged invention obvious to try?
   (b) Was there a reasonable expectation of success?

Conclusion

The advice we receive from the courts in the US and the UK and from the Appeal Boards in the EPO is surprisingly unanimous. The positive guidance we need to follow is simple and is that handed down by the US Supreme Court in *Carnegie Steel v Cambria Iron Company*. We should look for features associated with new and beneficial results, knowing that the courts are likely to give favourable treatment to claims based on such features. In the EPO features of this kind can be used to reconstruct the technical problem upon which problem/solution analysis is based. Furthermore, we should scrutinise the independent claims in our patent specifications for features that are not necessary for obtaining the new and beneficial results, since such features are likely to be redundant and could open routes for third parties to design around the claims.

A further source of unanimity between the US and the UK courts is a dislike of features given no prominence in the specification of the granted patent, but seized on during litigation as the key to inventive step. At the least, *every* feature from which an advantage flows should find its way into main or subsidiary claims. Very preferably the new functions, new results or other advantages should be highlighted and explained in the supporting description, because their credibility at the priority or filing date is many times greater than it is at if first identified post-grant. US courts have in recent years emphasised the public notice function of patents. Compliance with the public notice requirement, it is submitted, includes explaining what features contribute to the invention in its broadest and more specific aspects, and why they do so.

Qualifying subject-matter

"Innovation will die, and so will the rest of you once the EU begins allowing software patents"[110]

Coverage

This article explains briefly the range of subject-matter which may qualify for protection and considers in more detail how computer-related inventions are handled in the US and Europe.

When you have read this paper and the "must-read" materials, you should:

1. **Have a general understanding of the main features of European and US law on these topics.**

2. **Be aware of the need to investigate further than the usual "high level" explanation to identify the real difficulties involved in implementing computer-related and business method inventions and the technical problems to be overcome.**

3. **Be aware of the dangers of giving advice as to patentability in these fields from a purely local law standpoint.**

Introduction

The boundary between subject-matter that qualifies for patent protection and that which does not has been the subject of much debate.

Under US law, a very wide range of subject-matter qualifies for protection because the relevant statutory provision[111] is drafted in broad terms and is not subject to any further statutory qualification. It reads as follows:

> Whoever invents or discovers any new and useful process, machine, manufacture, or composition of matter, or any new and useful improvement thereof, may obtain a patent therefor, subject to the conditions and requirements of this title.

---

110. Quoted by Peter Zura, Patent Attorney, Chicago, Illinois, see
    http://271patent.blogspot.com/2005/04/eu-software-patent-directive-in-my.html

111. 35 USC 101

The European Patents Convention (EPC) also in principle allows grant for a wide range of patentable subject-matter provided that it is industrially applicable. The word "industrially" covers all kinds of industry including agriculture.[112] However, it applies a number of statutory exclusions which do not have counterparts under US law:

(1) discoveries, scientific theories and mathematical methods;

(2) aesthetic creations;

(3) schemes, rules and methods for performing mental acts, playing games or doing business, and programs for computers;

(4) presentations of information;

(5) methods for treatment of the human or animal body by surgery or therapy and diagnostic methods practised on the human or animal body;

(6) inventions the publication or exploitation of which would be contrary to "ordre public" or morality; and

(7) plant or animal varieties or essentially biological processes for the production of plants or animals.

It is beyond the scope of this general introduction to give more than a generalised guide to the often very complex statutory provisions and the jurisprudence under them. There are, however, two particular areas in which an introduction may be helpful in view of the significant number of cases which arise in these fields: computer program-related inventions and business method-related inventions.

Computer programs and related inventions

The idea that there is a world-wide prohibition on patenting computer program-related inventions is a fallacy. For example, in the early 1960s, IBM obtained a patent for a word processor[113] and subsequently for a spreadsheet.[114] Other famous patents that might be mentioned are those for public key cryptography,[115] the LZW compression algorithm used *inter alia* for PDF files[116] and the Eloas patent[117] which

---

112. Arts. 52, 57 EPCO.

113. US-A-3248705 (Damman *et al*; International Business Machines Corporation); believed to be the first word-processor patent.

114. US-A-3610902 (Rahenkamp *et al*; International Business Machines Corporation); see also US-A-4398249 (Pardo *et al*); see *In re Pardo*, 684 F. 2d. 912 (C.C.P.A. 1982); and also US-A-5247611.

115. US-A-4218582 (Hellamn *et al.,* The Board of Trustees of the Leland Stanford Junior University)

116. US-A-4558302 (Welch; Sperry Corporation)

117. US-A-5838906 (Doyle *et al.,* The Regents of the University of California); see US re-examination No 90/006831 (file available for inspection online), see also *Eloas Technologies Incorporated and The Regents of the University of California v Microsoft Corporation*, Fed. Cir. 2 March 2005.

claims features allegedly incorporated into *Windows Explorer* and which is currently the subject of litigation against Microsoft with a potential $500m damages claim. The Eloas patent allows a user of a browser program on a computer connected to an open distributed hypermedia system to access and execute a program object embedded into a hypermedia document much like an embedded data object.

Computer program patentability in US

An early US case which was appealed to the Supreme Court, *Diamond v Diehr*[118] made it clear that the mere presence of a mathematical step (a calculation according to the Arrenhius equation) did not preclude patentability.

The applicants filed a patent application claiming invention for a process for moulding raw, uncured synthetic rubber into cured precision products. While it was possible, by using well-known time, temperature, and cure relationships, to calculate by means of an established mathematical equation when to open the moulding press and remove the cured product, according to the respondents the industry had not been able to measure precisely the temperature inside the press, thus making it difficult to make the necessary computations to determine the proper cure time. The applicants characterised their contribution to the art as residing in the process of constantly measuring the temperature inside the mould and feeding the temperature measurements into a computer that repeatedly recalculated the cure time by use of the mathematical equation and then signalled a device to open the press at the proper time. See the following drawing:

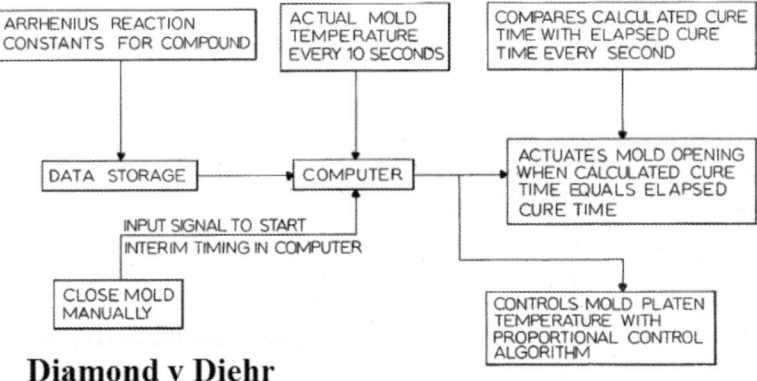

Diamond v Diehr

The claim in issue, which had been rejected by the US Patent Office on the ground of non-patentable subject-matter, read:

> A method of operating a rubber-moulding press for precision moulded compounds with the aid of a digital computer, comprising:
> providing said computer with a data base for said press including at least

---

118. 450 US 175; also available online (**required reading**).

natural logarithm conversion data (ln), the activation energy constant (C) unique to each batch of said compound being moulded, and a constant (x) dependent upon the geometry of the particular mould of the press,

    initiating an interval timer in said computer upon the closure of the press for monitoring the elapsed time of said closure,

    constantly determining the temperature (Z) of the mould at a location closely adjacent to the mould cavity in the press during moulding,

    constantly providing the computer with the temperature (Z),

    repetitively calculating in the computer, at frequent intervals during each cure, the Arrhenius equation for reaction time during the cure, which is

$$\ln v = CZ + x$$

where v is the total required cure time,

    repetitively comparing in the computer at said frequent intervals during the cure each said calculation of the total required cure time calculated with the Arrhenius equation and said elapsed time, and

    opening the press automatically when a said comparison indicates equivalence

The US Supreme Court held that the above claim contained patentable subject-matter notwithstanding the fact that the claimed process was tied to a mathematical formula and was implemented using a digital computer, and accordingly a patent was subsequently issued.[119] The key part of the opinion (which is quoted at length because it contains references to significant earlier US Supreme Court opinions) reads:

> That respondents' claims involve the transformation of an article, in this case raw, uncured synthetic rubber, into a different state or thing cannot be disputed. The respondents' claims describe in detail a step-by-step method for accomplishing such, beginning with the loading of a mould with raw, uncured rubber and ending with the eventual opening of the press at the conclusion of the cure. Industrial processes such as this are the types which have historically been eligible to receive the protection of our patent laws …

> Our conclusion regarding respondents' claims is not altered by the fact that in several steps of the process a mathematical equation and a programmed digital computer are used… Our recent holdings in *Gottschalk v Benson* … and *Parker v Flook* both of which are computer-related, stand for no more than these long-established principles. In *Benson*, we held unpatentable claims for an algorithm used to convert binary code decimal numbers to equivalent pure binary numbers. The sole practical application of the algorithm was in connection with the programming of a general purpose digital computer. We defined "algorithm" as a "procedure for solving a given type of mathematical problem," and we concluded that such an algorithm, or mathematical formula, is like a law of nature, which cannot be the subject of a patent.

> *Parker v Flook*… presented a similar situation. The claims were drawn to a method for computing an "alarm limit." An "alarm limit" is simply a number and the Court

---

119. US-A-4344142

concluded that the application sought to protect a formula for computing this number. Using this formula, the updated alarm limit could be calculated if several other variables were known. The application, however, did not purport to explain how these other variables were to be determined, nor did it purport "to contain any disclosure relating to the chemical processes at work, the monitoring of process variables, or the means of setting off an alarm or adjusting an alarm system. All that it provides is a formula for computing an updated alarm limit".

In contrast, the respondents here do not seek to patent a mathematical formula. Instead, they seek patent protection for a process of curing synthetic rubber. Their process admittedly employs a well-known mathematical equation, but they do not seek to pre-empt the use of that equation. Rather, they seek only to foreclose from others the use of that equation in conjunction with all of the other steps in their claimed process. These include installing rubber in a press, closing the mould, constantly determining the temperature of the mould, constantly recalculating the appropriate cure time through the use of the formula and a digital computer, and automatically opening the press at the proper time. Obviously, one does not need a "computer" to cure natural or synthetic rubber, but if the computer use incorporated in the process patent significantly lessens the possibility of "overcuring" or "undercuring," the process as a whole does not thereby become unpatentable subject-matter.

In *AT&T Corporation v Excel Communications Incorporated*,[120] the invention concerned a message record for long-distance telephone calls that was enhanced by adding a primary interexchange carrier (PIC) indicator. The addition of the indicator aided long-distance carriers in providing differential billing treatment for subscribers, depending upon whether a subscriber called someone with the same or a different long-distance carrier.

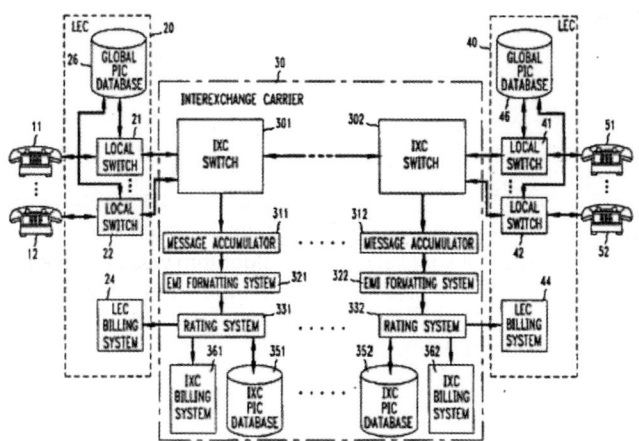

---

120. 172 F.3d 1352 (Fed. Cir. 1999); US-A-5331840.

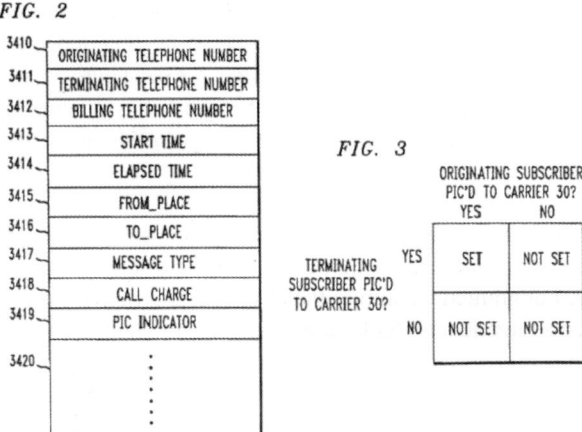

FIG. 2

FIG. 3

The claim in issue, which was held to be patentable subject-matter, read:

> A method for use in a telecommunications system in which interexchange calls initiated by each subscriber are automatically routed over the facilities of a particular one of a plurality of interexchange carriers associated with that subscriber, said method comprising the steps of:
>
> *generating a message record for an interexchange call* between an originating subscriber and a terminating subscriber, and
>
> *including, in said message record, a primary interexchange carrier (PIC) indicator* having a value which *is a function of whether or not the interexchange carrier associated with said terminating subscriber is a predetermined one* of said interexchange carriers."

The CAFC held that the above claim was not simply directed to Boolean logic and stated in its opinion:[121]

> It is clear from the written description of the '184 patent that AT&T is only claiming a process that uses the Boolean principle in order to determine the value of the PIC indicator. The PIC indicator represents information about the call recipient's PIC, a useful, non-abstract result that facilitates differential billing of long-distance calls made by an IXC's subscriber. Because the claimed process applies the Boolean principle to produce a useful, concrete, tangible result without pre-empting other uses of the mathematical principle, on its face the claimed process comfortably falls within the scope of §101.

---

121. Compare and contrast case EPO Appeal Board decision T 0641/00, note also that the Court was NOT considering inventive step.

Computer program patentability at the European Patent Office

Although the EPC formally prohibits the patenting of computer software, successive decisions of the EPO Appeal Boards have limited the application of this prohibition almost to vanishing point, providing that the software can be shown to solve a technical problem or produce a technical result which is not itself within one of the prohibitions of Art. 52 EPC.[122]

In the landmark *Computer-related invention/VICOM* case,[123] the EPO Appeal Board was not willing to grant a claim for all possible uses of a mathematical algorithm for processing data, but granted a claim to the algorithm as applied to real-world data in order to produce a technical effect on a physical entity represented by that data.

The invention related to an improved method for digitally filtering images by convolution which had the advantage that the volume of calculations required to be carried out was significantly less than in prior art methods. The key difference was that a conventional operator matrix was replaced by a "small generating kernel" e.g. of dimensions 3 elements by 3 elements which was iteratively scanned over the data matrix to approximate the result obtained when scanning with the full-sized operator matrix. The result was to bring about a significant reduction in the number of computations that was required for a conventional convolution. Furthermore, in conventional convolution the number of computations required rose as the square of the dimensions of the operator matrix, whereas in Vicom's method the required number of iterations rose only linearly in accordance with the size of the operator matrix it was required to emulate.

The original claim was to "*A method of digitally filtering data...*" This was held to be an abstract notion not distinguished from a mathematical method so long as it was not specified what physical entity was represented by the data and formed the subject of a technical process. The Board said:[124]

> There can be little doubt that any processing operation on a mathematical signal can be described in mathematical terms. The characteristics of a filter, for example, can be expressed in terms of a mathematical formula. A basic difference between a mathematical method and a technical problem can be seen, however, in the fact that a mathematical method or mathematical algorithm is carried out on numbers (whatever those numbers may represent) and provides a result also in numerical form, the mathematical method or algorithm being only an abstract concept prescribing how to operate on the numbers. No direct technical result is produced by the method as such. In contrast thereto, if a mathematical method is used in a technical process, that process can be carried out on a physical entity (which may be a material object but equally an image stored as an electric signal) by some

---

122. See Keith Beresford, *Patenting Software under the European patent Convention,* Sweet & Maxwell, London, 2000 which includes numerous examples of granted software patents and discusses the patenting of user interfaces, software for generating computer programs, business method patents and e-commerce. It is understood that a new edition is in preparation.

123. T 0208/84 (**required reading**); EP-B-00005954 US-A-4330833

124. Reasons, para. 5

technical means implementing the method and provides as its result a certain change in that entity. A technical means might include a computer comprising suitable hardware or an appropriately programmed general purpose computer.

The claim that was held to be allowable read:

A method of digitally processing images
in the form of a two-dimensional data array having elements arranged in rows and columns
in which an operator matrix of size substantially smaller than the size of the data array is convolved with the data array, including sequentially scanning the elements and the data array with the operator matrix,
characterised in that the method includes repeated cycles of sequentially scanning the entire data array with a small generating kernel operator matrix to generate a convoluted array and then replacing the data array as a new data array;
the small generating kernel remaining the same for any single scan of the entire data array and although consisting of at least a multiplicity of elements, nevertheless being of a size substantially smaller than is required of a conventional operator matrix in which the operator matrix is convolved with the data array only once
and the cycle being repeated for each previous new data array by selecting the small generating kernel operator matrices and the number of cycles according to conventional error minimisation techniques until the last new data array generated is substantially the required convolution of the original data array with the conventional operator matrix.

It should be noted that the wording of the claim was unchanged except for the italicised wording in the preamble which applied a field-of-use limitation to the otherwise unpatentable mathematical method. An important factor in the allowance of the above claim was that it was known in the prior art to process images by analog circuitry to improve their sharpness.

Claims to computer programs *per se* or on storage media, and claims to the transmission or electronic distribution of a program on the Internet are now in principle allowable following the decision of the EPO in *Computer related product/IBM*[125] in which the main claim, the allowability of which was not in dispute, read:

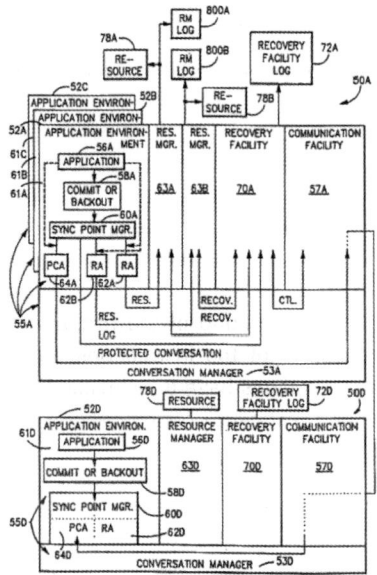

Computer-related product/IBM

---

125. T 1193/97 (**required reading**); EP-B-0457112.

1. A method for resource recovery in a computer system running an application which requests a work operation involving a resource, said method comprising the steps of:

implementing a commit procedure for said work request;

in case the said commit procedure is not completed due to a failure, notifying the application after some time that it can continue to run, whereby said application need not wait for resynchronization; and

while said application continues to run, re-synchronizing said incomplete commit procedure for said resource asynchronously relative to said application.

The claims that were objected to read:

20. A computer program product directly loadable into the internal memory of a digital computer comprising software code portions for performing the steps of claim 1 when said product is run on a computer."

21. A computer program product stored on a computer-usable medium, comprising:

computer-readable program means for causing a computer to control an execution of an application;

computer-readable program means for causing the computer to implement a commit procedure, especially a two-phase commit procedure for said application;

computer-readable program means for causing the computer to notify said application to continue to run in the event said commit procedure fails before completion, whereby said application need not wait for said commit procedure to be completed; and

computer-readable program means for causing the computer to resynchronise said incomplete commit procedure asynchronously relative to said application.

The Board held that claim 20 was in principle allowable, and that it was not appropriate to exclude all computer programs as such, irrespective of their contents. It now all depends on whether the software produces a "further technical effect" which is identified in the decision as follows:

It could be found in the further effects deriving from the execution (by the hardware) of the instructions given by the computer program. Where said further effects have a technical character or where they cause the software to solve a technical problem, an invention which brings about such an effect may be considered an invention, which can, in principle, be the subject-matter of a patent ...

Consequently a patent could be granted not only in the case of an invention where a piece of software manages, by means of a computer, an industrial process or the working of a piece of machinery, but in every case where a program for a computer is the only means, or one of the necessary means, of obtaining a technical effect within the meaning specified above, where, for instance, a technical effect of that kind is achieved by the internal functioning of the computer itself under the influence of said program.

The opinion went on to say that:

> The Board has analysed some aspects of the meaning of the expression 'computer programs as such', with the emphasis on the 'as such', and has arrived at the conclusion that a computer program product is not excluded from patentability if it possesses the potential to bring about a 'further' technical effect.

It also observed that from the standpoint of qualifying subject-matter, it was necessary for the technical effect to be novel. In reaching the above conclusion, the board distinguished the reasoning in the earlier decisions *X-ray apparatus/KOCH & STERZEL,*[126] *Editable document form/IBM,*[127] *Electronic computer components/ROBERT BOSCH*[128] and *System for generating software source code/ATT.*[129]

Although the allowability of claims to data structures has not yet been considered by the EPO Appeal Boards, it is believed that such claims may also be allowable under the EPO practice by analogy with *Television Signal/BBC*[130] where a signal of defined structure for a television picture was held to be patentable because it was a physical reality that could be detected by technical means. The claim read:

A colour television signal adapted to generate a picture with an aspect ratio of greater than 4:3, and in which the active-video portion of a line constitutes at least 85% and preferably 90% of the line period.

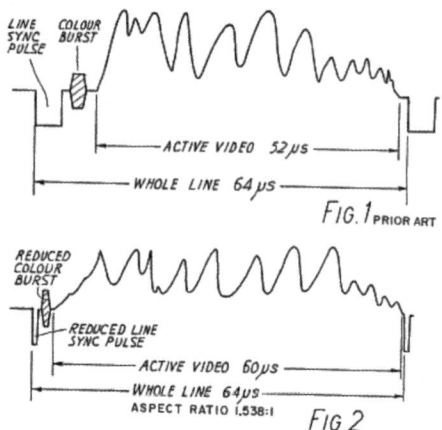

FIG.1 PRIOR ART

FIG.2

Television signal/BBC

In *Data structure product/PHILIPS,*[131] the question that had to be decided was whether a claim to a recording medium having stored information on it was precluded from protection. The Appeal Board followed the *BBC* decision and drew a distinction that had previously been identified by *Shannon* between *information* that can be protected and *content* which is excluded from protection and said:

---

126. T 0026/86
127. T 0110/90
128. T 0164/92
129. T 0204/93
130. T 0163/85; EP-B-0083352.
131. T 1194/97 (**required reading**); EP-B-0500927.

... the deciding board considered it appropriate to distinguish between two kinds of information, when discussing its presentation. According to this distinction, a TV signal solely characterised by the information per se, eg moving pictures, modulated upon a standard TV signal, may fall under the exclusion of Article 52(2)(d) and (3) EPC but not a TV signal defined in terms which inherently comprise the technical features of the TV system in which it occurs. The present board regards a record carrier having data recorded thereon as being in this respect analogous to a modulated TV signal and considers it appropriate to distinguish in a corresponding way between data which encodes cognitive content, e.g. a picture, in a standard manner and functional data defined in terms which inherently comprise the technical features of the system (reader plus record carrier) in which the record carrier is operative. The significance of the distinction between *functional data* and *cognitive information content* in relation to technical effect and character may be illustrated by the fact that in the present context complete loss of the cognitive content resulting in a humanly meaningless picture like "snow" on a television screen has no effect on the technical working of the system, while loss of functional data will impair the technical operation and in the limit bring the system to a complete halt. In particular the board sees no reason to ascribe less technical character to a synchronization signal recorded as digital data, e.g. a predetermined binary string, than to an analog synchronization signal transmitted or recorded as a pulse having a distinctive shape.

The Board supported its position by reference to Claude E. Shannon and Warren Weaver, *The Mathematical Theory of Communication* (1949):

The word information, in this theory, is used in a *special* sense that must not be confused with its *ordinary* usage. In particular, information must not be confused with meaning. In fact, two messages, one of which is heavily loaded with meaning and the other of which is pure nonsense, can be exactly equivalent, from the present (information technology) viewpoint, as regards information. Information in communication theory relates not so much to what you do say, as to what you could say. That is, information is a measure of one's freedom of choice when one selects a message.

The Board also held that the definition that it had put forward was consistent with the legislative history of Articles 52(2)(d) and (3) EPC. The phrase "presentation of information" in Article 52(2)(d) EPC had been adopted from PCT Rule 39.1(v). The records of the PCT Washington Conference 1970, page 572 showed that the intention of the provision was to remove tables, forms, writing styles and the like from what an International Searching Authority had to search. In the view of the board this was subject-matter which merely conveyed cognitive or aesthetic content directly to a human.

In the author's opinion, there is no better illustration of the boundary between technical and non-technical subject-matter than the waveform diagram from the *BBC* case. If, for any invention under consideration, we can find anything new and unexpected in the functional data area to the left of the picture we can be reasonably confident that potentially patentable subject-matter is present. If all the novelty falls within the realm of cognitive information content, then the presence of patentable subject-matter must be in severe doubt, at least so far as the UK and Europe is concerned. The alert patent draftsman should not be content with a high level explanation of the broad functions to be covered, supported perhaps by a few screen-shots and one or two simple flow-charts. Instead he should enquire in detail into the information to be processed and where and how it is held, and what software components are used at various times to receive, store, process and output that information, with particular attention to details of implementation and any difficulties that are overcome.

For example, in the *State Street* case described below at page 65, the patent in issue contains a superficially quite full description of the system and how it is intended to operate. However, could a skilled programmer really build a system on the basis of what is disclosed in the specification and his common general knowledge? What is the host computer which is to form the hub? Under what operating system did it operate? What were the computers at the spokes? What operating systems did they use and were there any compatibility problems if they used different operating system systems? How did the hubs and the spokes communicate together with sufficient security to meet the presumably stringent requirements of a financial institution? What if communication was incomplete or messages were missed? What files needed to reside on the hub? What files needed to reside on the spokes? What elements of the software were standard accounting/banking programs (and if so which?) and what elements were custom-written? What were the real problems involved in making everything work together with the required reliability, accuracy and speed? Two of the interesting black boxes are the general ledger 54 and the portfolio accounting system 56, which are said to be computer programs of types commonly used in accounting. If so, why are we not given actual examples of specific accounting programs that might be used? If the programs need adaptation (as almost certainly they do) broadly what are the changes that are necessary? Are there any real problems in making these programs operate as desired or is this an unusual case where everything is utterly straightforward? Can the skilled systems designer/programmer who has experience of working in a financial environment *really* select what he needs merely on the basis of his general knowledge of accounting software and without any additional guidance? Does the written description disclose sufficient structure to support these functional boxes and meet the requirements of 35 USC 112(6). For example, feature (d) of claim 1 refers to *second means for processing data regarding assets in the portfolio ...* Is this means-plus-function language sufficiently supported by specific disclosed structure? No view is expressed as to whether answers exist for these questions, but they exemplify the kinds of question that an alert draftsman should be asking as preparation for drafting a patent application, and which are likely to identify technical difficulties that might convince a European examiner that the application is grantable. Similar doubts were expressed by the hearing officer in *Raytheon Company's Application (inventory management)*.[132]

---

132. BL O/047/06, 13 February 2006, R. C. Kennel (Hearing Officer).

UK Patent Office – Computer program related inventions

UK practice has been in a state of flux following a series of events in 2005.

The first event was a series of "Technical Contribution" workshops run by the Patent Office in March and April 2005 in preparation for a proposed EU Directive concerning the patentability of computer-related inventions. Attorneys and interested members of the public were invited to participate. However, the proposed EU Directive was disapproved by a vote in the European parliament in May 2005 and no attempt to revive it appears likely.

A second set of events is decisions of the Patents Court in *CFPH LLC's application*[133] and *Halliburton Energy Services Inc v Smith International (North Sea) Ltd and others.*[134] The *CFPH* opinion, in particular, set forth new patentability tests. As interpreted by the UK Patent Office, patentability does not now depend on simple application of a "technical contribution" test. Instead the Patent Office should:

(1) Identify the alleged advance;
(2) Decide whether that advance is new and not obvious; and
(3) Decide whether the advance falls within a field excluded by section 1(2). For this purpose the following test propounded in CFPH at paragraph 104 is considered helpful:

> Would it still be new and not obvious in principle even if the same decisions and commands could somehow be taken and issued by a little man at a control panel, operating under the same rules? If yes, that suggests the invention is not really about computer programming at all.

The third event is an official notice dated 19 August 2005 which can be downloaded from the Patent Office website[135] and which announces that the Patent Office would in future apply the new test set out above and derived from *CFPH*.

Full copies of the case studies that were discussed in the Technical Contribution Workshops can be down-loaded by selecting a link in the online version of the *August 2005 Notice*. Since the EU directive is not proceeding, the Patent Office no longer considers these case studies to be of direct relevance. However, when it came to establish its current patentability standards, the Patent Office found it worthwhile to reconsider these case studies and compared the results using the *technical-contribution* test with those using the *CFPH* test. The case studies therefore provide a record of what was, and was not, considered to be patentable in 2005. For the patents draftsperson, it is advantageous to present an invention so as to correspond to one of the case studies that had a favorable outcome.

The studies and their outcomes are set out below.

---

133. [2005] EWHC 1589 Pat.
134. [2005] EWHC 1623 Pat.
135. www.patent.gov.uk/about/ippd/issues/cii-workshops-case-analysis.htm.

Case Study No 1 – Traffic light controller

Background: Traffic control is a vital part of urban highway management. In particular, the free flow of traffic has implications both for congestion and the environment. A system is proposed where data from traffic sensors is collected over a period of time and used to develop a program for the control of the traffic lights along a stretch of highway in order to optimise the flow of traffic along that stretch of road.[136]

Claim: A system for dynamically optimizing traffic flow along a highway by creating a traffic light control program from sensed data comprising:

- means for obtaining data from sensors relating to traffic along said highway;
- means for transmitting the collected data to a central control system;
- means for analysing the collected data at the control system to generate a control program for traffic lights on the highway;
- means for transmitting the generated control program to the correct traffic light; and
- means for installing the new control program in a traffic light and then operating the traffic light according to the new control program.

Outcome: Grant both under the *CFPH* approach and under the *technical contribution* approach.

Analysis: The advance in the art is the idea of creating a control program from real time data and its transmission to and installation in a set of traffic lights so as to dynamically optimise traffic flow. Assuming this is novel and inventive *per se*, the advance goes beyond the exclusions in Article 52(2) and the subject-matter is therefore patentable.

Case Study No 2 – Hazard warning device

Background: It has long been difficult to identify a noxious substance such as a poisonous gas until it is too late. The applicant has developed a tool that can be incorporated into a hazard warning device that can be connected to a central control station by a network. The device has a sensor that "sniffs" the air around it and extracts a chemical signature in a binary form. The device incorporates an embedded processor that creates a sliding window allowing chunks of the data to be analysed against known chemical compositions. If a match occurs then a positive identification signal is sent to a central control point which raises an alarm.

Claim: A hazard warning device connected by a network to a central control station for the detection of a noxious substance comprising:

- a sensor for sampling the air around the housing of the hazard warning device;
- a conversion means coupled to the sensor to provide a binary representation of the sample;

---

136. This study was clearly inspired by *Lux Traffic Controls Ltd v Pike Signals Ltd* [1993] RPC 107.

- ❑ a processor for receiving the binary representation from the conversion means, the processor being arranged to:
- ❑ create a data window of a predetermined size;
- ❑ apply the window to the binary representation;
- ❑ compare the data in the window against a list of predefined representations of known noxious substance;
- ❑ if a match occurs instruct a transmission means to transmit a signal to a central control station over the network and the central control system raising an alarm; or
- ❑ if no match occurs move the data window forward through the trace by a predetermined amount and repeat the comparison step until no more data is available.

Outcome: Grant both under the *CFPH* approach and under the *technical contribution* approach.

Analysis: The advance in this case is a new method of detecting a noxious substance by sampling the air, digitizing the sample and then comparing successive segments of the sample against a library of known noxious substances. If this is new and not obvious, then it is novel and inventive because it provides an improved detecting/alarm system that goes beyond the exclusions in Article 52(2). Whilst the program is clearly a major element of the advance it does not make up the entirety of the advance.

Case Study No 3 – Secure communication for mobile telephony

Background: Secure communications have become very important in the mobile telephone industry and the need to prevent someone listening into conversations is seen as requirement in many businesses. The applicant, a mobile phone manufacturer, has developed a new "discombobulation" chip[137] which is located in the phone between the wireless transmitter/receiver and the rest of the hardware. The device works by using the sending and destination addresses as a key to encrypting the contents of the message. On receipt of the message at the destination address the device is able to decrypt the message using the sender address. The device relies on an algorithm present in both devices that uses the addresses, date and time as an input.

Claim: A mobile telephony discombobulation device for ensuring secure communications between a sender and receiving device, the device being coupled to the wireless receiver/transmitter of the phone such that it modifies the transmitted/received message by encrypting/decrypting the body of the message using an algorithm based on the address of the sender, receiver and data and time of the call.

Outcome: Grant both under the *CFPH* approach and under the *technical contribution* approach.

---

137. For readers whose native language is not English, "discombobulation" is a made-up word to represent an arbitrary and imaginary technical function.

Analysis: The advance here is not simply a mathematical algorithm for taking an abstract digital sequence and encrypting it. Crucial to the advance is the fact that this is being done in a telephone system, because it is using features of that system – the sending and receiving addresses – to communicate in a secure way. Assuming this is novel and inventive, the advance goes beyond the exclusions in Article 52(2) and is thus novel and inventive. It is worth noting that this conclusion does not depend on whether the invention is implemented as a chip or as software.

Case Study No 4 – Digitally enhancing a photograph

Background: Photographic intelligence provides a large amount of information for data analysts in the security sector. However, given the nature of the work, large numbers of photographs in this business are taken at night or in conditions of low light. The applicant has defined a method of digitally filtering these photographs to adjust for the low light conditions and make them more readable.

Claim: Apparatus for digitally enhancing a photograph taken in low light conditions by applying a digital filter wherein the apparatus comprises:

☐ means for creating a two-dimensional array representing the photograph;
☐ means for identifying an operator matrix, the operator matrix representing a light enhancement factor;
☐ means for applying the operator matrix to the two-dimensional array representing the photograph; and
☐ means for reproducing the photograph after the application of the operator matrix.

Outcome: Grant both under the *CFPH* approach and under the *technical contribution* approach.

Analysis: This case study is based entirely on *Vicom*[138] As in case study 3, if the advance were simply a mathematical algorithm operating on abstract data, it would be unpatentable. However, following the reasoning of *Vicom* which the Deputy Judge in *CFPH* clearly thought to remain sound,[139] the practical application of an algorithm can be patentable. The advance in the art here would appear to be enhancing a photograph taken in low light conditions by applying an "operator matrix". Assuming this is both novel and inventive *per se*, it is novel and inventive under the description of an invention in Article 52 EPC because adjusting the quality of an image is an advance that goes beyond the exclusions in Article 52(2).

Case Study No 5 – Software component identification whilst upgrading

Background: The installation of software onto a computer is known to be difficult to achieve. This is made even more complicated when the computer to be updated is inside a television receiver system such as those in use with digital television signals. This

---

138. *Supra.*
139. Paragraph 64 of his decision.

presents the unique problem of a large number and variety of destination devices, each requiring different configurations. It is further complicated by some subscribers not needing some of the updates due to the subscription package they have. The applicant devised a way of issuing software upgrades that checks the existing version, evaluates this against the subscription package and identifies the required software components to be updated. The central system then issues the upgrades as an executable package which is auto-installed on the user device and schedules a reboot when the device is set to standby or reset by the user. This provides uninterrupted viewing to the applicant as the working memory of the device contains the current operating code.

Claim: A method of updating the configuration of a television receiver device comprising the steps of:

- ☐ identifying the subscription package appropriate to the device;
- ☐ identifying the software requirements for the said package;
- ☐ assembling the required software into an update package and creating a manifest;
- ☐ combining the manifest with the update package in an update routine for execution on the device;
- ☐ downloading the update routine to the device;
- ☐ executing the update routine, the update routine comparing the new manifest with the existing manifest on the device and installing only those software components requiring installation or update; and
- ☐ scheduling a reboot of the system on reset or when the device is set to standby mode.

Outcome: Grant both under the *CFPH* approach and under the *technical contribution* approach for the first scenario; second scenario refuse under the *CFPH* approach.

Analysis: If one assumes that previously users had to work out for themselves what upgrades they needed, order them and then install them, the advance lies in the idea of automatically working out what each user needs, sending it to them and then automatically installing the required components. Each of these is a software-controlled step, but the advance as a whole is not just in the details of the software and therefore goes beyond the exclusions in Article 52(2). However, if one considers a different scenario in which the prior art is more developed, the answer could well be different. For example, if the advance lay solely in the way in which a program identified the requisite software components, that would be an advance that is new and inventive only under a description that does not go beyond what is excluded under Article 52(2), namely, programs for computers.

[Case studies 6-8 relate to business methods, Case study 9 relates to bioinformatics. These are omitted.]

Case Study No 10 – Application program interface for operating system

Background: The applicant has developed a new computer-operating system, LinoDoors. The system is very secure and is platform independent. It uses sets of standard tools which are accessed by all programs. In use, it creates a virtual machine for each application. Each tool has its own data structure which when populated with data creates the environment for each application including menus and other screen display elements. In order to work with the operating system, the applicant has developed an application programming interface that is to be used by any application wishing to communicate with the operating system. This interface forms a major portion of the operating system, effectively acting as an interface layer to the internal operations of the system. In use it receives parameters from the application and populates the tool data structures before instantiating the appropriate data structure objects.

Claim: An application programming interface for an operating system, the interface comprising;

- ☐ means for receiving parameters from an application;
- ☐ means for populating a tool data structure with said parameters;
- ☐ means for instantiating a tool object using the populated data structure.

Outcome: Refuse both under the *CFPH* approach and under the *technical contribution* approach for the first scenario; second scenario refuse under the *CFPH* approach.

Analysis: This case study concerns an application programming interface (API). The advance is in the provision of a utility to allow any application to talk to the applicant's new operating system. An API is a program allowing other programs to talk to each other. Thus, even if the API is novel and inventive, the advance is novel and inventive only under descriptions that are excluded by Article 52(2) i.e. a program for a computer. The application of the "little man" approach suggested in paragraph 104 of the *CFPH* judgment confirms this since any novelty or inventiveness would lie only in the program and it could not be replaced by the little man at his console.[140]

Case Study No 11 – Automatic chip design method

Background: The advent of silicon conductor technology has allowed electronic devices to become smaller. Improved manufacturing techniques have also allowed for these to be manufactured more cheaply. Consequently, it is now possible to create specific chips (ASIC's) to undertake a specific function such as solving a quadratic equation. The applicant has identified a method of designing a chip specific to a calculation and manufacturing it. The chip is designed by undertaking a probability analysis of the scheduling of the functional components of the calculation to be performed by the chip. Once the order of the functional components has been determined the chip floor plan is designed accordingly.

---

140. This analysis appears directly contradictory to that of the EPO Appeal Board in *Editable document form/INTERNATIONAL BUSINESS MACHINES CORPORATION* T 0110/90. In that case control items, for example printer control codes included in a text which was represented as digital data were held to relate to technical features of the text processing system in which they occurred, and the transformation of control codes which are technical features of one text processing system into those belonging to another text processing system was a method having technical character.

Claim: A method of manufacturing an integrated chip to perform a particular calculation comprising the steps of:

☐ receiving a functional specification of the calculation;
☐ identifying the parameters and relationships between the parameters of the functional specification;
☐ scheduling the functional flow of the calculation by assessing the probability that a previous function will have completed;
☐ using the said schedule to create a chip floor plan; and
☐ manufacturing the chip by using the chip floor plan.

Outcome: Refuse under the *CFPH* approach (first scenario) but grant (second scenario). Refuse under the *technical contribution* approach (first scenario).

Analysis: If the design process does not result in chips of a new type, inclusion of the manufacturing step at the end of the claim is simply a guise to give the claim an air of technicality. The advance must lie in the particular design process itself. Even if this design process is novel and inventive, it is novel and inventive only under descriptions that are excluded, namely methods for performing mental acts and programs for computers.[141] The position might be different if the design process resulted in a new type of chip. In that scenario the advance would be a new chip with improved characteristics, and that would be patentable as the advance would be novel and inventive under descriptions that go beyond the excluded items.

[Case study 12 relates to a business method (online gaming) and is omitted; see the decision in Shopaloltto discussed below.]

Case Study 13 – Mobile telephony – dynamically allocating bandwidth

Background: Mobile phones operate in cells with each cell having a base station responsible for handling all traffic within that cell. As a mobile phone user moves they pass into other cells and it is necessary to "hand off" the call to the next base station. This "hand off" information is useful in determining the number of users in a cell and hence through the use of an algorithm developed for the task a useful indication of the likely demand for telephony services. The applicant has developed equipment which can use this information to make bandwidth dynamically available within a base station on this basis. The equipment also identifies flows of users enabling adjacent cells to be warned of the requirement for more bandwidth. For example, mobile phone demand after a major public event such as a cup final will be high in a single cell. However, as

---

141. See also *NMR Holdings No 2 Pty Limited* BL O/230/05, 16 August 2005. The applications in question related to methods for designing coils for magnetic resonance imaging. The analysis in this case study conflicts with that of the EPO in case T 0605/93 *Designing receptacles/DAI NIPPON*. It also appears to conflict with a decision of the German courts. The headnote of the German Federal Patents Court (Bundespatentgericht) of 21 March 2002 in case 21 W (pat) 24/00 Cable Harness explains that if the characterizing instructions of a claimed computer-implemented method provide the solution of a specific technical problem, in the case in issue the industrial production of cable harnesses without the usual construction of a prototype, then such programs are not excluded from patentability. Is not a process that reduces the manufacturing cost of a chip a technical process?

the crowd disperses, the flow of spectators will move in two different directions through a number of cells – all of which may require dynamic allocation of bandwidth.

Claim: A method of using "hand off" data in a mobile telephony system to dynamically allocate bandwidth to a base station according to demand and to identify adjacent cells where additional bandwidth may be required, the method using an algorithm comprising the steps of:

- ☐ identifying the number of devices in a cell;
- ☐ monitoring the hand off data and when the number of hand offs exceeds a predetermined value issuing a resource demand to a dynamic bandwidth allocator;
- ☐ storing the hand off path of a phone; and
- ☐ monitoring the hand off paths and when the number of devices following a specific path exceeds a predetermined value issuing a resource demand to the dynamic bandwidth allocator for an adjacent cell.

Outcome: Grant both under the *CFPH* approach and under the *technical contribution* approach.

Analysis: The advance here is using the limited bandwidth available to a mobile telephone network more efficiently by changing the bandwidth allocated to each cell on the basis of real-time demand. Assuming that is new and inventive *per se*, it is new and inventive under the description of an invention in the sense of Article 52 EPC because the advance goes beyond the exclusions in Article 52(2). In particular, the advance viewed as a whole is not just a computer program, though obviously it uses a program.

Case Study No 14 – Generating a test script for program QA

Background: The testing of software applications has long been fraught with difficulty. It is believed that only 2% of code is ever truly tested. This obviously presents a problem when safety systems are being developed. Consequently, there exists a need to provide a method of generating test scripts which can test all code in an efficient manner. The applicant has developed a software application which takes as its inputs a specification for a program and identifies test paths through the specification. The application then produces a test script that is applied to the written program. The program then further records any discrepancies in a report which can be used to quality assure the written program.

Claim: A method of generating a test script for quality assurance of a program written according to a specification comprising the steps of:

- ☐ parsing the specification to identify variables, relationships and an expected output;
- ☐ establishing a test script using a test case of variables;
- ☐ executing the test script against the program; and
- ☐ comparing the output with the expected output and using the results to quality assure the written program.

Outcome: Refuse both under the *CFPH* approach and under the *technical contribution* approach.

Analysis: The advance is deriving the test script by parsing the specification for the program. The final step of executing the program would not form part of the advance in the art since the execution of a program is known. While the advance may be novel and non obvious, it is novel and inventive only under the description of a computer program and thus fails the second CFPH test. This is confirmed by application of the "little man" approach (see case study 10 on page 55).

Case Study No 15 – Assessing health of farm animals

Background: Assessing the health of farm animals is often difficult given the large number of animals involved. The applicant has developed a method of using a known multi channel sensor with a number of sensors that are arranged to be distributed over the surface of the animal and provide a number of outputs relating to physiological data. These outputs are then fed to a processing means where they are compared to a known set of conditions which relate to a healthy animal. The processing means determines if there is a statistical deviation from the normal distribution of the readings and provides an immediate indication of the health to the farmer. The device has a specific use for assessing the health of milking cows as they are in a known location twice a day.

Claim: A method of permitting an indication as to the health of a farm animal [identifying an animal having abnormal skin indicia] by comparing selected physiological characteristics of the animal [skin indicia] to reference characteristics of a healthy condition for the animal [reference skin indicia], the method comprising:

- □ using a multi channel sensor having a plurality of sensor elements attached to a region of skin of the animal;
- □ transmitting the readings to a processor means and determining a statistical distribution;
- □ comparing the distribution with a known distribution for a healthy animal [a reference distribution of said skin indicia] to provide an assessment of any deviation between them; and
- □ where the deviation is above a statistical norm indicating that an animal is unhealthy [providing an indication for the animal].

Outcome: Refuse both under the *CFPH* approach and under the *technical contribution* approach.

Analysis: The advance lies in combining the various readings to provide a single assessment or measure, rather than merely giving the user all the individual readings and leaving them to work it out for themselves. The way in which the readings are combined is obviously important, but this is not simply a mathematical analysis carried out on abstract numbers – what the numbers signify is crucial. Were it not for Article 52(4), this advance would be novel and inventive under the description of an invention in the sense of Article 52 EPC because it goes beyond the "mathematical method" exclusion in Article 52(2). However, Article 52(4) states that a diagnostic method practiced on an animal is not considered to be susceptible of industrial application, and this is a generic exclusion.[142]

Case Study No 16 – Finding legal parking areas using GPS

Background: With the advent of GPS technology, obtaining the position of an object, such as a vehicle, can now be done far more accurately than traditional methods. Furthermore, the advance in geographical mapping systems now makes it possible to provide a highly accurate routing system. The applicant has developed a system which combines these two operations to determine whether a vehicle is legally parked. The system comprises a database of permitted parking locations, a central server and an in- vehicle device which incorporates a GPS location finder, a transmitter/receiver and a screen. In use the vehicle device obtains a GPS location for its current position, transmits it to a server. The server determines if it is legally parked by looking up the position in the database and returns an appropriate message to the vehicle for display on the screen. In the advent of an illegal parking operation the server will also transmit navigation instructions to the vehicle device giving guidance to the nearest available car park.

Claims: A method of determining if a vehicle is parked in a permitted location and if not guiding the vehicle to the nearest car park the method comprising:

☐ using an in-vehicle device obtaining the position of the car using a GPS locator and transmitting the position to a server;
☐ receiving the location at the server and looking up the positioning a list of positional data, the list of positional data being positional data of known valid parking spaces and;
☐ where the position is a valid parking space transmitting an "OK to Park Here" message for display on the screen of the in vehicle device, or where the position is an invalid parking space, implementing a navigation module to obtain a route to the nearest car par and transmitting the route to the vehicle for display on the in vehicle device screen.

Outcome: On the first scenario grant both under the *CFPH* approach and under the *technical contribution* approach. On the second scenario refuse under the *CFPH* approach.

---

142. As befits a patent office study, this is a claim with avoidable built-in weakness. The method of the invention provides a method for identifying animals whose skin data lie outside pre-defined norms. Diagnosis happens later. The apparatus does not perform any value judgment concerning the health of the animal: that is a matter for subsequent investigation. Astute European attorneys do not draft claims that fall into traps of this type by claiming more than the apparatus really achieves. Properly formulated, there is no reason why a patent should not be obtained for this invention, the [features] added to the claim providing an indication of how the prohibition on diagnostic method patents might be avoided. See also the EPO Enlarged Appeal Board decision G 0001/04 *Diagnostic methods/PRESIDENT'S REFERENCE* (16 December 2005) in which the requirements for exclusion under the diagnostic methods prohibition were construed narrowly.

Analysis: Given that GPS *per se* is known, the advance appears to be using GPS, in conjunction with a database of permitted parking locations, to advise a driver on where he/she can park. If the advance were merely giving information, it would fail the *CFPH* test, but it is not. The use of GPS in order to select the appropriate information is crucial. Assuming use of GPS in this way is not known, the advance goes beyond the exclusions in Article 52(2) EPC and is thus novel and inventive in the sense of Article 52. However, the answer would be different if it was already known to use GPS to advise drivers on other local facilities. In that scenario, the advance would lie merely in the provision of a different type of information, and that would not go beyond the "presentation of information" exclusion in Article 52(2). It would also have fallen foul of the previous "*technical contribution*" test. (Quite apart from this, the advance would probably also be obvious).

Case Study No 17 – Multi-processor compiler

Background: Compiling programs is often a complex and difficult task. This task is made even more difficult by the use of multiple processor technologies. In these circumstances the compiler has to consider if the program can be compiled into threads, where each thread can be executed on single or multiple processors. In order to do this, the compiler has to consider the scheduling of each thread and the visibility of both local and global variables. The applicant has developed a compiler which incorporates a data structure into the compiled code. In order for this to work the compiler inserts information tags into the code which read/write status values from/to the data structure to determine the next step for the program thus avoiding deadlocks due to the waiting of results from multiple processors. The main advantage of such a compiler is that it improves the efficiency of a program and hence the machine it is running on by making more effective use of resources.

Claim: A method of more efficiently using the processing capabilities of a multi processor computer by using a scheduling compiler, said compiler inserting a data structure to record the state of each thread into the compiled code to improve the efficiency of the compiled program comprising;

- ☐ receiving source code and parsing code into threads
- ☐ for each thread identifying the variables to be used;
- ☐ scheduling the threads to the number of processors in the system;
- ☐ updating a data structure for each thread and variable, wherein each complete record in the data structure acts as a state machine for each thread or variable;
- ☐ inserting a first instruction into the compiled code for instantiating a state object for each thread and variable;
- ☐ inserting information tags into the compiled code, each information tag when executed, providing update information to the state object the thread or variable; and
- ☐ executing the compiled code on a multi-processor computer.

Outcome: Borderline under the *CFPH* approach, grantable under the *technical contribution* approach.

Analysis: From the fact that deadlocks are avoided it would appear that the advance in this particular case is a compiler for generating a program which, when run, causes the computer to function differently at a technical, not just a program, level. Arguably, that just tips the balance towards an advance that is novel and inventive under a description that goes beyond the exclusions in Article 52(2). However, it is a borderline case, because one could also argue that a compiler is nothing more than a program and thus any advance in a compiler does not go beyond the computer program exclusion. Certainly compilers that do not result in a computer that functions differently at a technical level are unlikely to be patentable under the *CFPH* approach, though they would not have been patentable under the *technical contribution* approach either.[143]

Case Study No 18 – Spreadsheet recalculation using improved data structure

Background: Spreadsheets work by using cell references as inputs to a calculation procedure. When changes are made to a spreadsheet it is necessary to undertake a recalculation process to keep the information accurate. In a small spreadsheet this presents few problems but in larger spreadsheets with many calculations the time taken for recalculations to propagate through a spreadsheet can be long. The applicant has developed a new data structure that will in effect act as a multiple index to cells that are affected by a change. The structure works by holding a cell reference as an indexed value to a record of cells making up the inputs to that cell. It then becomes possible to "tree walk" using a source cell to identify all other cells affected. This method will improve the speed of the calculation.

Claim: A method of improving the speed of recalculation of a spreadsheet using an improved data structure the method comprising:

☐ establishing a data structure to hold a cell reference as an index value in a first field with further fields containing constituent cell references;

☐ establishing a second data structure to hold calculation chains reflecting the linking of cells in the spreadsheet, the structure using the last cell in the chain as an index value;

☐ instantiating a tree walker object to operate on the first data structure and inverting the chain before inserting the value chain into the second structure; and

☐ when a new value is entered into a cell, looking up the cell reference in the second data structure to identify the affected cells, recalculating the value in the cells, looking up the affected cell reference in the first data structure and if found repeating the above steps;

☐ executing the compiled code on a multi-processor computer.

---

143. It is submitted that this is not a borderline case. Comparre EPO Appeal Board decision in *Computer Program Product II/IBM* T 0935/97 which expressly states (Reasons, paragraph 6.5) that a patent may be granted not only where software manages an external process or machine, but also where the program produces a technical effect relating to the internal function of the computer itself, and *Computer Program Product/IBM* T 1173/97 where the same conclusion was expressed at paragraph 6.5 of the Reasons. Insofar as these cases, which are generally recognised as landmark decisions of the EPO Appeal Boards were not cited by counsel in *CFPH*, and are not discussed in that decision, it is arguable that the broader conclusions contained in it were reached *per incuriam* and should not be followed.

Outcome: Refuse both under the *CFPH* approach and under the *technical contribution* approach.

Analysis: The advance lies in storing information about relationships between cells and then using this information in a particular recalculation routine which allows the spreadsheet to be updated more quickly. This may well be novel and inventive but it is novel and inventive only under the description of a computer program and thus fails the second *CFPH* test. This is confirmed by application of the "little man" approach (see case study 10): the only reason that the advance may be novel or inventive is as a result of the use of the computer program which makes the changes easier to implement.[144]

Decisions immediately following the *CFPH* case showed that the UK Patent Office was applying the new test suggested in that case in a stringent manner, and possibly more stringently than the above case studies would suggest.

Mark-up language conversion/ORACLE CORPORATION[145] concerned a method of converting text from one markup language (eg. SGML) to a second markup language (eg. HTML) and was refused on the basis that the invention related to a computer program as such which should not be foreclosed to the public under the patent law. A similar decision was handed down in *Data Storage System/ORACLE CORPORATION*[146] which concerned a data structure for storing different versions of data objects, for example, computer program files or modular elements of computer programs. A third decision *Information retrieval system/OVERTURE SERVICES INC*[147] concerned a search engine for searching geo-coded records in a database. Conflict between at least the first two of these decisions and the EPO Appeal Board

---

144. The facts in this study mirror those in *Gale's Application* [1991] RPC 305 in which a patent was refused on appeal to the UK Court of Appeal for a ROM in which was stored instructions for carrying out an algorithm that permitted square roots to be calculated more accurately. Anyone who considers that such cases are distinguishable from the *Vicom* decision shows little knowledge of the history of technology. One of the principal reasons why the claim in *Vicom* was allowed was that the process that was being carried out digitally was a process that had previously been carried out using analog filter circuitry. Readers should cast their minds back to the early 1960s when the predominant calculating machines to be found in scientific laboratories were hand-cranked and difficult to use. Mains-powered mechanical calculators were available, but were the size of a fairly large cash register and heavy to carry about. Their ability to perform multiplication and division by entering numerals and commands on a keyboard seemed little short of miraculous, as did the first electronic calculators which started to appear in the late 1960s (the Inorganic Chemistry Laboratory at Oxford University had its first electronic calculator for student use in early 1968). Calculations were performed mechanically or electro-mechanically and then by dedicated electronic circuits before they were performed in software, and the analogy with the filter circuits of *Vicom* is direct and inescapable. Increased speed of calculation is clearly a technical achievement. Anyone who in the early 1960s made a mechanical desk calculator run twice as fast, probably with simplified mechanical components, would have been in no doubt that he had achieved something technical and would have expected to be able to patent his technology if it was inventive. In Case T 0461/03 *Calculation unit/TOSHIBA,* the EPO Appeal Board held that an application for a calculation unit for calculating a division or square root in which remainders could be determined simply by addition and subtraction allowing compact code and high speed was un-patentable because of non-enablement, but the Board did not object that the claimed subject-matter was a computer program as such; see WO 99/381412.

145. BL O/254/05 dated 13 September 2005; see GB-A-2385686.

146. BL 0/255/05 dated 14 September 2005; see GB-A-2383152.

147. BL O/331/05, 21 December 2005; see GB-A-2379062.

decision in *Editable document form/INTERNATIONAL BUSINESS MACHINES CORPORATION* and with the landmark decisions in *Computer program Product/IBM* and *Computer program product II/IBM* is clear and direct. Immediately following the *CFPH* case, the UK Patent Office was adopting a position which is significantly more restrictive than that applied by the EPO.

Subsequent decisions the Patents Court casts doubt on the appropriateness of a restrictive approach and pointed towards the continuing importance of the *technical contribution* test. Patent revocation proceedings in *Research in Motion UK Limited v Inpro Licensing SARL*[148] concerned a patent which was alleged to be infringed whenever a BlackBerry device downloads a web page including images. The claim in issue read:

> An internet proxy-server comprising: a first data port adapted for accessing other Internet servers; and a second data port adapted for connecting to a field computer; wherein the proxy-server is adapted to access the other Internet servers through the first data port, directed by commands and data received through the second data port from the field computer, to download data from the Internet servers thus accessed, to transpose the downloaded data by reducing information density, and to transfer the transposed data via the first data link in a TCP/IP format characterised in that upon connection, the field computer transfers to the proxy-server information particular to specific characteristics of the field computer including information identifying the specific size and resolution of the display of the field computer, and wherein the proxy-server downloads data comprising WEB pages and transposes the data in reliance on such information to match the specific size and resolution of the field computer.

The patent in issue was held to be infringed but invalid for obviousness. Validity was also challenged on the basis that the invention was in a field that was excluded from patentability. Pumfrey J rejected this objection for the following reasons:

> It is now settled, at least at this level, that the right approach to the exclusions can be stated as follows. Taking the claims correctly construed, what does the claimed invention contribute to the art outside excluded subject-matter? The test is a case-by-case test, and little or no benefit is to be gained by drawing analogies with other cases decided on different facts in relation to different inventions. RIM says that the point does not require elaboration. It contends that all that is claimed, as a matter of substance, is a collection of programs for computers. I think this is wrong. What the claims give is a technical effect: computers running faster and transmitting information more efficiently, albeit ultimately for the purpose of displaying part of that information.
>
> I am anxious that these exclusions are not given too wide a scope. All modern industry depends upon programmed computers, and one must be astute not to defeat patents on the ground that the subject-matter is excluded under Article 52 unless the invention lies in excluded subject-matter as such. The test proposed by RIM in this case (is a computer program accused of

---

148. Patents Court, Pumfrey J., 2 February 2006, [2006] EWHC 70, see EP-Bo-0892947.

infringement) proves too much. An offer of computer program may be an offer of a process for use in the United Kingdom (section 60(1)(b)) or it may itself be 'means relating to an essential element of the invention...' within section 60(2) even when the invention cannot be accused of residing in excluded subject-matter: it depends on the facts. Perhaps one can say that the invention does not lie in excluded subject-matter, even though it may be expressed in a computer program.

I agree with RIM, therefore, that the question does not call for elaboration, but disagree that invention lies in excluded subject-matter. This objection fails.

It remains to be seen whether further developments in UK case law will more closely align the UK Patent Office approach with that of the EPO Appeal Boards. Very recently there have been UK Patent Office decisions suggesting a more lenient approach[149] e.g. on the basis (a) that the invention concerns what the program must do rather than how it would be structured or written or (b) that the invention causes the computer to "*function differently at a technical level and not just at a program level*".

Business methods in the US

In this field, there is a major difference in approach between the USPTO and US courts on the one hand and the European patent offices and courts on the other hand, that difference flowing from the statutory prohibition in Europe but not in the US on business method patenting, and on the requirement in Europe for "technical effect".

The leading US authority, which favours grant of business method patents, is the decision of the US Court of Appeals for the Federal Circuit in *State Street Bank & Trust Company v Signature Financial Group.*[150] In that case, the input data was numerical information (financial data) and the output was also numerical information (a share price) and in contrast to the reasoning in *Vicom* the invention was held to be patentable.

---

149. *Sun Microsystems Inc's Application*, 2 March 2006, BL O/057/06 (rationalized set of Java Bytecode instructions giving more elegant and robust virtual machine, patentable), see WO 02/077806; *ARM Limited's Application*, BL O/066/06, GB-A-23913148 (Compilation of application code for generating instructions for execution by a processor; advance in the art was the use of data from a non-invasive trace unit to direct compilation of application code giving faster and more accurate compiler that can adapt and improve iteratively each time it is used, inventive and not excluded).

150. 149 F. 3d 1368 (Fed. Cir. 1998); US-A-5193056. The difference between the US and the European approach is sharply demonstrated by the file wrapper of the corresponding EP-A-0575519 (file available for inspection online). The EPO Examiner objected that no new technical effect was discernible. The disclosed problem was to reduce fund operating costs, and such a problem was associated with methods of doing business rather than a problem of a technical nature. The applicants argued that the data being manipulated represented physical entities (e.g. fund asset values), and that these entities corresponded to physical reality in the same way as the image data in *Vicom*. The Examiner replied that no technical skills or considerations were required for solving any explicit or implicit technical problem, and that fund asset values and the like were business objects, whose processing did not amount to a technical process. The EPO repeated its objection that the invention was non-technical in further correspondence, and the application was allowed to lapse by failure to respond to a communication from the Examining Division.

The patent in issue was directed to a data processing system for implementing an investment structure that had been developed for use in Signature's business as an administrator and accounting agent for mutual funds. In essence, the system, identified by the proprietary name *Hub and Spoke*, facilitated a structure whereby mutual funds (Spokes) pooled their assets in an investment portfolio (Hub) organised as a partnership. This investment configuration provided the administrator of a mutual fund with the advantageous combination of economies of scale in administering investments coupled with the tax advantages of a partnership. In particular, this system provided means for a daily allocation of assets for two or more Spokes that were invested in the same Hub.

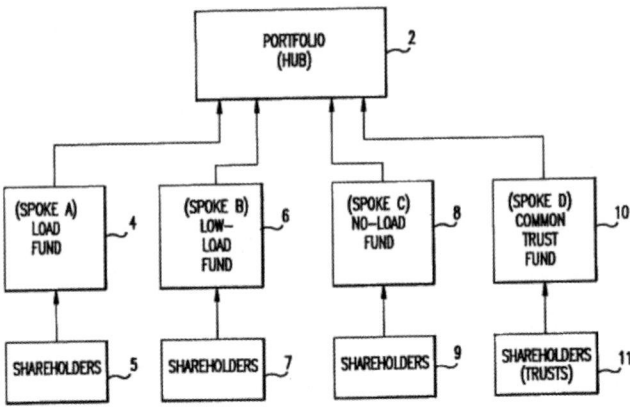

The system determined the percentage share that each Spoke maintained in the Hub, while taking into consideration daily changes both in the value of the Hub's investment securities and in the concomitant amount of each Spoke's assets. In determining daily changes, the system also allowed for the allocation among the Spokes of the Hub's daily income, expenses, and net realised and unrealised gain or loss, calculating each day's total investments based on the concept of a book capital account. This enabled the determination of a true asset value of each Spoke and accurate calculation of allocation ratios between or among the Spokes.

The system additionally tracked all the relevant data determined on a daily basis for the Hub and each Spoke, so that aggregate year end income, expenses, and capital gain or loss could be determined for accounting and for tax purposes for the Hub and, as a result, for each publicly traded Spoke. It was essential that these calculations were quickly and accurately performed. In large part this was required because each Spoke sold shares to the public and the price of those shares was substantially based on the Spoke's percentage interest in the portfolio. In some instances, a mutual fund administrator was required to calculate the value of the shares to the nearest penny within as little as an hour and a half after the market closed. Given the complexity of the calculations, a computer or equivalent device was a virtual necessity to perform the task. The claim in issue read:

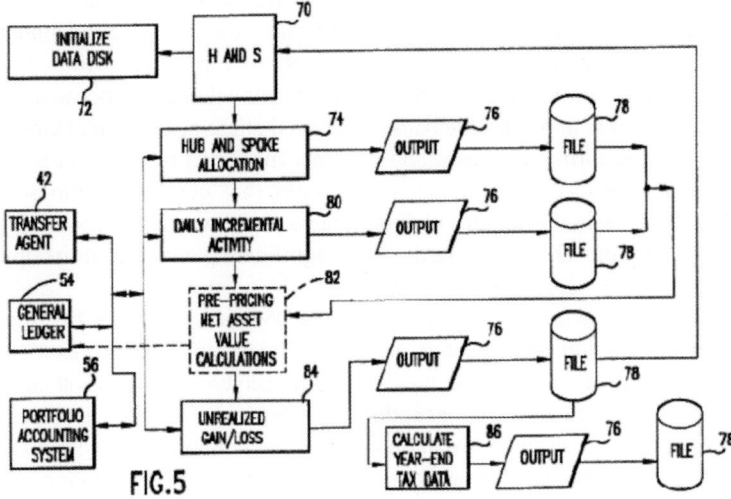

FIG.5

A data processing system for managing a financial services configuration of a portfolio established as a partnership, each partner being one of a plurality of funds, comprising:

(a) computer processor means [a personal computer including a CPU] for processing data;

(b) storage means [a data disk] for storing data on a storage medium;

(c) first means [an arithmetic logic circuit configured to prepare the data disk to magnetically store selected data] for initializing the storage medium;

(d) second means [an arithmetic logic circuit configured to retrieve information from a specific file, calculate incremental increases or decreases based on specific input, allocate the results on a percentage basis, and store the output in a separate file] for processing data regarding assets in the portfolio and each of the funds from a previous day and data regarding increases or decreases in each of the funds, [sic, funds'] assets and for allocating the percentage share that each fund holds in the portfolio;

(e) third means [an arithmetic logic circuit configured to retrieve information from a specific file, calculate incremental increases and decreases based on specific input, allocate the results on a percentage basis and store the output in a separate file] for processing data regarding daily incremental income, expenses, and net realised gain or loss for the portfolio and for allocating such data among each fund;

(f) fourth means [an arithmetic logic circuit configured to retrieve information from a specific file, calculate incremental increases and decreases based on specific input, allocate the results on a percentage basis and store the output in a separate file] for processing data regarding daily net unrealised gain or loss for the portfolio and for allocating such data among each fund; and

(g) fifth means [an arithmetic logic circuit configured to retrieve information from specific files, calculate that information on an aggregate basis and store the output in a separate file] for processing data regarding aggregate year-end income, expenses, and capital gain or loss for the portfolio and each of the funds.

The CAFC held that the above claim was patentable subject-matter and that the transformation of data, representing discrete dollar amounts, by a machine through a series of mathematical calculations into a final share price, constituted a practical application of a mathematical algorithm, formula, or calculation, because it produced *"a useful, concrete and tangible result"* – a final share price momentarily fixed for recording and reporting purposes and even accepted and relied upon by regulatory authorities and in subsequent trades. Furthermore the "business methods" exception to patentability was no longer available unless there was some more well-defined statutory objection. The CAFC said, in the significant passage from its opinion:

> As an alternative ground for invalidating the '056 patent under § 101, the court relied on the judicially-created, so-called "business method" exception to statutory subject-matter. We take this opportunity to lay this ill-conceived exception to rest. Since its inception, the "business method" exception has merely represented the application of some general, but no longer applicable legal principle, perhaps arising out of the "requirement for invention" – which was eliminated by §103. Since the 1952 Patent Act, business methods have been, and should have been, subject to the same legal requirements for patentability as applied to any other process or method.

> The business method exception has never been invoked by this court, or the CCPA, to deem an invention unpatentable. Application of this particular exception has always been preceded by a ruling based on some clearer concept of Title 35 or, more commonly, application of the abstract idea exception based on finding a mathematical algorithm. Illustrative is the CCPA's analysis in *In re Howard*, 394 F.2d 869, 157 USPQ 615 (CCPA 1968), wherein the court affirmed the Board of Appeals' rejection of the claims for lack of novelty and found it unnecessary to reach the Board's section 101 ground that a method of doing business is "inherently unpatentable." *Id.* at 872, 157 USPQ at 617.

> Similarly, *In re Schrader*, 22 F.3d 290, 30 USPQ2d 1455 (Fed. Cir. 1994), while making reference to the business method exception, turned on the fact that the claims implicitly recited an abstract idea in the form of a mathematical algorithm and there was no "transformation or conversion of subject-matter representative of or constituting physical activity or objects." 22 F.3d at 294, 30 USPQ2d at 1459 (emphasis omitted).

Furthermore, the CAFC approved the following passage from the US Examination Guidelines: "Claims should not be categorised as methods of doing business. Instead such claims should be treated like any other process claims." If the objection was that the claims were too broad to be patentable, that was a matter to be decided under 35 USC 102 (novelty), 103 (inventive step) or 112 (disclosure).

A recent and more extreme decision in favour of broad patentable subject-matter is in *Ex Parte Lundgren*[151], a decision of the Board of Patent Appeals and Interferences within the USPTO. The invention concerned a method of compensating a manager,

---

151. Appeal No. 2003-2088 (BPAI 2005)

and covered implementation of the method using pencil and paper. The Examiner objected that the claims were outside the technological arts and merely related to an economic theory expressed as a mathematical algorithm without the disclosure of a computer or automated apparatus of any kind and were therefore non-statutory. The Board held that there was no judicially recognised "technological arts" test to determine patent-eligible subject-matter under 35 USC §101, that it was inappropriate to create one and that accordingly the rejection could not be sustained. It is at present uncertain whether this decision will be subject to further judicial review, but it points to a widening of the gap between the US and Europe as regards business method patentability.

Business methods in Europe

Although the climate of opinion in Europe is strongly against the patenting of business methods, it should not be assumed that all objections of this type are certain of success. For example in *System for processing mail/PITNEY BOWES*[152], the patentees had noted that in the prior art, long-distance mail was sorted according to the destination zip code and not in accordance with the departure times of common carriers (aircraft), and that it would be better to pre-sort the mail and arrange for its delivery to common carriers in a "just in time" manner. According to a first auxiliary request submitted to the EPO during opposition proceedings, in its broadest aspect the invention related to:

> Apparatus for mailer processing of mail comprising:
> (a) a processor means;
> (b) means for sorting mail and separating local mail from non-local mail;
> (c) means for traying the non-local mail; and
> (d) means for delivering mail trays from the mailer to a common carrier, characterised in that
>   said processor means has or contains mail lists and time of departure data
> for a transportation system,
>   the apparatus further including means for shipping non-local mail to the common carrier in accordance with the times of departures of the transportation system so as to meet a just-in-time sequence for the mail.

Opponents argued that the just-in-time feature was not a genuine apparatus feature but was an administrative measure typical of a business activity, a just-in-time organization of work being a typical method of doing business. The patentees said that labeling of trays with destination codes and departure times to determine the sequence of their delivery was "mechanical" and that they had developed a non-obvious application of the just-in-time concept which selected certain mail pieces for delivery in advance of others and materially affected the flow of mail pieces. The Appeal Board noted that in the prior art the practice of processing mail in zip code numerical order resulted in a lower effective throughput in a given time period, and that the invention addressed this problem. The practical application of the mathematically-

---

152. T 0767/99 – 3.5.2; EP-A-0575109

based concept of just-in-time to the material expression or embodiment of mechanical handling and selective conveying of articles to different destinations was a technical process and accordingly the opponents' objection that it was a mere business method should not succeed. The patent was also held valid on novelty and inventive step grounds. An earlier decision in the transport industry on somewhat similar facts is found in *Method of material distribution/NAT SHIPPING*[153]

However, the very different approach of the EPO compared to that of the USPTO and courts is demonstrated by *Controlling pension benefits system/PBS Partnership*[154] *(Pension Benefits),* which has been followed by the UK Patent Office, though often using different reasoning. It precludes patents for business methods (whether expressed in terms of a method or an apparatus claim) where the novelty and ingenuity resided purely in the field of business administration and there was no **technical** effect involved.

The reasoning in *Pension Benefits* has subsequently been confirmed by the EPO Appeal Board in *Auction method/HITACH I*[155]. In the latter case, the EPO Appeal Board held that modification to a business method aimed at merely circumventing a technical problem rather than solving it by technical means does not contribute to the technical character of the claimed subject-matter and therefore does not lead to a patentable invention. The *Pension Benefits* doctrine has recently also been affirmed in *Discount Certificates/CATALINA.*[156]

Since these decisions, it has become clear that alleged inventions where the novelty and inventive character resides purely in the field of business administration are *not* patentable in the UK or Europe. Note that this does *not* preclude the filing of a business method application at the UK Patent Office or elsewhere in Europe for the purpose of claiming Convention priority in the USA and in other countries where seuch methods might be patentable.

In the *Pension Benefits* case,[157] the applicants, who were based in the US aimed to provide a computer-based system for administering employee pensions. The system was based on a master trust to which employees were to subscribe, which purchased insurance from life-insuring institutions and which permitted financial calculations for all the enrolled employees to be carried out centrally (see Fig. 1 of the patent below). The new system imposed low and fixed determinable financial burdens upon the employer and relieved him of administrative and fiduciary responsibility, while also providing expanded accurately predictable and increasing benefits to enrolled employees.

The EPO had to examine main independent method and apparatus claims reading

> 1. A method of controlling a pension benefits program by administering at least one subscriber employer account on behalf of each subscriber employer's

153. T 0636/88 – 3.2.1.; EP-B-0067064.

154. T 0931/95

155. T 0258/03

156. T 0531/03-3.4.3, 17 March 2005, opposition decision, see EP-B-0511463.

157. Application in issue published as EP-A-0332770, European counterpart to US-A-4750121.

enrolled employees each of whom is to receive periodic benefits payments, said method comprising:

providing to a data processing means information from each said subscriber employer defining the number, earnings and ages of all enrolled employees of the said subscriber employer;

determining the average age of all enrolled employees by average age computing means;

determining the periodic cost of life insurance for all enrolled employees of said subscriber employer by life insurance cost computing means; and estimating all administrative, legal, trustee, and government premium yearly expenses for said subscriber employer by administrative cost computing means;

the method producing, in use, information defining each subscriber employer's periodic monetary contribution to a master trust, the face amount of a life insurance policy on each enrolled employee's life to be purchased from a life insurer and assigned to the master trust and to be maintained in full force and effect until the death of the said employee, and periodic benefits to be received by each enrolled employee upon death, disability or retirement.

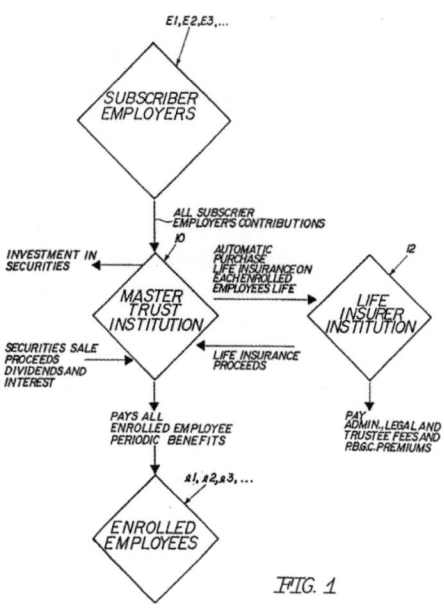

FIG. 1

5. An apparatus for controlling a pension benefits system comprising:

a data processing means which is arranged to receive information into a memory from each subscriber employer defining the number, earnings and ages of all enrolled employees, said data processing means including a processor which includes:

average age computing means for determining the average age of all enrolled employees;

life insurance cost computing means for determining the periodic cost of said life insurance for all enrolled employees of said subscriber employer;

administrative cost computing means for estimating all administrative, legal, trustee, and government premium yearly expenses for said subscriber employer;

the apparatus being arranged to produce, in use, information defining each subscriber employer's monetary contribution to a master trust; the face amount of each life insurance policy to be issued and made payable to said master trust by a life insurer on the life of each enrolled employee and to be maintained in full force and effect until the death of the said employee; and periodic benefits payable by said master trust to each enrolled employee upon death, disability, or retirement.

The examining division objected that the claimed invention was unpatentable since it related only to features of a commercial or managerial character and lacked any technical features. The applicants appealed, contending that the claims were directed to the processing of data which was a physical entity within the meaning set out in *VICOM*, that the requirement for technical character was now outdated having regard to the abandonment in a number of non-European countries of the exclusion of business methods as exemplified by the US decision in *State Street*, and that the field of business methods had been opened to patent protection in *General Purpose Management System/SOHEI*[158] and *Queueing System/PETTERSON.*[159]

The Appeal Board rejected the argument that a requirement for technical character had become obsolete, and commented that the requirement had been assumed to be necessary in the recent decisions in cases *Computer Program Product/IBM*[160] and *T 0935/97 Computer program product II/IBM*[161]*;* see also the decision of the German federal Court of Justice in case *XZB 15/98 Sprachanalyseeinrichtung.* The various method steps in claim 1 were of a purely administrative, actuarial or financial character, and the use of technical means for carrying out these steps did not impart technical character to them. In the *Vicom* case the claimed method produced the technical result of improving and sharpening an image, in *Sohei* the steps of the claimed method were closely related to the functional features of the computer system, and *Petterson* related to a three-dimensional apparatus which was clearly of a technical character. The subject-matter claimed in each of the above three cases was of a technical character whereas that claimed in claim 1 of the application in issue was not.

The Appeal Board held that the subject-matter of claim 5 was *not* excluded by the prohibition on patenting business methods In the Board's view a computer system suitably programmed for use in a particular field, even if that was the field of business and economy, had the character of a physical entity, man-made for a utilitarian purpose and was therefore an invention within the meaning of Article 52(1) EPC. This distinction with regard to patentability between a method for doing business and an apparatus suited to perform such a method was justified in the light of the wording of Article 52(2)(c) EPC, according to which "schemes, rules and methods" are non-patentable categories in the field of economy and business, but the category of "apparatus" in the sense of "physical entity" or "product" was not mentioned in Article 52(2) EPC. If a claim was directed to such an entity, the formal category of such a claim did in fact imply physical features of the claimed subject-matter which could qualify as technical features of the invention concerned and thus be relevant for its patentability. Note that in the subsequent *Hitachi* case this reasoning was criticised and the Appeal Board held that a method involving technical means (e.g. a computer) was also *not* excluded.

---

158. T 0769/92
159. T 1002/92
160. T 1173/97
161. T 0935/97

The applicant's problems were by no means over: the Board went on to decide that the subject-matter of claim 5 involved no inventive step. They concluded that the assessment had to be carried out from the standpoint of a skilled person who knew of the structure and concept of the improved pension benefits system and the underlying schemes for information processing. Use of computers in the economic sector had become widespread in the economic field at the priority date, and there was no *technical* contribution provided by the claimed subject-matter to the prior art Accordingly the EPO Appeal Board rejected the appeal and the application was refused.

In an opposition case, *Two Identities/COMVIK*,[162] the closest prior art against which the inventive character of the claimed subject-matter had to be judged was a paper describing the subscriber identity module for the European digital cellular system GSM. The differences between the subject-matter claimed in EP-B-0579655 and the prior art were that:

(i) The subscriber identity module was allocated at least two identities.
(ii) The user could select to which of the two or more identities a call was to be allocated e.g. by reversing the attitude of a SIM card shown diagrammatically below.
(iii) The selective activated identities were used for distributing the costs among service and private calls or among different users.

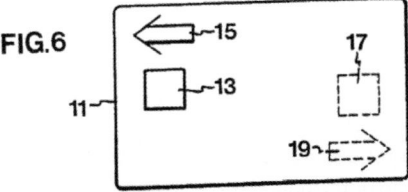

FIG.6

The Appeal Board held that these differences did not relate to the technical aspects of the network, but were financial and administrative concepts that did not require the exercise of *technical* skills and competence and did not involve the solution of a technical problem, the necessary commands already being available within the GSM system, and the discrimination required for cost distribution merely requiring minor modification of the network's home database. Accordingly, the patent was revoked.

Similar attitudes prevail in the UK Patent Office, although the reasoning used has in the past differed slightly from that in the US. In *Fujitsu's UK Application 9604003.5 (GB-A-2300284)*, the main embodiment was a reservation management system in which the relative importance of conflicting requests was assessed based on such factors as the reason for a meeting, the importance of the person making the booking, the number and seniority of attendees, how long it was until the meeting, for how long a meeting had already been booked, and the number of times a reservation had been rescheduled. An algorithm assessed the degree of importance using these

---

162. T 0641/00

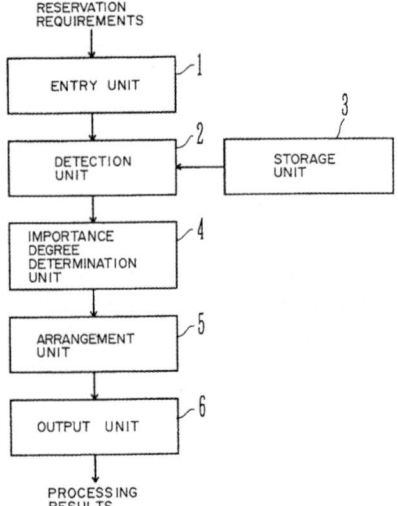

criteria and priority was given to the more important reservation. Existing reservations could be rescheduled. Fig. 1 of the application appears below:

Apparatus and method claims were presented, the apparatus claim in the form that it was examined during the hearing, reading as follows:

> A reservation management apparatus in an information processing system for receiving reservation requirements and determining automatically whether to accept the reservation requirements, comprising:
>
> entry means for entering requirements of a first reservation;
>
> storage means for storing information of a second reservation that was previously registered and storing predetermined standards for determining degrees of importance;
>
> detection means for determining whether there is a duplication between the first reservation and the second reservation, according to the information of the second reservation stored in said storage means and the requirements of the first reservation, when the requirements of the first reservation are entered;
>
> importance degree determination means for automatically calculating an importance degree of the first reservation according to the requirements of the first reservation, and an importance degree of the second reservation according to the information of the second reservation by referring to the predetermined standards for determining degrees of importance stored in the storage means; and
>
> arrangement means for determining whether to accept the requirements of the first reservation, based on a comparison between the importance degree of the first reservation and the importance degree of the second reservation, which are calculated by said importance degree determination means, wherein the first reservation is automatically accepted when the importance degree of the first reservation is greater than the importance degree of the second

reservation, and a time and date of the first reservation is automatically changed when the importance degree of the first reservation is lower than the importance degree of the second reservation.

Fujitsu argued that the problem being addressed by the invention was technical in that conflicting requests for entry to a database had to be handled efficiently and consistently according to criteria set up in advance. They added that the technical nature of the invention was demonstrated by the fact that the system permitted a plurality of input sources from multiple users over a network and highlighted the possible use of different input devices such as keyboard, mouse, telephone, microphone, fax and reading characters from a request form, which they said distinguished the present system from the traditional manual method of resolving conflicts. They pointed to the complex criteria for assessing priority which they said contributed to the technical character, and argued that the performance of the calculation to assess priority, the resultant changes to the database, and the rescheduling of other items were technical matters, as was the output of notification to the users. Examples of output notification given in the specification were e-mail, fax, electronic bulletin board, automatic calls using voice synthesis, mailing and circulating a printed notice. They concluded that while the operation of the invention might be underpinned by a business method, that should not of itself exclude the invention from patentability, and that that the claims were not directed to a business method as such.

The Patent Office (Mr Peter Marchant, Deputy Director) rejected the above argument and held that the claimed subject-matter fell within either the mental act or the business method objection to patentability, and that any claim that could be put forward based on the disclosed subject-matter would fall within one or other of these exclusions since it would involve merely the automation of a manual method of prioritizing human actions.

If there was an objection based on the mental act prohibition, then following the *Merril Lynch* decision,[163] the presence or absence of a technical effect was irrelevant to patentability. If this approach was wrong, however, the claimed apparatus and method did not in fact produce any technical effect. Mr Marchant summarised the conclusions of the Patent Office as follows:

> The specification makes clear that the invention originates in the automation of a manual reservation management system. A computer system is employed to do what was hitherto done manually. The steps in the manual method have been translated into steps in the computer system and the two systems would involve equivalent processing and produce equivalent outputs. The technical means for putting the method into effect are the conventional input, output and processing means of computer systems everywhere. Mr Mohun argued that these technical features rendered the claims patentable. I do not agree. Automation may make the method quicker, more accurate, more easily accessible to users and, in the network version, more widely available, but

163. [1989] RPC 561

these are the familiar benefits of computerisation, and I can see nothing further
in the present case, in any of the claims proposed or in the description, which
produces a modification of the technical operation of the computer system, or
any special interaction between the software and the physical computer system
which could produce a new technical result. The system is a technical system
as Mr Mohun says, but the technology is conventional and the system taken as
a whole does not in my view involve a technical effect; that is to say it does not
produce a new result in the form of a technical contribution.

Accordingly the application was refused.

Recently the UK Patent Office issued a notice[164] that for business-method related
applications, an applicant would in future receive a single Examination Report
inviting him to a hearing, and that if the Examiner remained of the opinion that no
patent should be granted, then the application would be referred to a Hearing Officer
immediately for a decision on whether the application should be refused. Any refusal
by the Hearing Officer could be in abbreviated form, merely referring back to
previous decisions of the same kind. A listing of the sort of applications that are
inherently un-patentable accompanies the notice and is reproduced below, the
references being to British Library accession numbers:

1. A computer system for optimizing an investment portfolio to reflect the investor's
   wishes on risk, investment spread and investment limits – *O/215/04*

2. An internet-based system for allowing individuals to club together to benefit
   from bulk purchase discounts: those who commit themselves early get a better
   price – *O/208/04*

3. A reminder system which sends a single consolidated reminder for all the actions
   necessary in the next week or month, rather than sending lots of separate
   reminders – *O/193/04*

4. A reverse auction system which also monitors a purchasers purchasing history so
   as to recommend further purchases that are likely to be of interest – *O/195/04*

5. An online betting system that automatically adjusts the odds to ensure that
   payouts will be of rounded amounts – *O/199/04*

6. An online trading system which allows a bid to have visible and concealed
   portions, so a bidder can enter the market without distorting it – *O/147/04*

7. A system for automatically optimizing the scheduling of airline crew – *O/125/04*

8. An internet-based grocery shopping system which tells customers how much
   freezer space their order will require – *O/121/04*

---

164. www.patent.gov.uk/patent/notices/practice/business.htm

9. A system for sharing information about semiconductor product design – *O/031/04*

10. A system for managing a debt-recovering process – *O/030/04*

What is striking about these decisions is the apparently pedestrian nature of the inventions in question, so that even if the problem of qualifying subject-matter were disregarded, it is difficult to identify a convincing argument that any of them contain inventive subject-matter.

UK and European law on this topic has recently been considered in relatively recent UK Patents Court decisions in *Shopalotto*[165] and *Crawford's Application*[166]. The consistent principle in these decisions is that the inventor must make a contribution to the art (i.e. the invention must be new and not obvious) and that the contribution must be of a technical nature (i.e. susceptible of industrial application and not within one of the areas excluded by Art 52(2) EPC). The differences between the legal reasoning of the UK Patent Office and courts and that of the EPO Appeal Boards on business-method related patents, though legally interesting, do not apparently make any significant difference to the scope of subject-matter that is excluded under the heading "business method".

In conclusion, as in the case of the computer-related cases, it is submitted that the drawings in the *BBC* case provide valuable insight, and that seeking functional data features may provide a way of avoiding qualifying subject-matter objections. Patenting business methods in Europe is, and will remain, difficult because of the statutory prohibition and the present political climate which is strongly against extension of patent protection into the business method field. The kinds of high-level description which are routinely accepted by the USPTO will *not* usually do in Europe. However, there is no reason why computer systems and software that make such business methods possible by providing technical solutions to real technical problems arising in the implementation of a business method should not be patentable. Making business software workable in a stable and reliable manner on real computer systems implemented using complex networks with security and conflict implications is very difficult, as those who install computer systems and software in their own businesses are only too well aware. These difficulties must be even greater for financial institutions where reliability, security and stability are of paramount importance. It is submitted that going beyond the high-level description and looking at how the software really works and how the program modules and data are organised to allow this to happen will enable genuine technical problems that have ingenious solutions not in a prohibited area to be identified, and that patent applications written with this additional care will have a much greater chance of acceptance by the EPO or the national patent offices in the EU contracting states.

165. [2005] EWHC 2146, Pumfrey J, 23 June 2005
166. [2005] EWHC 2417, Kitchin J, 24 October 2005

Clarity, enablement and utility

*"Whatever we well understand we express clearly,
and words flow with ease."*
(Nicholas Boileau-Despréaux)

Coverage

This article introduces a number of "internal" grounds of invalidity which present serious challenges for the patents draftsman because objections under these grounds are often fatal.

When you have studied the contents of this article, and the "required reading" you should during your drafting be able to:

1. Avoid relative terms in the claims wherever possible.

2. Avoid reciting apparatus features and method steps in a single claim if doubt is thereby created about whether what is claimed is an apparatus or a method.

3. Avoid indefinite terms e.g. "aesthetically pleasing", "improved characteristics" or "substantially pure" which may give rise to clarity and enablement problems.

4. Avoid parameters in claims where possible. Where a parameter is unavoidable, ensure that it is precisely and accurately defined, and that any necessary test(s) to determine that parameter are adequately disclosed in the written description.

5. Ensure that all relevant starting materials and process conditions are disclosed so that the skilled person can start from materials he has available or knows to make, and can produce embodiments of the invention according to the disclosed methods and without having to bridge any gap in the disclosure.

6. Ensure that "black-boxes" are supported by sufficient disclosed structure and technical discussion, including references to, and brief précis of, any relevant cited literature.

7. Check for errors and omissions of technical information and ensure that the inventors do likewise (they should have a greater depth of knowledge about their invention than the patent attorney and are in a better position to detect errors if they set their minds to doing so).

8. **Ensure that there is no wilful concealment of critical technical information.**

9. **Bear in mind the legal and practical consequences of non-compliance with any of the above.**

Relative terms and indefiniteness (UK, EPC)

It is inadvisable for applicants before the EPO and the UK Patent Office to rely in their claims on relative terms which have no generally accepted meaning, or on imprecisely defined parameters, and such issues have counterparts in US practice.

The EPO Examination Guidelines provide the following instructions concerning relative terms:

> It is preferable not to use a relative or similar term such as "thin", "wide" or "strong" in a claim unless the term has a well-recognised meaning in the particular art, e.g. "high-frequency" in relation to an amplifier, and this is the meaning intended. Where the term has no well-recognised meaning it should, if possible, be replaced by a more precise wording found elsewhere in the original disclosure. Where there is no basis in the disclosure for a clear definition and the term is not essential having regard to the invention, it should normally be retained in the claim, because to excise it would generally lead to an extension of the subject-matter beyond the content of the application as filed – in contravention of Article 123(2). However, an unclear term cannot be allowed in a claim if the term is essential having regard to the invention. Equally, an unclear term cannot be used by the applicant to distinguish his invention from the prior art.

It should also be remembered that during litigation, one of the principal tasks facing the court will be to construe the claims. The ambit of relative expressions such as "thin" will inevitably require expert testimony and could involve foreseeable expenditure of perhaps £100,000 if the meaning turned out to be important during infringement proceedings. The advice against using such terms is not mere over-zealousness on the part of Patent Offices; the problem is real and such language should be avoided.

Under the EPC, where claimed subject-matter involves definition by an imprecise parameter, the patent will be wholly or partly invalid for lack of enabling disclosure. For example, in *Coatings/UNION CARBIDE*,[167] the invention concerned a curable coating composition comprising a hydroxy functional acrylic monomer and an alkoxylated melamine. The only characterizing feature of the invention was that the ratio of the equivalent weight of the alkoxylated melamine to the total hydroxy equivalent weight of the acrylic monomer had to be in the range 1.0-1.8. If the ratio was too low, the coating would be soft and lack solvent resistance, and if it was too high, the coating would be brittle. However, no information was given concerning how to measure the equivalent weight of the alkoxylated melamine. The patentees

---

167. T 0654/90

alleged that there were standard methods for determining this quantity, but this argument was not accepted because equivalent weights were not quoted on data sheets from manufacturers of alkoxylated melamine, and because one such brochure said that these were not determinable because the equivalent weights might vary within a wide range, or because the materials might self-condense. Accordingly the claim was declared invalid for non-enablement.

A further example from case law under the EPC is provided by *Pure terfenadine/ALBANY*,[168] where the invention covered a class of *substantially pure* piperidine derivatives of a defined generic structural formula and amongst which desired isomers were difficult to separate from other isomers. The description provided no quantification of what was meant by substantial purity. The Appeal Board rejected the applicant's argument that the term referred to a pharmaceutical standard of purity and held that it had no generally accepted meaning and that pharmaceutical purity was a hazy concept that shifted in time and with progress in analytical chemistry. Since purity was the only distinction over the cited prior art, the claimed subject-matter was held to lack clarity.

In *Rubber Compositions/BRIDGESTONE CORPORATION*,[169] the EPO Appeal Board drew a distinction between the information needed to support an objectively measurable characteristic and an effect-related functional feature. The Background and the reasoning of the Board are apparent from the following passage:

> It is apparent and was not denied by the Examining Division that the information in the application enables the skilled person to practice the invention by subjecting available carbon black varieties to a screening program. However, in the Division's view this exercise involved undue burden, possibly because the application was considered to lack instructions as to how to purposefully pre-select promising candidates and turn initial failure into success.

> The Board is not convinced by these arguments. In its judgment, the application-in-suit comprises all the information – in the form of *directly measurable structural component characteristics* – that is necessary to put the skilled person in a position of being able to carry out the invention and of knowing when he is working within the forbidden area of the claims... The present situation is different from the one where an invention is characterised by *effect related functional features* used to "round up" the definition of the claimed subject-matter in order to limit a feature (e.g. component) to those of its meanings which belong to the invention if a characterisation of this feature cannot be made (or would be too narrow) by directly measurable objective attributes. In this situation the skilled person depends on a reliable and practically feasible method in order to ascertain the exact scope of the claimed subject-matter... In the case of present Claim 1, however, there is no need to resort to experiments to assess the exact scope of the claimed subject-matter... because the invention is unambiguously characterised by *directly measurable*

---

168. T 0728/98 – 3.3.1
169. T 0769/02 – 3.3.3

structural component characteristics which allow their reduction to practice in an objective fashion. In this situation the necessity to carry out chemical and physical measurements which are then mathematically converted to numerical values in order to find out those carbon black varieties which meet the characteristics of Claim 1 does not amount to undue burden. (emphasis added)

The above decision has a UK counterpart in *Kirin-Amgen Inc v Hoechst Marion Roussel*[170] where the specification failed to describe with sufficient accuracy a criterion for distinguishing erythropoietin falling within the claim from that derived from urinary sources. The claim in issue specified that the product has "*a higher molecular weight by SDS-PAGE than erythropoietin derived from urinary sources.*" Erythropoietin according to the invention from recombinant technology is referred to as rEPO, and that from urinary sources is referred to as uEPO. It turned out that the molecular weight of uEPOs depended on source and method of isolation and that some rEPOs had the same molecular weight as some uEPOs so that molecular weight did not always provide an effective distinction. The House of Lords held that the specification was insufficient and expressed its reasons as follows:

> The claim appeared to assume that all uEPOs had effectively the same molecular weight, irrespective of source and method of isolation. This had been shown not to be the case. So which uEPO did the claim require to be used for the test? Simply to use the first uEPO which came to hand would turn the claim into a lottery. On the other hand, it would be burdensome to have to work one's way through several specimens of uEPO (which were, as I mentioned at the beginning of my speech, extremely hard to come by) and even then the result would be inconclusive because *non constat* that some untried specimen did not have a different molecular weight.

> The judge decided that the lack of clarity made the specification insufficient. It did not merely throw up the possibility of doubtful cases but made it impossible to determine in any case whether the product fell within the claim. The invention was not disclosed "clearly enough and completely enough for it to be performed by a person skilled in the art": section 72(1)(c).

> The Court of Appeal disagreed. They said that it was sufficient that some uEPO could be tested against eEPO by SDS-PAGE. The fact that it did not specify which uEPO and that choosing one uEPO would bring the product within the claim and another would not was "lack of clarity dressed up to look like insufficiency." For my part, I do not think that can be right. If the claim says that you must use an acid, and there is nothing in the specification or context to tell you which acid, and the invention will work with some acids but not with others but finding out which ones work will need extensive experiments, then that in my opinion is not merely lack of clarity; it is insufficiency. The lack of clarity does not merely create a fuzzy boundary between that which will work and that which will not. It makes it impossible to work the invention at all until one has found out what ingredient is needed.

---

170. [2005] RPC 169

The patentees argued that the skilled person would be trying to make the invention work, but the House of Lords held that this approach was inapplicable to the situation it had to consider, and said:

> In the present case, however, the choice of uEPO has nothing to do with making the invention work. It is simply a criterion against which one tests whether the rEPO falls within the claims. The very concepts of "success" or "failure" seems irrelevant to the choice of uEPO. What counts as "success"? Ex hypothesi the skilled person does not know in advance whether any given uEPO will bring his rEPO within the claim or not. From the point of view of success or failure, one is as good as another. All the skilled man can do is try to guess which uEPO the patentee had in mind and if the specification does not tell him, then it is insufficient.

The lesson for the patents draftsman is self-evident: if a particular technical criterion is to be made a feature of a claim, then that criterion must be clearly and accurately defined and must be reproducible, otherwise the claim will be invalid.

Relative terms and indefiniteness in US

In the US, every patent specification must conclude with one or more claims *particularly pointing out and distinctly claiming* the subject-matter which the applicant regards as his invention.[171] The purpose of the definiteness requirement is to ensure that the claims delineate the scope of the invention using language that adequately notifies the public of the patentee's rights. However, the definiteness requirement does not demand absolute clarity. Only claims "*not amenable to construction*" or "*insolubly ambiguous*" are indefinite.[172] However, language which is relative, or even worse subjective, may give rise to unenforceability in the US.

Process features in apparatus claims were objected to by the CAFC in the recent and important case of *IPXL Holdings L.L.C. v Amazon Com Inc.*[173] The invention related to the 1-click system which customers of Amazon who have previously stored information including credit card numbers and shipping addresses could use to place an order without having to re-enter that information. A subsidiary claim which was potentially important to novelty was held by the District Court to be indefinite because it attempted to claim both a system and a method of using that system. It recited:

> The *system* of claim 2 [including an input means] wherein the predicted transaction information comprises both a transaction type and transaction parameters associated with that transaction type, and *the user uses the input means* to either change the predicted transaction information or accept the displayed transaction type and transaction parameters.

---

171. 35 U.S.C. §112, (2)

172. *Novo Indus., L.P. v Micro Molds Corp.*, 350 F.3d 1348, 1353 (Fed. Cir. 2003); *Honeywell Int'l*, 341 F.3d at 1338; *Exxon Research & Eng'g Co. v United States*, 265 F.3d 1371, 1375 (Fed. Cir. 2001).

173. Fed. Cir., 21 November 2005, see US-A-6149055

The Federal Circuit held that it was unclear whether infringement of claim 25 occurred (a) when a system was created that allowed the user to change the predicted transaction information or accept the displayed transaction, or (b) when the user actually used the input means to change transaction information or used the input means to accept a displayed transaction. Because claim 25 recited both a system and the method for using that system, it did not apprise a person of ordinary skill in the art of its scope, and it was invalid under §112(2). The CAFC also noted that claims of this type were contrary to the USPTO *Manual of Patent Examining Procedure*[174] and were condemned in *Landis on Mechanics of Patent Claim Drafting.*[175]

In *Datamaze, LLC v Plumtree Software, Inc,*[176] the invention related to an authoring system for creating a desired uniform and "*aesthetically pleasing*" look and feel to custom interface screens. The Court held that the term *aesthetically pleasing* was not covered by an objective standard from which a skilled person could determine the scope of the claimed invention, nor was there anything in the written description or prosecution history which defined objectively when an information screen was *aesthetically pleasing.* Although beauty might be in the eye of the beholder, a claim term, to be definite, required an objective anchor. Accordingly the defendant's application for summary judgment of invalidity succeeded. In a similar category is *STX, LLC v Brine, Inc*[177] which concerned a head for a lacrosse stick which provided "*improved handling and playing characteristics*", which are purely subjective qualities. In *Union Pacific Resources Company v Chesapeake Energy Corporation,*[178] the word "*comparing*" was held to be indefinite and non-enabling in the absence of any explanation in the specification of the basis of comparison.

The word "about" does not necessarily introduce indefiniteness, but it is liable to be challenged in litigation and may give rise to difficult and expensive argument. For example, it was considered in *BJ Services Company v Halliburton.*[179] The claimed invention related to:

> A method of fracturing a subterranean formation, comprising the steps of:
>> blending together an aqueous fluid and a hydratable polymer to form a base
> fluid, wherein the hydratable polymer is a guar polymer having carboxymethyl
> substituents and a *C* value* of *about 0.06 percent by weight*;
>> adding a crosslinking agent to the base fluid to form a gel; and
>> injecting the gel into at least a portion of the subterranean formation at high
> pressure to form fractures within the formation.

---

174. § 2173.05(p)(II) (1999)

175. Robert C. Faber, at § 60A (2001) ("Never mix claim types to different classes of invention in a single claim.").

176. Fed. Cir.., 04-1564, 5 August 2005, Clevenger J, Bryson J. and Prost J. (**required reading, if only for the shock value**)

177. 211 F.3d 588, 54 USPQ2d 1347 (Fed. Cir. 2000, Mayer J., Lourie J. and Schall J.) (**required reading**)

178. 236 F.3d 684, 694 (Fed. Cir. 2001, Michel J. Lourie J. and Rader J.)

179. 338 F.3d 1368 (Fed. Cir. 2003, Mayer J, Dyk J. and Prost, J)

Halliburton objected to the reference to C* value on the ground that it was not enabled, the specification containing no instructions as to the method and the conditions to be used to make the measurement. They also objected to the word "about" as being indefinite, since a person skilled in the art having made his measurement and calculated C* would not know when the result was "about 0.06". The question as regards definiteness was whether one of ordinary skill in the art would understand what was claimed when the claim was read in light of the specification. BJ Services argued that a skilled person would understand that the term "about" was intended to cover the range of experimental error that occurs in any measurement. To that end, they presented experimental results obtained by their expert, all of which were slightly above or below 0.06, with an average of 0.0596. In an effort to contradict this testimony, Halliburton presented the results of its expert, which varied wildly and conveniently ranged as high as the prior art. However, BJ Services presented evidence that Halliburton's expert had tampered with his measuring equipment by substituting his software for that of the machine, had improperly mixed the test solutions, and had specifically chosen imbalanced data points to measure C*. BJ went on to show that if the raw data were analysed without the tampering, the results would be very similar to those of their expert. All of this undermined the credibility of Halliburton's expert, and the Court concluded that substantial evidence supported the jury's finding that the patent in issue was not invalid for reasons of indefiniteness or lack of enablement.

Starting materials and process conditions

If essential starting materials and process conditions are lacking, a patent will be wholly or partly invalid. This point is illustrated by the decision in *Badische Anilin und Soda Fabriek v La Societe Chimique des Usinea du Rhone and Wilson*.[180] The invention concerned the production of a particular dyestuff in an autoclave. During trial it emerged that this process failed unless the autoclave used was made of iron, as was often the case, but that enamelled autoclaves were also commonly used. The patent was held invalid for insufficiency because the description did not mention the use of an iron autoclave and, therefore, did not contain the necessary instruction which turned out to be essential for the performance of the invention.

Deficiency of the above type is especially common in specifications of an inter-disciplinary character written by a specialist from a single subject-matter area. Mechanical engineers, for example, can be depended on to produce good descriptions of structure but are at risk of omitting details of the materials used, which sometimes prove to be important. Chemists may, for example, devise a new liquid crystal or electro-luminescent material for use in displays, but omit detail about desirable changes to the driving waveform for displays embodying that material.

In *Pyridine Herbicides/ICI*,[181] the issue arose as to whether a document effectively disclosed certain chemical compounds when it did not disclose how the necessary

---

180. (1898) 15 RPC 359 (HL)

181. T 0206/83 (**required reading**)

starting materials could be made. The patentees had failed to identify sources by which a skilled person could have remedied this deficiency. The Appeal Board held that it did not and stated:

> It is the view of the Board that a document does not effectively disclose a chemical compound even though it states the structure and the steps by which it is to be produced, if the skilled person is unable to find out from the document or from common general knowledge how to obtain the required starting materials or intermediates. Information which can only be obtained after a comprehensive search is not to be regarded as part of common general knowledge.

We should not assume that questions of availability of required starting materials are confined to the field of chemistry. For example, in *Deep UV Lithography/AT&T CORP*,[182] the invention concerned an optical system that differed from previous systems using longer wavelength light insofar as that the bandwidth of the light used was narrowed and the optical system used lenses made of quartz only, whereas previous optical systems had used lenses of multi-materials differing in refractive index and dispersion. The missing element was a projection lens marked 109 in the accompanying figure which is shown as a single-component biconvex lens. In reality such lenses are multi-component and of complex design, and a suitable projection lens made wholly of quartz for use in UV lithography was not commercially available and had not been disclosed in any scientific paper or patent. The patentees adduced evidence that a suitable lens could be designed by a reasonably skilled lens designer using commercially available lens design software. However, the Appeal Board accepted evidence from the opponent that the lens had to be of very high resolution and low distortion, that it should be corrected for all monochromatic lens aberrations, should have an increased depth of focus compared to a lens working at longer wavelengths to deal with the steps that occur on a wafer, should have large object and image sizes and should produce a flat image. It also accepted the opponent's evidence that the design of such single-material lenses was more difficult than designing a multi-material lens working at a longer wavelength, and that there was no starting point available to the public from which a lens with the required combination of properties could be designed. The Appeal Board did not need to decide, but apparently would have decided, that even if such a starting point had been available to a skilled lens designer, no suitable design methodology was known for going from that starting point to a workable single material lens. Accordingly, the patent was revoked for non-enablement. Another way of regarding the case is that the lens 109 was in effect a "black box" (see the discussion at page 91), the contents of which were not adequately disclosed. The lesson is that it is as necessary in mechanical, optical or electronic engineering cases to check for the availability of critical components and design methods as it is in the fields of chemistry, biochemistry and medicine where such issues more frequently arise.

---

182. T 0376/95 – 3.4.2; EP-B-0183827; compare the decision of the Federal Circuit in *Bruning v Hirose* 161 F.3d 681, 686, 48 USPQ2d 1934, 1938 (Fed. Cir. 1998) where in relation to the corresponding US patent the experimental evidence of the patentee that a suitable lens could be designed within a period of eight hours using conventional lens design software was accepted.

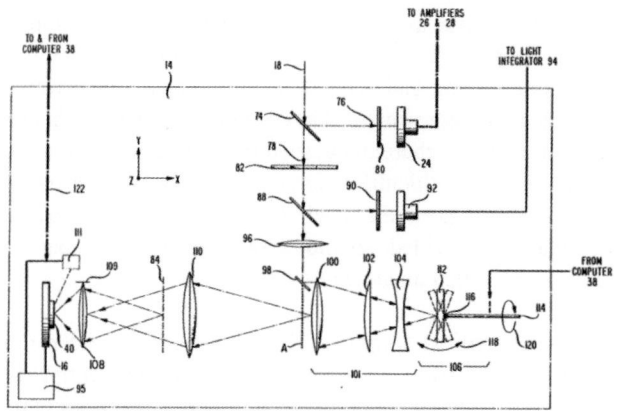

Deep UV lithography/AT & T Corp. The
disputed "Black box" is the projection lens 109.

As an example of inadequately disclosed process conditions, in *Impact resistant resin composition/JSR*,[183] the invention concerned an impact resistant composition including a graft copolymer having a degree of grafting of 70-120% by weight and an intrinsic viscosity of 0.55-0.80 dl/g. During EPO opposition proceedings, the patentees had distinguished their invention from a citation based on an experimental report showing that the process of the citation did not produce the required degree of grafting, and the opponents submitted that this difference must have arisen from a particular feature of the process which had not been disclosed in the patent. The patentees attempted to answer this point by reference to three earlier patents showing degrees of grafting above 70%. The opponents replied that the disclosure should enable the *whole range* of 70-120% grafting to be achieved, that the patents only disclosed achieving 72% grafting and that there was no information available which would have instructed a skilled person how to raise this to 120%. They also argued that degree of grafting should not be considered in isolation, and that there was no disclosure how other required features such intrinsic viscosity were to be achieved at the same time. The Appeal Board accepted these arguments and commented that to find the necessary specific combination of operative features from the many parameters mentioned in the earlier patents would place an undue burden on the skilled person and "practically require him to make the invention again".

In *Calculation unit/TOSHIBA*,[184] an application for a high-speed division and square root calculation unit was refused for lack of enablement because it was not possible to assess the correctness of the calculation result *inter alia* since no overall concept or algorithm had been disclosed in relation to the claimed hardware structure. Available prior art documents showed the level of detail to be expected which included disclosure of the algorithms used and of numeric examples.

---

183. T 0079/88
184. T 0461/02

Although both European and US law refer to undue burden or undue experimentation, it is submitted that these terms are not effective stand-alone objections. The fact that trial and experiment called for by the patentee may be time-consuming and expensive is not enough to amount to non-enablement, and if pursued in that way often looks to the EPO or to a judge as a mere whinge. They are likely to ask: "What precisely is the information that you say is not there in the specification, and ought to be there, for the specification to be enabling?" Identification of that missing information is the most promising route to a non-enablement attack. For the draftsman avoiding any obvious gap in the information provided should avoid hostile third parties from even attempting to put forward such an attack.

It should be noted that critical technical features should not be referred to in the written description solely by a trade mark or catalogue entry, and that it is inappropriate to use trade marks in claims. One reason is that a trade mark is a mere badge of origin and says nothing about what is made available under that mark, which is often a trade secret so that use of a trade mark is at best an imperfect disclosure of what is made available under that mark. For example, a manufacturer's data sheet for a chemical product often contains only a general description of the nature of the product without detailed information about its composition. Data sheets and manuals for microprocessors and other integrated circuits or chipsets give considerable detail about how the products in question might be used, the instruction set that they obey and sufficient information about the internal architecture to enable the product to be used effectively. This may nevertheless fall well short of a full product description. A further reason is that what is supplied under a trade mark may change with time, and in certain consumer products also with place of supply[185] and the patent specification may then give inadequate instructions concerning how to practice the invention. Under US law, the view taken is similar to that in Europe, and the relationship between a trade mark and the product that it identifies is regarded as "*sometimes indefinite, uncertain, and arbitrary.*"[186]

Inadequate disclosure – US

The approach adopted by the US courts is generally similar to that under the EPC and under the UK *Patents Act, 1977*. For example in *Genentech v Novo Nordisk*[187] the CAFC observed that "*tossing out the mere germ of an idea does not constitute enabling disclosure*" and went on to explain that:

> However, when there is no disclosure of any specific starting material or any of the conditions under which a process can be carried out, undue experimentation is required; there is a failure to meet the enablement requirement that cannot be rectified by asserting that all of the disclosure related to the process is within the skill of the art. It is the specification, not the

---

185. Apparently, as explained in a passing-off decision some years ago, the composition of toothpaste is dependent on locally available ingredients so that there may be significant differences in the composition of what is sold in Europe and what is sold e.g. in the Caribbean.

186. USPTO Manual of Patent Examining Practice at para. 608.01(v).

187. 13 March 1997

knowledge of one skilled in the art that must supply the novel aspects of an invention in order to constitute enablement. This specification provides only a starting point for further research.

Recently in *Enzo Biochem v Calgene*,[188] the CAFC affirmed a conclusion that certain claims concerning antisense technology were unduly broad and non-enabled because they related to a mere germ of an idea and were not supported by practical directions and examples. The Court referred to so-called *Wands factors*, all of which have also been approved in one form or another in decisions of the EPO Appeal Boards, and which are:

(1)   the quantity of experimentation necessary;
(2)   the amount of direction or guidance presented;
(3)   the presence or absence of working examples;
(4)   the nature of the invention;
(5)   the state of the prior art;
(6)   the relative skill of those in the art;
(7)   the predictability or unpredictability of the art; and
(8)   the breadth of the claims.

Error and its effects

Insufficiency can arise as a result of error, i.e. the invention cannot be made to work and the disclosed embodiments do not solve the technical problem described in the specification. For that to be put right, the patentee has to prove that the existence of the error was obvious to the skilled person, and that only common general knowledge was needed to correct it. The relevant principles are apparent from the following examples.

In *ExxonElectrically conductive polymeric compositions/EXXON*,[189] the length of fibres used in the single example contained in the specification had been incorrectly stated. Neither the alleged error nor the correction required was apparent on the face of the document. A skilled person who repeated the experiment disclosed in that example would not have been able to obtain the results reported and would not have known what was wrong. The Appeal Board refused the application on the grounds that:

(1)   the error involved misinformation, not merely miscalculation;
(2)   the only permissible amendment to the example would be its complete excision; and
(3)   it would not be proper for the application to proceed to grant with a misleading example or without any example.

In *Redox Catalyst/AIR PRODUCTS*,[190] the invention related to an aqueous polymer resin for making waterbased paints. Opponents adduced experimental evidence that the only example given in the specification did not work because the yield of polymer

---

188. 24 September 1999
189. T 0134/82
190. T 0171/84 mentioned above (**required reading**)

was much less than alleged. In reply, the patentees adopted a strategy of confession and avoidance. They adduced evidence that the amount of catalyst stated to have been added in the example was wrong, and recognizably so because it was many times less than that recommended in *Ullmann's Encyclopaedia,* which is a well-known reference work. They also said that because the polymerization reaction was well known, a skilled person would have realised that something had gone wrong, and would have identified what it was. The Appeal Board accepted this evidence and held that the objection of insufficiency did not succeed. However, it issued a warning that:

> Applicants are well advised not to be unduly influenced by their excessive experience in the field to which the invention relates, so as to neglect providing all the detailed instructions in the specification which are necessary for carrying out the invention without difficulties and to rely immoderately on using common general knowledge to fill gaps and to rectify any deficiency in the disclosure.

In *Fusion proteins/HARVARD,*[191] the Appeal Board held *inter alia* that a skilled person could not be expected to use a restriction enzyme to cleave a plasmid where the known and published restriction map for that plasmid did not show the restriction sites for that enzyme, and commented that choosing a restriction enzyme involved a considerable amount of skill and of trial and error.

Reference documents for remedying non-enablement (EPC)

If an application or patent suffers from a deficiency of the kind set out above, the range of documents or things that can be used to put matters right is restricted by the requirement that they should be within the common general knowledge. A very hard-line view, which has nevertheless been followed in a number of subsequent cases, was put forward by the Appeal Board in *Pyridine Herbicides/ICI:*[192]

> Basically any cure of insufficiency lies with the addressee of the document, i.e. the person skilled in the art who has common general knowledge at his immediate disposal. It would be unfair to the public if more were to be expected from him, i.e. an awareness of the whole state of the art. It is normally accepted that common general knowledge is represented by basic handbooks and textbooks on the subject in question. The skilled person could well be expected to consult these to obtain clear advice as to what to do in the circumstances since the skills of such persons not only include knowledge about particular basic prior art but also knowledge as to where to find such information. Such books may refer him to articles describing specifically how to act or at least giving him a fairly generally applicable method for the purpose, which can be used without any doubt. Normally patent specifications are not part of the common general knowledge and cannot therefore cure apparent insufficiency... The indexes of Chemical Abstracts cover virtually the whole state of the art, and represent therefore much more than what is assumed to be the common general knowledge of the addressee of the specification. Reliance on the contents of Chemical Abstracts to rectify insufficiency might be tantamount to leaving the skilled reader to carry out a search in the whole state of the art, which would be an unacceptable burden on the public.

---

191. T 0060/89
192. T 0206/83 (**required reading**)

In *Starting Compounds/MERCK*,[193] a different appeal board held that *Pyridine Herbicides/ICI* was distinguishable on its facts, and that in a new field a patent specification could be common general knowledge. It stated:

> In the present case, the C-076 starting compounds are highly elaborated microbial metabolites opening a new field of research, so that any technical knowledge acquired in this field at the beginning, through basic pioneering work, has not been distilled into the form of textbooks. By contrast, in the prior decision T206/83 the situation was quite a different one, namely that the person skilled in the art was a person working in the field of classical herbicide chemistry, which was not a new developing field like that of the chemistry of the C-076 compounds. The man skilled in the art, therefore, cannot be presumed to possess the same common general knowledge in both cases.

The lesson for the patents draftsman is that if there is a deficiency in disclosure, the range of documents that can be relied on to remedy the deficiency is less than commonly thought, that reliance on particular documents may involve lengthy and expensive challenge in *inter partes* situations, and that such deficiencies of disclosure are *very unsafe* and should be guarded against. Deficiencies of this kind are particularly attractive for an opponent or defendant in infringement proceedings because of their fatal character.

Black boxes (UK, US)

Black boxes unsupported by adequate description are risky, as is apparent from the recent UK High Court decision in *Halliburton Energy Services, Inc v Smith International (North Sea) Limited*.[194] The proceedings involved two patents relating to the design of roller-cone drill bits using computer simulation. The drawings below are taken from one of the patents in issue, and are a view of a drill bit and a diagrammatic view of a toothed roller cone. An illustrated algorithmic design procedure is also shown: in the patent specification the description is relatively short and provides only the barest outline of the mathematical theory without describing any of the steps in detail.

The following claim appeared in one of the patents in issue:

> A method of designing a roller cone drill bit comprising a plurality of arms, rotatable cutting structures mounted on respective ones of said arms and a plurality of teeth on each of said cutting structures, the method comprising the steps of:
> (a) *calculating the axial force acting on each tooth (18) on each cutting structure (16) of the roller cone drill bit;*
> (b) *calculating the axial force acting on each cutting structure per revolution of the drill bit;*
> (c) comparing the axial force acting on each of said cutting structures with the axial force on the other ones of said cutting structures of the bit;
> (d) adjusting at least one geometric parameter on the design of at least one of said cutting structures; and

---

193. T 0051/87

194. [2005] EWHC 1623 (Pat), Pumfrey J., 21 July 2005 (**required reading**).

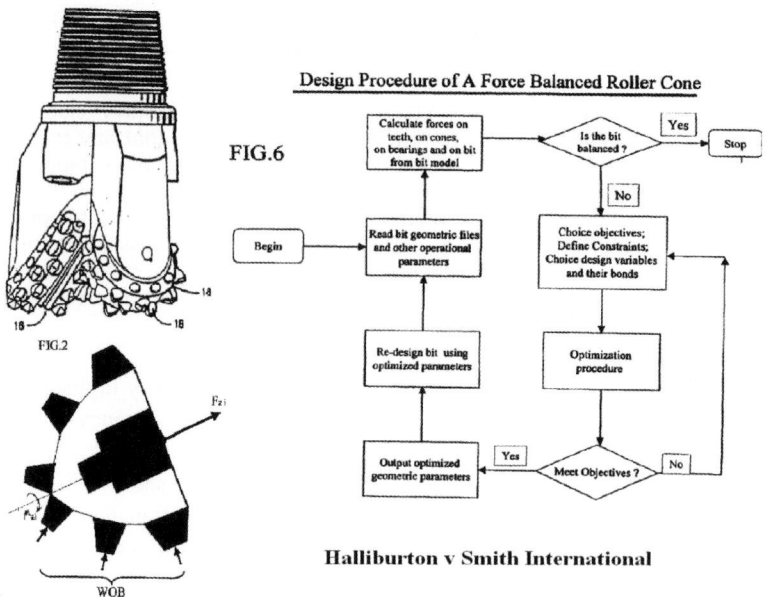

(e) repeating steps (a) through (d) until substantially the same axial force will act on each cutting structure when the drill bit (10) is drilling into a formation.

The patented method was based on computer-modeling of the cutting operation to be performed by the drill bit, but there was no clear description in either specification of how to construct the model. The expert evidence was that it would be difficult to model the drill bit from a geometric and kinematic standpoint, that there was no common general knowledge enabling the force on a drill tooth to be calculated and that an accurate cone/bit speed ratio which was essential for calculating the "swept-out volume" for each cone was difficult to obtain. The Court held that both patents were "grossly insufficient" and hence invalid. The particular disclosed information relating to the two italicised functionally-defined *calculating* steps was the single black box in the flow chart and a sketchy mathematical outline of what needed to be done.

The dangers of black boxes are further highlighted by the US decision in *Atmel Corp v Information Storage devices, Inc*,[195] where the patentees had used means-plus-function claim language to refer to an element in a circuit. Under 35 USC §112, they were obliged to disclose structure corresponding to that element, and mere depiction of a black box in the circuit did not satisfy the requirement to disclose corresponding structure even if the circuit in question were well known. Nor could the structure be disclosed by a mere cross-reference, because such a cross-reference did not amount to disclosure of the structure required by the statute.

The facts in *Atmel* merit more detailed explanation since they demonstrate how easy it is to take too much for granted, to provide insufficient supporting structural detail

---

195. 198 F.3d 1374 (Fed. Cir. 1999)

and so to fall foul of 35 USC §112(6). The invention concerned a charge pump for raising the voltage of a memory array word line to a desired high value during memory array programming operations. In MOS floating gate storage devices, because the amount of time required to program any individual storage device located along a given word line depended upon the amount of charge applied to the storage device floating gate, the ability to increase the voltage present on the associated word line during memory programming operations, and thus to provide a greater charge enabled programming times to be significantly reduced. The trend towards the provision of self altering intelligent systems created a need for memory devices that did not require external high-voltage power supplies for programming. However, voltages higher than the standard five volt power supplies were still necessary for programming purposes. It had been proposed that these higher voltages necessary to achieve acceptable programming times could be generated on the memory chip itself and circuits for voltage multiplication readily adaptable to integration on a memory array chip had been proposed. However, in order for capacitor sizes in those circuits to be reasonably sized for practical integration on a memory array chip, current drive capabilities had to be sacrificed. Consequently, such on-chip high-voltage generation techniques could not be implemented where conventional programming circuits were used, especially in larger arrays, since the DC current leakage through unselected word lines would cause an unacceptable current drain on the high-voltage generation circuit. The invention provided a solution to that problem. The claim in issue read as follows, the disputed feature being shown in italics:

> An apparatus for selectively increasing the voltage on one or more of a plurality of conductive lines having inherent distributed capacitance disposed in a semiconductor circuit comprising:
>   means disposed on said semi-conductor circuit for selecting one or more of said conductive lines;
>   *high-voltage generating means disposed on said semiconductor circuit for generating a high voltage from a lower voltage power supply* connected to said semiconductor circuit;
>   voltage pulse generating means disposed on said semiconductor circuit for generating voltage pulses;
>   means for capacitively coupling voltage pulses from said voltage pulse generating means to a voltage node in said semiconductor circuit;
>   transfer means responsive to said selecting means and connected to said voltage node for transferring increments of charge from said high voltage generating means to the inherent distributed capacitance in selected ones of said conductive lines in response to said voltage pulses;
>   said transfer means including switching means cooperating with said selecting means for blocking substantially all of the flow of current through and transfer of charge from said high-voltage generating means to said conductive lines which are unselected.

The structure disclosed for the high-voltage generating means was the box 114 (see the accompanying figure on page 94), and this was supplemented by the written description which stated that known circuit techniques could be used to implement high-voltage circuit 114, for example as described in an article entitled *On-Chip High-Voltage Generation in NMOS Integrated Circuits Using an Improved Voltage Multiplier Technique* and published in *IEEE Journal of Solid State Circuits*. At issue was whether the contents of this article could be used to supplement the disclosure

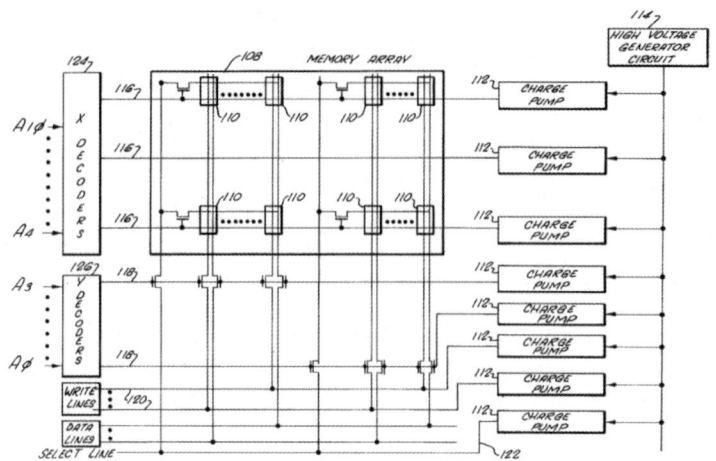

Amtel Corp v Information Storage,
see the black box 114

of the specification, and whether the specification was invalid through indefiniteness or non-enablement. The specification itself suffered from a total absence of disclosed structure corresponding to the *high-voltage generating means* feature, although it will be appreciated from the technical explanation given above that such circuits were in principle well known, and that the precise form of circuit was incidental to the invention.

The CAFC held that the written description did not have to describe explicitly the structure, material or acts corresponding to a means-plus-function limitation, and that such structure could be implicit in the written description if it would have been clear to those skilled in the art what structure must perform the function. What mattered was whether structure *was* disclosed in the specification, and if so whether a skilled person would identify the structure from that description. In the present case (with a dissenting opinion on this point) a published document incorporated by reference did not assist the patentees because the statutory requirement to disclose structure could only be met by what was disclosed in the specification itself.

The patent was only saved from invalidity because Atmel's expert testified that the title of the cited article was in itself sufficient to indicate to one skilled in the art the precise structure of the means recited in the specification, and that testimony was unrebutted. Accordingly the CAFC held that summary judgment of invalidity for indefiniteness under §112, was improper. How close the patent came to invalidity for indefiniteness notwithstanding the cross-reference is self-evident – if the title had been omitted and only the literature reference had been given the specification would have been incurably invalid under 35 USC §112.

Concealment of critical detail

A grantable specification requires an enabling disclosure,[196] and if an applicant cannot or will not provide such disclosure, then he should rely on the law of trade secrecy and not use the patent system.

Deliberate concealment of essential information while hoping to obtain a valid patent has an enduring attraction for inventors, but has not been a successful strategy in the UK since *R v Arkwright*[197] where the evidence that had been given concerning lack of clarity was summarised as follows:

> He admits in that he has not properly specified how the machine was made, and he says that he purposely (in prevention of an evil, that foreigners might not get them) omitted to give so full a description of his inventions in the specification attending the last patent as he otherwise would have done.

Deliberate concealment works no better in the EPO. In *Inadequate description/ Hakoune*,[198] the invention concerned marking a gemstone by cathode bombardment through a patterned mask to produce an etched pattern on the gemstone. Cathode bombardment had previously been disclosed as a means of cleaning the surface of a gemstone prior to metal coating. The specification did not disclose what different bombardment conditions were needed for etching as opposed to mere cleaning. A memo from the applicant's technical staff came to light which said:

> Details of the actual production process have been kept secret to prevent them being copied straight from the patent.

The application was refused for lack of enabling disclosure.

The US courts treat deliberate concealment with equal disfavour, especially having regard to the statutory requirement[199] to disclose best mode contemplated by the inventor for carrying out his invention. In *Union Pac. Res. Co. v Chesapeake Energy Corp*,[200] the invention concerned horizontal drilling for the exploration of oil or natural gas and related to a method for determining the location of a borehole relative to strata in a subterranean formation by (a) providing information from said borehole, which information characterises the strata, (b) providing characterizing information of said

---

196. The concepts of disclosure and enablement are distinct and should not be confused. For a review of UK law in this area, see the decision of the House of Lords in *Synthon v Smithkline Beecham* [2005] UKHL 59, 20 October 2005.

197. 1 WPC at p 68 (1785)

198. T 0218/85

199. 35 USC §112(1). Evidence of concealment (accidental or intentional) is to be considered. If the best mode is *not* disclosed at the time of filing, that defect cannot be cured by amendment and any resulting patent may be invalid. It should be noted, however, that the statute requires that the best mode should be disclosed in the specification, but that where a number of embodiments are disclosed, there is no obligation to disclose which of them is best. For example, patent specifications in the fields of chemistry, pharmacy and dyestuffs commonly contain numerous examples but there is no necessity to single out a best single example or examples forming a best group.

200. 236 F.3d 684 (Fed. Cir. 2001); US-A-5311951

strata from an offset location, and (c) *comparing* said characterizing information from said borehole to said characterizing information from said offset location to determine the location of selected points along said borehole relative to said strata. The disclosed comparison required correlation of selected points along a horizontal borehole log to selected points of an offset log and testimony at the trial established that getting *true stratigraphic depth* (TSD) information through comparison was the novel feature of the invention, TSD describing the location of a borehole relative to a target zone. The District Court found that the patent as a whole failed to explain to one of ordinary skill in the art how to select points for correlation, how to select sections to consider, how to "stretch and squeeze" or manipulate the horizontal log in an attempt to match it to the vertical, how to determine when an adequate match has been achieved and how to use that information to develop a display that would provide directional information. It also found that the inventors had deliberately concealed computer program details, and this was supported by an e-mail between two of the inventors which read:

> None of the GR/NAV type stuff is included [in the patent]; this type of expertise (and especially the software, manuals, examples, etc.) are "trade secrets"...

The finding by the District Court that the specification did not meet the enablement requirements of 35 USC §112 was affirmed by the CAFC.

The absence of critical detail is usually very obvious to those sufficiently alerted to look for it. For example, in *Insulating magnetic toner/MITA,*[201] the critical ingredient of a toner was stated to be magnetite of defined particle size, water content and impurity content. In the examples, the magnetite used was simply referred to as "Type A" and "Type B" and although the water and impurity contents were stated, details concerning preparation or source from which the magnetite was obtained were not given. It emerged during opposition proceedings that the preparative process could give variable results, and that the detailed method used was important. The Appeal Board revoked the patent for insufficiency. The bare references to "Type A" and "Type B" in circumstances where new and better properties of the magnetite were the whole basis of the invention were a signal to any experienced attorney that critical information was either unknown to the patentee or was being deliberately withheld, and that in either case there was an anomaly that merited investigation.

In a case where an inventor may be planning to withhold critical information, it is best practice to inform him that not only will this jeopardise the validity of any resulting patent, but that even attempting to withhold such information is pointless because the fact that critical information is missing (either because it was unknown to the inventor or because it was deliberately concealed) is usually self-evident. In order to avoid difficulties of this kind it is essential to check that adequate structure is disclosed for each "black-box" feature.

---

201. T 0199/91

Claim construction: implications of recent US, UK and EPO Appeal Board decisions for patent drafting and prosecution

"No foresight can anticipate nor any document of reasonable length contain express provisions for all possible questions."[202]

Coverage

This paper compares and contrasts the approach to claim interpretation in the UK, in the EPO and in the US.

After you have read this paper, you should be aware of:

1. The main features of "purposive construction" as applied by the UK courts.

2. The problems that can be created by geometrical definitions in claims (which can be classified as structural rather than functional definitions).

3. The strict interpretation normally given to numerical ranges.

4. The US approach to claim interpretation, and the tests for literal infringement and equitable infringement on the doctrine of equivalents.

5. Concerns in the US about "patent profanity" and over-selling the invention and their implications for the handling of US-originating applications in Europe.

6. The *Festo* decisions in the US, and the implications for the patents draftsman of the foreseeability standard adopted by the US Supreme Court.

---

202. Abraham Lincoln, *First Inaugural Address*. Readers will remember that Lincoln had just ended a long and successful career as an attorney.

Introduction

Claim interpretation has long been controversial. In the UK, we have seen the House of Lords decisions in *Catnic*[203] and more recently in *Kirin-Amgen*.[204] In the US, the Supreme Court has considered the applicability of the doctrine of equivalents in *Warner-Jennkinson*[205] and then in *Festo*.[206] More recently a dispute between those who construe patent claims relying primarily on the wording of the specification and those who consider that the primary source for interpretation should be dictionaries has been resolved by the CAFC sitting *in banc* in *Phillips*.[207] The increasingly frequent consideration of claim construction in *Markman*[208] hearings highlights the importance of issues which can arise under US law and which are understood in the UK and Europe insufficiently widely and in insufficient detail.

This paper explains briefly the UK and EPO approaches to claim construction, and in particular the approach that the UK courts have adopted in *Kirin-Amgen*. It uses these as starting points for comparison with the US approach, hopefully enabling important differences to be highlighted and appropriate action to be suggested. The result should be an overall improvement in our approach to drafting, but unfortunately as we shall also see, an increase in the necessary length and cost of the specifications that we write, especially where we adopt wholly or partly functional claim language.

Although some issues that arise in the EPO and in UK national practice have counterparts in the US, there are many considerations and difficulties in the US that have no such counterparts in the EPO or in the UK.

Principles of claim construction before the EPO are largely settled and claim construction has never been a major issue, a main reason being that the EPO has no infringement jurisdiction. Although new points continually arise, there is nothing corresponding to the intense debate that has been seen in recent years in the US.

In UK national practice, infringement actions naturally focus on issues of construction, and the recent House of Lords decision in *Kirin-Amgen* has placed these issues within a more logical framework, without, it is submitted, affecting the prevailing judicial approach which is likely to be adopted in most cases.

---

203. *Catnic Components v Hill and Smith,* [1982] RPC 183 (UK House of Lords) (**Required reading**).

204. *Kirin-Amgen v Hoechst Marion Roussel,* [2004] UKHL 46 (UK House of Lords; Lords Hoffmann, Hope of Craighead, Roger of Earlsferry, Walker of Gestingthorpe and Brown of Eaton-under-Heywood, 21 October 2004) (**Required reading**).

205. *Warner Jenkinson v Hilton Davis Chemical Co.* (95-728), 520 U.S. 17, 41 USPQ2d 1865 (US Sup. Ct., 1997) (**Required reading**).

206. *Festo Corp. v Shoketsu Kinzoku Kogyo Kabushiki Co.*, 62 USPQ2d 1705 (US Sup. Ct., 2002) (**Required reading**).

207. *Edward H. Philips v AWH Corporation* 75 USPQ2d 1321., Fed. Cir. 12 July 2005 (**Required reading**).

208. *Markman et al. v Westview Instruments, Inc., et al.* (95-26), 517 U.S. 370 (US. Sup. Ct., 1996) (**Required reading**).

Variants in UK infringement proceedings

At present, infringement proceedings in Europe are heard by the relevant national courts. In England and Wales these are the Patents Court and the Patents County Court. National procedures, cultures and traditions differ and this has in the past led to differences in approach, but the effects of these differences should not be over-emphasised. Courts decide the cases before them according to the evidence, and if the outcome in Germany is different from that in the UK one possible explanation is national differences, but another equally possible reason, which is often overlooked, is that the evidence before the courts may have been materially different.

UK courts have, at least since *Catnic*, moved away from an over-literal approach to an approach based on "purposive construction" which in appropriate circumstances gives language an extended meaning. The doctrine is of general application, and interpretation of patent claims is only one particular area where it has been applied. A recent and instructive example of purposive construction as applied outside the field of IP appears in *Regina v Secretary of State for Health (Respondent) ex parte Quintavalle (on behalf of Pro-Life Alliance) (Appellant)*.[209] It exemplifies how far the UK courts are prepared to depart from the literal wording of statutes, where circumstances demand, in order to deal with technology developed after the statute was enacted. The proceedings required interpretation of the *Human Fertilization and Embryology Act, 1990,* which regulates the treatment of live human embryos. An embryo is defined to mean a live human embryo *where fertilization was complete.* At issue was whether the Act protects live embryos produced by the subsequently developed technology of cloning, which does not require fertilization. The House of Lords unanimously held that it did, and the Court's approach to construction is of general interest. The lead judgment was handed down by Lord Bingham of Cornhill. In relation to the general principles of statutory construction he said:

> The basic task of the court is to ascertain and give effect to the true meaning of what Parliament has said in the enactment to be construed. But that is not to say that attention should be confined and a literal interpretation given to the particular provisions which give rise to difficulty. Such an approach not only encourages immense prolixity in drafting, since the draftsman will feel obliged to provide expressly for every contingency which may possibly arise. It may also (under the banner of loyalty to the will of Parliament) lead to the frustration of that will, because undue concentration on the minutiae of the enactment may lead the court to neglect the purpose which Parliament intended to achieve when it enacted the statute. Every statute other than a pure consolidating statute is, after all, enacted to make some change, or address some problem, or remove some blemish, or effect some improvement in the national life. The court's task, within the permissible bounds of interpretation, is to give effect to Parliament's purpose. So the controversial provisions should be read in the context of the statute as a whole, and the statute as a whole should be read in the historical context of the situation which led to its enactment.

> There is, I think, no inconsistency between the rule that statutory language retains the meaning it had when Parliament used it and the rule that a statute is always

---

209. [2003] UKHL 13

speaking. If Parliament, however long ago, passed an Act applicable to dogs, it could not properly be interpreted to apply to cats; but it could properly be held to apply to animals which were not regarded as dogs when the Act was passed but are so regarded now. The meaning of "cruel and unusual punishments" has not changed over the years since 1689, but many punishments which were not then thought to fall within that category would now be held to do so. The courts have frequently had to grapple with the question whether a modern invention or activity falls within old statutory language: see Bennion, *Statutory Interpretation,* 4th ed (2002) Part XVIII, Section 288. A revealing example is found in *Grant v Southwestern and County Properties Ltd* [1975] Ch 185, where Walton J had to decide whether a tape recording fell within the expression "document" in the Rules of the Supreme Court. Pointing out (page 190) that the furnishing of information had been treated as one of the main functions of a document, the judge concluded that the tape recording was a document.

On the construction of the statute, the Court held that the words *where fertilization is complete* were not intended to define what amounted to an embryo, but instead to the time when it should be treated as such i.e. when a two-cell zygote appeared, as stated later in the statute. The purpose of the Act was to protect live human embryos created outside the human body. Lord Bingham went on to formulate more detailed questions that he considered should be answered in reaching a decision:

(1) Does the creation of live human embryos by cloning (CNR) fall within the same genus of acts as those to which the expressed policy of Parliament has been formulated?

(2) Is the operation of the 1990 Act to be regarded as liberal and permissive in its operation or restrictive and circumscribed?

(3) Is the embryo created by CNR different in kind or dimension from that for which the Act was passed?

In answer to the first question, Lord Bingham's opinion was that it plainly did, because an embryo created by *in vitro* fertilization and one created by CNR were similar organisms. Whether the 1990 Act was liberal or restrictive was a more difficult question but following its evident purpose in the present case required regulation of activities that differed only insignificantly from those regulated by the Act. As regards the third question, there was plainly no such difference. It was permissible to ask whether Parliament, faced with the difficult religious, moral and scientific issues, could rationally have intended to leave live human embryos created by CNR outside the scope of regulation had it known of them as a scientific possibility. There was only one possible answer to this question and it was negative.

It will be apparent that when construing statutes, the UK courts are prepared both to give words figurative rather than literal meanings (e.g. *document* covering tape recording) and to depart from specific wording (e.g. *when fertilization was complete* in the 1990 Act). Their willingness to do so is greater for newly developed circumstances than it is for circumstances existing when the statute was enacted. Purposive construction of patents could in principle give similar results, but patent cases in which the courts have been prepared to give claim language the wide figurative meaning seen in *Quintavalle* have been very rare.

The latest explanation by the House of Lords of the UK approach to patent claim interpretation is given in *Kirin-Amgen*. Lord Hoffmann handed down the leading judgment, and his opinion, which is of general importance to the profession in both the UK and throughout Europe, is summarised below:

1. Under Art. 69 EPC, the extent of protection conferred by a European patent is determined by the scope of the claims. Consequently the patent gives *no* protection beyond the terms of the claims. That had already been decided by the House of Lords under the common law in *Catnic*, and when the EPC came into effect Art. 69 precluded protection extending beyond the claims by reference to 'pith and marrow' or the doctrine of equivalents. There is now no difference between the approach of the UK courts and those of the courts in Germany and the Netherlands, where the claims are recognised as the decisive basis for determining the extent of protection.[210]

2. The *Protocol on the Interpretation of Article 69* governs the rules for construction of patent claims under Art. 69, and not the construction of individual claims. The first sentence excludes the former common law rule as it had applied up to *Catnic* that the context provided by the description and drawings and the background or "extrinsic evidence" could only be used to construe claims in which there was an ambiguity. Under the EPC these matters were to be available for the interpretation of all claims. The "purposive construction" required in *Catnic*, which rejects a meaning different from what would have been understood by the person to whom the words were addressed, is precisely in accordance with the *Protocol*. The second sentence excludes the former German approach that claims could treated simply as a point of departure and that it was legitimate to go beyond their terms to derive an inventive concept. The third sentence called for fair protection for the patentee combined with reasonable certainty for third parties, and this could only be achieved by not disappointing the reasonable expectations of either side:

    > What principle of interpretation would give fair protection to the patentee? Surely, a principle which would give him the full extent of the monopoly which the person skilled in the art would think he was intending to claim. And what principle would provide a reasonable degree of protection for third parties? Surely again, a principle which would not give the patentee more than the full extent of the monopoly which the person skilled in the art would think that he was intending to claim. Indeed, any other principle would also be unfair to the patentee, because it would unreasonably expose the patent to claims of invalidity on grounds of anticipation or insufficiency.

---

210. see *Batteriekastenschnur* [1989] GRUR 903, 904) and *Ciba-Geigy/Oté Optics* (1995) Nederlandse Jurisprudentie 39, see also the EPO Appeal Board decision in T 0208/88 *Plant growth regulating agent/BAYER* [1990] EPOR 257, 261.

3. *"The question is always what the person skilled in the art would have understood the patentee to be using the language of the claim to mean."*[211] That is an objective question depending on the words in the claim, the context of and background to those words, the identity of the person skilled in the art, and the knowledge and assumptions to be attributed to him:[212]

> There will be occasions upon which it will be obvious to the skilled man that the patentee must in some respect have departed from conventional use of language or included in his description of the invention some element which he did not mean to be essential. But one would not expect that to happen very often.... It has been suggested that in the absence of any explanation for a restriction in the extent of protection claimed, it should be presumed that there was some good reason between the patentee and the patent office. I do not think that it is sensible to have presumptions about what people must be taken to have meant but a conclusion that they have departed from conventional usage obviously needs some rational basis.

4. It is legitimate to take equivalents into account as an aid to construction because they are an important part of the background facts known to a skilled person. Taking account of equivalents in order to determine the extent of protection is specifically required by the new *Article 2* of the *Protocol to Article 69* introduced under the 2000 revisions to the EPC (not yet in force). Guidance about how to do so is given by the so-called *Protocol Questions* derived from *Catnic,* and further explained in *Improver v Remington*[213] as follows:

> If the issue was whether a feature embodied in an alleged infringement which fell outside the primary, literal or acontextual meaning of a descriptive word or phrase in the claim ("a variant") was nevertheless within its language as properly interpreted, the court should ask itself the following three questions:
>
> (i) Does the variant have a material effect upon the way the invention works? If yes, the variant is outside the claim. If no?
> (ii) Would this (i.e. that the variant had no material effect) have been obvious at the date of publication of the patent to a reader skilled in the art? If no, the variant is outside the claim. If yes?
> (iii) Would the reader skilled in the art nevertheless have understood from the language of the claim that the patentee intended that strict compliance with the primary meaning was an essential requirement of the invention? If yes, the variant is outside the claim. On the other hand, a negative answer to the last question would lead to the conclusion that the patentee was intending the word or phrase to have not a literal but a figurative meaning (the figure being a form of synecdoche[214] or

---

211. Compare the more restrictive criterion for construction of a US claim as discussed below.

212. See also the detailed explanations that had previously been given in *Mannai Investment Co Ltd v Eagle Star Life Assurance Co Ltd* [1997] AC 749 *and Investors Compensation Scheme Ltd v West Bromwich Building Society* [1998] 1 WLR 896.

213. [1990] FSR 181, 189 (**Required reading**).

metonymy[215]) denoting a class of things which include the variant and the literal meaning, the latter being perhaps the most perfect, best-known or striking example of the class.

However, in those cases where the *Protocol* questions are helpful, instead of asking whether the variant works in the same way, it may now be better to follow the German courts and ask whether the variant solves the problem underlying the invention by means having the same technical effect.[216]

5. The *Protocol* questions may be helpful where the decision to be made is between strict compliance with the conventional meaning of a word or phrase or a looser figurative interpretation and also for decisions (as in the "quintet" of German cases and in *Catnic* in the UK) as to whether figures and measurements are used in a strict conventional sense or as approximations. However, they should be treated as guidelines more useful in some cases than in others and should not be treated as legal rules

> No doubt there will be patent lawyers who are dismayed at the notion that the *Protocol* questions do not provide an answer in every case. They may feel cast adrift on a sea of interpretative uncertainty. But that is the fate of all who have to understand what people mean by using language. The *Protocol* questions are useful in many cases, but they are not a substitute for trying to understand what the person skilled in the art would have understood the patentee to mean by the language of the claims.

---

214. A figure of speech in which a part of something is used for the whole (e.g. hands to refer to workers or head to refer to cattle), the whole of something is used for a part (e.g. the police for an individual officer or a small group of officers), a species is used for the genus, (e.g. bread for food), a genus is used for the species (creature for person), or the stuff of which something is made is used for the thing (willow for cricket bat; plastic for credit card).

215. The use of a single characteristic to refer to a complex entity e.g. the White House to refer to the US administration, or the Crown to refer to the UK government. In the expression: "The pen is mightier than the sword" the pen denotes the written word and the sword denotes military force.

216. See the *"quintet"* of cases before the *Bundesgerichtshof*, for example, *Kunstoffrohrteil* [2002] GRUR 511 and *Schneidemesser* 1 [2003] ENPR 12 309 (which concerned questions whether figures or measurements in a claim allow some degree of approximation) and see also a paper by Judge Peter Meier-Beck (currently a judge of the 10th Senate), now published in the International Review of Intellectual Property and Competition Law (IIC) 3/2005. Judge Meier-Brink explains in his paper (apparently written before the House of Lords decision in *Kirin-Amgen*) that: "*A variant only has the same technical effect if it brings about all the results that a person skilled in the art understands from the claim to be brought forth by every single feature and by the mutual connection of all features of the claim. Determining the technical effect means determining those effects that the person skilled in the art understands to be the result of the technical teaching of the claim. Therefore the first question already does not relate to technical facts viewed in isolation and separately from the patent claim. The objective technical identity is only relevant if it constitutes an identity of all effects that the person skilled in the art understands to be the effects of the inventive technical teaching.*" He goes on to explain that the equivalent must be an obvious equivalent, and that not all obvious equivalents are covered but only those that are sufficiently close to the technical teaching of the patent claim. It will be apparent that there is a convergence of view between the UK and the German courts, and possibly a greater consistency in decision-making, but that a common approach has not yet been arrived at. At the time of writing, the reaction of the German courts to *Kirin-Amgen* has not yet become apparent.

6. In particular, the *Protocol* questions are not helpful:

(a) where it is first necessary to construe the claim and decide what the person skilled in the art would understand was the level of generality of the invention, i.e. what the invention really is, the *Protocol* questions answering themselves when that issue had been decided; or

(b) for new technology, in which case the question is whether the claims can properly be construed sufficiently generally to cover that technology or whether they are restricted to existing technology because of doubts about sufficiency rather than lack of forethought about future developments:

> There is no difficulty in principle about construing general terms to include embodiments which were unknown at the time the document was written. One frequently does that in construing legislation, for example, by construing "carriage" in a 19th century statute to include a motor car. In such cases it is particularly important not to be too literal. It may be clear from the language, context and background that the patentee intended to refer in general terms to, for example, every way of achieving a certain result, even though he has used language which is in some respects inappropriate in relation to a new way of achieving that result: compare *Regina (Quintavalle) v Secretary of State for Health* [2003] 2 AC 687.

Despite the length of the *Kirin-Amgen* judgment, the key point is simple. In order to establish infringement, Kirin-Amgen had to succeed on the basis of a claim which included the words *product of eukaryotic expression of an exogenous DNA sequence.* The word *exogenous* implied that the DNA being expressed was introduced into the cell from an exterior source. The accused process relied on later-developed technology to bring about expression of a sequence coding for the same protein but naturally occurring in the cell (an *endogenous* sequence). Lord Hoffmann was not prepared to treat *exogenous* as a figurative expression additionally covering *endogenous* DNA because he considered that it would give the patentee a monopoly for the use of the sequence information as such, and that was over-broad. It will be noted that in order to find infringement, it would have been necessary for the House of Lords to vitiate the express limitation *exogenous* and hold that its meaning extended to its opposite *endogenous*: UK courts, like their US counterparts are rarely willing to adopt such a course.

However, UK courts have on occasions proved significantly more flexible than their reputation for strict construction would suggest. For example, it is possible to identify a sequence of cases where UK courts have been prepared to give extended figurative meanings to geometrical language where the difference is irrelevant to function.

In *Barking Brassware Co. Ltd v Allied Ironfounders*,[217] the invention concerned kitchen mixer taps (see accompanying figure) for connection to a mains water supply

---

217. [1962] RPC 210; GB-A-0669295

and simultaneously to a domestic hot water tank, and for avoiding the risk that the mains water supply might become contaminated with hot water from the water tank, e.g. in the event of loss of mains pressure in hilly districts during the summer. The solution claimed (with reference numerals added) was:

> Apparatus for mixing fluids from two sources which comprises a body portion (1) divided into two parts by a partition (4) and an outlet member consisting of two co-axial members (7,8), one of which (8) passes through the partition and communicates with one of the parts while the other (7) communicates with the other part and in which each of the two parts is connected to one of the sources of fluid, the disposition of the two co-axial members (7,8) being such that there is no physical contact between the fluids until they have left the apparatus.

In the accused device, one tube was offset relative to another so that their axes did not coincide, but the Court held that this variant was within the ambit of the claims, and set out its reasoning in terms which anticipates much subsequent debate in the UK and in the US:

> In approaching the resolution of the conflict between the contentions of the parties, it must be stated at the outset that the conception of the court as a depository of dictionaries and encyclopaedias for the elucidation of technical terms is wholly erroneous. Reference to such works may be and frequently is of assistance in assessing the comprehensiveness and reliability of the evidence of witnesses of opinion, but the primary duty of the court is to identify itself with the knowledgeable persons in the particular art to whom the specification is deemed to be addressed, to seek to understand the terms used in the specification in the sense that he and his kind would attribute to them, and thus to arrive at an ascertainment of the alleged invention as it would present itself to a competent potential user of it. This is not to decry the merit of intellectual criticism of language, but merely to mark the bounds within which it will be found of advantage.

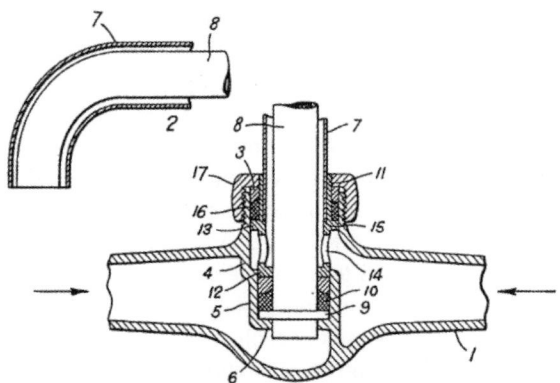

Barking Brassware

In *Catnic*, the invention concerned a box girder for fitting as a lintel over a window or door opening, and the claim referred to a back plate *extending vertically*. In the accused device, the back plate was inclined at 6° or 8° from the vertical, and the question was whether this difference was sufficient to remove it from the ambit of the claims. The House of Lords decided that the accused device did indeed infringe, and analysed the relevant facts as follows:

> Put in a nutshell the question to be answered is: "Would the specification make it obvious to a builder familiar with ordinary building operations that the description of a lintel in the form of a weight-bearing box girder of which the back plate was referred to as 'extending vertically' from one of the two horizontal plates to join the other, could not have been intended to exclude lintels in which the back plate although not positioned at precisely 90° to both horizontal plates was close enough to 90° to make no material difference to the way the lintel worked when used in building operations?" No plausible reason has been advanced why any rational patentee should want to place so narrow a limitation on his invention. On the contrary, to do so would render his monopoly for practical purposes worthless, since any imitator could avoid it and take all the benefit of the invention by the simple expedient of positioning the back plate a degree or two from the exact vertical.
>
> It may be that when used by a geometer addressing himself to fellow geometers, such expressions descriptive of relative position as "horizontal", "parallel", "vertical" and "vertically" are to be understood as words of precision only; but when used in a description of a manufactured product intended to perform the practical function of a weight-bearing box girder in supporting courses of brickwork over window and door spaces in buildings, it seems to me that the expression "extending vertically" as descriptive of the position of what in use will be the upright member of a trapezoid-shaped box girder, is perfectly capable of meaning positioned near enough to the exact geometrical vertical to enable it in actual use to perform satisfactorily all the functions that it could perform if it were precisely vertical; and having regard to those considerations to which I have just referred that is the sense in which in my opinion "extending vertically" would be understood by a builder familiar with ordinary building operation. Or, putting the same thing in another way, it would be obvious to him that the patentee did not intend to make exact verticality in the positioning of the back plate an essential feature of the invention claimed.
>
> My Lords, if one analyses line by line the ways in which the various expressions are used in the specification, one can find pointers either way as to whether in particular lines various adjectives and adverbs descriptive of relative position are used as words of precision or not. Some of these are discussed in the judgments of the majority of the Court of Appeal who found the pointers in favour of precision stronger than those to the contrary, of which one example is the description of the two "horizontal" plates as being only "substantially parallel". For my part I find the result of such analysis inconclusive and of little weight as compared with the broad considerations to which I have referred and which are a consequence of giving as I think one should, a purposive construction to the specification.

In *Dyson v Hoover*,[218] the patent in issue addressed the problem that a vacuum cleaner based on high-efficiency frusto-conical cyclones connected in series did not work well under normal domestic conditions when dirt particles of larger size and other extraneous objects were present, and what was needed was an upstream cyclone deliberately constructed to be of lower efficiency by omitting the usual downwardly convergent taper or by providing a reverse taper. The main claim was directed to:

> A vacuum cleaning appliance including cyclone units of successively higher efficiency, in the capability of depositing fine dust, in series connection, the highest efficiency cyclone having a frusto-conical part (15) tapered away from its entry (18) and means for generating an air flow from a dirty air inlet sequentially through the cyclone units characterised in that a lower efficiency cyclone unit upstream of the highest efficiency unit has a body (13) without the taper away from the air entry, being either cylindrical or having a reverse taper.

In the accused device (HTV), the high-efficiency cyclone was "trumpet-shaped" rather than precisely frusto-conical and the defendants averred that this was a variant which should not be held to fall within the ambit of the claim. The High Court rejected this argument, and commented:

> The apparently trivial difference between a geometrically perfect frusto-conical profile and that of the relevant portion of the HTV was dramatically highlighted at trial by the drawing put forward by Dyson in chief as Document X-9. This was a blown-up photocopy of the relevant portion of a sectional drawing of the relevant part of the HTV appliance. Upon this, two geometrically correct frusto-conical profiles had been superimposed in red, showing a slightly different notional angle corresponding to the "top" and "bottom" of Hoover's "trumpet". I have held that properly construed, the phrase "frusto-conical" does not demand such geometric exactitude since to do so would be to indulge in the sort of strict literal interpretation which is forbidden by the Protocol. For this reason alone, I would be hesitant to hold that the separating zone in SU3 is not in fact "frusto-conical" within the proper meaning of the claim. And I feel sure that the skilled reader would so regard it.

It was accepted that the trumpet-shaped cyclone worked in the same way as a frusto-conical cyclone, as the following passage from the cross-examination of the defendant's expert witness shows:

> Q. The skilled person in 1980 would understand that the effect of the frusto-conical cone is to reduce the diameter of the vortex and consequentially increase the tangential velocity of the particles as they pass down the cone?
> A. Or at least maintain it, yes.
>
> Q. You would expect that also with the trumpet shape?
> A. That is going to happen of course at a different rate.

---

218. [2001] RPC 473 (HC), [2002] RPC 465 (CA); EP-B-0042723

Q You would expect it to happen?

A. It would happen but at a different rate.

The Patents Court said that it would have been obvious to a skilled reader with a basic knowledge of cyclone separation that the trumpet shape would work in the same way as a frusto-conical separator, that there was no plausible reason why a rational patentee would have wished to confine the scope of protection to geometrical precision, and that the claim extended to a surface which was *sufficiently frusto-conical to do its job*. This approach was affirmed by the Court of Appeal, which said:

> It is clear from reading the specification that the purpose of the cone is to concentrate the vortex and to separate the fine particles from the air. The specification never suggests that the cone should have a precise shape which had to accord with the mathematical definition of a cone. To the contrary, it envisages that "a body of substantially frusto-conical shape tapering away" would be sufficient. Further the specification did not attempt to teach that any particular shape was better than another. The skilled reader would understand, to adopt the evidence of Professor Allen that the purpose of the frusto-conical shape was to generate a centrifugal force by concentrating the vortex. The trumpet shape of Hoover did just that.
>
> In my view the words frusto-conical as used in the patent are not to be given the precise mathematical definition. They must be construed purposively so as to encompass a shape, generally frusto-conical, which achieves the desired concentration and separation of fine particles. The trumpet shape of Hoover is a frusto-cone in the way that those words are used in the specification.

The above decisions may be compared with the classic US decision in *Winans v Denmead*,[219] where the patentee claimed a railway truck for transporting coal. It had

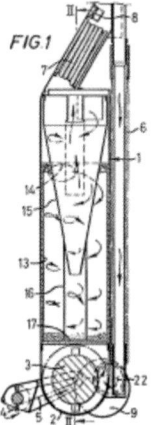

Dyson v Hoover

---

219. See US Patent 5175 issued 26 June 1847 and 56 US (15 How.) 330 (1853); the case is discussed in Peter D. Rosenberg, Patent Law Fundamentals, Clark Boardman Company, Ltd, New York.

a coal hopper of inverted *frusto-conical* shape to give a relatively small base that could extend below the frame of the truck and between its axles to give a low centre of gravity. The defendant's truck was similar, except that their hopper had the form of a *hexagonal pyramid*, i.e. it had a number of straight walls instead of the required single curved wall. The resulting infringement controversy reached the US Supreme Court before it was finally resolved in the patentee's favour.

The lesson, in both jurisdictions, is that geometrical definitions are best avoided – it should *not* be the objective of a draftsman to use wording that will only be held to cover an accused device on appeal to the House of Lords or to the Supreme Court. Nor is the *Winans v Densmead* decision necessarily in accordance with current US judicial thought.

The lenient UK attitude to geometrical terms apparently does not apply to numerical ranges, see *Auchincloss v Agricultural and Veterinary Supplies.*[220]

By the 1960s, if not before, it was a misrepresentation to say that the reason why the UK courts almost never applied the doctrine of equivalents was because of an anachronistic devotion to literalism. It is reasonable to assume that the UK cases that created concern amongst Continental European practitioners and prompted drafting of the Protocol were *Van der Lely v Bamfords*[221] and *Rodi & Wienenberger v Showell.*[222] In *Van der Lely,* the claimed inventive concept was converting a side delivery rake to a swathe turner by moving a "hindmost" group of rake wheels. The decision of the House of Lords that only movement of that group of wheels was covered was contextual because only that group had ever been disclosed as movable. The House of Lords was satisfied that the patentee had never thought of the alternative of moving the foremost group of wheels, and it was not prepared to broaden the claimed inventive concept with retrospective effect to cover an undisclosed embodiment. It is submitted that it would be equally difficult today to persuade a UK court that a reasonable engineer would have understood "hindmost" to be a figurative expression also covering movement of the foremost group, and that many engineers would regard this as an outrageous extension of the originally claimed subject-matter. It may be compared with the rule under US law, discussed below, that the doctrine of equivalents cannot apply if the result would be to vitiate an entire claim limitation or a specific exclusion. Similarly, the reason why *Rodi & Wienenberger* could not enforce their patent was not an acontextual claim interpretation, but belief that what the patentees had invented was limited to the flexible inexpensively assembled bracelet structure defined in some detail in the main claim, so that it was not legitimate to omit the detail with retrospective effect in order to cover the defendant's differently constructed embodiment. In both cases, the temptation to broaden the inventive concept came not from the patentee's disclosure or his contemporary foresight definition of his invention, but from hindsight knowledge of the defendant's redesign. Although these decisions created surprise in other European countries given their different pre-EPC judicial approach, the recent case law quoted by Lord

220. [1967] RPC 649
221. [1963] RPC 61
222. [1969] RPC 367

Hoffmann shows that such judges would now have greater understanding of the reasoning applied in *Van der Lely* and in *Rodi & Wienenberger*.

Has purposive construction as restated by Lord Hoffmann opened patent claims for wider interpretation in the UK? Notwithstanding the negative result in *Kirin-Amgen* it should be remembered that only the underlying principles in an earlier case was binding in a later case, and that each case is decided on its own facts. The task facing the patentee is to persuade the court that it can adopt a broad or figurative meaning for the claim language in question without either going outside what the patentee has truly invented or adopting an interpretation which gives the ambit of the claim undue breadth. One promising approach for a patentee may be to emphasise (where possible) that the accused variant relates to unforeseeable subsequently discovered technology. It remains to be seen whether a sequence of cases along these lines will develop, perhaps initially in the mechanical or electrical arts. However if the *"one compulsory question"* (Lord Walker) under Article 69 EPC is what the skilled reader would have understood the claim to mean, then the almost invariable answer up to now is that a UK court will not go beyond the natural meaning of the words in the claim, interpreted in context perhaps, but not stretched to some broader generality that can be discerned with hindsight from the disclosure but is not found in any claim.

A European draftsman's viewpoint

The task for the European practitioner is to select the appropriate set of features to include in his claims, and to define those features and the relationships between them in appropriate broad language. UK practitioners in particular have a settled expectation that to establish infringement, the accused product or process must fall within the literal wording of the claims as granted, and do not expect that an inappropriately worded claim will be rescued by the doctrine of equivalents or by the more modern approach of extended figurative construction. That expectation dates back to the decision in *Nobel Explosives Co., Ltd v Anderson*.[223] In that case, the invention was for the manufacture of explosives and was claimed in terms of a combination of nitroglycerine with "soluble nitro-cellulose". The defendant used, in combination with nitroglycerine, a form of nitro-cellulose which was not soluble and all judges held that this was not an infringement. The following statement of Romer J who was the judge at first instance was approved both in the Court of Appeal and subsequently in the House of Lords and is often quoted:

> In order to make out infringement, it must be established, to the satisfaction of the Court, that the alleged infringer dealing with what he is doing as a matter of substance, is taking the invention claimed by the patent; not the invention which the Patentee might have claimed if he had been well advised or bolder, but that which he has in fact and substance claimed on a fair construction of the Specification.

However, the constraints on the language used are few. As explained above, functional claiming is not frowned on, and although some limits are imposed by the

---

223. (1895) 11 RPC 115 (Romer J); (1895) 11 RPC 520 (CA); (1896) 12 RPC 164 (HL).

requirements of rule 29 EPC that the claim should define "the technical features of the invention", functional features can qualify as technical features. The word "means" is not yet a profanity in Europe. The facts and arguments submitted to the Patent Office during prosecution do not usually return to haunt us during infringement litigation – file wrapper estoppel is not considered by the European courts. The liberalization of the rules on post-grant amendment throughout Europe following the changes being introduced by EPC 2000 have moved the spotlight further away from the activities of the prosecution attorney. The landscape is significantly different from that which faces our US colleagues.

Principles of claim interpretation in the US: another common law system, another universe?

How US patent claims should be interpreted has been the subject of intense debate, and has been considered by the US Supreme Court three times since 1996. The decision of the Supreme Court in *Festo* which seemingly gave an authoritative overview of the how the doctrine of equivalents should be applied seems to have raised as many questions as it has settled. The purpose of this section is to summarise the main points that can be gleaned from recent US decisions, to highlight differences from the law under the *UK Patents Act, 1977* and the *EPC* and to consider their implications for European practitioners in their day-to-day work of drafting applications and providing instructions to their colleagues in the US. The differences are especially significant in the context of functional claim language, which is the subject of the following paper. Of course, where there is any difficulty, or where a legal opinion is required, there is no substitute for the advice of a US practitioner.

The infringement provisions of the US Statute[224] are generally similar to those in Europe and provide for both direct and induced or contributory infringement. A significant difference is that contributory infringement applies when a product is supplied in disassembled kit form for final assembly outside the US, or when key components are supplied for use outside the US. In the case of a "distributed invention"[225] the desirability of having both system claims and claims to the individual components is understood in the US as in Europe because direct infringement is more straightforward to establish than literal infringement. However, in Europe, a patentee cannot control the supply of critical components or kits for export unless he also has patent protection in the country where they are to be assembled and used, and without *per se* claims to the components and kits the rights of the patentee may be significantly diminished. US practitioners may not be fully aware of this difference and its implications when instructing the filing of US-originating applications in Europe. European attorneys receiving US-originating applications should therefore routinely check for claims to components and kits and should advise the addition of such claims when necessary. It should also be noted that, as in Europe, import into the US of the product of a patented process for commercial purposes amounts to infringement unless subsequent processing has materially changed the product or it has become a trivial or non-essential component of another product.

---

224. 35 USC § 271

225. See the discussion of distributed inventions at page 218

US test for infringement

A determination of infringement of a utility patent requires a multi-step analysis:[226]

(1) The court determines the scope and meaning of the claims asserted, which is a question of law.[227]
(2) The properly construed claims are compared to the allegedly infringing device: determination whether every claim limitation or its equivalent is to be found in the accused device.[228] For literal infringement, the properly construed claim must read onto the accused device exactly.[229] If literal infringement is not established, then:
(3) Infringement is reconsidered on the basis of the doctrine of equivalents.
(4) For a "means-plus-function" or "step-plus-function" feature, equivalents are considered in two stages: firstly legal equivalents whose coverage is required by the wording of 35 USC § 112(6), and secondly a further group of equitable equivalents whose coverage is derived from decisions of the Supreme Court in e.g. *Graver Tank*,[230] *Warner-Jenkinson* and *Festo* (see the paper below on functional claims).

Issues of patent construction in US patent infringement proceedings have taken centre-stage following the decision of the US Supreme Court in *Markman et al. v Westview Instruments, Inc., et al.*[231] At issue in that case was whether the construction of a patent, including terms of art within the claims was for the court to decide, or whether it should be decided by a jury. The right to a jury trial in any action where the value in dispute exceeds $20 is preserved by the US Constitution, seventh amendment. The Court decided that the construction of patents, as of other written documents, should be left to the judge since common law practice at the time of framing of the US Constitution and early cases from England both showed that judges, not juries, construed terms in patent specifications, and because this which a task that a judge, from his training and discipline, was in the better position to perform. Following that decision, pre-trial hearings to construe the patent's claims following motions by defendants for summary judgment (so-called *Markman* hearings) have become a routine feature of infringement trials and now account for a major part of the work of the Federal Circuit. It seems that once there was a clear decision that claim interpretation was for the judge alone and did not have to be put to a jury, then there was no obstacle to asking the judge to make a preliminary ruling on claim interpretation, and *Markman* hearings have escalated in popularity because they provide defendants with a means for potentially bringing protracted infringement litigation to an abrupt end.

---

226. *Sybor Corp. v FAS Techs., Inc.*, 138 F.3d 1448, 1454 (Fed. Cir. 1998) (*en banc*)

227. *Markman v Westview Instruments, Inc.*, 52 F.3d 967, 970- 71 (Fed. Cir. 1995) (*en banc*), aff'd, 517 U.S. 370 (1996)

228. *Warner-Jenkinson Co. v Hilton Davis Chem. Co.*, 520 U.S. 17, 29 (1997); *Bai v L & L Wings Inc.*, 160 F.3d 1350, 1353 (Fed. Cir. 1998).

229. *Amhil Enters., Ltd. v Wawa, Inc.*, 81 F.3d 1554, 1562, 38 USPQ2d 1471, 1476 (Fed. Cir. 1996).

230. *Graver Tank & Manufacturing Co Inc v Linde Air Products Company* 339 US 605, 607 (US. Sup. Ct., Jackson J, 1950)

231. *supra.*

Claim construction to determine literal infringement

Claim construction begins with the words of the claim[232] which are given their ordinary and customary meaning, i.e. the meaning that the term would have to a person of ordinary skill in the art in question at the time of the invention, i.e. as of the effective filing date of the patent application. It is considered unjust to the public as well as an evasion of the law to construe a claim in a manner different from its plain import or its terms.[233] During examination, the USPTO gives claims their broadest reasonable interpretation.[234] A patentee may claim an invention broadly and expect enforcement of the full scope of that language unless there is a clear disavowal or contrary definition in the specification.

To ascertain the meaning of a claim term, the court looks to those sources available to the public that show what a person of ordinary skill in the art would have understood disputed claim language to mean. Those sources include:
  (1) The words of the claims themselves.
  (2) The remainder of the specification.
  (3) The prosecution history.
  (4) Extrinsic evidence concerning relevant scientific principles, the meaning of technical terms, and the state of the art.

As an example of extrinsic evidence, when prior art that sheds light on the meaning of a term is cited by the patentee, it can have particular value as a guide to the proper construction of the term, because it may indicate not only the meaning of the term to persons skilled in the art, but also that the patentee intended to adopt that meaning.[235] However, extrinsic evidence cannot be used to alter a claim construction dictated by a proper analysis of the intrinsic evidence.[236]

A significant difference from European statute law and the statute law of the US is that whereas Article 69 EPC requires the description and drawings to be used as an aid to determining the meaning of the claim wording, there is no such explicit requirement under US law (under which there is no requirement that the description be amended to conform to any amendments in the claim wording). Thus, only

---

232. *Vitronics Corp. v Conceptronic, Inc.*, 90 F.3d 1576, 1582 (Fed. Cir. 1996); *Tex. Digital Sys., Inc. v Telegenix, Inc.*, 308 F.3d 1193, 1201 (Fed. Cir. 2002).

233. *White v Dunbar*, 119 U.S. 47, 52 (1886); see also *Cont'l Paper Bag Co. v E. Paper Bag Co.*, 210 U.S. 405, 419 (1908) ("the claims measure the invention"); *McCarty v Lehigh Valley R.R. Co.*, 160 U.S. 110, 116 (1895) ("if we once begin to include elements not mentioned in the claim, in order to limit such claim... , we should never know where to stop"); *Aro Mfg. Co. v Convertible Top Replacement Co.*, 365 U.S. 336, 339 (1961) ("the claims made in the patent are the sole measure of the grant").

234. *Burlington Indus., Inc. v Quigg*, 822 F.2d 1581, 1583 (Fed. Cir. 1987*); In re Am. Acad. of Sci. Tech. Ctr.*, 367 F.3d 1359, 1364 (Fed. Cir. 2004).

235. *Kumar v Ovonic Battery Co.*, 351 F.3d 1364, 1368 (Fed. Cir. 2003); *Arthur A. Collins, Inc. v N. Telecom, Ltd.*, 216 F.3d 1042, 1045 (Fed. Cir. 2000)

236. *Intel Corp. v VIA Techs., Inc.*, 319 F.3d 1357, 1367 (Fed. Cir. 2003); Frank's *Casing Crew & Rental Tools, Inc. v PMR Techs., Ltd.*, 292 F.3d 1363, 1374 (Fed. Cir. 2002); *Bell & Howell Document Mgmt. Prods. Co. v Altek Sys.*, 132 F.3d 701, 706 (Fed. Cir. 1997).

recently in the *en banc* decision of the *Federal Circuit in Phillips v AWH Corp.*[237] have the appellate courts indicated the importance of using the specification in preference to dictionaries to determine the meaning and effect of claim wording.

In *CCS Fitness, Inc. v Brunswick Corp,*[238] the following ways were identified by which the ordinary meaning of a claim term might be restricted, if:
   (1) The patentee acted as his own lexicographer and clearly set forth a definition of the disputed claim term in either the specification or prosecution history.
   (2) The intrinsic evidence shows that the patentee distinguished that term from prior art on the basis of a particular embodiment, expressly disclaimed subject-matter, or described a particular embodiment as important to the invention.
   (3) The term chosen by the patentee so deprives the claim of clarity as to require resort to the other intrinsic evidence for a definite meaning.
   (4) If the patentee phrased the claim in step-plus-function or means-plus function format.[239]

A significant difference in approach between the US and the UK courts is signaled by the emphasis on the ordinary and customary meaning of claim terms:[240] the US courts focus on the meaning to the skilled person of the *words* in the claim, whereas following *Kirin-Amgen* the UK courts focus on *what the skilled person would have understood the patentee to have used the words to mean.* The subtlety of the distinction should not obscure its importance. US courts often adopt a strict constructionist approach to literal infringement, whereas, as explained above, UK courts sometimes adopt a more flexible purposive construction. As working European practitioners it is *not* our job to say which approach is better but to be aware of the differences and to craft our specifications so that wide enforceable claims are obtained in both the US and Europe.

The strict constructionist approach is exemplified by *Chef America, Inc. v Lamb-Weston, Inc.,*[241] where the claim required heating dough *to* a temperature of 400°F to 850°F. The problem was that if the batter-coated dough was heated *to* a temperature in this range it would be burned to a crisp. Instead of the *dough products suitable for freezing and finish cooking to a light, flaky, crispy texture* which the patented process was intended to provide, the resultant product of such heating would be something that resembled a charcoal briquette. To avoid this result and to ensure that the patented process could accomplish its stated objective, Chef America urged the court to interpret the claim as if it read *heating the... dough at a temperature in the range of –* i.e. to apply the heating requirement to the place where the heating took place (the oven) rather than the item being heated (the dough). The court however, refused to adopt this interpretation on the ground that it could not redraft claims, whether to

---

237. Fed. Cir. 2005.

238. 288 F.3d 1359, 62 U.S.P.Q.2d 1658 (Fed Cir., 2002, Michel J).

239. See the discussion of functional definitions in the following paper.

240. Figurative meaning does not yet seem to have been explored by the US courts as an avenue of escape from potentially unjust consequences of the literal construction.

241. 358 F.3d 1371, 69 USPQ2d 1857 (Fed. Cir. 2004)

make them operable or to sustain their validity, even where the result was a nonsensical construction. It is submitted that a UK court would have looked at what would have been understood by the words of the claim rather than what the literal meaning of the words actually was, and would have construed the claim in a way that would achieve the specified result. As is well known, however, when considering post-filing or post-grant amendment, the EPO has a similar strict constructionist approach, as shown in the closely similar recent decision in *Great Lakes Chemical (Europe) GmbH*[242] where opponents averred that by specifying cooling conditions with the term *cooling at room temperature* instead of *cooling to room temperature*, as in the disclosure of the application as filed, the final temperature of cooled extrudate was no longer restricted to room temperature but could be higher, thus giving the patentee an unwarranted advantage over third parties contrary to the purpose of Article 123(2) EPC as set out in Enlarged Appeal Board decision G 0001/93.[243] The EPO Appeal Board held that the claim had been inadmissibly broadened, but that the word *at* could not be deleted without contravening Article 123(3). The patentees were therefore in an "inescapable trap" and the patent should be revoked. The lesson, of course, is that it is better to avoid getting involved in such arguments and to ensure that the language of the claims is correct from the technical standpoint.

A further example of strict construction is to be found in *Alltrade Tools LLC. v Olympia Group, Inc,*[244] which concerned an application for an interlocutory injunction to restrain infringement of a patent relating to a so-called "prying bar". The main claim with reference numerals added read:

A prying bar comprising an elongate shank (11) having a predetermined cross section and defining a *longitudinal* axis (As) and having a prying hook (16) at one end and a prying chisel (14) at the other end, said prying hook having a tapered portion (18) and a generally U-shaped portion (16) integrally formed with said shank and said tapered portion generally defining a common plane, said tapered and U-shaped portions forming a prying footprint surface (19) facing a direction away from said shank, said prying footprint surface having a minimum transverse dimension which is substantially greater than the minimum cross sectional dimension of said shank, and said predetermined cross section having a major axis generally parallel to said plane and a minor axis generally normal to said plane, whereby the strength of the prying bar in applying forces at said prying hook and said prying chisel can be maximised and the bending of said prying bar shank can be minimised while enhancing the comfort gripping said prying bar shank by a user.

The Federal Circuit held that the word *axis* within the phrase *longitudinal axis* required the shank 11 to be linear or straight, this definition being consistent with the dictionary meaning of *axis* and its use in a number of references which were cited to the court. The accused device had a curved shank and although Olympia adduced evidence that the curvature was *de minimis*, they did not put in evidence of the

---

242. T 0657/01 – 3.3.3; EP-B-0565184
243. Reasons 16
244. 04-1090, 8 February 2005, Fed. Cir., Newman J., Clevenger J., and Gajarsa J., see US-A-6257553.

deviation. Consequently Olympia had not demonstrated a likelihood of infringement, and the motion for an interlocutory injunction was denied. It may be noted that precise straightness, or otherwise, of the shank was not relevant to what appears from the patent specification to have been the main novel feature, which was the angle between the hook and the shank, or to the advantage flowing from that feature which was that increased leverage was obtained when using the bar. The case demonstrates the danger accompanying the inappropriate use of words of geometrical precision: as explained above it is doubtful whether a UK or German court would have arrived at a similarly restrictive interpretation.

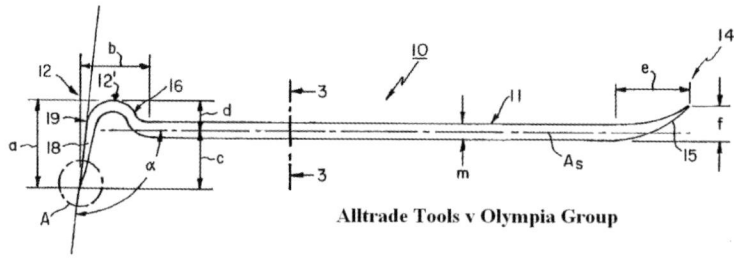

Alltrade Tools v Olympia Group

A yet further example is found in *Norian Corporation v Stryker Corporation*[245] where the patent in issue related to a rapidly setting calcium phosphate composition to be used as a bone cement and required as one ingredient a solution consisting of water and *a* sodium phosphate. The accused kit contained two different sodium phosphates, monobasic sodium phosphate monohydrate and dibasic sodium phosphate heptahydrate. The District Court held that the words "consisting of" coupled with the indefinite article should be interpreted to mean that the solution contained only water and a single solute. The Federal Circuit affirmed this interpretation and gave summary judgment of non-infringement, pointing out that all the disclosed solutions contained a single solute and that there was no reference anywhere in the specification, expressly or implicitly, to making the solution from a mixture of sodium phosphates. The prosecution history confirmed this interpretation, and the Federal Circuit observed that if during prosecution a patentee surrendered more than he had to in order to avoid prior art, the patentee was held to the scope of what he had claimed and could not post-grant argue for a broader interpretation.

Pedantry of the *Chef America* kind is not the invariable approach of the US courts, and an opposite approach was adopted in *Merck & Co., Inc v Teva Pharceuticals USA, Inc*[246] where *acid* was held to cover *salt*. For the patent draftsman, however, what matters is not whether the US courts might adopt a liberal approach to claim construction, but whether there is a significant risk that they may adopt a restrictive approach.

In the US, as in the UK, ranges, e.g. of amounts in a chemical composition, will normally be construed "*with numerical precision*", see *Jeneric/Pentron, Inc v Dillon*

245. Fed. Cir. 6 December 2005.

246. 347 F.3d 13677 (Fed. Cir., 2004, Rader J)

Company Inc.[247] The approach may be compared to that of the UK courts in *Lubrizol v Esso*[248] where the finding below (excluded from the abridged report[249]) was upheld that a claim parameter specified to have a minimum value of 1.3 was infringed by a product in which the parameter had a value of 1.25+, the figure specified not being 1.30 (i.e. two significant figures) so that a figure of 1.25 should be rounded up to the nearest significant one-decimal place under the usual convention of this type of parameter, i.e. to 1.3.

The disclosure in the written description of only a single embodiment does not limit the claimed invention to the features described in that embodiment[250] unless there was a clear intention to limit the claim scope by words or expressions of manifest exclusion or restriction. It is axiomatic that without more, the court will not limit claim terms to a preferred embodiment described in the specification.[251] A claim interpretation that excludes a preferred embodiment from the scope of the claim is rarely, if ever, correct.[252] However, inclusion of only a single embodiment does not assist in extending claim scope, and inclusion of additional embodiments and mention of possible equivalents for structures corresponding to claimed features is self-evidently desirable.

An instance where the CAFC felt obliged to exclude a preferred embodiment despite the observations in *Globetrotter*[253] occurred in *Elekta Instrument S.A. v O.U.R. Scientific International, Inc.*[254] The claimed invention was a γ-unit in which there was a radiation shield having a space for receiving the head of a patient and having an opening having a diametrical plane extending across the opening, wherein radiation sources and beam channels were required to be located *only within a zone extending between latitudes 30° and 45°* as seen from the diametrical plane. The preferred embodiment in the patent had its radiation sources and beam channels at latitudes of 0°-45°, and the accused device had radiation sources and beam channels at latitudes of 14°-43°. The court held that the words *only* and *extending* were key, and that the unambiguous language of the amended claim controlled over any contrary language in the written description. This interpretation was also supported by the prosecution history, and the court commented "*this is the rare case in which such an interpretation is compelled.*" Accordingly, there was no literal infringement: the case was remitted to the district court for consideration of infringement based on the doctrine of equivalents.

---

247. 205 F.3d 1377, 1382, 54 USPQ2d 1086, 1090 (Fed. Cir. 2000).

248. [1997] RPC 195 (HC), [1998] RPC 727 (CA)

249. [1977] RPC 195

250. *Liebel-Flarsheim Co. v Medrad, Inc.*, 358 F.3d 898, 906 (Fed. Cir. 2004)

251. *Virginia Panel Corp. v Mac Panel Co.*, 133 F.3d 860, 866, 45 USPQ2d 1225, 1229 (Fed. Cir. 1997) ("*[I]t is well settled that device claims are not limited to devices which operate precisely as the embodiments described in detail in the patent.*"); *Laitram Corp. v Cambridge Wire Cloth Co.*, 863 F.2d 855, 865 (Fed. Cir. 1988)

252. *Globetrotter Software, Inc. v Elan Computer Group, Inc.*, 362 F.3d 1367, 1381 (Fed. Cir. 2004); *Vitronics Corp. v Conceptronic, Inc.*, 90 F.3d 1576, 1583 (Fed. Cir. 1996); *Int'l Rectifier Corp. v IXYS Corp.*, 361 F.3d 1363, 1371 (Fed. Cir. 2004); *Modine Mfg. Co. v U.S. Int'l Trade Comm'n*, 75 F.3d 1545, 1550 (Fed. Cir. 1990).

253. *Supra.*

254. 242 F.3d 1302, 1306, 54 USPQ2d 1910, 1912 (Fed. Cir. 2000, Lourie J, Rader J and Bryson J)

When a claim term understood to have a narrow meaning when the application is filed later acquires a broader definition, the literal scope of the term is limited to what it was understood to mean at the time of filing. This approach may result in claim interpretations that might be unexpected from a European standpoint. As an example, see *PC Connector Solutions LLC v Smartdisk Corporation*[255] in which the invention was concerned with the connection of peripherals into a computer via a coupler inserted into a diskette drive. Claim 1 of the patent in issue, which dated from 1988, required in combination with a computer having a diskette drive *"an end user computer peripheral device having an input/output port normally connectible to a **conventional** computer input/output port."* The input/output ports of vintage 1988 computers used multi-pin connectors. The accused device was a diskette-shaped, sleeve-like adapter for flash memories and smart cards that allowed such media to be accessed through a diskette drive. There was no literal infringement because flash memories and smart cards use flat planar contact electrodes unknown in 1988 and incapable of fitting to a 1988 vintage I/O port. Furthermore, to find infringement on the doctrine of equivalents would foreclose the limitation of the I/O ports to what was *normal* in 1988 and accordingly summary judgment of non-infringement was granted.[256] This approach may be contrasted with the "always speaking" approach adopted by the UK courts to the construction of statutes and discussed above, and the similar approach suggested by the EPO Appeal Board in *Synergistic herbicides/CIBA GEIGY*[257] and in *Polypeptide Expression/Genentech.*[258]

The preamble of a claim generally limits the claimed invention if it recites essential structure or steps, or if it is necessary to give life, meaning, and vitality to the claim.[259] When limitations in the body of the claim rely upon and derive antecedent basis from the preamble, then the preamble may act as a necessary component of the claimed invention. However, if the preamble offers no distinct definition of any of the limitations of the claimed invention, but instead merely states the purpose or intended use of the invention, then the preamble cannot be read as a limitation on a claim. An example of a limiting preamble is quoted in *NTP v Research In Motion, Ltd*[260] and reads: *"A system for transmitting originated information from one of a plurality of originating processors in an electronic mail system to at least one of a plurality of destination processors in the electronic mail system comprising:..."*, the originating and destination processors being essential parts of the claimed system.

255. Fed. Cir., 04-1180, 6 May 2005, Michel, Lourie and Prost

256. The opinions of the EPO Appeal Board in *Synergistic herbicides/CIBA GEIGY* and *Polyepeptide expression/GENENTECH* point towards the opposite conclusion, although the EPO does not itself have jurisdiction covering infringement.

257. T 0068/85, OJEPO 1987, 228; [1987] EPOR 302

258. T 0292/85, OJEPO 1989, 275; [1989] EPOR 1

259. *C.R. Bard, Inc. v M3 Sys., Inc.*, 157 F.3d 1340, 1350 (Fed. Cir. 1998); *Pitney Bowes, Inc. v Hewlett-Packard Co.*, 182 F.3d 1298, 1305 (Fed. Cir. 1999); *Catalina Mktg. Int'l, Inc. v Coolsavings.com, Inc.*, 289 F.3d 801, 808 (Fed. Cir. 2002); *Eaton Corp. v Rockwell Int'l Corp.*, 323 F.3d 1332, 1339 (Fed. Cir. 2003).

260. Fed. Cir., 03-1615, 12 December 2004, concerning RIM's BlackBerry system, see also the recent decision in *Bicon, Inc et al v The Straaumann Company et al.,*20 March 2006, Fed. Cir. where the preamble was also held to be limiting.

Reading features from the written description into the claims

It is wrong to read into the claims an extraneous limitation from the written description – to do so was identified as a cardinal sin in the *en banc* decision in *Phillips*. A party wishing to use statements in the written description to confine or otherwise affect a patent's scope must, at the very least, point to a term or terms in the claim referring to those statements. Without any claim term that is capable of clarification by the written description, there is no legitimate way to narrow the property right. In other words, there must be a textual reference in the actual language of the claim with which to associate a proffered claim construction.[261]

For example in *Anheuser-Busch Companies, Inc. v Crown Cork & Seal Technologies Corporation*[262] the patent in issue was directed to a can end having a chuck wall that is inclined to an axis perpendicular to the central panel of the can end. Figure 4 of the patent, shown below, illustrates a sectioned side view of an embodiment of the claimed can end with a chuck wall (24), a chuck wall angle (C°), and a central panel (26):

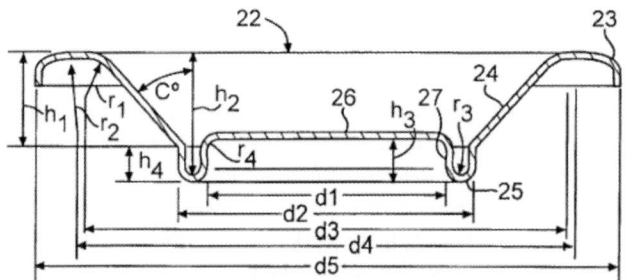

Anheuser-Busch v Crown Cork
(Fig. 4 of the patent in issue)

The claim of the patent in issue required the chuck wall to be inclined to an axis perpendicular to the exterior of the central panel at an angle between 40° to 60°. The defendants argued that the reference to inclination at an angle implied that the chuck wall must be flat since only a flat wall would be described as inclined at an angle, and also that the only disclosed embodiment illustrated a flat chuck wall, and that the only disclosed process resulted in cans with flat chuck walls. These arguments were accepted by the US District Court which handed down summary judgment that the defendant's arcuate chuck wall was non-infringing. On appeal, the Federal Circuit vacated this judgment on the ground that neither the specification nor the prosecution history required the wall to be flat: the word *incline* did not require flatness and, for example, steps of a stair are commonly said to incline at an angle without being flat.

---

261. *Renishaw PLC v Marposs Societa' per Azioni*, 158 F.3d 1243, 1248 (Fed. Cir. 1998); *Johnson Worldwide Assocs., Inc. v Zebco Corp.*, 175 F.3d 985, 990 (Fed. Cir. 1999); *McCarty v Lehigh Valley R.R. Co*, 160 U.S. 110, 116 (1895)

262. Fed. Cir., 04-1185, -1188, December 23, 2004; US-A-6065634

In a further example the US Patent Office refused, when examining the term "hair brush", to import from the specification a limitation that would apply the term only to hairbrushes for the scalp, and held that it was not limited to the brushing of any particular kind of hair. This interpretation was affirmed on appeal.[263]

However, the claims are read in the context of the specification as a whole, and as shown in the recent decision in *Ron Nystrom v Trex Company, Inc*[264] this may lead to a term having a narrower meaning in context than it might be given acontextually in dictionaries and other extrinsic works. The patent in issue was concerned with boards for constructing an exterior floor, and explained that:

> Construction materials and methods for exterior decks and porches changed dramatically with the advent of chemically treated lumber, which enabled exterior structures to be fully exposed to the weather. The chemically treated lumber used in these structures is generally produced by subjecting untreated lumber to a process whereby the chemicals are caused to penetrate into the lumber by a vacuum or pressure technique. This makes them weather-resistant, and provides much greater flexibility in architectural style than previously used materials for exterior construction.
>
> However, very little change has been made in the basic design of the wood building materials used in such exterior constructions. For instance, flooring or decking used in exterior decks comes in essentially only two configurations, 2×4 and/or 2×6 or 2×8 lumber, and so-called 5/4 decking boards. All of these flooring materials are essentially rectangular in cross-sectional configuration. Additionally, the 5/4 decking boards have slightly rounded top edges.
>
> In all conventional flooring materials known to applicant, the top and bottom horizontal surfaces of these flooring materials are flat and planar. As a result, water tends to stand on the surface of the decking material, causing it to deteriorate more quickly than it otherwise would.

The summary of the invention included object clauses reading as follows:

> Accordingly, it is an object of this invention to provide a board for use in constructing flooring, wherein the board is shaped to shed water from its upper surface and which, at the same time, is comfortable to walk and stand on.
>
> Another object is to provide a decking board for use in exterior deck constructions, wherein the board has a convex upper surface to shed water, but which at the same time is comfortable to stand and walk on, and which includes a concave configuration in its bottom surface to facilitate stacking of the boards one on top of the other during storage and handling.
>
> A further object of the invention is to provide a decking board which is shaped to shed water from its upper surface, and which also yields a superior

---

263. *In re Bigio*, 381 F.3d 1320, 1324 (Fed. Cir. 2004, Newman J., Rader J. and Schall J.).

264. 03-1092, 14 September 2005, Fed. Cir., Mayer J, Gajarsa J. and Linn J.; US-A-5474831, this decision was handed down after the *en banc* decision in *Phillips v AWH Corp* and may be a guide to the approach being adopted by the Court since that decision.

product when cut from a log, reducing the amount of scrap in the outermost boards cut from a log.

These and other objects and advantages of the invention are achieved by shaping at least the top surface of a board through cutting or milling and the like, so that the board has a very slightly rounded convex upper surface sloping off to each side of the board for shedding water. In a preferred embodiment, the board has a concave bottom surface shaped complementally to the top surface to facilitate stacking of the boards on top of one another. The shaped top surface also results in a board configuration which enables more usable boards to be obtained from a log, and the shaped bottom surface lends a slight cushioning effect to the board...

The main claim was directed to *a board for use in construction of a flooring surface for exterior use* and the accused boards were made not from wood but from a composite of wood fibres and recycled plastic. The Federal Circuit construed *board* to mean *a piece of elongated construction material made from wood and cut from a log* and said that this conclusion was the inevitable result of considering the term in the context of the written description and the prosecution history. The meaning of an expression which was revealed by the intrinsic record (which in this instance was also the ordinary meaning) could not be broadened by reference to dictionaries, treatises or other extrinsic sources. Accordingly, the District Court's grant of summary judgment of non-infringement should be affirmed.

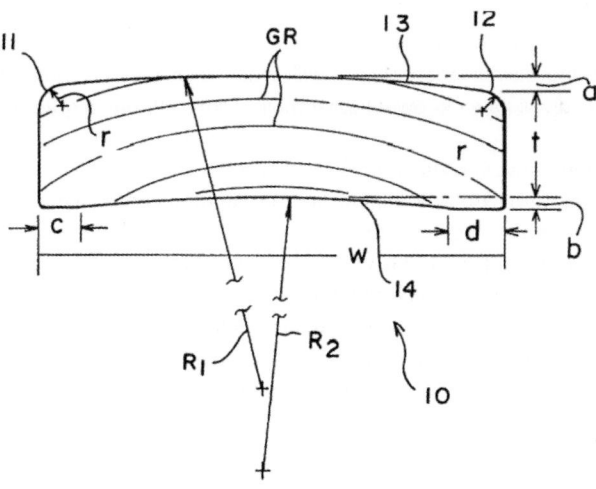

Ron Nystrom v Trex

Infringement on the doctrine of equivalents (US)

Under US law, infringement under the doctrine of equivalents occurs when a claimed limitation and the accused product perform substantially the same function in substantially the same way to obtain substantially the same result.[265] It should be noted that following the decision of the House of Lords in *Kirin-Amgen* discussed above, these provisions have *no* counterpart in the law of the UK or (if the logic of that decision is accepted elsewhere) in other EU contracting states, the issues addressed being covered by the willingness of UK courts to give claim language an extended or figurative meaning on the basis of purposive construction.

The doctrine of equivalents continues to be of practical importance in the US. It is routinely considered by the courts after issues of literal infringement have been disposed of. In an attempt to show whether an affirmative finding of infringement through equivalents is commonplace or rare, reference is made to a paper by Benjamin Hershkowitz[266] of Kenyon & Kenyon. From the figures he quotes, the chances of success in proving literal infringement are about 30%. The doctrine of equivalents provides a second bite at the apple, and the odds of proving infringement under the doctrine of equivalents are about 15%. George Wheeler[267] reviewed the precedental cases of the Federal Circuit for 1999-2002 and concluded that the chance of proving infringement on the doctrine of equivalents was relatively small, with no successful case in 2000. He explains that the doctrine of equivalents continues to be an exceptional remedy to right a manifest wrong at the expense of the notice function of claims, and draws attention to the following passage from the *Festo* opinion;

> Application of the doctrine of equivalents is the exception, however, not the rule, for if the public comes to believe (or fear) that the language of patent claims can never be relied on, and that the doctrine of equivalents is simply the second prong of every infringement charge, regularly available to extend protection beyond the scope of the claims, then claims will cease to serve their intended purpose. Competitors will never know whether their actions infringe a granted patent.

On either view, however, the significance of the doctrine and the success rate in the US has *no* counterpart in UK patent law: the author's information and belief is that there were only two-three reported cases in the UK where infringement on the basis of equivalents or "pith and marrow" was established in the whole of the twentieth century. The significant success rate in what are inherently the more difficult cases explains why the ability to assert infringement on the basis of equivalents is so highly regarded in the US and why we are advised to exercise so much care during the prosecution stage in order to preserve that ability.

---

265. *Warner-Jenkinson Co. v Hilton-Davis Chem. Co.*, 520 U.S. 17, 40 (1997), affirming the earlier US Supreme Court decision in the 1950s in *Graver Tank.*.

266. WHAT ARE MY CHANCES? From Idea through Litigation,
 http://www.kenyon.com/files/tbl_s47Details%5CFileUpload265%5C54%5CChances.pdf

267. *Creative Claim Drafting: claim drafting strategies, specification preparation, and prosecution tactics,* 3 J. Marshall Rev. Intell. Prop. l. 34

The continued existence of the doctrine of equivalents was challenged in both *Warner Jenkinson* and in *Festo* in the face of indications that the judges of the Federal Circuit would prefer to phase it out. In both cases it was held not to have been rendered obsolete by the entry into force of 35 USC 112 in 1952. In *Festo*, the Court explained that:

> The language in the patent claims may not capture every nuance of the invention or describe with complete precision the range of its novelty. If patents were always interpreted by their literal terms, their value would be greatly diminished. Unimportant and insubstantial substitutes for certain elements could defeat the patent, and its value to inventors could be destroyed by simple acts of copying. For this reason, the clearest rule of patent interpretation, literalism, may conserve judicial resources but is not necessarily the most efficient rule. The scope of a patent is not limited to its literal terms but instead embraces all equivalents to the claims described. See *Winans v Denmead*, 15 How. 330, 347 (1854).
>
> It is true that the doctrine of equivalents renders the scope of patents less certain. It may be difficult to determine what is, or is not, an equivalent to a particular element of an invention. If competitors cannot be certain about a patent's extent, they may be deterred from engaging in legitimate manufactures outside its limits, or they may invest by mistake in competing products that the patent secures. In addition the uncertainty may lead to wasteful litigation between competitors, suits that a rule of literalism might avoid. These concerns with the doctrine of equivalents, however, are not new. Each time the Court has considered the doctrine, it has acknowledged this uncertainty as the price of ensuring the appropriate incentives for innovation, and it has affirmed the doctrine over dissents that urged a more certain rule.

The Court explained both in *Warner-Jenkinson* and in *Festo* that the doctrine of equivalents was settled law, and that:

> ... the lengthy history of the doctrine of equivalents strongly supports adherence to our refusal in *Graver Tank* to find that the Patent Act conflicts with that doctrine. Congress can legislate the doctrine of equivalents out of existence any time it chooses. The various policy arguments now made by both sides are thus best addressed to Congress, not this Court.

However, in *Warner-Jenkinson*, the court responded to concerns that the doctrine of equivalents had taken on a life of its own, unbounded by the patent claims, which conflicted with the definitional and public notice function of claims. It concluded that the doctrine was applicable to the individual elements in a claim, and not to the claim as a whole, and that a claimed element should not be eliminated in its entirety ("vitiated").[268] The essential inquiry was whether the accused product or process contained elements identical or equivalent to each claimed element of the invention:

> An analysis of the role played by each element in the context of the specific patent claim will thus inform the inquiry as to whether a substitute element

---

268. See the discussion of the UK decisions in *Van der Lely v Bamfords* and *Kirin-Amgen*, *supra*.

matches the function, way, and result of the claimed element, or whether the substitute element plays a role substantially different from the claimed element.

The doctrine of equivalents is applicable equally to claims that were allowed unamended and to claims that were rewritten during prosecution. As the court explained in *Festo*:

> By amending the application, the inventor is deemed to concede that the patent does not extend as far as the original claim. It does not follow, however, that the amended claim becomes so perfect in its description that no one could devise an equivalent. After amendment, as before, language remains an imperfect fit for invention. The narrowing amendment may demonstrate what the claim is not; but it may still fail to capture precisely what the claim is … The amendment does not show that the inventor suddenly had more foresight in the drafting of claims than an inventor whose application was granted without amendments having been submitted. It shows only that he was familiar with the broader text and with the difference between the two. As a result, there is no more reason for holding the patentee to the literal terms of an amended claim than there is for abolishing the doctrine of equivalents altogether and holding every patentee to the literal terms of the patent.

How, then, could the law establish the most appropriate balance between the competing interests of protection for the patentee and certainty for the public? In *Festo*, the Court was provided with a range of options advanced by the parties and by various *amici*. The question is presented in terms of claim amendment, but there is no reason why the underlying logic should not apply to any claim:

(1) There should be an *absolute bar* on coverage of equivalents where a restriction had been introduced into a claim during prosecution because such restriction was a disclaimer. This "bright-line" approach which had been adopted by the Federal Circuit in *Festo* was supported by a number of major US companies including IBM, Eastman Kodak, Ford, Intel, Cypress Semiconductor Corporation and United Technologies Corporation.

(2) There should be a *flexible bar* that denied coverage of otherwise patentable subject-matter only where it had been clearly and unmistakably surrendered by the patentee. This approach was supported, amongst others, by the American Intellectual Property Law Association (AIPLA).

(3) There should be a *foreseeable bar* which permitted equivalents to be covered unless the limiting effect of amended language with respect to an accused device would have been foreseeable at the time of the amendment to a reasonable person skilled in the art. The foreseeable bar was said to avoid each 'parade of horribles' put forward by respective opponents of the flexible bar and the absolute bar, while simultaneously giving effect to the policy considerations advanced by their respective advocates. Thus a patentee could argue for an extended meaning by showing that the alleged infringement was a later development or that a person of ordinary skill in the art could not reasonably have drafted a patent claim that

literally encompassed the alleged equivalent. That approach was advocated by IEEE and by the US Government.

The Supreme Court adopted a foreseeable standard and concluded that the claims could cover equivalents that were unforeseeable or that for some other reason the patentee could not reasonably be expected to have described. Since the patentee has, as explained above, the same level of foresight at the time of drafting the application as at the time of submitting amendments, this standard implicitly applies equally to un-amended claim language and to claim language that has been amended during prosecution.

Subject-matter that is contained in the written description but not claimed is "dedicated to the public" and cannot be recaptured on the doctrine of equivalents. The leading authority on this point is now the *en banc* decision of the Federal Circuit in *Johnson & Johnson Associates Inc. v R. E. Service Co.*[269] The patent in issue concerned a PCB in which during manufacture a copper foil was attached to a protective substrate sheet to facilitate handling. The written description stated:

> While aluminium is currently the preferred material for the substrate, other metals such as stainless steel or nickel alloys may be used. In some instances … polypropylene may be used.

However the claims in issue all specified that the substrate was of aluminium. The US District Court found that there was infringement by use of a steel sheet on the basis of the doctrine of equivalents, and on appeal there was no dispute about factual equivalency. However, the defendants argued that by limiting their claim to an aluminium substrate, the patentees had dedicated to the public the use of other substrates, and this argument was accepted by the Federal Circuit which emphasised the notice function of patent claims both to the USPTO during prosecution and to the public at large, including potential competitors after the patent had been issued. In a concurring opinion, Rader J and Mayer CJ offered the alternative reasoning that the doctrine of equivalents cannot be invoked to capture subject-matter that the patent draftsman could reasonably have foreseen during the application process, and said:

> Perhaps more than each of these other restraints on non-textual infringement, a foreseeability bar would concurrently serve both the predominant notice function of the claims and the protective function of the doctrine of equivalents. Where one of ordinary skill in the relevant art would foresee coverage of an invention, a patent drafter has an obligation to claim those foreseeable limits. This rule enhances the notice function of claims by making them the sole definition of invention scope in all foreseeable circumstances. When the skilled artisan cannot have foreseen a variation that copyists employ to evade the literal text of the claims, the rule permits the patentee at attempt to prove that an "insubstantial variation" warrants a finding of non-textual infringement. In either event, the claims themselves and the prior art erect a foreseeability bar that circumscribes the protective function of non-textual infringement. Thus a foreseeability bar sets an objective standard for assessing when to apply the doctrine of equivalents.

---

269. 285 F 3d 1045 (Fed. Cir. 2002) (**required reading**); see US-A-5153050.

A foreseeability bar places a premium on claim drafting and enhances the notice function of claims. To restate, if one of ordinary skill in the relevant art would reasonably anticipate ways to evade the literal claim language, the patent applicant has an obligation to cast his claims to provide notice of that coverage. In other words, the patentee has an obligation to draft claims that capture all reasonably foreseeable ways to practice the invention. The doctrine of equivalents would not rescue a claim drafter who does not provide such notice.

Definitions and the notice function of claims

Because of the complexity and expense that claim construction can generate in the course of litigation, US colleagues now strongly recommend the inclusion in the description of definitions of the terms used in the claims, since it is:

> ... the failure of applicants to define such terms that has been at the root cause of the need for dictionaries and expert testimony... Where the patentee as lexicographer has a clear opening of his specification with a section on definitions with the defined technology bracketed by quotation marks, here, there is no special burden placed on the interpreter of the technology: to the contrary, it should be favoured to have terms defined in the specification which can only make the instrument a more precisely understood instrument.[270]

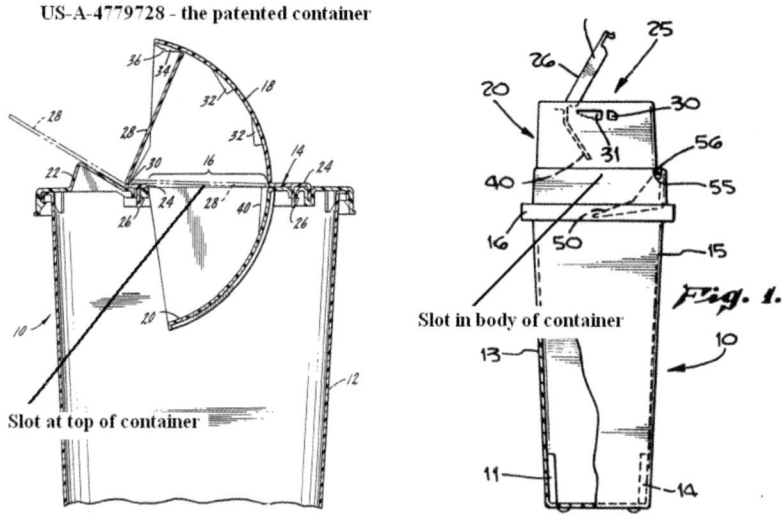

US-A-4779728 – the patented container

Slot at top of container

Slot in body of container

Fig. 1.

---

270. Harold C. Wegner, *Claim Construction: the En Banc Phillips Case*, downloadable from the www.foleylaw.com. Harold Wegner is a former Professor of Law at George Washington University Law School.

The above recommendation is supported by the leading case of *Sage Products, Inc v Devon Industries, Inc*[271] which was cited with approval in the *Johnson & Johnson* case mentioned above. The proceedings covered three patents concerning a disposal container for hazardous medical waste or "sharps", including hypodermic needles. One of the three patents was US-A-4779728, whose only independent claim read in part:

> A disposal container comprising: (a) a hollow upstanding container body (10, 12), (b) *an elongated slot (16) at the top of the container body* for permitting access to the interior of the container body ...

The accused device is shown in the Figure (page 126) from the defendant's US-A-5080251. It was a medical instruments disposal container for surgical sharps, syringes, and the like. It comprised a hollow bin 10 and a hollow top member or housing 20. A tortuous path was defined within top housing 20 to normally block entry to the interior of hollow base member or bin 10, so that a doctor or hospital personnel could not place their fingers into the interior of the container. The tortuous path was defined by a first barrier wall 40 and a second barrier wall 50 within the top housing 20 such that medical instruments, discards or waste dropped into the top housing through the entry port 25 would fall through a direction-changing, tortuous passage provided by the surfaces of walls 40 and 50 to the interior of bin 10 while, at the same time, inadvertent manual entry of the user's hands into the interior of bin 10 is prevented.

The Federal Circuit held that there was no literal infringement because the relevant slot in the accused device was defined between the elements 40 and 50 and was located within the container body and not at the top of that body as required by the claim. The Federal Circuit then considered infringement on the doctrine of equivalents and was not prepared to vitiate the limitation "*at the top of the container body.*"[272] The Federal Circuit went on to make some observations regarding the requirements for claim drafting that are universally applicable, difficult to answer effectively and foreclose the possibility of an effective "quick and cheap" patent application:

> The doctrine of equivalents prevents an accused infringer from avoiding infringement by changing only minor or insubstantial details of a claimed invention while retaining their essential functionality ... Applied more broadly, the doctrine would conflict with the primacy of the claims in defining the scope of a patentee's exclusive rights ... Thus, for a patentee who has claimed an invention narrowly, there may not be infringement under the doctrine of equivalents in many cases, even though the patentee might have been able to claim more broadly. If it were otherwise, then claims would be reduced to functional abstracts, devoid of meaningful structural limitations on which the public could rely...
> ...The claim at issue defines a relatively simple structural device. A skilled

271. 126 F.3d 1420, 44 USPQ2d 1103 (Fed. Cir., 1997, Rader J).

272. See *Warner-Jenkinson*, 117 S. Ct. at 1049 ("It is important to ensure that the application of the doctrine, even as to an individual element, is not allowed such broad play as to effectively eliminate that element in its entirety."); *Pennwalt*, 833 F.2d at 936, 4 USPQ2d at 1741 ("[If] even a single function required by a claim or an equivalent function is not performed [by the accused device], the [district] court's finding of no infringement must be upheld."); *Dolly, Inc. v Spalding & Evenflo Cos.*, 16 F.3d 394, 400, 29 USPQ2d 1767, 1771 (Fed. Cir. 1994) ("The concept of equivalency cannot embrace a structure that is specifically excluded from the scope of the claims.").

patent drafter would foresee the limiting potential of the "over said slot" limitation. No subtlety of language or complexity of the technology, nor any subsequent change in the state of the art, such as later-developed technology, obfuscated the significance of this limitation at the time of its incorporation into the claim ... If Sage desired broad patent protection for any container that performed a function similar to its claimed container, it could have sought claims with fewer structural encumbrances. Had Sage done so, then the Patent and Trademark Office (PTO) could have fulfilled its statutory role in helping to ensure that exclusive rights issue only to those who have, in fact, contributed something new, useful, and unobvious. Instead, Sage left the PTO with manifestly limited claims that it now seeks to expand through the doctrine of equivalents. However, as between the patentee who had a clear opportunity to negotiate broader claims but did not do so, and the public at large, it is the patentee who must bear the cost of its failure to seek protection for this foreseeable alteration of its claimed structure...

This court recognises that such reasoning places a premium on forethought in patent drafting. Indeed this premium may lead to higher costs of patent prosecution. However, the alternative rule – allowing broad play for the doctrine of equivalents to encompass foreseeable variations, not just of a claim element, but of a patent claim – also leads to higher costs. Society at large would bear these latter costs in the form of virtual foreclosure of competitive activity within the penumbra of each issued patent claim. Because the doctrine of equivalents blurs the line of demarcation between infringing and non-infringing activity, it creates a zone of uncertainty, into which competitors tread only at their peril ... Given a choice of imposing the higher costs of careful prosecution on patentees, or imposing the costs of foreclosed business activity on the public at large, this court believes the costs are properly imposed on the group best positioned to determine whether or not a particular invention warrants investment at a higher level, that is, the patentees ...

Prosecution history estoppel

The doctrine of prosecution history estoppel requires the claims of a granted patent to be interpreted in the light of events during prosecution so that subject-matter that has been surrendered cannot be recaptured. Unlike European practice, in the US the written description is not normally amended to correspond to the claims as granted and to remove inconsistencies, so that where inconsistencies are present it is necessary to consult the file wrapper in order to determine their significance. In *Festo* the court decided that any narrowing amendment made to satisfy a requirement of the Patent Act could give rise to an estoppel. However, the purpose of the estoppel doctrine was to hold the applicant to the representations made during prosecution and the inferences that might reasonably be drawn from any amendment that had been made. Reading the *Warner-Jenkinson* and *Festo* decisions together shows that there is a rebuttable presumption that estoppel applies, subject to the following rules:

(i) The onus is also on the patentee to prove that the amendment could not reasonably be viewed as surrendering a particular equivalent, for example because:
   - the equivalent was unforeseeable at the time of the application or amendment, or
   - the reason for the amendment was irrelevant to the equivalent in question; or

- there was some other reason why the patentee could not reasonably have been expected to have covered the equivalent in question.[273]

(ii) If the patentee is unable to explain the reasons for an amendment that narrows an element, then estoppel bars the application of the doctrine of equivalents and the patentee is presumed to have surrendered all subject-matter between the broader and the narrower language.

As previously explained, the doctrine of equivalents is subject to the limitation that it cannot apply if the result would be to vitiate an entire claim limitation[274] or a specific exclusion.[275] For example, in *Asyst Technologies, Inc v Emtrack, Inc*,[276] the claimed invention was a wafer processing system having first and second two-way communication means, the first two-way communication means involving first microcomputer means mounted on a transportable container and a second two-way communication means involving second microcomputer means mounted on a work station. The defendant's system had a microprocessor electrically connected to the work station by a serial cable but not otherwise attached to it. The defendants averred that this cable connection was not covered by the word *mounted* which meant *fastened into position* or *fixed securely on a support,* this averment being supported by the prosecution history. The District Court concluded that *mounted* was binary in nature and that to hold that *mounted* covered *unmounted* would effectively read the *mounted* limitation out of the patent. This conclusion was upheld by the Federal Circuit which affirmed the summary judgment of non-infringement.[277]

One of the frequently cited cases on prosecution history estoppel is *Bayer AG v Elan Pharm. Research Corp*[278] in which the subject-matter claimed was:

A solid pharmaceutical composition comprising as the active ingredient an effective amount of nifedipine crystals with a specific surface area of 1.0 to 4 m²/g, in admixture with a solid diluent, to result in a sustained release of nifedipine.

The patent in issue had a lengthy prosecution history, from August 1981 to November 1993, in which the criticality of the claimed range of specific surface area was emphasised. The range originally claimed was from 0.5 to 6 m²/g, but the examiner did not accept that this gave unexpected results. The range was, therefore, narrowed, and Bayer explained that there was an unexpected plateau-like effect of the newly claimed range, with high bioavailability dropping off outside the claimed range. Bayer asserted that it claimed a special form of nifedipine, namely, having a specific surface area of 1.0 to 4 m²/g, and it stated that 1.0 to 4 m²/g was a superior, inventive range. Thereafter,

---

273. See also the decision of the Fed, Cir., *en banc*, in *Festo III*, 344 F.3d at 1368.

274. *Warner-Jenkinson Co. v Hilton Davis Chem. Co.*, 520 U.S. 17, 29 (1997)

275. *SciMed Life Sys. v Advanced Cardiovascular Sys.*, 242 F.3d 1337, 1346 (Fed. Cir. 2001*); Moore U.S.A., Inc. v Standard Register Co.*, 229 F.3d 1091, 1106 (Fed. Cir. 2000); *Athletic Alternatives, Inc. v Prince Mfg., Inc.*, 73 F.3d 1573, 1582 (Fed. Cir. 1996)

276. Fed. Cir, 04-1808,-1048,-1064, 22 March 2005; US-A-4974166 and US-A-5097421

277. This decision appears directly comparable to that of the UK House of Lords in *Van der Lely* discussed above.

278. 212 F.3d 1241, 1253, 54 U.S.P.Q.2d 1711 (Fed Cir., 2000)

Bayer cited an article that supported the proposition that "the claimed upper limit of 4 m^2/g is a reasonable upper limit for obtaining high bioavailability". In a brief to the Board of Patent Appeals and Interferences Bayer argued that nifedipine crystals with a SSA range of 1.0 to 4 m^2/g provided the *"peculiar"* effect of maintaining a high blood level of nifedipine for a long period of time. This was also supported by declarations supporting the advantages associated with the claimed range. The Federal Circuit held that this was a clear and unmistakable surrender of subject-matter outside the claimed range, which was not now available for re-expansion using the doctrine of equivalents.

A further example is provided by *Pharmacia & Upjohn Co.*[279] That case concerned a pharmaceutical formulation of which the use of spray-dried lactose was a feature. In a declaration filed with a response to the first office action, one of the inventors stated:

> The key feature of the present invention is the particular type of lactose employed in the composition. The claims in the specification clearly indicate the need for spray-dried lactose. If ordinary or non spray-dried lactose is employed in place of the spray-dried lactose, then the advantages of the present invention are lost.

Unsurprisingly, the court held that the patentees were bound by this statement and that coverage of other forms of anhydrous lactose had been surrendered.

For an example of a contrary decision, where the question concerning equivalence in the accused device had only a tangential relationship to the amendments made during prosecution, see *Insituform Techs., Inc. v Cat Contracting, Inc.*[280] Again the test for the patents draftsman is not what a court *will* do in a particular case, but what it *could* do.

"Patent profanity"

Bryan C. Diner *et al*[281] have commented that:

> Some practitioners call it "patent profanity," others call it "selling the invention," and still others, particularly in Europe, might even call it "describing a solution to a technical problem." Whatever its moniker, the Federal Circuit has consistently seized on a patentee's use of words like "critical," "essential," "important," and the like to steadfastly deny a claim for equivalency.

At the Mid-Winter Institute, 2005 of AIPLA, Tom Irving *et al*[282] questioned in their written presentation whether an applicant should use the term "preferable" and in their oral presentation stigmatised it as "patent profanity", citing *inter alia* the

279. 170 F.3d at 1377-78, 50 U.S.P.Q.2d at 1037-38 (Fed. Cir. 1999)

280. 385 F.3d 1360, 72 U.S.P.Q.2d 1870 (Fed. Cir. Oct. 4, 2004)

281. *Festo: The Tip of the Iceberg*, Bryan C. Diner, C. Gregory Gramenopoulos, and Anthony C. Tridico, Ph.D., LES Benelux Newsletter, December 2002, downloadable from the website of Finnegan, Henderson, Farabow, Garrett & Dunner, LLP

282. *Advanced Wizardry:The Magic Of Claim Drafting, Claim Construction, and Patent Prosecution*

opinion in *Wang Laboratories v America Online, Inc*[283] for the proposition that when the "preferred embodiment" is described as the invention itself, the claims are not entitled to a broader scope than that embodiment. However, it is not clear that any particular meaning of the word "preferable" was a key issue in *Wang*. The main point was whether disclosure of an invention in terms of character-based technology could cover bit-mapped technology which was known to be equivalent but which was more difficult to implement. The court's reasons for limiting the claim to character-based technology appear to be based more on the limited capabilities of the disclosed technology than on an expressed preference for that technology.

Most European practitioners would agree that words which clearly disavow claim scope and introduce specific definitions of the claimed subject-matter should be introduced with caution at the filing stage, and that the word "preferably" should be used only where there are identifiable advantages associated with the preference and not as a mere synonym for an embodiment of the invention. Great caution should be adopted in the use of the phrase "*this invention relates to...*" or "*according to the invention...*". In the case of *Honeywell v ITT Industries, Inc.* (Fed. Cir. 22 June 2006), the claim in issue referred to a "*fuel-injection system component*". However, the description only disclosed a fuel filter and the inventor stated "*this invention relates to a fuel filter for use in fuel line that delivers fuel to a motor vehicle engine*". The Federal Circuit held that the public is entitled to take the patentee at his word and the word was that the invention was a fuel filter. The accused device did not meet this limitation and hence avoided infringement.

However, it is unfair to judges, either in the UK or in the US, to suggest that the avoidance of particular restrictive words or words of preference or advantage is a panacea that will enable the correct claim scope to be obtained. Most decisions referred to above do not show a wooden concentration by the courts on particular words, but instead show careful and detailed analysis of the subject-matter disclosed in the patent specification and subsequently claimed using a paradigm which at least in outline is well established notwithstanding controversy about detail. What really makes the difference between success and failure in obtaining useful claim scope and enforcing the resulting patent is correct technical analysis at the time of filing, and including in the initially filed application at least one definition of the invention with the correct level of generality together with generalised fall-back definitions that can be used as required during prosecution or during litigation. It is the inclusion in the specification as originally filed or as granted of features that prove to be unnecessary accompanied by representations that they are essential (over-selling the invention) or failure to derive from the specific embodiments appropriate generalizations of intermediate scope, and failure to discuss the advantages of particular features (e.g. the surfboard hull in *Windsurfer*) that it is submitted are likely to be underlying reasons why desired claim scope will not be obtained or superficially broad claim wording will be interpreted more narrowly than intended.

---

283. 197 F.3d 1377, 1383, 53 U.S.P.Q.2d 1161,1165 (Fed. Cir. 1999); see also *Applying Recent Case Law to Daily Practice,* Erik R. Puknys, Published in the Proceedings of the 2001 AIPLA Spring Meeting, March 2001, available on the website of Finnegan, Henderson, Farabow, Garrett & Dunner, LLP.

Action points for the European practitioner

The different approaches discussed above have relevance firstly for the European applications which our US colleagues ask us to file and prosecute and secondly for the cases we ask them to file in the US.

It will be apparent from the discussions of patent profanity that some senior colleagues in major US firms distrust the technical problem approach used before the EPO and fear that the European specification or file history may grow to contain statements that could result in an unnecessarily restrictive interpretation of the corresponding US patent. Our best response is firstly to do what is necessary to achieve grant of a European patent with the broadest possible claims consistent with the instructions we receive, and secondly to say and do no more than is necessary to achieve the desired result. Harm should not flow from correct European prosecution practice, where possible based on a single difference from the closest prior art, and a single advantage flowing from that difference. It is more likely to flow from failure to identify the closest prior art, unnecessary inclusion of multiple differences or unnecessary references to the simultaneous achievement of multiple advantages that over-sell the invention.

A Europe-based prosecution attorney could also respond that there should be a balanced approach: a litigator whose primary concern is width of claim might prefer what is in effect a white image on a white sheet of paper, offering the greatest scope for development, but unfortunately conveying no information. Patent prosecution, like politics, is the art of the possible. The desirability of building flexibility into the specification at the time of filing by having a variety of independent claims directed to different potentially novel features or combinations of potentially novel features and the need for care during prosecution when we select the particular feature or features which provide the important distinction over the prior art are well-recognised. However, when we approach the grant stage, the need to prosecute applications based on a specific advantage and the technical problem reconstructed from that advantage is hard-wired into the European system.

Ideas concerning patent profanity have become fashionable in the US and have resulted in a generation of issued US patents of a bland character, with no object or technical problem set forth, few or no advantages disclosed, and no preferences, only references to embodiments of the invention and no reasons for preferences in subsidiary claims that might support useful fall-back positions. European practitioners who have lived with the problems of Article 123(2) EPC for nearly three decades are experienced in preparing specifications which on initial filing do not irreversibly commit an inventor to a particular view of what his invention is, but at the same time support inventive step by discussions of problem and advantage. It is submitted that European practitioners should not blindly follow the current US fashion and should continue to explain the advantage of the invention as a whole and the relative advantages of various embodiments, as has been our practice for many decades. In future years, the battleground may shift from construction issues, for instance to issues of inventive step, and the present generation of patents whose positive merits are not immediately apparent simply by reading the patent specification are likely to give the courts at least as much trouble as their predecessors. One US practitioner told the author during a recent AIPLA conference that he had the first 1200 words of the patent specification within which to convince a judge or the members of a jury of the merits of the invention, which argues against the fashion for bland anecdotal presentation. It should be borne in mind that an important part of the public notice function of patents is to explain what features are considered inventive, and why.

What should we in Europe do in response to the *Festo* line of decisions as regards our cases to be filed in the US? It is suggested that if we follow the steps set out below, which should already be part of our routine practice, we should be able to send applications and subsequent instructions for amendment to our US colleagues whilst avoiding our clients ending up with unduly narrow claims. These steps are:

(1) For our specifications to be filed in the US, for each term in the claims ensure that the written description:

(a) identifies those disclosed components of the detailed description and drawings which are related to that term;

(b) provides a generic definition of the term in the claim to minimise the need for consideration in subsequent enforcement, and the risk of the court adopting a narrower definition at the suggestion of the defendant; and

(c) lists all known equivalents of the components defined by the claim term in order to minimise the risk that the patent does not cover such equivalents. This is a practical necessity for a means-plus-function feature as discussed in the following paper; it is arguably also best practice for *all* claimed features.

(2) Avoid using means-plus-function language, or at least provide independent claims with alternative claim language.

(3) During prosecution check for equivalents lying outside the scope of the claims as proposed to be amended. The US Examiner's well-meaning suggestion that patentable subject-matter could be found e.g. if claim 1 were combined with claims 14 and 23, or that he would allow the claim if limited to the use of anhydrous solvents, though inexpensive to follow, may not be wise. It is not just a question of what it costs to obtain a granted patent but also what it could cost to have a patent that is unenforceable. As *Festo* and *Sage Products* explain, the doctrine of equivalents is not an aid for patentees who cut corners during prosecution and introduce limitations that they later regret.

(4) Ensure that the client or inventor understands any proposed amendments, and has appreciated what subject-matter is being given up and what is not. The need for the attorney to work closely with the client in deciding on claim scope and language is emphasised by the *Festo* decision.

(5) Explain the reasons that have prompted amendment, and the intentions

underlying the amendment, emphasizing where appropriate the limited nature of those reasons and intentions. Hopefully that will avoid third parties or a court giving the claim an unintentionally narrower meaning when the claims are read, or miss-read.

The *Festo* and *Sage Products* opinions should serve as a reminder that the patent specifications that we prepare and the prosecution files that we generate have to be fit to place before a judge, and this applies no less in the UK and in other European countries than it does in the US. Those who have been involved in litigation will appreciate how high a standard that implies, and what severe criticism and/or fatal consequences can follow from failing to meet that standard. *Festo* demonstrates that courts may be prepared to help patentees in unforeseeable difficulty, but that they will have little sympathy for patentees who come with ill-prepared specifications and claims with limitations that it could have been foreseen were unnecessary. Notwithstanding the express inclusion of equivalents in the amended Protocol to Article 69 EPC, the *foreseeable* standard adopted by the Supreme Court is bound to have influence, explicitly or tacitly, in Europe and elsewhere. Those who criticise the costs of patent drafting and prosecution (usually in the name of the small inventor) should reflect on the effort and skill needed to marshal all the relevant facts, explain them in a coherent manner and provide a clear definition of the rights to be protected. Legally effective patents, like other legal documents, cannot come cheap.[284]

---

284. There have been proposals to out-source patent specification drafting e.g. from the US to India. For budgetary reasons, other corporations when using outside counsel have sought to impose fixed and relatively low fees for patent drafting. It is difficult to see how such approaches can be reconciled with the forthrightly expressed judicial requirements for close contact with the inventors during drafting and prosecution and care during the drafting process, or with the knowledge of domestic and international jurisprudence which is essential for successful drafting. At most such approaches should be applied only to those inventions that can be foreseen to be of minor importance and unlikely to be litigated. For an invention whose importance justifies a multi-national filing programme, a well-drafted specification supports the whole programme but gives rise to only a small fraction of the overall cost. Therefore, the benefits of squeezing cost at the drafting stage are small and create disproportionate risks to a successful outcome.

Functional claims

" ... a patentee cannot obtain greater coverage by failing to describe his invention than by describing it as the statute commands."[285]

Coverage

In the mechanical, electrical and computer arts, the broadest ambit for a claimed feature is provided by functional claim language. In the UK and Europe, the use of such language has not given rise to significant difficulty. In contrast in the US, judicial concern about functional claims was followed by legislative action during the 1952 legislation, but the resulting statutory remedy created further difficulties which have no counterpart in the UK or other EPC contracting states. However, because of the significance of the US market, the provisions of US national law merit detailed study. Furthermore, the measures which should be taken to avoid or mitigate the effects of the US statute can profitably become drafting habits of general application and which will result in specifications of improved quality though also of increased length.

When you have studied this paper and the "required reading" references, you should know:

1. Authorities permitting a broad scope of functional and means-plus-function or step-plus-function expressions in Europe.

2. The provisions of 35 USC §112(6) concerning claims in means-plus-function or step-plus-function format.

3. The requirements under US law for legal infringement (equivalent structure, identical function) and equitable infringement on the doctrine of equivalents (equivalent structure, equivalent function, but *only* for subsequently developed technology).

4. How to support such claims effectively in the written description by (a) ensuring that there is clearly identifiable structure for each claimed element, and (b) identifying equivalents for each claimed element.

5. How to avoid the provisions of 35 USC §112(6) by using nouns requiring generic structure (connector, circuit, etc.) and the desirability, for consistency, of using this type of claim format in Europe as well as in the US.

---

285. Black J in *Halliburton Oil Well Cementing Co. v Walker* 329 U.S. 1 (1946) **(required reading)**

Functional claims in the UK and Europe.

In the UK both functional claims and claims limited by result are in principle allowable, the latter form of claim being approved in frequently-cited decision in *No-Fume v Pitchford.*[286] It is, however, salutary to recall that in the *No-Fume case,* although the result-limited claim was held in principle to be allowable, the patented ashtray did not work as claimed since it allowed smoke to escape, and the action was dismissed with the dry judicial retort that the court would not enforce *"this puffing patent".*

In the practice of the EPO functional claims or in appropriate circumstances claims limited by result are also considered allowable when necessary for giving fair protection to the patentee. This principle was established in *Synergistic herbicides/CIBA GEIGY,*[287] whose logic has been applied in many subsequent cases, and which in effect gives positive approval both for functional claiming and for claiming by result. The problem with which the invention was concerned was to reduce the quantity of herbicide used for cereal and soya bean crops while improving the safety margin. The claimed solution was:

> An agent for selective weed control, characterised in that, in addition to carriers and/or other additives, it contains as active ingredients [a first component] *in an amount producing a synergistic herbicidal effect* and [a second component].

Objections under art 84 EPC by the Examining Division were rejected by the Appeal Board, which held that the requirement for synergism was a technical feature, that it was sufficiently precise and that it complied with the clarity requirements of Article 84 EPC. Its analysis was as follows, matters of principle being identified in *italics*:

> 8.4 This form of words is a *"technical feature"* within the meaning of Rule 29(1) and (3) EPC.
>
> 8.4.1 A technical feature is one that can be read by a skilled person as an instruction as to the technical procedure to be followed to achieve a given result. Such an instruction may be *explicit* - for example in chemistry where "ethanol is the solvent" or "starting material substance having the formula X" - or *functional, i.e. defined in terms of the result*, as in expressions such as *"fat-dissolving solvent"* or *"compound with a reactive hydrogen atom"*. Applied to the present case, the feature "weight ratio between 1:1 and 1:4" in Claim 3 is explicit, and the feature "... in [an amount] ... effect" in Claim 1, functional. A functional feature is usually chosen out of the legitimate desire to couch the invention in the most general terms possible in order to secure adequate and reasonable protection. While in chemistry explicit features are often chosen in preference to functional ones, the latter occur far more frequently in other technical fields. Thus a claim relating to a mechanical invention would be unlikely to refer to a *nail* or a *rivet*, but to *fastening means* - a functional feature. Since patent law is indivisible there is no reason why functional features should not occupy their rightful place beside explicit features in chemistry too.

---

286. (1935) 52 RPC 231.(**required reading**)
287. T 0068/85 – 3.3.1

8.4.2 However, the applicant cannot simply define a feature in a claim as he wishes; he must choose the form that is objectively more precise .... This requirement is met in the present case as the Board does not see how the limits within which the two herbicide couples combine to give a synergistic effect could be defined more precisely than has been done without limiting the scope of the invention. Accepting the Examining Division's suggestion and including in Claim 1 as it then stood the features expressed numerically in Claim 3 so as to render the former more precise would mean limiting the scope of the invention unjustifiably to a particular range of weight ratios and thus *unacceptably restricting protection to only part of the invention as disclosed.*

8.4.3 On the other hand, the effort to define a feature in functional terms must stop short where it jeopardises the clarity of a claim as required by Article 84 EPC. That clarity demands not only that a skilled person be able to understand the teaching of the claim but also that he be able to implement it. In other words, the feature must provide instructions which are sufficiently clear for the expert to reduce them to practice without undue burden, if necessary with reasonable experiments.

8.4.4 The *clarity* requirement is met in the present case: In interpreting the instruction in Claim 1 to combine compound (II) with compound (Ia) or (Ib) "in an amount producing a synergistic herbicidal effect", a skilled person will even on the basis of his general knowledge of the art, rule out combinations involving vastly different proportions. He will also be guided by the preferred weight ratios mentioned in Claims 2 and 3 in seeking other suitable ratios, which may vary considerably according to the crop to be protected or weed to be destroyed. Moreover, the skilled person is given *precise directions* - should he need them - as to how he can by means of various *tests* (Colby method) recognise and even calculate a synergistic effect when [the active ingredients] have been used in "an amount producing a synergistic herbicidal effect" .... While the tests take a long time, since the plants first have to germinate and there is then a waiting period of 15 to 20 days for the results, all things considered, *the effort called for on the part of a skilled person* must be regarded as reasonable, since such tests are quite normal in the art and those used in the present case no more elaborate than usual. (emphasis added)

A further leading authority on this issue is *Polyepeptide expression/GENENTECH*[288] in which the Appeal Board explained the need for functional claims to be allowed in order to give fair coverage to embodiments of the invention created with future technology:

3.1.2 ... The suggested features in the claims are essentially functional terms in this particular context, in spite of structural connotations, and may cover an unlimited number of possibilities. It follows that *the features may generically embrace the use of unknown or not yet envisaged possibilities, including specific variants which might be provided or invented in the future.* This Board concurs with the decision of another Board (T 68/85 -3.3.1., "Synergistic herbicides", OJ EPO 1987, 228) in which the possibility of using functional

---

288. T 0292/85 – 3.3.2

terminology in claims was approved if "such features cannot otherwise be defined more precisely without restricting the scope of the invention" and their reduction to practice was not an undue burden. The Board sees no valid reason why this should not be equally true for the field of biotechnology as in other fields of technology. In appropriate cases, such as the present, it is only possible to define the invention … in a way which gives a fair protection having regard to the nature of the invention which has been described by using functional terminology in the claims.

3.1.3 What is also important in the present case is the irrelevancy of the particular choice of a variant within the functional terms "bacteria", "regulon" or "plasmid". It is not just that some result within the range of polypeptides is obtained in each case but *it is the same polypeptide which is expressed, independent of the choice of these means*. A term of this kind must, of course, be clear and enable the skilled person to find suitable specimens without undue difficulty. In the present application enough choice is available, although some vehicles and hosts are preferred for practical reasons.

3.1.4 The objection raised against the terms *"plasmid"* and *"bacteria"* that they are too broad since some of them rely on yet unavailable entities is untenable. The Board is of the opinion that this is quite normal practice in many technical fields where terms as *"carriers"*, *"resilient means"*, or *"amplifying means"* are commonplace and *embrace new components, be they inventive or not*. This is not to mention that very often the generic indication of a kind of an article in the claim is followed by the non-exclusive term "comprising" and the characteristics of modifying features, leaving completely open the actual features of the rest of the article, apart from the necessity that its functioning should be as expected.

3.1.5 The above examples show that the need for a fair protection governs both the considerations of the scope of claims and of the requirements for sufficient disclosure. Unless variants of components are also embraced in the claims, which are, now or later on, equally suitable to achieve the same effect in a manner which could not have been envisaged without the invention, the protection provided by the patent would be ineffectual. Thus it is the view of the Board that an invention is sufficiently disclosed if at least one way is clearly indicated enabling the skilled person to carry out the invention. Consequently, any non-availability of some particular variants of a functionally defined component feature of the invention is immaterial to sufficiency as long as there are suitable variants known to the skilled person through the disclosure or common general knowledge, which provide the same effect for the invention. The disclosure need not include specific instructions as to how all possible component variants within the functional definition should be obtained.

3.1.6 The Examining Division's tentative suggestion that such terms should be restricted to those available in the art has no basis in existing law. Unless broad, yet proper terminology is allowable, subsequent investigations by third parties might be encouraged to concentrate on finding alternatives outside the claims instead of trying to pursue progress through dependent inventions. The lack of recognition of the full significance and the interdependency of technical contributions could adversely affect progress in the area of microbiology and biochemistry.

It is noteworthy that the EPO considers that claim language can automatically cover future technology on the "*always speaking*" approach that UK courts apply to the interpretation of statutes.[289] Significantly, US courts may depart from an *always speaking* approach, so that it cannot be taken for granted that in the US claim language as literally interpreted will cover future technology, as discussed above.

A yet further EPO Appeal Board case demonstrates the approach applied in the mechanical and electrical arts. In *Focus control/SONY CORPORATION*,[290] the problem with which the invention was concerned was how to provide automatic focus control of the lens of a video camera without overshooting.

One of the claims in issue (which our US colleagues would nowadays advise could be narrowly interpreted under 35 USC §112(6))[291] read (see the accompanying drawing):

Focus control apparatus for a video camera in which a component of a video signal is maximised for performing focus control, the apparatus comprising:

means (5A, 5B) for extracting a signal having a predetermined frequency component from a video signal;

means (2) for moving a position of a lens (1) of the camera; and

means (8, 9) for sampling the signal of predetermined frequency component extracted from the video signal at continuous, successive at least first, second, and third lens positions (1m, 1m+1, 1m+2); *characterised by:*

means (10) for determining a first gradient (s0) in response to a change in value of the signal of predetermined frequency component for a change in lens position between said first and second lens positions (1m, 1m+1) from the signal of the predetermined frequency component sampled at the first lens position (1m) and the signal of the predetermined frequency component sampled at the second lens position (1m+1);

means (10) for determining a second gradient (s1) in response to a change in value of the signal of predetermined frequency component for a change in lens position between said second and third lens positions (1m+1, 1m+2) from the signal of the predetermined frequency component sampled at the second lens position (1m+1) and the signal of the predetermined frequency component sampled at the third lens position (1m+2); and

means (11) for controlling the speed of movement of the lens (1) at said successive lens positions *in response to a comparison* of said first and second gradients (s0,s1).

The Examining Division objected that the term "in *response to a comparison*" was vague and indefinite, so that the function of the "*means for controlling the speed of movement...*" was not clearly defined. The way in which the gradients were

289. See the *Quintavalle* case concerning the *Human Fertilization and Embryology Act, 1990* discussed in the paper on claim construction, see page 99.

290. T 0630/93 – 3.5.1 [1993.10.27]

291. As discussed below this means-plus-function language is now inappropriate, at least in the US. However, the present case highlights the utility and practicality of the means-plus-function format that we are now urged to abandon.

compared and the way in which the means responded to the result of comparison remained undefined and a precise definition was indispensable for a clear technical teaching. The applicants argued that it was unnecessary to specify the method of comparison in detail: the disclosed embodiment described comparison in terms of a *ratio*, but the skilled person would appreciate that there was an alternative method of comparison by calculation of the *difference*, so that limiting the claim to calculation by ratio would leave the claim open to easy avoidance. The Appeal Board, after consideration of the cited prior art, accepted this argument on the basis that there was novelty and inventive step in the principle of determining successive gradients, and it was not necessary to define in detail the way in which the comparison was performed in subsequent speed control. The outcome may be contrasted with the decisions of the US courts on indefiniteness discussed below.

European and US colleagues would agree, however, that arguments of the above kind are best avoided. In hindsight, the logical sequence of questions to the inventor which would have avoided the need for an appeal was: "How do you compare the gradients? Oh! By calculating a ratio. Is there any other method of calculation that can be used?"

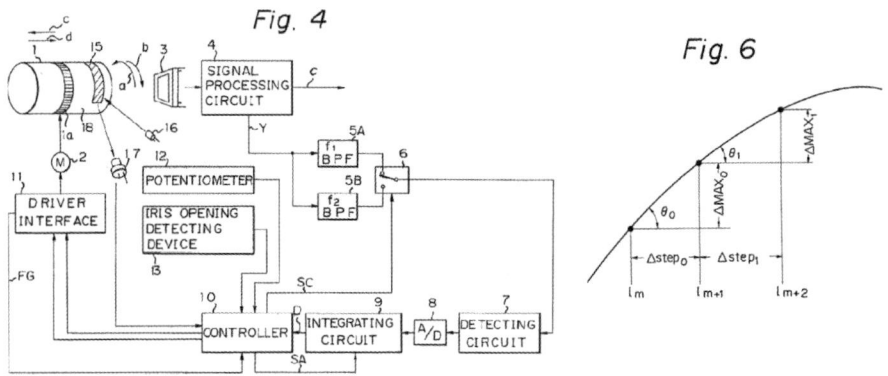

Focus Control/SONY CORPORATION

Functional claiming – the US position

European practitioners are trained to regard means-plus-function or step-plus function claims as the broadest possible claims. It comes as a shock to find that in the US their scope is often comparable to that of so-called "omnibus" or picture claims in the UK.

The problem can be traced back to a decision of the US Supreme Court in *Halliburton Oil Well Cementing v Walker*[292] which concerned depth measurement in oil wells, and where the claimed invention was:

> In an apparatus for determining the location of an obstruction in a well having therein a string of assembling tubing sections inter-connected with each other by coupling collars,

---

292. 329 U.S. 1 (1946) mentioned above, see US-A-2156519

means communicating with said well for creating a pressure impulse in said well,

echo receiving means including a pressure responsive device exposed to said well for receiving pressure impulses from the well and for measuring the lapse of time between the creation of the impulse and the arrival at said receiving means of the echo from said obstruction, and

means associated with said pressure responsive device for tuning said receiving means to the frequency of echoes from the tubing collars of said tubing sections to clearly distinguish the echoes from said couplings from each other.

The patent in issue disclosed as the device for tuning the echo receiving means to make the echoes from the tubing collars more prominent a mechanical acoustic resonator in the form of a tube having a length of one third of that of a tubing joint, and that in effect is what the Supreme Court considered was the contribution to the prior art. The accused *Halliburton* device employed an electrical filter for the same purpose. The Supreme Court held that there was no infringement and that means-plus-function language could not be employed at the exact point of novelty in a combination claim. It went on to comment that nowhere in the patent was there any indication that the patentee contemplated any specific structural alternative for the acoustical resonator or for the resonator's relationship to the other parts of the machine, and to criticise the breadth of the claim in the following terms (citations omitted):

Under these circumstances the broadness, ambiguity, and overhanging threat of the functional claim of Walker become apparent. What he claimed in the court below and what he claims here is that his patent bars anyone from using in an oil well any device heretofore or hereafter invented which combined with the Lehr and Wyatt machine performs the function of clearly and distinctly catching and recording echoes from tubing joints with regularity. Just how many different devices there are of various kinds and characters which would serve to emphasise these echoes, we do not know. The Halliburton device, alleged to infringe, employs an electric filter for this purpose. In this age of technological development there may be many other devices beyond our present information or indeed our imagination which will perform that function and yet fit these claims. And unless frightened from the course of experimentation by broad functional claims like these, inventive genius may evolve many more devices to accomplish the same purpose. Yet if Walker's blanket claims be valid, no device to clarify echo waves, now known or hereafter invented, whether the device be an actual equivalent of Walker's ingredient or not, could be used in a combination such as this, during the life of Walker's patent. Had Walker accurately described the machine he claims to have invented, he would have had no such broad rights to bar the use of all devices now or hereafter known which could accent waves.

The 1952 legislation statutorily overruled the finding that means-plus-function language could not be used at the point of novelty, but responded to the objection that the ambit of such language was unduly wide by placing a statutory restriction on the ambit of such language, whether at the point of novelty or elsewhere in a claim. The relevant provision, 35 USC §112(6), reads as follows:

An element in a claim for a combination may be expressed as a means or step for performing a specified function without the recital of structure, material, or acts in support thereof, and such claim shall be construed to cover the corresponding structure, material, or acts described in the specification and equivalents thereof.

The landmark case of *In re Donaldson Co. Inc*[293] concerned the interpretation of the above provision for pending patent applications. In that case the Board of Patent Appeals and Interferences of the USPTO had interpreted the expression "*means, responsive to pressure increases in said chamber caused by said cleaning means for moving particulate matter in a downward direction*" in broad general terms and said that it was axiomatic that the particular features or limitations of the specification were not to be read into the claims of an application, On appeal, the Federal Circuit rejected an argument by the USPTO that 35 USC §112(6) applied only in the context of post-issuance infringement and validity actions, and further held that there was no conflict between this finding and the doctrine that during prosecution claims were to be given the broadest reasonable interpretation. The broadest interpretation that an Examiner was entitled to give a means-plus-function limitation was that mandated by statute and the USPTO could not disregard the structure disclosed in the specification corresponding to such language when making a patentability determination. The Court's reasoning is explained as follows (citations being omitted):

Our holding similarly does not conflict with the second paragraph of section 112.7. Indeed, we agree with the general principle that §112(6) does not exempt an applicant from the requirements of the first two paragraphs of that section. Although paragraph six statutorily provides that one may use means-plus-function language in a claim, one is still subject to the requirement that a claim "particularly point out and distinctly claim" the invention. Therefore, if one employs means-plus-function language in a claim, one must set forth in the specification an adequate disclosure showing what is meant by that language. If an applicant fails to set forth an adequate disclosure, the applicant has in effect failed to particularly point out and distinctly claim the invention as required by the second paragraph of section 112.

Also contrary to suggestions by the Commissioner, our holding does not conflict with the general claim construction principle that limitations found only in the specification of a patent or patent application should not be imported or read into a claim. The Commissioner confuses impermissibly imputing limitations from the specification into a claim with properly referring to the specification to determine the meaning of a particular word or phrase recited in a claim. What we are dealing with in this case is the construction of a limitation already in the claim in the form of a means-plus-function clause and a statutory mandate on how that clause must be construed.

---

293. 16 F. 3d 1189, 29 USPQ2d 1845 (Fed. Cir. 1994, *en banc*)**(required reading)**

Avoiding the provisions of 35 USC §112(6)

To fall within the ambit of this statute, the alleged means-plus-function claim element must lack recitation of a definite structure which performs the described function and must be a purely functional placeholder in which structure is filled in by the specification.[294] Patent drafters conventionally find themselves in this position by using only the words *means for* followed by a recitation of the function performed. If the claim uses the word *means* without specifying any structure or material for performing the recited connecting function, this element calls for interpretation under 35 USC §112(6).[295] Merely because a named element of a patent claim is followed by the word *means*, however, does not automatically make that element a *means-plus-function* element under 35 USC §112(6). The converse is also true; merely because an element does not include the word "means" does not automatically prevent that element from being construed as a means-plus-function element. The decision is made on an element-by-element basis whether §112(6) applies based upon the description and the prosecution history.

A claimed element that does not use 'means' will trigger the rebuttable presumption that §112(6) does not apply.[296] The party alleging that §112(6) applies in the absence of a 'means' claim term can rebut this presumption if it demonstrates that the claim term fails to recite sufficiently definite structure or else recites a function without reciting sufficient structure for performing that function.[297]

In order to maximise protection without being caught by §112(6), it appears desirable to use a noun that specifies a genus of structures known to those skilled in the art and capable of performing the specified function, which may be followed by functional language further specifying features of the element in question. The following decisions provide examples of the above:

■ *Interspiro, Inc. v Figgie Int'l.*[298] ("*detent means* for [function]" found within §112(6)): compare with *Greenberg v Ethicon Endo-Surgery, Inc.*[299] ("*detent mechanism*" for [function] found to refer to particular structure and hence to be outside §112(6) – small changes of language can have significant practical effects!).

■ *John D. Watts v XL Systems Inc*[300] ("the joints each having a second end formed with tapered external threads dimensioned such that one such joint may be *sealingly connected* directly with another such joint"; term not a means-plus-function limitation because "tapered external threads" has a well-defined structural meaning and because "sealingly connected" it is reasonably well understood in the art).

---

294. *Phillips v AWK Corporation,* 03-1269, – 1286 (12 July 2005, Fed. Cir.)

295. *Al-Site Corp. v VSI Int'l, Inc.,* 174 F.3d 1308, 1318, 50 USPQ2d 1161, 1166 (Fed. Cir. 1999)

296. *CCS Fitness, Inc. v Brunswick Corp.,* 288 F.3d 1359, 1369 (Fed. Cir. 2002); *Personalized Media,* 161 F.3d at 703.

297. *Watts v XL Sys., Inc.,* 232 F.3d 877, 880 (Fed. Cir. 2000); see also *Apex Inc. v Raritan Computer, Inc.,* 325 F.3d 1364, 1371-72 (Fed. Cir. 2003); *CCS Fitness,* 288 F.3d at 1369

298. 815 F. Supp. 1488 (D. Del.1993)

299. 91 F.3d 1580, 1583 (Fed. Cir. 1996)

300. 232 F.3d 877, 882 (Fed. Cir. 2000, Bryson, J., Gajarsa J. and Linn J.)

■ *TurboCare Div. of Demag Delaval Turbomachinery Corp. v Gen. Elec. Co*[301] ("*compressed spring*" not a means-plus-function limitation).

■ *CCS Fitness, Inc. v Brunswick Corp*[302] (*reciprocating member* not a means-plus-function limitation; *member* had a dictionary definition to mean a structural unit such as a beam or tie or combination of these).

■ *Linear Technology Corporation v Impala*[303] (circuit for controlling a switching voltage regulator including a first *circuit* for monitoring a signal from the output terminal to generate a first feedback signal, a second *circuit* for generating a first control signal during a first state of circuit operation, the first control signal being responsive to the first feedback signal to vary the duty cycle of the switching transistors to maintain the output terminal at the regulated voltage; *circuit* implies well understood structure and is not a means-plus-function limitation).

■ *Lighting World, Inc v Birchwood Lighting*[304] (lighting fixture comprising a *connector assembly*; term defines a genus of structures and is not a means-plus-function limitation).

■ *Edward H. Philips v AWH Corporation*[305] (*baffles* is structural even though clearly intended to perform several functions).

■ *Carl Landers v Sideway, LLC*[306]: (*cutter head* not a means-plus-function limitation but a term encompassed by a number of different cutting mechanisms; term not limited to the disclosed ball cutter).

■ Useful guidance is derived from the dissenting judgment of Schall J. in *Alloc v ITC*[307] where he explained that "to lock" is a function but "a lock" is a structure that took its name from a function. Similarly with other devices that take their names from the function that they perform e.g. a filter, a brake, a clamp or a screwdriver.

There is evidence from recent patents of major US corporations that the US profession has responded to the jurisprudence concerning the ambit of 35 USC §112(6), by opting for a generic structural noun-plus function format in preference to a means-plus function format. The following four examples of issued US patents illustrate this trend:

US-A-6957140 (Bauerle *et al*, General Motors Corporation) concerns an electronic throttle control for replacing a mechanical pedal assembly used in a vehicle and is concerned with compensating for build-up of throttle body coke deposits during the

301. 264 F.3d 1111, 1121 (Fed. Cir. 2001)

302. 288 F.3d 1359, 62 U.S.P.Q.2d 1658 (Fed. Cir., 2002)

303. 379 F.3d 1311, 72 USPQ2d 1065 (Fed.Cir. 2004, Newman J., Schall J. and Linn J.)

304. 382 F.3d 1354, 1366 (Fed. Cir. 2004, Bryson J., Plager J. and Linn J.)

305. 03-1269, -1286 Fed. Cir., 12 July 2005

306. Fed. Cir., 04-1510, -1538, 27 July 2005, Lourie J., Rader J. and Gajarsa J.

307. 342 F. 3d 1361 (Fed Cir. 10 September 2003).

life of the vehicle leading to reduced idle quality. The main claim of the granted US patent refers to *a driver input device* and *a control module* that at least arguably are generic for a range of structures known to the art, the remaining features of the claim being functional. The granted claim reads:

> A throttle control system for a vehicle, comprising:
> *a driver input device* that generates a control signal; [and]
> *a control module* that generates a throttle control signal based on said control signal, that determines whether said throttle control signal is within one of a first and a second region, that determines a compensation factor from a first look-up table when said throttle control signal is within said first region, that determines said compensation factor from a second look-up table when said throttle control signal is within said second region and that calculates a compensated throttle control signal based on said compensation factor.

US-A-6959451 (Ramanathan, Intel Corporation) is concerned with broadcast equipment for an interactive broadcasting system that is capable of supporting multiple broadcast signals having different transmission rates and different protocols. The main claim as granted uses nouns generic to classes of structure: *data management module, transmitter module* and *transport medium*, these generic structural expressions supporting very extensive functional definitions. It reads:

> A transmission system, comprising:
> *a data management module* capable of managing data flow;
> *a first transmitter module* coupled to a transport medium and to the data management module, the transmitter module to contain first configuration information specifying at least one predefined transmission characteristic; and
> at least an *additional transmitter module* containing second configuration data,
> the data management module to access the first configuration information to determine the at least one predefined transmission characteristic and to modify data flow management based on the at least one predefined transmission characteristic and
> the data management module to access the second configuration information to determine at least one predefined transmission characteristic associated with said additional transmitter module,
> wherein each transmitter module is associated with a different *transport medium*, and the first configuration information is retrieved by the data management module at startup of the first transmitter module or data management module, and
> wherein the first configuration information comprises at least one of information to indicate if the first transmitter module is able to assign priorities to data, and information to indicate if the first transmitter module is able to perform bandwidth management.

US-A-6957733 (Mazur *et al*, Cummins-Allison Corp) concerns a versatile currency evaluation device, and uses in its main claim generic noun phrases such as *input receptacle, output receptacle, transport mechanism, discriminating unit, detector* and *processor*. These structural expressions all support much functional language concerning the way in which the device is arranged to discriminate recognised bills from various forms of anomalous bill. The main claim as granted reads:

A compact, high-speed United States currency evaluation device for receiving a stack of currency bills and rapidly processing all the bills in the stack, the device comprising:

an *input receptacle* adapted to receive a stack of United States currency bills of a plurality of denominations to be processed;

two or more *output receptacles* adapted to receive the bills after the bills have been processed;

a *transport mechanism* adapted to transport the bills, one at a time, along a transport path from the input receptacle to the output receptacles at a rate of at least 800 bills per minute;

a *discriminating unit* adapted to count and denominate the bills including United States bills of a plurality of denominations at a rate of at least 800 bills per minute, the discriminating unit including a *detector* positioned along the transport path between the input receptacle and the output receptacles; and

a *processor* programmed to flag bills meeting or failing to meet any of certain non-piece count related criteria, a bill meeting or failing to meet any of the criteria being termed a flagged bill, the processor being adapted to cause the transport mechanism to halt in response to a determination that a bill meets or fails to meet at least one of the criteria;

wherein the certain criteria include a criterion of the discriminating unit determining the denomination of a bill, a bill failing to meet the criterion of having its denomination determined by the discriminating unit being termed a no call bill, the processor being programmed to flag no call bills,

wherein the discriminating unit is further adapted to determine whether a bill has a denomination other than a target denomination, a bill having a denomination other than the target denomination being termed a stranger bill and

wherein the certain criteria include the discriminating unit determining whether a bill is a stranger bill and

wherein the processor is programmed to flag stranger bills,

wherein the discriminating unit is further adapted to determine whether a bill is a suspect bill and

wherein the certain criteria include the discriminating unit determining whether a bill is a suspect bill and

wherein the processor is programmed to flag suspect bills,

wherein stranger bills and no call bills are directed to a first set of one or more output receptacles and suspect bills are directed to a second set of at least one or more output receptacles, the output receptacles of the second set being different from the output receptacles of the first set.

US-A-6957354 (Uzelac *et al*, Intel Corporation) discloses a CMOS circuit for low leakage battery operation which connects the real time clock to the power supply when available or to a low leakage source when the power supply is not available, and uses the expressions *clock circuit* and *associated circuit* to denote generic structure. The main claim as granted reads:

An apparatus comprising:

    a *real time clock circuit*; and

    an *associated circuit* that operates in a first mode when a power supply voltage is present and operates in a second mode when battery power is present,

        said second mode providing a biasing condition that reduces a sub-threshold off current for the real time clock circuit during battery operation by adjusting source voltage levels for the real time clock circuit.

The examples given above exemplify the view of our US colleagues that provided that there is *some* generic structural language to remove a claimed element from the ambit of 35 USC §112(6), then much about the claimed element can still be specified in functional language.

Supporting a means-plus-function or step-plus function feature

If means-plus-function or step-plus-function language is used in a claim, the description must adequately disclose what is meant by that language. A structure disclosed in the specification qualifies as *corresponding* structure only if the specification or prosecution history clearly links or associates that structure to the function recited in the claim. This duty to link or associate structure to function is the *quid pro quo* for the convenience of employing §112(6). While the patentee need not disclose details of structures well known in the art, the specification must nonetheless disclose some structure. Self-evidently, the trade-off of §112(6) is not fulfilled when there is a total omission of structure;[308] see the detailed discussion of this case under the heading "black boxes" in the enablement chapter. The sanction is that if the description fails adequately to disclose the corresponding structure of a means-plus-function limitation, then it fails to particularly point out and distinctly claim the subject-matter which the applicant regards as his invention as required by §112 (2)[309] and the claim is unenforceable for indefiniteness. That deficiency cannot be remedied by subsequent expert testimony: that testimony cannot rewrite the specification. Furthermore, the corresponding structure to a function set forth in a means-plus-function limitation must be necessary to perform the claimed function.[310] While corresponding structure need not include everything necessary to enable the claimed invention to work, it must include all structure that actually performs the recited function.

---

308. *Atmel Corp v Information Storage Devices Inc*, 198 F.3d 1374 at 1382; 53 USPQ2d 1225 (Fed. Cir., 1999).

309. *In re Donaldson Co.*, 16 F.3d 1189, 1195 (Fed. Cir. 1994) (en banc); *Medtronic, Inc. v Advanced Cardiovascular*, 248 F.3d 1303, 1311 (Fed. Cir. 2001; *Budde v Harley-Davidson, Inc.*, 250 F.3d 1369, 1379 (Fed. Cir. 2001); *B. Braun Med. v Abbott Labs.*, 124 F.3d 1419, 1424 (Fed. Cir. 1997); *O.I. Corp. v Tekmar Co.*, 115 F.3d 1576, 1583 (Fed. Cir. 1997); *Cardiac Pacemakers, Inc. v St. Jude Med., Inc.*, 296 F.3d 1106, 1119 (Fed. Cir. 2002).

310. *Omega Eng'g, Inc. v Raytek Corp.*, 334 F.3d 1314, 1321 (Fed. Cir. 2003)

Legal and equitable interpretation
of a means-plus-function element

To determine whether a claim limitation is met literally, where expressed as a means or step for performing a stated function, the court must compare the accused structure *with the disclosed structure*, and must find (a) equivalent structure and (b) *identity* of claimed function for that structure.[311] §112(6), rules out the possibility that any and every means which performs the function specified in the claim literally satisfies that limitation.[312]

The proper test is whether the differences between the structure in the accused device and any disclosed in the specification are insubstantial.[313] A literal or "legal" equivalent provided by §112(6) results from an insubstantial change which adds nothing of significance to the structure, material, or acts disclosed in the patent specification.[314] The legal equivalence analysis requires a determination of whether the *way* the assertedly substitute structure performs the claimed function, and the *result* of that performance, is substantially different from the *way* the claimed function is performed by the *corresponding structure described in the specification*, or its *result*.[315] A finding of known interchangeability, while an important factor in determining equivalence, is not decisive.[316] Such evidence does not remove the statutory requirement to compare the accused structure to the corresponding structure.

Legal equivalents under §112(6), and equitable equivalents under the judicially-created *Graver Tank* doctrine both relate to insubstantial changes. There is an important difference, however, between legal equivalents and equitable equivalents, which relates to timing:[317]

(1) Equitable equivalents are necessary because of the unpredictability of the future. Due to technological advances, a variant of an invention may be developed after the patent is granted, and that variant may constitute so small a change from what is claimed in the patent that it should be covered. Such a variant, based on after-developed technology, could not have been disclosed in the patent. Even if such an element is found not to be a legal equivalent because it is not equivalent to the

---

311. *Pennwalt Corp. v Durand- Wayland, Inc.*, 833 F.2d 931, 934, 4 USPQ2d 1737, 1739 (Fed. Cir. 1987) *(in banc)* (emphasis in original); *Laitram*, 939 F.2d at 1536.

312. *Pennwalt Corp.*, 833 F.2d at 934, 4 USPQ2d at 1739

313. *Valmont Indus., Inc. v Reinke Mfg. Co.*, 983 F.2d 1039, 1043, 25 USPQ2d 1451, 1455 (Fed. Cir. 1993); *Chiuminatta Concrete Concepts, Inc. v Cardinal Indus., Inc.*, 145 F.3d 1303, 1309, 46 USPQ2d 1752, 1756 (Fed. Cir. 1998).

314. *Alpex Computer Corp. v Nintendo Co.*, 102 F.3d 1214, 1222, 40 USPQ2d 1667, 1673 (Fed. Cir. 1996)

315. *Odetics, Inc. v Storage Tech. Corp.*, 185 F.3d 1259, 1267, 51 USPQ2d 1225, 1229-30 (Fed. Cir. 1999).

316. See, e.g., *Graver Tank & Mfg. Co v Linde Air Prods. Co.*, 339 U.S. 605, 609, 85 USPQ 328, 331 (1950) (stating in reference to the doctrine of equivalents that consideration *"must be given to the purpose for which an ingredient is used in a patent, the qualities it has when combined with the other ingredients, and the function which it is intended to perform. An important factor is whether persons reasonably skilled in the art would have known of the interchangeability of an ingredient not contained in the patent with one that was."*).

317. *Al-Site Corp. v VSI Int'l, Inc.*, 174 F.3d 1308, 1321 n.2 (Fed. Cir. 1999)

structure disclosed in the patent, that should not prevent it from being an equitable equivalent.

(2) Where equivalence involves technology that predates the invention, non-equivalence for §112(6) purposes precludes equitable equivalence because the accused device could have been disclosed in the patent. There is no policy reason why a patentee should get two bites at the apple. If he or she could have included in the patent what is now alleged to be equivalent, and did not, leading to a conclusion that an accused device lacks an equivalent to the disclosed structure, why should the issue of equivalence be litigated a second time?

It should be noted, however, that the finding of no equitable equivalence for existing technology applies *only* to means-plus-function features. In *Kraft Foods, Inc. v Int'l. Trading Co,*[318] the Federal Circuit explained:

> Where the patentee does not use the means-plus-function format, the resolution of infringement under the doctrine of equivalents would not allow the patentee "two bites at the apple," since the resolution of the literal infringement question would not address the issue of equivalence in a claim drawn to structure rather than to a means-plus-function. Thus, for a claim limitation not drafted in means-plus-function language, the mere fact that the asserted equivalent structure was pre-existing technology does not foreclose a finding of infringement under the doctrine of equivalents.

Examples of how elements are interpreted

An example of where protection given in the US by a means-plus-function claim of this type was narrowly construed as regards literal infringement is provided by *Catalina Marketing International v Coolsavings.com, Inc.*[319] In that case, the invention concerned apparatus for distributing coupons from electronic terminals at point of sale, which included *activation means for activating the terminal for consumer transactions* and *selection means operatively connected with a display means provided to permit selection of a desired displayed coupon by the consumer.* The Court construed the *activation means* to be a magnetic card reader since the specification contained numerous references to a magnetic card reader, and neither the specification nor the prosecution history identified any other structure as the *activation means* for the terminal. The *selection means* was construed to be a touch screen since no alternative structure was disclosed. On this basis the claims did not cover the defendant's Internet web site, and the infringement proceedings were summarily dismissed.

An example where a means-plus-function limitation was satisfied neither literally nor on the doctrine of equivalents is provided by *Chiuminatta Concrete Concepts,*

---

318. No. 99-1240, Fed. Cir., 14 Feburary 2000

319. Fed. Cir., 03-1548-1627, Michel, Raeder and Prost, 19 November 2004; for a further example see *Franks Casing Crew and Rental Tools, Inc v Weatherford International, Inc* Fed. Cir., 03-1519,-1563, 30 November 2004, Raeder, Freidman and Dyk.

Chiuminatta Concrete Concepts v Cardinal Industries

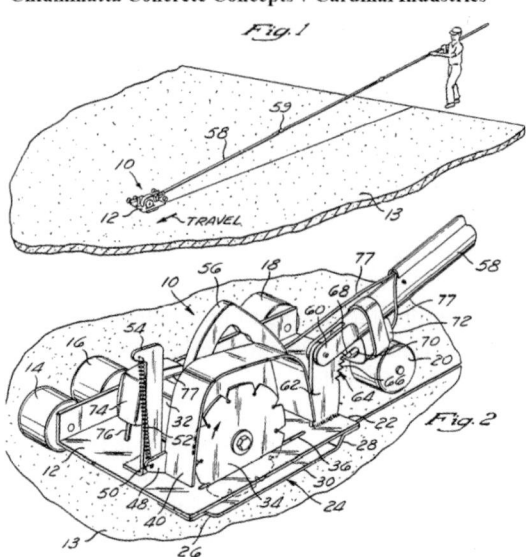

Inc v Cardinal Industries, Inc.[320] The invention concerned a saw for cutting concrete before it had fully hardened; there were method and apparatus patents[321] and the present discussion concerns only the apparatus patent. A feature of the claimed saw was *means connected to the saw for supporting the surface of the concrete adjacent the leading edge of the cutting blade to inhibit chipping, spalling, or cracking of the concrete surface during cutting.* The only structure disclosed for supporting the surface of the concrete was a skid plate, whereas the accused device had two small soft compressible wheels mounted adjacent to the leading edge of the saw blade. The court construed the corresponding structure for the functionally defined feature to be the skid plate which was a small hard plate that straddled the leading edge of the cutting blade. The wheels of the accused device were held to be substantially different. The Court summarised its conclusion as to literal infringement as follows:

> The assertedly equivalent structures are wheels, and the differences between the wheels and the skid plate are not insubstantial. The former support the surface of the concrete by rolling over the concrete while the latter skids. The former are soft, compressible, and round; the latter is hard and predominantly flat (albeit with rounded edges to prevent gouging of the concrete). Additionally, the wheels rotate as opposed to skid as the saw moves across the concrete and thus have a different impact on the concrete. Since the wheels and the skid plate are substantially different from each other, they cannot be equivalent, and no reasonable jury could so find...
>
> ... Moreover, Chiuminatta has not alleged that those of ordinary skill in the art recognised the interchangeability of metal plates with wheels for supporting

320. Fed. Cir., 97-1194,-1401, 14 May 1998, Michel, Plager and Lourie (**required reading**).
321. US-A-4889675 (method); US5056499 (apparatus)

the surface of concrete. Significantly, the patent discusses the use of wheels in the context of supporting and stabilizing the saw, but never once suggests that wheels could perform the function of the skid plate. Notwithstanding the discussion in the specification regarding the inherent drawbacks of a skid plate, including potential gouging of the concrete and increased drag against the concrete, there is no hint in the specification that the skid plate could be replaced by small wheels adjacent to the blade for supporting the concrete.

The court further held that there could be no infringement on the basis of the doctrine of equivalents because the structure in the accused device, the wheels, operates in a substantially different way compared with the structure of the claimed device, the skid plate, and because there was no question of infringement being based on future-developed technology.

As a further example, in *The Toro Company v Deere & Company*[322] the claimed structure included a functionally defined control mechanism for which the structure disclosed in the description was a cam and follower. The accused apparatus had a solenoid system which was considered to perform the specified function in a fundamentally different way, and infringement could be established neither literally nor under the doctrine of equivalents.

An example where literal infringement of a means-plus-function requirement was denied but infringement on the doctrine of equivalent was affirmed is found in *WMS Gaming Inc v International Game Technology*[323] which related to technology for a virtual reel slot machine that is now fitted to the majority of such machines throughout the world and in which the critical novel feature is the non-uniform mapping of numbers to stop positions (i.e., assigning a plurality of numbers to stop positions where the plurality of numbers exceeds the number of stop positions) to decrease the odds of winning. The Claim 1, with the key disputed feature italicised, reads as follows:

A game apparatus, comprising:

a reel mounted for rotation about an axis through a predetermined number of radial positions;

means to start rotation of said reel about said axis;

indicia fixed to said reel to indicate the angular rotational position of said reel;

means for assigning a plurality of numbers representing said angular positions of said reel, said plurality of numbers exceeding said predetermined number of radial positions such that some rotational positions are represented by a plurality of numbers;

means for randomly selecting one of said plurality of assigned numbers; and

means for stopping said reel at the angular position represented by said selected number.

---

322. Fed. Cir., 03-1160, -1161, 24 January 2004, Michel, Lourie and Linn
323. 184 F.3d 1339 (Fed. Cir. 1999).

The US district court construed the *"means for assigning"* limitation of claim 1 to cover any table, formula or algorithm for determining correspondence between the randomly selected numbers and rotational positions of the reel. On appeal the Federal Circuit held that this interpretation was too broad because in a means-plus function feature, the corresponding structure was a special purpose microprocessor programmed to execute the described algorithm. In this case the microprocessor was programmed to assign a plurality of single numbers to stop positions such that (i) the number of single numbers exceeded the number of stop positions, (ii) each single number was assigned to only one stop position, (iii) each stop position was assigned at least one single number, and (iv) at least one stop position was assigned more than one single number. The test for literal infringement under §112(6) was equivalence in structure and identity in function. In the accused device, what was assigned was a combination of numbers, not a single number. The difference in the way that the microprocessors were programmed amounted to equivalent structure but the claimed function was not identical to that of the accused device because the function of assigning and selecting a single number was not the same as that of assigning and selecting a combination of numbers. Accordingly, the accused device did not literally infringe the claim. However, the doctrine of *Graver Tank* equivalence was broader insofar as it only required substantially the same function rather than identity of function as in §112(6), and the insubstantial differences in the accused device were insufficient to avoid infringement.

Conclusions

Should we change our habits for claim drafting for our EPO or UK national patent applications? In principle, means-plus-function is the best way of defining a claimed feature in Europe, but a US audience will interpret such claims narrowly, and by the time we have an opportunity of explaining the error business negotiations may have been concluded under a misunderstanding of the true scope of protection in Europe. Caution and client relations suggest that we should use the word *means* on fewer occasions than we do now, and instead substitute nouns representing generic structures whenever possible, along the lines of the examples quoted above.

As regards support in the written description, in effect, we are now being asked to foresee all possible questions and include express provisions for dealing with them. Best practice is expressly to state in the written description the known equivalents we wish to cover both for features expressed in ordinary structural language and for features expressed in means-plus-function or step-plus-function form, otherwise there is a risk that an equivalent may not be covered, or may be the subject of prolonged and avoidable argument in court. If our patent specifications become unreasonably long and tell those skilled in the art at length what they already know, that is an unavoidable response to the decisions made by the US courts and the need to reduce doubt during litigation. Furthermore, although the skilled addressee already has knowledge of equivalents, other addressees including management, judges and members of a US trial jury may not, and the more that is included in the specification, the less that is left to argument and chance. The above advice, of course, is also appropriate for Europe: definitions in the written description of features in the claims increase certainty and may reduce the time and cost of litigation.

DRAFTING SKILLS

Historic Papers

Brushing up our drafting

E.W.E. Micklethwait

This paper first appeared in *Trans. CIPA*, LXV (1946-47), page 72, and was re-published in *The CIPA Journal* at [2003] *CIPA* 320 and 379. Editorial comments appear in footnotes where the paper has become dated by virtue of changes in the law since 1977. The basic principles that Mr Micklethwait so clearly sets out remain the bedrock of a good patent drafting even today.

Introduction

Drafting patent specifications is a subject likely to be of interest to patent agents at any time as it occupies most of their time, but I think that the present time is particularly appropriate for discussing it as we are getting back into gear after the disturbance of the war.[324] The profession to-day includes three classes each of which has some reason for brushing up its drafting.

First there are those who have never fully qualified as drafters of specifications and who have yet to pass the final examination. They will find food for thought in Mr Leistikow's admirable paper on the final examinations,[325] but although he dealt with his subject in general terms he was mainly concerned with interpretation and many candidates may welcome some further remarks on drafting. Secondly there are those who have been in the Forces or in Government service for a number of years and have recently returned to patent work. They may well feel somewhat rusty after all this time and may accept some discussion of the subject as a kind of informal refresher course. Finally there are those who have been at it all through the war, battling with shortage or complete absence of staff, absence of partners on Government service, shortage of office materials, delays in the mails, countless restrictions to be studied, permits to be obtained, and forms to be filled in, to say nothing of the nervous strain, danger and material damage and inconvenience caused by bursting bombs and rockets. Such conditions are not conducive to work of the highest standard, especially work needing great concentration; and the choice must often have been not between first-class work and second-class work, but between second-class work and nothing at all. So it seems a good time for us all to re-examine our work and ask ourselves whether it is really up to the highest possible standard.

I propose to divide my remarks into two parts. I think most people will agree that the points dealt with in the first part under the heading ***Shoddy Drafting*** are faults which should be avoided if they can be detected. After eliminating all such faults there is still room for considerable difference of opinion on points of drafting, there are cases where drafting may be influenced by circumstances and cases where a compromise may have to be adopted. Such cases I discuss in the second part under the heading ***Drafting Policy***.

---

324. The reference is to the Second World War, 1939-45.

325. Leistikow, F.W.R., "*The Institute Final Examination*", Trans. C.I.P.A. LXIV (1945-46), 41

Shoddy drafting

Procedure for drafting – two phases.

Drafting a patent specification is a very specialised form of writing English and is an art which, like painting a picture or playing the piano, depends partly on natural aptitude and partly on acquired skill. In acquiring such skill there is room for some instruction and system as well as long practice aided by self-criticism and outside criticism.

In drafting claims no amount of system and no amount of practice will obviate the necessity for hard work and concentrated thinking, but it may be helpful to adopt certain methods of directing one's thought so that it may be used to the best advantage. As Mr Tennant said in an excellent paper on claim drafting some years ago, it is no use gazing dreamily at a blank piece of paper and hoping for inspiration.

Although in detail everyone may have a different method of procedure I think that in all drafting there are certain broad fundamental principles to be borne in mind. At each stage, as in any engineering problem, one should have a clear idea what one is trying to do and should work out the most direct and efficient method of doing it, so as to achieve the optimum result with no unnecessary effort. In this connection it is generally useful to consider the problem from first principles.

In drafting a main claim I think the problem can usefully be tackled in two phases, although these phases overlap and may at times be almost indistinguishable.

The first phase consists of making up one's mind what the invention is, or forming a mental picture of what is to be claimed, while the second phase consists of putting that mental picture into words. In most cases the mental picture of what is to be claimed will probably undergo development and change as it is put into words, but none the less the conception may be useful for two reasons; firstly as helping one to realise that at each phase faults may creep in and must be corrected; and secondly as helping one to adopt the most direct method of procedure at each phase.

With regard to avoiding or correcting faults I think it is fairly obvious that the mental picture one forms of the invention may not be the correct mental picture. It may be too narrow or it may be too broad or it may not embody essential features. The mental picture chosen will probably be no matter of scientific correctness but a matter of opinion depending on such arbitrary factors as the policy of the client and it may involve some sort of a compromise between conflicting interests. In general it is a question very much of the judgment of the individual draftsman. These aspects are discussed more fully in Part 3. On the other hand the possibility of faults in the second phase i.e. not saying what one means, is perhaps less obvious. We shall return to this later.

The first phase – the mental picture.

Some people consider that a satisfactory way of drafting a claim is, to write down a list of integers appearing in the specific construction designed by the inventor and then to cross out those features which are not essential. To be content with the claim so drafted is in my view very shoddy drafting. If in addition one goes on to scrutinise the integers remaining, alter and reword them as necessary, and perhaps add one or two others until the final product is quite unrecognizable, the result may be a perfectly good claim. My own view is that this is an indirect way of reaching one's goal and one can develop a more direct method by going to first principles.

To arrive at the mental picture, it seems to me essential to ask at the start what is the point of the invention. I believe too many people just look at the instructions and say to themselves vaguely, "So and so looks rather an essential feature". *The point of an invention is to secure certain advantages, and the features to which the claims must be directed are the features which enable those advantages to be obtained* . So in drafting I think one should ask: "What is the point of the invention? Why should any sane person ever choose to use the inventor's apparatus in preference to what is already known?" In cases where the answer is "Nobody ever would", one can only draw upon a fertile imagination and hope for the best. In most cases some general answer is clear, such as that it gives a totally new result which is advantageous, or it may be only that it as neater, stronger, more efficient or cheaper. Why is it stronger or cheaper? Because he uses so and so. Could he omit so and so or use something else instead? After chatting to oneself on these lines for a short time one will have made some progress towards getting a mental picture of the invention.

The time is then probably ripe for beginning to convert one's mental picture into words, and as soon as a first draft wording has been put down it becomes necessary to scrutinise and criticise this wording. This scrutiny will obviously give a further check on the mental picture. Again, in criticizing a claim one must consider the function it is to fulfill. It is useless to hold it up to the light, inhale its bouquet or munch it; like a connoisseur appraising a vintage. The test of a claim is not whether it produces a pleasant sensation, reminiscent of silk dresses rustling in the Mediterranean moonlight, or a symphony conducted by Toscanini, or whether it produces an unpleasant sensation, like a visit to the headmaster's study, or the putrefying corpse of a leprous polecat (although such sensational claims may be encountered). The test of a claim, as of anything else, is fitness for its purpose, and the direct way of scrutinizing one's wording is to go to first principles and ask: "What is the purpose of this claim?" *The answer is that it is to make it as difficult as possible for a potential infringer to get the advantage of the invention without infringing the claim.*[326]

Surely then the logical method of testing the claim is to put one's self in the position of a potential infringer and see if one can readily get the benefit of the inventor's work and ideas without infringing the claim. This must involve a measure of inventive ingenuity and design, and it seems to me incontestable that a patent agent cannot draft a satisfactory claim to an invention without directing his mind to the possibility of constructions alternative to that suggested by the inventor. Obviously this process can be overdone, and it is no part of the patent agent's business to design in detail any modification of the applicant's construction.[327] It is sufficient to reach the stage of saying it seems probable that something on those lines could be done.

---

326. [Editor's emphasis]. Mr Micklethwait's proposition is substantially the same as that set out at the conclusion of the inventive step chapter at page 37, The fundamentals of good patent drafting have remained little changed.

Nor am I suggesting that any description of such modified constructions need necessarily be put into the specification.

Personally, I often find it helpful to make very diagrammatic little line sketches in the margin indicating possible modifications, when deciding which should be included and which should be excluded, for lack of novelty or because they do not really come within the invention envisaged.

Let us assume that, either by this process, or in any other way the individual drafter may prefer, the mental picture of the invention is now crystallised into something like its final form and appears *prima facie* to be tolerably well represented by the draft wording.

The second phase – saying what you mean.

At this stage many people are content to pass on to Claim 2, but in so doing they are neglecting to check what I have termed the second phase of claim drafting. Both from reading printed specifications and from marking examination papers, I am convinced that it never occurs to a large number of people that they have not said what they mean and certainly do not mean what they said. This second phase of drafting is, or should be, much more a question of scientific accuracy than the first, since, in conception at all events, it is a matter of reproducing in words an accurate definition of the mental picture that has been conjured up.

Perhaps I might digress for a moment to give one or two examples of the type of fault that may occur in what I have called the second phase of drafting. In examination paper J for 1936 (below) there was a question concerned with a tube bent into the form of a closed figure and containing a quantity of liquid to serve as a gradient-meter for use in a motor car. Many candidates referred to this as a closed tube, thinking that they had thereby limited the claim to a tube in the form of a closed figure or in other words an endless tube, but if they had thought about it they would have realised that the term "closed tube" would include a straight tube closed at both ends. Again, many candidates stated that the tube was filled with liquid. Since the indication of the gradient was given by the surface of the liquid, the instrument would obviously have been quite useless if it had been filled with liquid. It was about that time that Mr Leistikow and I motored across Europe and we often found it prudent to carry a few bottles of beer. Some of the candidates' claims would have been invalidated by this prior user, but had one said to any candidate: "Do you intend your claim to include a bottle of beer in the back of a car?" I feel confident he would have said: "No!" This was an example of a drafter not saying what he meant, or in other words not making his wording coterminous with his mental picture. It is therefore also necessary to scrutinise the claim carefully to see whether it includes something which it is not intended to include and to see whether it incorporates all the features which appear to be essential to the invention and does not introduce any undesirable limitation.

---

327. [Editor's note: many of us have contributed suggestions in outline. Bur we are *not* persons skilled in the art, and straying into detailed design is indeed dangerous.]

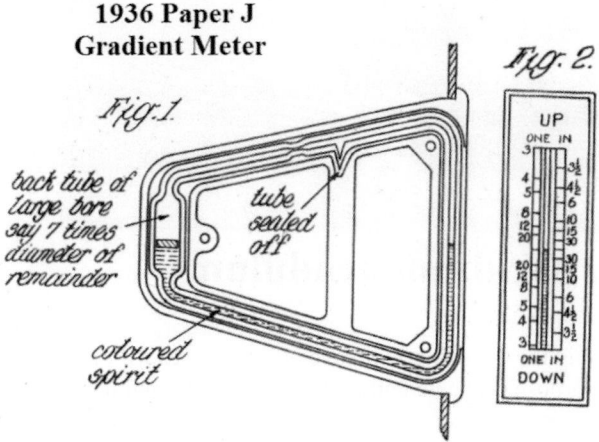

**1936 Paper J
Gradient Meter**

One method of doing this is to read through the claim, trying as far as possible to banish from one's mind the construction actually employed and to make a rough diagrammatic sketch of what the claim defines. Generally it is best to attempt to be rather stupid when doing this, and imagine oneself a rather obstinate artist drawing just what was not intended, but always complying with what is required by the wording of the claim. In this way it is probable that the candidates who referred to a closed tube would in many cases have drawn a straight closed tube and realised that something more was required in their claim. This process of translating the words into little diagrams is the converse of that described previously which involved translating little diagrams into words.

It may also be useful at this stage to make a list of all the elements of the specific construction and see whether the essential ones are represented in the claim. This should be done with caution as the claim may be such that individual integers are not recognizable in it.

Let us consider, as another example, a claim to a pendulum compensated for temperature (below) reading as follows:

> Apparatus comprising an iron rod rotatable about its top end, two or more brass rods supported vertically from its bottom end, and an iron rod depending from the top of each brass rod, the last mentioned iron rods being yoked together at their lower extremities.

In the first place the claim starts: "Apparatus". This may be satisfactory in some cases but it gives no clue to what it is all about, or how it is to be arranged. It leaves the whole burden of defining the invention to what follows. Why not call it a pendulum?[328] There is always a danger that something quite different will possess the

---

328. [Editor's note: "Pendulum" is a field-defining feature, whereas the iron rods, brass rods and yoke are other technical features. The relationship between these aspects of a claimed invention is discussed under Technical Field beginning at page 185.]

Gridiron pendulum

features enumerated in the claim but will have other features which at once render it impossible for the purpose of the invention. If a claim is drafted in such broad terms as to include a five-barred gate or a grand piano or a gridiron, what justification is there for saying the inventor (or his agent) never intended it to include such things. He should say what he means. If the claim starts with the words "A pendulum" one can say of such a red herring: "It is obviously not a pendulum."

Now let us look again to see if the claim includes all we wish to include and excludes all we wish to exclude. The whole point of the pendulum claimed is that the weight is not to go up or down with changes of temperature. But the claim has no reference to any weight at all. Surely we ought to include a reference to a weight.[329] It is limiting the claim to an essential and excluding constructions which would be pointless and inoperative.

Now does the claim cover all one wants to cover? Putting oneself in the shoes of an infringer and selling one's ingenuity to work to devise a construction which falls outside the claim and yet enjoys the advantages of the invention; we have not far to seek. What if we turn the thing upside down and attach the pivot to the yoked iron rods and the weight to the single iron rod?

This illustrates a common fault, namely, describing or claiming a construction only in one position or condition. In a specific description it is often convenient, and probably permissible, to describe a structure in its normal position if it has one, and there can be no possible objection to this if it is stated that the description assumes the structure is in the normal position or the position shown in a particular drawing. In a claim this becomes more doubtful and a claim would be on very doubtful ground if it referred to the upper and lower ends, for example, of an engine cylinder which is described with its axis vertical but could be arranged with it horizontal. The pendulum example quoted above is even worse than this, since only part of the structure is inverted. If the thing is to work at all as a pendulum the weight must be below the pivot and hence it is not possible to argue that you have only to invert the complete article to make the claim read on to it. If the connection to the weight is specified in the claim then when it is one way up it is excluded by one limitation and

---

329. [Editor's note: Or to a fixing for a weight if the pendulum body and the weight are components that might come from different suppliers and be assembled together subsequently.]

when it is the other way up it is excluded by another limitation. This aspect of accuracy is discussed further in a later section, but it may be said at once that in its most serious form it may render the patent very nearly useless.

Before leaving Claim 1, the wording must be checked for inaccuracies, inconsistencies, *non sequiturs*, carts before horses, and other similar faults. We will leave these questions to Section 2.6 in which we discuss the general question of accuracy.

The broad fighting claim – nicely graded subsidiary claims.

Let us assume now that we have arrived at our final wording for Claim 1. As discussed in Part 3, this may have involved some decisions as to policy or some compromise. It may be that we have decided to risk a claim broad to the borderline of vagueness, and possibly in somewhat functional form. We may want to draw a comprehensive search, but of course we cannot be certain that the claims initially filed will not be accepted as they stand.

This leads on to the question of the second claim of the specification, which is often the weakest part of a shoddily-drafted specification. This is particularly apt to be the case where the first claim is a broad functional claim. It may be that the client has himself set out the purpose of the invention and the agent sees fit to claim in his first claim any structure achieving this purpose. Or it may be that the agent has himself dug out the matter for a broad first claim. Then he heaves a sigh of relief, like a man on the completion of an arduous and unpleasant task, and settles down lightheartedly to draft a series of constructional claims packed with arbitrary limitations and describing in more or less pictorial detail the specific constructions. This is no good at all. If he sees fit to put in a broad functional first claim to anything fulfilling a given function, he must then analyse the specific constructions to see what in them represent the essential features for achieving that function. In this way a nicely-graded series of claims can be drafted, each of which introduces some perhaps minor but definitely advantageous feature as compared with earlier claims.

Here again one may go to first principles. The question is what is the point of a subsidiary claim, and I take it the answer is to give protection, either under Section 32A[330] or by amendment, if the broader claims are found to be invalid. So one may check for too great or too small a gap between claims by asking: "If Claim 1 were just anticipated, could one support a broader claim than that?" or, on the other hand: "If Claim 1 were found to lack novelty or patentable subject-matter is there any chance of Claim a being upheld?"

This last point brings me on to consider the incidence of one claim on another. It has been emphasised before and I will emphasise again that the wording of an appendant claim may affect the interpretation of an earlier claim in a way quite unintended by the shoddy drafter. Thus, if claim 1 refers to a peg and claim 2 says: "in which the peg is of circular cross-section" claim 1 will be interpreted as covering square pegs, and if they have to fit into round holes claim 1 may be bad. Such a claim has been well

---

330. of the Patents and Designs Act 1907, as amended by the Patents and Designs Act 1932

described by Mr Gill as "worthless but not harmless".[331] I think this trouble only arises from slack drafting and will not do so if one has a really clear idea of what are the added features of each claim and what advantages follow from them. Again the little marginal sketches may be used to indicate what each claim covers and how they differ.

One other point I might mention is the undesirability in general of including in any claim features which are not essential and which introduce limitation but no subject-matter. People sometimes feel that a claim is rather weak and decide to narrow it down by limitation to a feature that has nothing whatever to do with what is already claimed, and without considering whether the subject-matter is in any way strengthened. If both claims are equally weak one might as well have the broader one.

The introduction

I think most people agree that in normal cases it is desirable to include in the early part of the specification some broad statement of the invention. Some suggest that the statement should not adhere to the words of the claim but I think any departure is liable to be dangerous.[332] If one has spent time and thought bringing the claim to the best wording one can think of, it seems illogical to employ a second best for the statement of invention. If its meaning is identical why not use the same words, and if not, surely it introduces grave danger of ambiguity. On the other hand the introduction to the specification close to the statement of invention is just the place to put in chatty explanations, examples of rather obscure generalised phrases, references to purpose and so forth. On the same basis there may even be occasions for putting some sort of restatement of invention at the end of the specification to be read only by those initiated into the mysteries of the specific examples.

On the other hand there are cases when I think drafters often err in not putting the statement of invention very early in the specification, but waiting until they have completely stolen all their own thunder. Some inventions are the solution of a problem which has cost many a pint of midnight oil. In such a case by all means make a song about the problem. But many inventions are just a bright idea (perhaps more are just an idea). A *dress shirt with a zip fastener.* The more we elaborate the annoyances of being late for dinner and the expense of the consequent taxi, the convenience of the well-known zip fastener on the ladies dress, tobacco pouch, brief case, hand bag and even golf jacket, the less epoch-making seems the idea of putting a zip fastener on the dress shirt. If you put it all in after the statement of the invention it makes just as good a legal document and much better window dressing.

---

331. The Effect of Recent Decisions in Patent Cases. Trans. C.I.P.A., 1936-7, at p.63. Note that the same point is referred to by US practitioners as "claim differentiation" and can be important for the construction of the claims of a UK patent.

332. [Editor's note: Mr Micklethwait's comments were made before the entry into force of the Patents Act, 1977, Section 76 or Art. 123(2) EPC. His comments remain applicable for the patent as granted, but may be inadvisable for the specification as filed, where some elements inconsistency between the written description and the claims may be deliberately introduced in order to preserve flexibility. Furthermore, some US practitioners now omit a statement of the invention in order to minimise the risk of the US courts reading unintended limitations into the claims.]

Perhaps I might include a reminder that a specification is not an advertisement, and inventors, like mothers, often think nobody has ever produced anything quite so beautiful. In blowing the trumpet of an invention phrases guarded to the extent of vagueness are in my view permissible. I regard as most dangerous phrases like: "*The object is to obtain 100 per cent. efficiency*", and much prefer: "*The object is to improve the efficiency and certain constructions may achieve an efficiency approaching 100 per cent*". It must be remembered that even if the claim made is true of the inventor's preferred construction or even of all the inventor's constructions, it may well be quite untrue of many constructions coming within the claims, and even some marketed by an infringer. In the case of the liquid level mentioned above some candidates said the sensitivity was enormously increased whereas a little consideration would have made it clear to them that the greatest possible improvement (involving a limb of infinite cross-section) would only have doubled the sensitivity.

To give another example, paper J of 1935[333] was about a centrifugally variable drive for a windscreen wiper. The object was to keep the speed of the wiper more nearly constant than that of the car.
  "How constant?"
  "The more constant, the better."

In these circumstances it is shoddy drafting to say, as the majority of candidates did, "substantially constant at all car speeds". First of all, what is meant by "substantially constant"? Then when the car stops the wiper stops so we can only consider a certain range of car speeds. Suppose we say 5-60 m.p.h. existing wipers have presumably been usable with a speed variation of 1,200 per cent. Actually the range of the gear ratio was about 3 or 4 to 1 and the wiper speed variation might be reduced from 1,200 per cent to 300 per cent, which could hardly be called substantially constant. The question merely said the device prevented the wiper speed rising in proportion to that of the car.[334]

Accuracy

It may seem merely a statement of the obvious to say that everything in the specification must be accurate and true, but it is an aspect of drafting that requires continual watchfulness. I have referred above to the fault of saying that the object of the invention is to achieve results that are not, or need not be, in fact achieved. Then again one must avoid saying, for example, that the object is to produce a cheaper article when in fact the article is more expensive but possibly worth it due to its higher efficiency.

For the rest there is little to say of a general nature, but a few examples may be mentioned.

---

333. Published in CIPA Transactions for 1935.

334. See also *Kraft Cheese Co. v McAnulty*, (1931) 48 R.P.C., p.536; *No Fume, Ltd. v Frank Pitchford and Co., Ltd.*, (1935) 52, R.P.C., p.231.

In the gradient meter question already referred to it was perhaps permissible in the specific description to refer to the *vertical* and *horizontal* limbs of the tube, although the instrument's primary function was in connection with hills where this description was not strictly accurate. But it was definitely shoddy drafting to go a stage further and refer to the horizontal limbs being *inclined to the horizontal* to prevent air locks, or to *fluid* when *liquid* was essential, *filled* when *containing* was intended, *parallelepiped* when *trapezium* was intended, or to refer to the difference between the levels of the two ends of the liquid column, or the *diameter* of a tube that was not necessarily of circular section and of which one part was definitely described as flattened.

Then again consider the claim quoted above to a compensated pendulum, which starts by referring to an iron rod rotatable about its top end. This is putting the cart before the horse for if the rod is horizontal it has no top end. It may be argued that the reference to a top end implies that the rod is not horizontal, but if possible it would be better to say so directly, and not merely by implication. Then the phrase gives no clue as to the axis of rotation, so the obstinate artist may draw a picture of a sloping rod pivoted about a vertical axis.

Jargon and wordiness

Accuracy throughout the specification is essential, but not high-sounding pomposity. Some people seem to think that in the pendulum claim one could not be scientifically accurate without saying: "a rod disposed with its length extending vertically or substantially vertically and mounted at its upper extremity so as to be rotatable about an axis which is substantially horizontal and which passes through that extremity". I think we should not be far wrong if we said: "hanging from a horizontal pivot near one end". Mr Tennant used to say something to the effect that: "Sesquipedalian expressions of a redundant character inherently introduce a tendency towards obfuscation, but: "short words make things clear".

In my paper on *"Clarity and Brevity in Legal Documents"*[335] I made some references to the unfortunate choice of language (I will not call it English) adopted by some patent agents. No doubt there are those who feel that their first duty to their client is to alter the wording he has used to describe his invention, and that once they have altered the client's clear but specific description into a vague and ambiguous but high sounding jargon their fee is earned. There are those who cannot bear to call a spade a spade and the handle of a spade the handle of a spade, but must cloak such rude implements in the guise of, "said first aforementioned cultivating member associated with said second aforementioned cultivating member". It is as if they purposely use obscure language in order to make the specification a mystery unintelligible to the uninitiated, but they should remember that their client will be among the latter class, and if an agent has not perfectly understood his client's intention the client may point it out when he has the specification for approval, but only if he can understand it, and not if it appears to him so much unintelligible jargon. Even to the agent himself clear language goes with clear thinking, and if the invention is expressed in an obscure and

---

335. *Trans C.I.P.A* LX (1941-42) p. 220

roundabout way it will probably be thought out in a similar way. So too a judge is less likely to condemn for ambiguity a definition which strikes him with vivid clarity than one which he has to read a dozen times and then ask Counsel to explain before he begins dimly to discern what is intended. Most people are familiar with plain English, so let us use plain English wherever plain English will do the job.

There are certain words I have never heard used in conversation or in a book, but somehow they are always cropping up in patent specifications. Words like *"thereto, therefrom, thereafter or thereup,"* sound more pompous than *"to it, from it, after it or up it,"* but are they really any clearer? In this connection one must also have regard to its effect on the sentence in which it occurs. Such words as I have mentioned often make a sentence more cumbersome than it otherwise might be. Then again the word "said" meaning "the" is largely peculiar to specifications, though it has infiltrated into technical jargon generally. *"A wheel on said shaft"*, conveys very little more than the English equivalent *"A wheel on the shaft"*.

Christening of individual parts is often a great help towards achieving a clear and easy style rather than a heavy and cumbersome one. In many cases this can be done without introducing any restriction, and in such cases the part's nickname can be used both in the claims and description. In other cases a broader term may be required in the claims, but the nickname will none the less be of great value in the description. It should be unnecessary to add that having chosen a name one should stick to it.

I believe one cause of cumbersome and wordy expressions is the attempt to correct a fault such as ambiguity by adding words rather than rewriting the sentence or if necessary the paragraph. It appears as if the writer, dissatisfied with a word or phrase, seeks to correct it by adding a further word or phrase, and if still dissatisfied adds still more words until he has built up a monstrous edifice of tangled verbiage. In many cases this could be avoided by cutting out the faulty phrase and substituting a better one. A horrible example of this occurs in the *Trading with the Enemy Act, 1939 (c. 89)*.[336] Here the drafter has used the phrase *"in particular"*. This phrase is inherently ambiguous as nobody seems to know whether what precedes it is limited to what follows it or whether the latter is merely by way of illustration. The drafter has seen this, but instead of cutting out the ambiguous phrase he has inserted further words until he has built up the monstrous phrase *"in particular but without prejudice to the generality of the foregoing provision"*. In fairness to him he has removed the ambiguity, but at what cost? We all know what he means. In two words, he means *"for example"*. It may be thought pedantic to criticise a phrase such as this, since, if carefully examined, its meaning is quite clear. But if every phrase in a specification is inflated with windy jargon in this manner the result becomes most indigestible. This is an aspect of the choice of words which needs to be borne in mind throughout a specification, or indeed any other document. Whereas a single cumbersome word or roundabout phrase may seem adequately clear and reasonably concise when standing alone, the cumulative effect of a number of such phrases put together in a specification may be intolerably cumbersome.

---

336. Section 1.2a, see also *Trade Marks Act, 1938, Section* 37.3.

Arrangement of description – keeping the reader in blinkers

Some specifications seem to be drafted with the object of keeping the reader as much as possible in the dark as to what it is all about, although ultimately it may be impossible not to reveal the secret of what is being described. This seems to apply particularly to specifications drafted in the United States.

It may be partly that what we regard as plain English is regarded by our friends in America as an obscure and archaic dialect, but I think the chief explanation lies in certain rules of US practice. I have received official objections on the ground that I have described the function of a mechanism before describing the mechanism.[337] This in itself may seem quite reasonable and undoubtedly it prohibits what is an undesirable extreme. But if it is made a rigid rule the natural tendency is to force practice to the opposite extreme to be quite certain of avoiding objection. This means never saying what a mechanism is for, until every nut and bolt of it has been described. The effect is aggravated by another feature of US practice. I will quote a letter from America commenting on a 67-page US specification; it said:

> To understand this it must be remembered that the value of a US patent is also linked with the extent of the description, and the technical contribution that it gives to the art. That means that the courts are more likely to sustain patents where the applicant has been liberal and efficient in his efforts to describe everything he knows. Such policy, as far as I know, is not used by the courts in Europe.

His last sentence is not of course quite correct as British courts attach very great importance to sufficiency of description, but the difference is that they measure disclosure by facts and not by folios. I am not for a moment criticizing the practice of another country or suggesting that they should alter it to suit me. But the question assumes relevance when a British Specification has to be prepared corresponding to a US, and it would naturally save trouble to adopt the same wording for the description.

It is interesting to try to analyse the reasons why certain such descriptions seem less clear than they might be. To begin with, the mechanism is not described as a whole, starting with a main framework indicating the main parts and what they are for, and later describing the details of the parts and how they perform these functions. If this is done the reader can appreciate at every stage how the details fit into the general picture. This is impossible if the description starts in one small corner of the mechanism with minute details the significance of which is veiled in mystery until the end of the last chapter. (It is of course possible the writers of these specifications are more familiar with the writing of detective novels.) This is carried to an extreme in the case of phrases such as "the function of which will presently appear". Surely in most cases one could indicate the purpose very briefly, even if details are to follow later, by using some phrase such as "to hold the baby as described in more detail below". If this is not done, the reader is expected to carry in his head details of a mass of meaningless structure; shafts and wheels, first-mentioned members and second-mentioned members, until at the last moment, after wading through pages of description, he is let into the secret of what it is all for.

---

337. [Editor's note: The approach to drafting has changed, and such objections are nowadays uncommon.]

A very good test of a description is that it should be intelligible without any reference to drawings. In fact if the description relies entirely on drawings it is not really pulling its weight, and there is no doubt that the labor of following a description is enormously increased if every phrase has to be interpreted by searching the drawings to find the corresponding reference letter. Perhaps the worst type of description is that which starts, "A is a shaft, B is a wheel, C is another shaft". Such a description gives no idea at all of the relationship between the various parts referred to, and in the absence of drawings conjures up no mental picture of any sort at all. The length of the specification is not unduly increased by employing a phrase such as "the mechanism includes a driving shaft A carrying a wheel B and mounted coaxially with a driven shaft C". This gives at any rate some idea of the arrangement and makes it very much easier to identify the parts on the drawing without searching about for the reference letters concerned. Even if the length of a specification is slightly increased by adopting a pictorial style it must be recollected that the length of a specification is really unimportant. Again going to first principles the purpose of the specification is to convey a description of the apparatus as clearly as possible, and in fact a reader may obtain a clear picture more rapidly from two pages of clearly-worded pictorial description, than from a single page which he has to read three times.

Inspection and checking

Some patent agents, who have been concerned with the methods of inspection used by industry during the war, such as the multiple gauge which with a single blast of air checks a dozen dimensions of a cartridge case with incredible accuracy, may sometimes wish they could subject their patent specifications to some such automatic scrutiny, inserting Claim 1 into a neat little slot and reading on a huge dial, too narrow, too broad or OK. Although I cannot offer anything of this sort it may be worth summarizing certain questions which can usefully be asked in reviewing a specification to help one judge whether it covers the invention as well as possible. No doubt many other questions may be added but it seems that some of the more important are as follows:

1. Has Claim 1 utility; i.e. does it include the features from which the advantages of the invention follow?

2. Can Claim 1 be avoided by any obvious modification?

3. Has Claim 1 patentable subject-matter or does it cover something obvious?

4. If Claim 1 is weak are there strong, independent sub-claims?

5. Do the claims say what they mean and mean what they say; i.e. do the mental picture and verbal counterpart agree?

6. Can the claims be avoided by selling subordinate integers?

7. Do the claims cover the construction when empty, idle, placed on its side, upside down, etc.?

8. Do the claims include any limitations which lend no patentable subject-matter and are not essential to the purpose aimed at?

9. Are the claims based on any doubtful theory?

10. Are the claims accurate in substance and terminology?

11. Can the claims be made less pompous and more succinct, for example, by making them more colloquial or pictorial without sacrificing accuracy?

12. Are all the client's information, modifications and remarks included (if this is desirable)?

13. Is there sufficient explanation of parts, operation and terms, and mention of advantages, bearing in mind the state of the art and the need for clarity to a judge?

14. Are any doubtful terms defined, in particular "the type specified"?

15. Is the description of the drawings complete in itself?

16. Is the technology consistent throughout the specification, especially if the claims have been amended?

17. Does the description lead up to and amplify the claims and set forth the purposes and points of the features claimed?

18. Is any unnecessary or doubtful theory included, and if so is it guardedly introduced?

19. Is any unnecessary or doubtful modification described, and if so is it guardedly referred to?

20. Are there any superlatives or are results claimed which need not be obtained, or worse still are not even obtained by the preferred construction?

21. Is everything stated in the specification true?

22. Are there reference letters to all parts of the drawings likely to be pointed at in Court?

Policy in drafting claims

Form of claim to suit each case

The question of the form of claim to be adopted is included in this part of the paper since some members may make it their policy to prefer one type of claim to another. One man may always start: "*In a so and so the combination with...etc.*", another starts: "*A so and so comprising in combination*", another prefers: "*A so and so in which or wherein*", while others use the word *"characterised"*. The question of functional claims is discussed more fully in Section 3.2. My own view is that the patent agent should have all these forms of claim in his repertoire and in each case should select the form which best suits the particular invention. I would suggest using the term "characterised" only when a single feature really does characterise the invention, and one of the combination forms when a combination of features is involved, especially if each feature by itself is already known. But even here there is no hard and fast rule and each case should be considered on its merits.

How broadly to claim

In some cases it is fairly obvious that the invention enables certain clear-cut advantages to be obtained; and it is relatively easy to complete one's mental picture of the invention to be covered. In other cases it may be extremely difficult to decide how broadly to claim the invention, and there may be no limit to the possible breadth beyond the fact that the claim becomes impossibly vague and functional.

One example of this difficulty is where the invention is a case of, for example, *"the hotter the better"*. It is clearly asking for trouble on the ground of ambiguity to limit the claim by a phrase such as *"very hot"* and the only way to make the claim definite is to select an arbitrary limitation such as *"above 1000°C."* Then, of course, if the nearest prior art was just under 500°C an infringer may get much of the advantage of the invention by using 950°C. On the other hand if our claim specifies *"above 500°C"* it includes at its extreme limit a case having no appreciable advantage over the prior art. Presumably the best makeshift is to select an adequate breadth of no man's land between the claim and the known prior art and be content to let the infringer into this territory.[338] Further limitation can, of course, be brought into later claims. It may be desirable to make it clear that there is no magic about the limits chosen, by stating specifically that the precise temperature is not critical. The matter is, of course, made worse if the prior art is vague about the exact temperature, and uses phrases such as "heated to a high temperature". If any members have a real solution to this problem I should very much welcome it.

The question of functional claims is another about which opinions differ, but my own view is that this again can be usefully viewed from first principles. If this is done it will at once be clear that functional claims cover a wide range of very different types. The purpose of the claim is to tell the reader as clearly as possible what he is prohibited from doing, and if this is done most easily, most clearly and most unambiguously by means of a functional claim there seems no reason why a functional claim should not be adopted. On the other hand if the functional claim merely sets the reader a problem, and purports to prevent him from adopting any solution that he may devise, with whatever ingenuity and research, then it is clearly not defining an invention that the inventor has made, but calling upon the reader to make an invention himself and then telling him he may not use it. A claim of this type

---

338. [Editor's note: It is very often *not* desired to leave a no-man's land. Then a phrase such as *more than 500°C* excludes 500°C itself and covers all temperatures above this value; this format is extremely useful, especially for process-related inventions.]

was once described by Mr Ballantyne by the term "Free beer," covering, as it does, something which many people regard as highly desirable, but which nobody has so far found a process of producing. Since the *No Fume* decision[339] the profession in general views functional claims more favourably.

This brings me on to one of the most general questions of policy in relation to the drafting of claims, namely its dependence on decided cases. Naturally enough the interpretation of specifications is to a considerable extent affected by High Court decisions in particular cases, and we should be foolish not to give due weight to such decisions and to any advice we may from time to time be fortunate enough to receive from those closely connected with court work. At the same time I suggest that such decisions need not be followed too slavishly in drafting specifications. The vast majority of specifications never come into Court at all. For example, in the five years from 1934 to 1938 the number of complete specifications accepted was about 100,000 whilst the number of patents forming the subject of cases reported in the R.P.C. (including applications for extension) was about 60. Admittedly the remainder are viewed in the light of court decisions, but there is always a margin of doubt as to the decision that would be obtained, and the deterrent effect of the cost and trouble involved in infringement proceedings. A gloomy counsel may well advise a prospective plaintiff that a certain claim is weak, but at the very same moment a cautious patent agent may be advising a potential defendant that it would be most inadvisable to risk an infringement action. Moreover, one must consider the alternative. It would of course be very nice to have a claim which was much stronger and was also infringed, but too often if the doubtful claim were not there the patentee would be advised without any doubt at all that the patent was not infringed.

A further point is that the Court decision may subsequently be over-ruled, or altered by statute.

In brief, there is one over-riding consideration which applies to the drafting of claims, namely that it is easy to cancel them later on, and utterly impossible to put them in [after grant]. Naturally there is a limit to the extent to which this policy should be carried, but if there is any serious doubt it would appear that the cautious policy is to include the claim rather than leave it out. A doubtful claim may present a difficult task to counsel or experts. The lack of it may present an impossible task.

Mullard v Philco[340]

We are all familiar with the decision in the pentode valve case in which the claim to a valve in its circuit was upheld, but the claim for the valve *per se* as an article of manufacture was held not to involve patentable subject-matter although it was new. It would be impertinent for me to question the decision of all the Courts which decided this case, but from my limited knowledge of the case I entirely disagree with the decision. It is a principle which if carried to its logical conclusion would result in the most ludicrous absurdities and render all patent protection worthless. A chair would be unpatentable except in combination with a person sitting on it, since it

---

339. *No Fume Ltd. v F. Pitchford and Co., Ltd.*, (1935) 52 R.P.C. at p.231.

clearly fails to perform its function when there is nobody sitting on it. A sparking plug would not be an infringement of a patent when made by the manufacturer or when sold by the vendor, nor even when fitted to a motor car if the motor car contained no petrol. It might even be argued that the sparking plug would cease to be an infringement every time the user of the motor car switched off his engine. Be this as it may the decision has been given and cannot be altered merely by my disagreeing with it.

But this does not mean that it must necessarily be followed in drafting claims. In the first place it may be over-ruled or altered by statute long before the patent expires or comes into Court. Secondly it is not suggested that the claims to a subordinate integer should be substituted for claims to the complete combination but that they should be included in addition. If it is not intended to rely upon them in an action they can always be cancelled.

Sufficiency of claims

It is sometimes suggested that a claim is liable to be held invalid if it does not specify all the features which are necessary for the mechanism to be operative. In a chemical case if the claim refers generally to halogens and one of the halogens will not give the desired result it is generally agreed that the claim is invalid. On the other hand there must be a limit to the extent to which this is applied, at all events to mechanical cases. If a claim refers to a piston and cylinder it will generally be unnecessary to state in the claim that the piston must fit the cylinder, and that if it were either too large or too small the desired result would not be obtained. The body of the specification must describe one means of carrying the invention into effect in sufficient detail to enable a competent technician to do it, and clearly the claims cannot be expected to go into the same detail nor need the claims be limited to that one embodiment.

No doubt members will have various opinions on this question but it is suggested that there is a distinction between the extent of detail required in connection with features which are germane to the invention and features which are well known. For example, if the invention related to a shock absorber in which the whole point was that the piston did not fit in the cylinder, it would clearly be essential to specify this in the claim, whereas in the ordinary way a reference to a piston and cylinder would be assumed to refer to a cylinder with a piston fitting it.

---

340. (1936) 53 R.P.C., p.323 discussed below. [Editor's note: The *Mullard* decision which gave concern to Mr Micklethwait did not prove influential and is nowadays seldom cited. Such an invention could be treated as a "distributed invention" (see the discussion on this topic at page 218 onwards) with the main independent claim being for the pentode valve in place in an amplifying circuit for which the valve was intended, with a second independent claim to the pentode valve for use in the previously defined amplifier. In order to use the distributed invention format, however, the claim to the component must be novel and inventive. The problem for *Mullard* was that there had been a progressive increase in the number of electrodes within an evacuated glass envelope from the single electrode lamp of Edison to the two electrode rectifier of Sir Ambrose Fleming, then to the three-electrode amplifier of Lee DeForest, and again to four electrode thermionic valves. Against this background the House of Lords did not find it credible that there was inventive step in adding a further electrode, especially since a pentode valve might find utility in circuits whose design owed nothing to Mullard's invention, and on this basis their decision is understandable.]

Subsidiary claims

We have discussed in part 2 the purposes of subsidiary claims, one of which is to obtain the benefit of Section 32A.[341] The question arises whether this section applies to a portion of a claim; for example, an alternative or a preferred or optional feature.[342] It is thought that the Court might reasonably be expected to give relief where preference is expressed, or even an optional feature included, on the ground that this implies selection, and in fact a claim of this form is merely a more concise way of writing what could be equally well covered by two separate claims. On the other hand a direct alternative is merely a means of expanding the scope of a claim; for example, a reference to the right hand or the left hand could be expressed generically by the phrase "*one hand*". It is therefore thought that where a direct alternative is included in a claim there is no suggestion of selection, and if one limb of the alternative lacks novelty the Court would not grant relief in respect of the other limb.

One of the most widespread forms of alternative embodied in British claims is that caused by making claims appendant to "any one of the preceding claims" and this is discussed in the next section.

Permutations and combinations of claims

It is not always realised what a lot of claims a British specification contains. Claim 1 is of course only one claim, and so is Claim 2. When we come to Claim 3, if it includes the phrase "as claimed in Claim 1 or Claim 2", it is obviously in fact two different claims. Similarly, if Claim 4 contains the phrase; "as claimed in any one of the preceding claims", it is in fact four claims, since it may be appendant to Claim 1 or Claim 2, or either of the two Claims 3. And so it goes on until when we get to Claim 21 we have totted up no less than 1,048,576 separate claims, and Claim 22 adds a further 1,048,576. It is not suggested that this is necessarily a reason for not adopting this form of wording for appendant claims. It is not the arbitrary result of adopting a particular form of words, but is a natural mathematical outcome of the fact that, if we have 22 separate features which can be combined in different ways, there are over a million separate combinations of these, bearing in mind that they must all possess unity of invention, in that every combination must include the first feature.

We must therefore take the responsibility either of including all these combinations or of ignoring some of them. In either case it is necessary to consider the results very carefully. In the first place with regard to the question of selection it seems clear that it cannot possibly be said that if one of these combinations is novel and inventive, or even if a little group of a few thousand are novel and inventive, the claim can support a selective interpretation covering just that combination or group. For example, if Claims 1, 2, 3 and 4 respectively introduce features A, B, C and D it is quite conceivable that A + B + C would be old and A +B +D would be old, but that A + C + D might be new and useful and used by an infringer. In short, the first three claims would be anticipated and

---

341. Of the 1907 Act as inserted by the 1932 Act.

342. See Williamson, E., "Alternatives in Claims", *Trans. C.I.P.A.*, LXII (1943-44), p. 44

Claim 4 would be anticipated as appendant to Claims 1 and 2, but not as appendant to Claim 3. This is an instance where the drafter of the specification, if he had foreseen how things would turn out, could have drafted the specification so as to include the alleged infringement in a valid claim, but in fact has not done so. This emphasises the desirability of concentrating on combinations of claims which are likely to be of importance and which co-operate with one another in some particular way, although it is quite clearly impossible to include claims directed to all the combinations and in many cases it will be out of the question to hope to foresee what combinations will ultimately prove novel or be adopted by competitors.[343]

The omnibus claim[344]

The question of the omnibus claim, directed to the particular construction shown in the drawings, is one that has already been discussed very fully, and I do not propose to add to what has already been said about it.[345] Indeed it appears to be a never failing topic for argument and might be described as "A widow's cruse filled with bones of contention."

Concluding remarks

In conclusion I must apologise for having taken up so much of your time and yet being so far from having exhausted the subject. I can only hope that my remarks may suggest new trains of thought and resurrect old ones, and that a discussion will follow that will represent a real contribution to the subject of drafting, which occupies so much of our lives.

---

343. [Editor's note: The law has developed since Mr Micklethwait wrote his paper. Sections 27 and 75 of the Act now require the Court or the Comptroller in considering whether or not to allow the application to amend to consider any relevant principles under the EPC, which is being amended to allow the claims of granted specifications to be amended as of right provided that they comply with Articles 84, 123(2) and 123(3) EPC. In the circumstances he postulates, an application to amend will be necessary but should be available as of right.]

344. [Editor's note: This comment was made before the decision of the House of Lords in *Raleigh v Miller* (1948) RPC 141, (1950) 67 RPC 226, afterwards referred to as the "hub dynamo" case. The patent in issue related to a commercially valuable invention, and the only claim that has held to be valid and infringed was the omnibus claim. For a more recent example of a patent that was saved from ineffectiveness by the omnibus claim see *Rotocrop v Glenborne* [1982] FSR 241. The continued availability of "omnibus claims" in the UK is out of line with EPO practice and is questioned periodically. The Editor's view is that such claims provide valuable fall-back protection for a patentee, and should be included whenever appropriate. It is submitted that their scope is neither broad nor narrow but, when carefully drafted, the same scope as a Court would have accepted for the patent in issue if it had been granted under the nineteenth-century UK law where the inclusion of detailed claims was not required and the ambit of protection was decided by the court on the basis of the specification as a whole. Omnibus claims should be written as independent claims with an informative preamble, but should *not* be made dependent on one of the independent claims, otherwise the opportunity to argue for broadened scope as in *Rotocrop* may be lost. Both of the above cases are **required** reading for students.]

345. Williamson, E., "The Omnibus Claim", *Trans. C.I.P.A.*, LX (1941-42), p. 113

Claim drafting – the British tradition

By M.J. Daley

This paper was first published in (1981-82) 11 *CIPA* 110 and was recently republished at [2003] *CIPA* 431. It builds upon the earlier Micklethwait paper and provides useful introductory material for students as well as advice that all of us in the profession should follow.

Over the last ten years much emphasis has been laid on change in our profession and the need to seek new skills and possibly even a new role. Implicit in this emphasis has been the suggestion that the traditional skills of claim drafting and interpretation have somehow become less important. I am in strong disagreement with this. I believe, on the contrary, that as a claim can now define protection in a number of countries the drafting of that claim needs the very greatest care and skill.

A patent agent should, by way of introduction, acknowledge his [Ed.: Throughout the masculine includes the feminine!] principal source and this I have much pleasure in doing. I have been considerably influenced in the preparation of this Paper and indeed through my professional life by Mr E.W.E. Micklethwait's Paper[346] (entitled "Brushing up our Drafting" and I will refer to this Paper specifically from time to time. Everyone here who has not already done so should read Mr Micklethwait's Paper and the account of the discussion which followed the Paper.

It is perhaps of value to reflect, by way of introduction, on the nature of the exercise of claim drafting. Those seeking to instruct patent law and practice on an academic basis have, in my view quite correctly, avoided claim drafting as a conceptual exercise and rather concentrated on the form and possible effect of claims. Most practitioners, I believe, take the view that claim drafting though requiring without doubt acquired knowledge and intellect is essentially a skill or craft only properly learned by carefully supervised practice over a considerable period of time. One of the attractive features of our work is that this learning process only stops when we retire. It follows from this that no-one has produced, or is likely to produce, a credible and effective rigorous analysis of the craft of claim drafting and hence a means of learning the craft on an academic basis. Most of us owe such skill as we have to our teachers and colleagues. In this spirit I offer some comments based on my own experience.

The drafting of a patent claim is an exercise which can be divided into several stages.

Stage I: The analysis of the received disclosure to produce a mental picture of the invention which it is desired to monopolise. The phrase "mental picture" was used

---

346. *Trans. CIPA*, LXV (1946-47), Page 72, reprinted above.

by Mr. Micklethwait and seems quite apt and is so familiar to me that I propose using it in this Paper. I apologise to those of you who do not think, as I do, in pictorial terms and offer respects to those who are able to develop concepts in terms of words without the need for intermediate steps. The opening phase of the analysis must be a thorough technical comprehension of all the material communicated to you by the inventor or your correspondent, and I stress the word "all" for it is a common error to come to a view of the invention too early and to consider only material which seems to fit our own premature conclusions. It is sometimes tempting to pick out a few prominent features which seem at first sight essential and to organise them into claim language which looks professional and may even satisfy a client and the Patent Office. The drudgery of reading through much unnecessary material seems to be avoided. It will be purely fortuitous if such a claim, drafted without a proper analysis of the received disclosure, does have the correct scope. Only when all the communicated material has been totally understood, preferably to an extent such that it can be held in the mind while distanced from your written information, should the work of synthesising the mental picture begin.[347]

For this vital early stage of receiving and comprehending information the draftsman needs a good technical background but more importantly he requires an appetite for technology. He should have a genuine interest in the subject-matter in question and a desire to expand his knowledge. I believe, with the undoubted need to acquire new legal, linguistic and other skills, there has been a certain tendency to under-emphasise the technical and scientific side of our work. The view seems to be that, if we insist on very high technical entry qualifications, the technical side of work can be put behind an entrant to the profession on admission and before he undertakes his formal training. We also see this tendency in the departure of the Manufactures Paper from our own Chartered Institute Examinations. A patent practitioner must not only enter the profession with adequate technical qualifications but also maintain an abiding interest in technical matters, preferably not merely those confined to those of his own academic disciplines. A wide range of technical interests and hence knowledge is a symptom of the vital quality of what I have called "technical appetite".

Let us assume that the inductive work of thorough comprehension, which may involve dialogue with the inventor or our correspondent, is behind us and we can embark on the analysis of the invention and the production of our mental picture which will include all that is essential and nothing more. It is here that the fascinating quintessence of our work lies and we have all observed how some of our colleagues seem to be able to produce this vital synthesis rapidly and indeed almost instinctively both as a result of their innate mental ability and the application of their experience. For most of us, however, some specific mental techniques are required here and whilst referring you to Mr Micklethwait's Paper may I suggest two techniques that I have personally found helpful.

---

347. [Editor's note: A good test for whether you have understood an inventor's description or the disclosure of a reference is whether you can explain it orally to a colleague without notes or reference to the original, possibly some days after you have studied it. The work needed to fully understand disclosures and documents is easily and frequently underestimated.]

Firstly there is the technique of problem and solution. An inventor usually has some purpose in mind and finds it possible to give a reasonably clear indication of the problem with which he was grappling. The realised embodiment of the invention is before you so you can address yourself to the vital question of how has the solution been achieved. Expressed as two short questions:

    (i) What is the inventor trying to do?

    (ii) How has he achieved his solution?

Very often in my experience this line of questioning will at least catalyse the production of the vital mental picture.

The second technique calls for a careful and critical assessment of the invention as perceived by the inventor; what has he achieved in actuality? I have always been profoundly impressed with some remarks made by an eminent barrister at the Holborn College Lectures. Addressing himself to the question of "broad" and "narrow" claims he told us that breadth of claim monopoly should be coterminous with understanding of the invention; breadth beyond understanding is mere speculation and will result in invalidity on one ground or the other. As I recall, the example used was that of the notional discovery that common table salt killed dandelions growing on a lawn, leaving the grass unharmed. If that statement genuinely indicated the limits of the inventor's understanding then that is all that he is entitled to claim. Any extension would be mere speculation; "sodium chloride or the like" would not do as there was no knowledge as to the property of sodium chloride which achieved the desired result. Was it the fact that table salt was white and granular or what? There was no basis to construct the mental picture in other than totally specific terms. If it is known, however, either by evidence or soundly based deduction, that the solubility of the halogen ion is involved, as is the fact that dandelions have broad leaves, then we can do a little better.[348] It may be that we will have to prod and question an inventor and even make him do more work but this must ultimately benefit the patentee.

Let us take a mechanical example where often we are confronted with a machine stated to have an improvement in performance arising from a specific modification. The modification may be the mere insertion of a spring linkage for a previously rigid connection but by relating the modification to the result and discussion with the inventor it is usually possible to advance our understanding. Inventors in the mechanical arts have the habit of immediately translating quite broad conceptual invention to operational hardware and we must "understand back" from the hardware and not merely speculate.

Now these are two techniques that I personally find helpful and I will briefly refer to another which is so widely used that it must be mentioned. That is the systematic consideration of alternatives.[349] In broad aspect this consideration can be helpful. The question: "Why has the inventor arrived at this solution rather than another?" may enlighten. However at this stage I prefer to attempt an accurate identification based on

---

348. [Editor's note: see the paper on *Empirical Research Inventions*, page 249, where this theme is further developed without in any way impugning the correctness of the opinions expressed here.]

349. [Editor's note: see the paper on *Functional Claims* at page 135, which explains that to support a US patent claim with an element in means-plus-function or step-plus-function format, not only is systematic consideration of alternatives required but also specific mention in the written description of all alternatives which it is intended to cover, in order to comply with the "public notice" requirement.]

the material I have digested and tend to be confused by hypothetical exercises. After all, if my mental picture is clear and correct any alternatives will not have the invention and thus need not be conceived and subsequently discarded. The consideration of alternatives may be more helpful when we come to check our claim in the finished form

Implicit in my remarks is my incorrigible belief, supported by experience, that most inventions are susceptible of precise definition and arbitrary choices between "broad" and "narrow" claims do not have to be made as often as the columns of CIPA might suggest. It is my view that work at this synthesis exercise should continue until a clear and well-focused mental picture is produced. This mental picture represents the invention to be protected. At this time it is not my practice to occupy myself with the problems of expressing this mental picture into claim language and I commend this negative practice of not writing too early. In Imperial China it was customary for a craftsman, before undertaking an important piece of work, to travel to a remote location and remain there for at least a week without written information, tools or writing materials. During this week he organised his mind so that he had a complete conception of the work that he was attempting to undertake. I commend this attitude, if not the specific practice.

Stage II: When you have the mental picture, reduce it to a written statement quite rapidly using language which comes naturally to you. It is at this stage that your experience will be of value to you and I have found that undue attention to wording at this stage hinders what I might term the intuitive influence of this experience. If you adopt this technique you may be surprised at how often you do choose without effort the correct wording. Too much linguistic struggling at this stage may blur your carefully produced mental picture. This plain language statement of the invention fixes the mental picture.

Stage III: Now review and revise your Statement of Invention in a careful and critical way. One of the necessary skills of a patent agent is to be able to read his own work and to receive the message of the written word rather than to have the words act as a mere trigger to bring into his mind what it was he intended to write. This review is an important occasion in which this skill of self-criticism should be brought to bear. Obviously what you are seeking to do here is to satisfy yourself that your words create exactly the mental picture that you have so carefully prepared.

Whilst the words that you finally select should be appropriate and accurate, the solution to successful claim drafting does not, in my estimation, lie in the over-careful selection of particular words and one must strive to identify the thoughts that you have by description rather than by mere labelling with a word which may seem to you to be particularly apt. I incline to the view that neutral words such as "parts" and "members" are to be preferred in a claim and words which, though in common usage, have a number of meanings both literal and metaphoric are better avoided. "Bars" and "plates" are examples of such words. If your carefully assembled mental picture really requires a part to be characterised as solid, long in relation to its width and rigid, then it is probably better described as such than labelled as a "bar". The problem with descriptive words, particularly if they are metaphoric in character, is that they are capable of conveying different impressions to different people.

Stage IV: Now with a clear and accurate Statement of Invention in the English language you can consider matters of form and presentation. The exercise of organizing claim wordings into accordance, for example, with Rule 29 EPC can be carried out at this stage.

I do not wish to belittle the knowledge and skill which is involved in the organizing of a claim into a form appropriate to a particular country. What I am saying is that once you have your claim drafted for example in the British form in the manner envisaged in this Paper then the exercise of preparing claims for other countries is essentially a conversion exercise. If there is a totally different way of approaching invention for claim preparation in, say, the US, then I regret that I am not familiar with it. My impression is that when we come down to a bedrock such as an assessment and definition of invention there is not a great difference from country to country. What is different is the way the protection enforced is achieved and certainly there is still a strong body of opinion on the Continent of Europe that feels that claim drafting as envisaged in this Paper is an impossible exercise and therefore an unfair and essentially futile one. Obviously I do not share that view. In my estimation poor claims tend to be produced when these organizational considerations of claim form are brought to bear too early in the exercise and before the draftsman has a clear notion of the invention he is striving to protect.

A criticism of the claim drafting technique outlined above which involves "total immersion" in the received disclosure followed by a synthesis of the mental picture is that not sufficient account of prior art is taken. It could be argued that an inventor and his patent agent could evolve a perfectly drafted claim to a well-known device. I would say to this that the prior art, whether received from the inventor or discovered by searching, should form part of the disclosure to be digested and if necessary discussed before the mental picture is drawn. Quite often the patent draftsman synthesises his mental picture in the form of a "step" from a piece of prior art. This usually arises when the inventor has been working to improve a known construction or process. In this event, with the step properly identified, the drafting of the claim may be quite simple and certainly the organisation into EPC or other "Continental" form is straightforward. If, after filing, more relevant prior art is revealed then the claim drafting exercise may have to be repeated but experience tells me that prosecution redrafting is rarely as difficult and as time consuming as original drafting, as the task of understanding the disclosure is behind.

Although this is beyond the scope of this Paper, I should briefly state that claims drafted as envisaged in this Paper must accompany a specification which has a very full disclosure of all the material imparted by the inventor and not merely that which tends to support the invention as originally envisaged.

Let me address a few words on some adjectives which are often used to describe claims or even schools of claim drafting. Amongst others there are "broad", "narrow", "functional", "structural", "peripheral" and "central" as applied to claims. For myself I do not find these adjectives particularly enlightening or helpful; the identification and definition of invention seems to me a sufficient and complete operation. I have already stated my view that the arbitrary choice between "broad" and "narrow" claims for a particular invention occurs rather rarely. With regard to functionality most inventions have a functional aspect in that invention rarely resides in the choice of a specific component or integer. Thus you will tend to have in your mental picture the introduction of resilience in a particular part of a machine rather than the provision of a metal helical spring, or the maintenance of a certain degree of alkalinity rather than the addition of a specific chemical.

A very convenient form of claim wording has a recitation of the integers of your mental picture together with a statement explaining how the integers interact. This statement of interaction is often called a functional statement but one must beware of functional statements that are mere speculative statements of desired results and reveal only lack of proper analysis and consideration.

Turning to "peripheral" as applied to claim drafting, according to my understanding the proposition is that as the purpose of a claim is solely to define the outer limits of a monopoly rather than to identify an invention, all that is needed is to identify and eliminate the inessential features from a constructional embodiment. This seems rather a negative approach and one dealt with by Mr Micklethwait in the following words:

> Some people consider that a satisfactory way of drafting a claim is to write down a list of integers appearing in the specific construction designed by the inventor and then to cross out those features which are not essential. To be content with a claim so drafted is in my view very shoddy drafting. If in addition one goes to scrutinise the integers remaining, alter and reword them as necessary, and perhaps add one or two others until the final product is quite unrecognizable the result may be a perfectly good claim. My own view is that this is an indirect way of reaching one's goal and one can develop a more direct method by going to first principles.

With regard to the so-called "central" style I had thought that that was the one adopted by me but contemporary usage has ascribed a pejorative sense to characterise a claim that is a slightly generalised description of an embodiment with a consequent appeal to the mercy of any Court which might interpret the patent. In fact the view has been expressed that certain decisions of the Courts are rendering the skills of claim drafting unnecessary. I do not feel that the pyrrhic victories of *Catnic*[350] or even *Barking Brassware v Allied Ironfounders*[351] justify this point of view. Although it is perhaps unfair to use hindsight, I believe it reasonable to say that in each of the two cases a claim could have been drafted which would have achieved a successful result without the expensive controversy. It is, in my view, a mistake to emulate claims which have narrowly and expensively succeeded in the Courts; rather our function is to prepare claims which will protect our clients' interests in a less public way.

In passing I have heard it said that the relative decline in numbers of patent cases reported at the expense of copyright and other intellectual property matter indicates a decline in the importance of patents in industry. I do not accept this proposition. Cream is not the only substance which floats to become visible on the surface and a

---

350. [1981] FSR 60, [1982] RPC 183.

351. [1962] RPC 210.

properly drafted patent specification with good claims and relating to a genuine invention seldom needs to be considered by a Court to achieve its purpose, be that to restrain competition or to attract licence royalties.

May I deal briefly with sub-claims, and state that in my view these should be arrived at in a rather similar but perhaps not so exhaustive manner as the main claim or claims. That is to say we should produce a mental picture of the preferred but optional features of the invention and express them in claim wordings as before. One should be wary, however, of introducing features into a sub-claim to cover indecision as to whether these features should really be incorporated into the main claim. There is the implication that the expression of a feature as preferred in a sub-claim is a statement that the invention can function without that feature and it may be safer in the rare case of real doubt to express that feature as a statement in the body of the specification rather than as a claim. Each and every feature supporting a sub-claim should, in my estimation, introduce some minor but definitely advantageous feature and I do not favour a list of all conceivable preferred constructional variants.

How can the skills of claim drafting be acquired? The traditional training route of dealing with Examiner's objections forces one to consider claims prepared by others and to see to what extent these claims discharge their functions. The reading of reported cases is also extremely helpful as the Courts are our ultimate audience and more importantly the patent specifications which we prepare will be read by others in the context of decided cases. Ultimately however, supervised practice is the only route to success and here I stress the word "supervised". One does not become experienced simply by doing a thing for a long time. The trainee must receive and indeed seek out criticism, even if this runs contrary to his personal inclination which may be to practise solo as soon as possible. However I am quite confident that claim drafting is only really effectively learned by putting best efforts to a careful and critical principal.[352] I may say that this exercise will not only benefit the pupil but ensure that your principal maintains his own high standards.

The imparting of a skill to a pupil from a teacher is much more than the mere transfer of information. A skill such as drafting a claim involves the exercise of unconscious as well as conscious mental operations. A pupil learns partly by imitation, partly by listening and partly by the interaction of minds in the mysterious process of the dialectic. Thus progress will not be a steady advance from one defined objective to another but more in the nature of an organic growth. Not uncommonly the arrival at a good professional standard of claim drafting seems to be quite sudden; one day after months, or even years of endeavour the pupil finds that he can analyse disclosure, produce the all important synthesis which is at the heart of a well drafted claim and express this synthesis in clear language. When this does happen there is rare satisfaction for both teacher and pupil.

---

352. [Editor's note: The benefits of discussion do not end with qualification. At least in the case of a newly drafted specification covering a potentially important invention, it should be routine to discuss the claim with one or more colleagues. They can read the claim without the original draftsman's assumptions and with a different knowledge base, and are therefore in a strong position to suggest improvements. Patent attorneys work alone for much of the time, and the value of collaboration and teamwork in our profession is underestimated.]

DRAFTING SKILLS

More Detailed Papers

Technical field

Contents

This further paper discusses the relationship between the applicant's field(s) of endeavour and the scope of protection that can be obtained for other technical features. UK, US and EPO decisions relating to technical field are discussed and the difference between defined field of endeavour and the field of search of an examiner is explained.

After studying this paper, you should

1. Understand the effect that a selected definition of field of endeavour within a class has on the ambit available for other technical features within a claim.

2. Understand the importance of questioning the inventor as to field of endeavour and agreeing with him the field that should be claimed.

3. Understand when it is appropriate to define a narrow field of endeavour, a broad field of endeavour or a range of fields of endeavour of different scope.

4. Be able to identify features that should be inserted into the main independent claims and into dependent claims in order to define the applicant's field of endeavour.

The underestimated significance of technical field

An applicant is free to define in his specification the width of the field of endeavour ("technical field") to which his invention relates. That is a key decision because it influences the scope of protection that is likely to be available for other technical features.

It is advantageous to treat field of endeavour and other technical features as independent variables that together define the available scope of protection. An invention within a relatively narrow field of endeavour is likely to be definable relatively widely in respect of other technical features, whereas an invention covering a wide technical field is likely to require narrower definition in respect of other technical features. Scope is plotted against width of field to illustrate a solution space in which inventions will normally appear as rectangles, the height of an inventive rectangle within that space depending on the width of the field selected (see the accompanying Figure).[353]

---

353. The distinction between "Invention A" and "Invention B" and the idea that Invention A is usually the more valuable were suggested by Keith Beresford.

**Relationship between available claim scope
and width of inventor's field of endeavour**

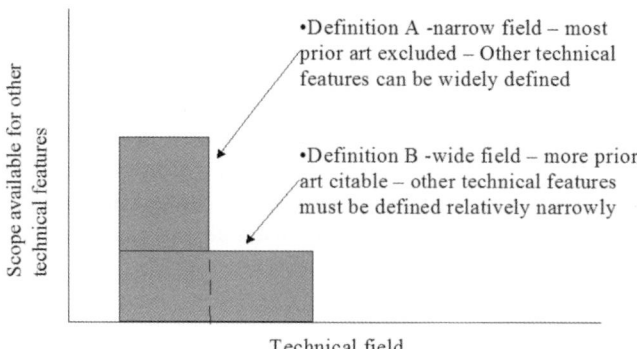

What width of field is it appropriate to select in a given case? The relevant factors are:
(1) The technical nature of the invention; and
(2) The field of endeavour or business in which the inventor is working.

The decision about width of field should not be left to an examiner or to the court but instead requires active consideration on the part of the draftsman in consultation with the inventor and inclusion of field-specific features in the main independent claims and/or in subsidiary claims.

Field of endeavour is not coterminous with examiner's search field

An effective field-specific limitation can be a relatively small feature within a known class of devices provided that the feature distinguishes those devices that fall within the inventor's field of endeavour from other devices that though superficially similar are nevertheless sufficiently distinct that the problem facing the inventor does not arise. The UK Court of Appeal decision in *Molins v Industrial Machine Co., Ltd*[354] provides an example. The specification of the patent in issue explained the invention as follows, with an amendment allowed by the Court of Appeal being shown in italics:

> This invention relates to cigarette-making machines of the continuous rod type wherein tobacco is fed from a hopper and showered so as to be directed downwardly into a trough by a picker roller extending lengthwise of the trough, the said trough having a travelling band or web of cigarette paper capable of moving at a high speed *(i e, equivalent to more than 900 cigarettes per minute)* relatively thereto (hereinafter called "the type described") The invention has for its object the provision of means for improving the consistency of the cigarette rod produced upon such machines running at high speeds.

354. (1938) 55 RPC 31; GB-A-325265 (Molins)

In cigarette making machines of the above type, the tobacco is showered vertically into the trough of the machine, and it will be understood that where the same meets a web of paper running at a high speed there is a tendency for variations to occur in the density of the rod, due to the vertically falling tobacco suddenly assuming a horizontal movement.

The present invention consists of a cigarette making machine of the type described wherein the tobacco showered into the trough of the machine is given a movement having a component in the direction of movement of the cigarette rod, prior to the showered tobacco engaging with the said band or web of cigarette paper as the said band or web moves through the trough.

The invention as claimed was directed to:

A cigarette-making machine of the type described wherein the tobacco showered into the trough of the machine is given a movement having a component in the direction of movement of the band or web of cigarette paper prior to the showered tobacco engaging with the band or web of cigarette paper as the said band or web moves through the trough.

The necessary component of movement was imparted to the tobacco by means of an inclined chute, and a similar inclined chute had been disclosed in an earlier patented cigarette-making machine of an inventor called Bonsack.[355] However, the Bonsack machine could only run at a relatively slow speed at which the problem of irregularity in the tobacco filling of the cigarette rod did not arise. Without the amendment in the written description (which became incorporated into the claim by the reference to *"the type described"*) the claimed subject-matter was anticipated. After the amendment had been allowed the claimed subject-matter was neither anticipated not obvious because a machine capable of running at a speed of over 90 cigarettes a minute was a different machine from Bonsack's machine.[356] In other words, the field or class of product of high-speed machines was distinguishable from the field or class of product of earlier low-speed machines and involved new and different technical problems.

It is apparent from this decision that the inventor's field of endeavour does not necessarily correspond to the technical field suggested by the official classification used by the national or regional patent office under which an application will be examined and granted. Both the Molins and the Bonsack machines were cigarette-making machines of similar structure, would be expected to be classified within the same official class, and would therefore be listed in the same file list for official searching purposes. However, the UK Court of Appeal accepted that the inventor's field of endeavour was concerned with the high-speed machines which were subject

---

355. GB 1896/00198

356. Interestingly, although the *Molins* specification in its un-amended form referred to *high speed* there was no reference to the particular speed of more than 900 cigarettes/minute. Insertion of the speed limitation was apparently permissible under the 1907 Act by way of explanation and/or disclaimer. A similar amendment might be permissible under current disclaimer practice, see the EPO Enlarged Appeal Board decision in *Disclaimer/PPG* G 0001/03, although it might be more difficult and open to question.

to the problem of density variation and not to the low-speed machines where this problem was not apparent. It was the inventor's field of endeavour which was decisive, not the scope of the relevant official Patent Office classification. It will be found in practice that most examiners are receptive to arguments of this kind when considering novelty and inventive step. For such arguments to be available for use, however, the appropriate definitions must appear in the application as filed, since it will usually be impossible to add them later during prosecution or during post-grant amendment proceedings. That is especially true in Europe having regard to the prohibitions on added subject-matter in section 76 of the UK Patents Act, 1977 and Article 123(2) EPC.

A further UK example of the importance of field of endeavour is provided by the *Workmate* case[357] where again a field-specific limitation made the difference between validity and invalidity. In that case, the critical field-defining element was the word *workbench.* That element distinguished the claimed product from the closest prior art which was a mere attachment for a workbench.

In *Haberman v Jackel*[358] the field of the inventor's endeavour was a drinking vessel *suitable for use as trainer cup or the like.* These words were held to distinguish the claimed invention from a baby feeding bottle which was a product of a different class for use with infants at an earlier stage of development.

EPO cases concerning field of endeavour

Under the jurisprudence of the EPO Appeal Boards, the scope of the inventor's field of endeavour as defined in the claims is fundamental to problem/solution analysis, because the starting point prior art on the basis of which the technical problem which the inventor has solved will almost always be within the applicant's defined field of endeavour and not in some allied or more remote field.[359]

The applicant or patentee has the option to decide whether to claim the invention within a broad or narrow field of endeavour and correspondingly to increase or decrease the range of citations which are potentially relevant. That proposition is supported by the following extract from the decision in *Pistons/AE PLC:*[360]

> If... a person skilled in the art prefers and decides to start from a specific compressor piston, he can further develop that piston but at the end of that development the normal result will still be a compressor piston and not an [internal combustion engine] piston. In other words, the chosen closest prior art

---

357. *Hickman v Andrews* [1983] RPC 147, see the paper in this volume at page 271.

358. [1999] FSR 683, see the paper in this volume beginning at page 297.

359 There is a well-known joke about a man asking the way to X and receiving the reply: "Well, I definitely would not start from here!" This reply should constantly be borne in mind when considering possible starting-point references against which inventive character of subsequently developed subject-matter should be judged – it is essential to select a fair and appropriate starting point.

360. T 0570/91

must be able or at least potentially able, perhaps after modifications, to obtain the same effects as those resulting from the claimed embodiment... Otherwise, such starting point prior art could not lead a skilled person in an obvious way to the claimed invention.

An alternative way of expressing the proposition is that a generically different document cannot provide a technically realistic starting point for evaluating inventive step: see, for example, *Optical Illumination System/PHILIPS*.[361]

It should be noted that in order to be effective, a field-related restriction should appear in or be introduced by amendment into the claims, and a mere statement in the description will not suffice.

US cases concerning field of endeavour

In the US, field-related arguments arise less frequently than in Europe but the same drafting considerations apply so that field-related arguments are available to be deployed when appropriate. The US Supreme Court has approved[362] proximity or remoteness as a criterion for evaluating inventive step:

> But, where the alleged novelty consists in transferring a device from one branch of industry to another, the answer depends upon a variety of considerations. In such cases we are bound to inquire into the remoteness of relationship of the two industries, what alternations were necessary to adapt the device to its new use, and what the value of such adaptation has been to the new industry. If the new use be analogous to the former one, the court will undoubtedly be disposed to construe the patent more strictly, and to require clearer proof of the exercise of the inventive faculty in adapting it to the new use, particularly if the device be one of minor importance in its new field of usefulness. On the other hand, if the transfer be to a branch of industry but remotely allied to the other, and the effect of such transfer has been to supersede other methods of doing the same work, the court will look with a less critical eye upon the means employed in making the transfer. Doubtless, a patentee is entitled to every use of which his invention is susceptible, whether such use be known or unknown to him; but the person who has taken his device, and, by improvements thereon, has adapted it to a different industry, may also draw to himself the quality of inventor.

In re Clay[363] is a frequently cited example of a case where a prior art reference was held to be non-analogous and therefore not citable. The invention concerned the storage of refined liquid hydrocarbons in a tank, and used a gel to reduce the dead space in the tank. The gel was known, but only from a reference concerning the reduction in permeability of subterranean hydrocarbon-bearing formations. The

---

361. T 0870/96; see *Case Law of the Boards of Appeal of the European Patent Office*, 4th Ed. at p. 104.

362. *C & P Potts & Co v Creager*, 155 U.S. 597 (1895)

363. 966 F.2d 656, 23 USPQ2d 1058 (Fed. Cir. 1992)

CAFC held that the reference describing the gel was irrelevant to inventive step because it was neither within the field of the invention nor relevant to the technical problem. *In re Oetiker*[364] provides a further example where a reference disclosing a garment fastener was held not to be analogous art citable against the inventive character of an invention relating to a hose clamp.

A US examiner has an absolute right to rely on a reference in support of an objection of lack of inventive step if that reference falls within the field of the applicant's endeavour. If it lies outside the field he has a only qualified right to rely on that reference depending on whether that reference is relevant to the particular problem with which the inventor is concerned.[365]

Field of endeavour during prosecution

The effect of a field-specific limitation is often that the prior art reference disappears both from the standpoint of lack of novelty and from the standpoint of lack of inventive step.

For example, in *Second Medical Indication/EISAI*[366] the invention related to the *use of [a chemical compound] in the preparation of a pharmaceutical composition against deafness and tinnitus.* By definition the field of the invention became restricted to medicaments for treating deafness and tinnitus, and a reference unrelated to that field was unlikely to provide a plausible primary reference, and had little persuasive power even when considered as a secondary reference. Likewise in *Friction reducing additive/MOBIL OIL III*[367] the claimed invention was *use of [a defined amount by weight of a compound of a defined genus] as a friction reducing additive in a lubricant composition comprising a major portion of a lubricating oil.* Once the claim had been limited in this way, documents disclosing the compounds as rust inhibiting additives became irrelevant, as is apparent from the following passage from the decision of the Technical Board of Appeal concerning inventive step:[368]

> In the present case, in relation to the issue of inventive step, the technical problem underlying the subject-matter claimed… is to provide a further additive for a lubricant composition for directly reducing the friction between sliding surfaces in engines. In the Board's judgement none of the prior documents relied upon in the opposition are concerned with this problem, and a skilled man wishing to solve that problem and reading these prior documents would receive no relevant teaching.

---

364. 977 F.2d 1443, 24 USPQ2d 1443 (Fed. Cir. 1992).

365. MPEP at para. 2141.01

366. G 0005/83

367. G 0002/88)

368. T 0059/87: this was the decision of the EPO Appeal Board in which it decided to refer the question of second non-medical use claims for consideration by the Enlarged Appeal Board.

Narrowing defined scope for inventor's field of endeavour is often better than limiting other technical features

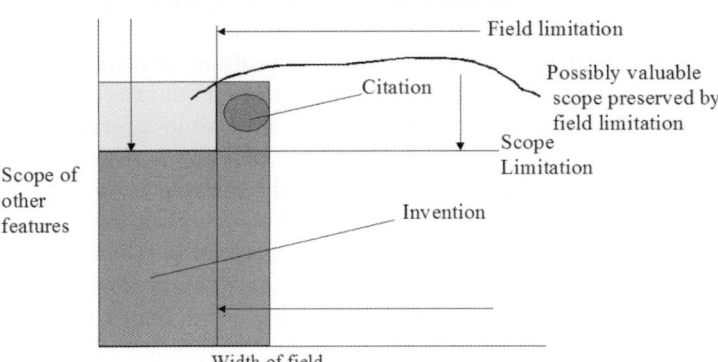

When you encounter prior art that requires limitation in a previously desired claim scope, it is usually preferable first to consider whether limitation of the technical field can avoid the citation, and only after that possibility has been eliminated to go on to consider the limitation of other technical features. That sequence reduces the likelihood of spuriously limiting claim scope in the technical fields which are of greatest commercial importance to the applicants and accidentally opening the way for third parties to design around the patent (see accompanying Figure).

For example, suppose that an inventor has disclosed a genus of compounds which are useful as dental cements. A citation which comes to light during prosecution discloses a species of compounds within that genus for bonding together the layers of glass in a laminated automobile windscreen. An inexperienced attorney focusing on the patentability of the compounds *per se* may be tempted to limit the genus of compounds covered so as to exclude the previously disclosed species. The effect is to set competitors free to use the disclaimed species as dental cements: the excluded compounds may not be the preferred compounds but they have previously been regarded as fit for purpose, and that may indeed prove to be the case, opening a way for designing around the patent in the very field of endeavour with which the inventors are concerned. It is much better to specify in the main independent claims that the invention concerns dental cements, thereby covering *all* the compounds within the original genus for this end us for example in a method of treatment claim (US) or in a Swiss-form use claim (Europe) restricted to dentistry. A further independent claim to novel compounds *per se,* which it is desirable to maintain, will still have to be restricted to avoid the novelty-destroying citation by disclaiming the previously disclosed species, but not with the effect of opening up the compounds within that species for dental use.

Practical steps

It is essential that the draftsman makes himself aware of the field of endeavour in which the invention originated, possible allied fields where there is a foreseeable possibility that the invention could be used, and more remote and speculative fields of use which it is not. The appropriate scope of claim is set by

(1) the technical nature of the invention; and

(2) the nature of the business within which the inventors are engaged.

It is therefore critical to investigate both the technical and the marketing implications of field of endeavour, and to incorporate appropriate definition(s) in the application as filed. New post-filing generalizations may be difficult to achieve.

In the dental cement example referred to above, the compounds can in principle have any utility and may, for example, be good for adhering laminated glass in automobile windscreens or panels in aircraft structures. Their generic field of endeavour is therefore as adhesive compositions. However, in the example, the invention originated in the dental supplies division of a pharmaceutical company, in which case the more restricted utilities that should be disclosed in the application as filed are as medical or dental adhesives, and then even more specifically as dental adhesives. The latter utilities may call for particular standards that are not applicable to general engineering adhesives, for example standards of purity or sterility. Furthermore, the dental use may call for packaging in particular forms, and with particular volumes of the compounds. All of these features assist in defining technical field and can be made the subject of useful dependent claims. However, they will not be available for use unless the relevant information has been included in the application as filed, and necessary to cover or which could be abandoned during prosecution without detriment.

Omission or inadequate disclosure of field of use is a recurrent fault found in specifications drafted by inexperienced attorneys, and examples of this fault can be found in nearly every technical field with which our profession is concerned. Where such a fault occurs, it may have significant adverse effects on the scope of claims obtainable during prosecution. For example, a draftsman may be so fascinated with the motion produced by a particular hinge structure and the details of the linkage that produces that motion that he omits to mention that the hinge structure is for doors attached to kitchen cabinets. If he is confronted during prosecution with a reference disclosing a similar linkage for controlling an aircraft door, he may lack basis for a more specific claim to a kitchen cabinet structure incorporating the hinge, and either the patent may issue with claims of unnecessarily restricted scope or the application may be refused.

The background section and the closest prior art

Contents

This further paper reviews approaches to identification of the closest prior art, and drafting styles based on an anecdotal approach (no prior art discussed), a specific approach (closest known prior art discussed) and a review approach (prior art extensively reviewed as in an academic thesis).

After you have studied this paper and the "must-read" materials you should be:

1. Aware of the opportunities for keyword-based and classification-based searches and the general nature of the IPC.

2. Aware of the different approaches adopted by European and US practitioners to the identification of prior art at the time of filing.

3. Able to identify closest starting point prior art from a European standpoint.

4. Able to draft a concise Background section based on a specific starting point prior art reference.

Investigating prior art

Sources of the prior art to be considered when drafting the background section may come from the inventor's own knowledge, especially if he is an academic who keeps up to date with the literature in his field of research or an inventor in a large corporation with in-house information specialists.

The ability of an attorney to make pre-filing checks for background art cost-effectively has been transformed by the Internet, which has put simple and rapid keyword-based prior art searching on our desktops, and enabled investigations to be carried out in a matter of minutes which only a few years ago would have taken hours or days of professional time. It has created a minor revolution in the quality of service that we can routinely offer clients, and in the quality of the patent specifications that we can routinely prepare.

The readily available databases have their individual strengths and limitations, and it is routine to consult several of them during the information gathering process which should be a preliminary to specification drafting. The USPTO enables full text keyword searching of US patent specifications published since 1976 and of published US patent applications, and the published text contains links to cited prior art. The *esp@cenet* database of the European Patent Office (EPO) allows keyword searching of the title and abstract, and when a reference has been found enables the full text to be downloaded and images of the published document to be printed, at present page by page. Coverage includes EPO, PCT and a wide range of national patent applications, and is particularly good for early published specifications. The Delphion database enables patent specifications to be downloaded as single pdf files (particularly convenient for sending by e-mail) and has links both to prior art citations and to forward references so that once a relevant reference has been found it is easy to search both forwards for subsequently developed prior art and backwards for previous cited references. In particular fields, specialised databases such as Chemical Abstracts or the NCBI database may be helpful. Search engines such as Google provide further assistance to supplement and cross-check what is found in the patent databases. Keyword investigations in these databases and search engines cannot hope to produce a comprehensive result: for example a search for banknote printing will not reveal references in which the patentee has referred only to the printing of security paper (sometimes used as a synonym for banknotes). However, it is possible relatively quickly to build up a collection of relevant prior art in the selected field, which can provide invaluable background information to assist the drafting process, reveal the general trends of development in the field in question, often suggest alternative embodiments or additional lines of enquiry for the inventor, and provide a starting point for identification or confirmation of novel features in the client's invention.

The information gathering process will normally not be limited to checking overall novelty, but will also include checks into the availability of key components or starting materials, possible manufacturing materials, and variants that may achieve the same or similar technical effects to the invention. Much information can be gleaned from visiting the website of the applicant or his employer, competitor websites, and component supplier websites. If the practitioner is told the basic information about a new invention in advance of the first meeting, relatively straightforward investigations can provide useful insight and permit focused and informed questioning.

The preliminary keyword-based searches may be backed up by systematic subject-matter searching based on classified file lists produced by the patent offices. Patent classification is a massive subject in itself, and the details are outside the scope of this book but for the sake of completeness a bare outline of the subject will be presented.

The most commonly used classification is the International Patent Classification (IPC) organised and maintained by the World Intellectual Property Organization (WIPO) which classifies on a hierarchical structure. At the top level, the whole body of knowledge that may be regarded as proper to the field of patents for invention, divided into eight sections entitled as follows:

A   HUMAN NECESSITIES

B   PERFORMING OPERATIONS; TRANSPORTING

C   CHEMISTRY; METALLURGY

D   TEXTILES; PAPER

E   FIXED CONSTRUCTIONS

F   MECHANICAL ENGINEERING; LIGHTING;
     HEATING; WEAPONS; BLASTING

G   PHYSICS

H   ELECTRICITY.

Each section is subdivided into classes, a class symbol consisting of a section symbol followed by a two-digit number. The class title indicates the content of the class to which it refers, for example A 01 AGRICULTURE; FORESTRY; ANIMAL HUSBANDRY; HUNTING; TRAPPING; FISHING.

Each class comprises one or more subclasses whose symbol consists of the class symbol followed by a capital letter, and is associated with a title indicating as precisely as possible the content of the subclass, for example A 01 B SOIL WORKING IN AGRICULTURE OR FORESTRY; PARTS, DETAILS, OR ACCESSORIES OF AGRICULTURAL MACHINES OR IMPLEMENTS, IN GENERAL.

Each subclass is broken down into subdivisions referred to as "groups", which are either main groups or subgroups. Each group symbol consists of the subclass symbol followed by two numbers separated by an oblique stroke. Each main group symbol consists of the subclass symbol followed by a one- to three-digit number, the oblique stroke and the number 00, and is associated with a title, for example A 01 B 1 /00 Hand tools.

Subgroups form subdivisions under the main groups. Each subgroup symbol consists of the subclass symbol followed by the one- to three-digit number of its main group, the oblique stroke and a number of at least two digits other than 00. Any third or subsequent digit after the oblique stroke is to be understood as a decimal subdivision of the digit preceding it, e.g., 3/426 is to be found after 3/42 and before 3/43, and 5/1185 is to be found after 5/118 and before 5/119. The subgroup title defines a field of subject-matter within the scope of its main group considered to be useful for search purposes. It is preceded by one or more dots indicating the hierarchical position of that subgroup, i.e., indicating that each subgroup forms a subdivision of the nearest group above it that has one dot less. The subgroup title is often a complete expression, in which case it begins with a capital letter. A subgroup title begins with a lower case letter if it reads as a continuation of the title of the next higher, less indented group i.e. having one dot less. In all cases, the subgroup title must be read as being dependent upon, and restricted by, the title of the group under which it is indented, for example:

A 01 B 1 / 00	Hand tools
1.16	– Tools for uprooting weeds
1 / 24	– for treating meadows or lawns.

The EPO operates a classification system called ECLA which is an extension of the IPC with additional subgroups being added to the IPC symbol.

Once an appropriate IPC or ECLA symbol(s) have been identified, they may be entered into the *esp@cenet* database to retrieve documents falling into that classification. For example, using the *Advanced Search* facility of *esp@cenet*, entering WO to select specifications published under the PCT and under the IPC symbol A01B1/16 produced a list of 18 results, of which WO 2005/011355 (Weed Removal Tool) and WO 2004/052082 (Gardening Implement) are typical.

A number of directories are available online from WIPO. These include an *Official Catchword Index* and an *International Patent Classification: Guide*. A good way of finding useful classifications to search is by identifying one or more relevant specifications using keyword searching, noting the IPC symbols under which they are classified, and looking up these symbols in the classification guide. It should be emphasised, however, that searching using these classified indexes is a specialised skill best performed by an information specialist working under the direction of a patent attorney, and that a search by a beginner working on his own is likely to be neither complete nor cost-effective. Guidance as to the appropriate selection of headings may be available from the UK Patent Office through their classification section or from the EPO but the level of assistance that they can give for instance during a short telephone conversation is limited.

The USPTO has its own classification system based on classes and subclasses which it operates in parallel with the IPC classification.

The question then arises which you should do: keyword searching or classification-based searching. The answer, ideally, is both and iteratively using early results to shape and refine the subsequent investigation. Particularly effective results can sometimes be achieved by using a generic heading in combination with a keyword. For example, to find specifications disclosing garden tools made of stainless steel it would be worth searching the esp@cenet database using the general heading A01B1/00 in combination with the keywords *stainless, chromium* or *nickel*.

In larger corporate organizations, information specialists will routinely conduct classified patent searches, prior, for example, to referring a proposal to file a patent application to an internal review committee. Arranging such searches through private search firms or through patent offices such as the UK Patent Office, the EPO and the Swedish Patent Office which are willing to perform searches on a contractual basis for inventors in SME's and for private individuals is less routine because it introduces delay and adds to cost. In the UK, it may be preferable to make a first filing accompanied by a request for a search, the results of the UK official search typically being made available within about two or three months from the initial filing date. Thereafter during the priority year it may be wise to arrange an in-house search, a search using a private firm of searchers, or a contractual search by the EPO. Even if time and resources do not permit a pre-filing classified search, it should be an objective to have completed such a search before the end of the priority year so that the results are available before expensive foreign filing decisions have to be considered.

It should also be realised that searches within the financial resources available at the application stage are invariably less than fully comprehensive: it impossible to advise that the invention is new on the basis of a pre-filing search, merely that a screening investigation has been carried out and that the invention has not yet been shown to have been anticipated. Experience shows that however much effort is devoted to pre-filing novelty searches, the official searches carried out during prosecution and/or the further searches carried out by an opponent or defendant in infringement proceedings are likely to reveal additional relevant material. Furthermore, pre-filing searches are document-based and do not cover potentially very relevant disclosures by prior use, which are more likely to come to light at the opposition stage.

The European view of an appropriate starting-point reference

Throughout the search process, and when investigations have been completed, we should be preparing to decide what shall be our primary reference used as a basis of comparison with the invention, and what are the most relevant secondary references.

Inventors do not work in a vacuum. As Markey J, a former chief judge of the US Court of Appeals for the Federal Circuit, memorably said: *"Only God works from nothing. Man must work with old elements."*[369] Creating an invention normally involves selecting a starting point and following a creative process that brings in additional elements and relationships to achieve a new function or result that lies at the heart of the invention. Reconstructing that process and in particular identifying a starting point within the field of endeavour to which the invention relates that can be used as a basis of comparison permits differences between the invention and the prior art to be more readily identified.

The EPO Examination Guidelines explain that in order to assess inventive step we should determine that combination of features, disclosed in one single reference, which constitutes the most promising starting point for an obvious development leading to the invention. In the UK High Court, Pumfrey J has suggested[370] that the above approach may not be universally appropriate:

> There are… possible difficulties with this approach… its concentration on the closest prior art… must stem from a belief that if an invention is not obvious in the light of the closest prior art it cannot be obvious in the light of anything further away. This runs the risk of offending against the principle that a skilled man must be permitted to do that which is obvious in the light of each individual item of prior art seen in the light of the common general knowledge.

The logic of this criticism is difficult to understand. If an invention is obvious over "something further away" but not over the apparently closest prior art, then that which was further away must by definition have been a more promising starting

---

369. *"Why not the Statute?"* 65 Journal of the Patent Office Society 331.

370. *Rambaxy UK Limited v Warner-Lambert Company*, [2005] EWHC 2142 (Patents), 12 October 2005

point. The difficulty is therefore not with the existence of the starting point but with its correct identification.[371]

In *Soild stabilizer composition/ENICHEM,*[372] the EPO Appeal Board suggested the following basis for selecting the starting point disclosure:

> It seems that in most cases it is appropriate to look particularly at those prior art disclosures which have something to do, be it explicitly or implicitly, with the problem set out in the application or opposed patent. These disclosures will normally either be capable of being further developed to arrive at the claimed invention or at least point thereto. The closest prior art, i.e. that which provides the strongest basis for an obviousness objection, will then be selected from the above-mentioned disclosures.

In *Hydroxypolyalkylene amine/DOVER,*[373] the EPO Appeal Board explained that:

> It is case law of the Boards of Appeal that the starting point for the assessment of inventive step should be one which is at least "promising"… in the sense that there was some probability of a skilled person arriving at the claimed invention. Quite apart from the fact that a skilled person would normally not consider an obviously defective disclosure at all, the Board deems it in particular artificial to select such defective disclosure as a starting point for evaluating inventive step, when there exists other prior art which is not doubted with regard to its disclosure but is also directed to the same purpose or effect as the patent in suit.

The best starting point is therefore not necessarily the disclosure that happens to be structurally closest if it does not concern properties that are relevant to the technical problem. It is often necessary during prosecution of an application to argue that the primary reference should be a different document from that selected by the examiner, and to base the preamble or classifying part of a two-part claim on what is disclosed in that other document. For such an argument to be effective, it is necessary to put forward to the examiner a specific alternative primary reference.

It is essential to select the starting point disclosure, in a way that is fair to the patentee. Fields where research is systematic so that later inventions truly build on the work of earlier inventors are distinguishable from fields where research is empirical, and it is misleading to assume that successive disclosures build one on

---

371. Second-best is not usually attractive. Second-best endeavours in a contract are unlikely to be a good business proposition. We do not offer employment to the second-best available candidate for a job. After our investigations are complete, we do not prosecute the second most likely suspect in a criminal case, nor do we prosecute a group of suspects in the alternative for the crime of a single individual in the hope that we can obtain a conviction against one of them. Why should patent cases be different? The only reason for the deference given to less relevant references in patent cases is fear that our investigations may be incomplete or that our technical analysis may be incorrect. Confidence in the work we do, and positive selection of a best starting point based on technical analysis and knowledge of the relevant jurisprudence leads to a shorter, more direct and more positive approach.

372. T 0590/91

373. T 0211/01 – 3.3.6

another. The UK decision in *Beecham Group's (Amoxycillin) Application*[374] illustrates the latter situation. The field of the invention was semi-synthetic penicillins. Prior to the patent, the leading compound in the field was Ampicillin which had been medically and commercially successful, and there had been intense research aimed at finding an even better compound. That research had given rise to a large body of literature, but no better compound had emerged. The patent in issue was based on the discovery that Amoxycillin had a better combination of properties that Ampicillin and was the hoped-for better compound. It is submitted that when defining the technical problem addressed by the Amoxycillin inventors, the proper starting point was Ampicillin itself because that was the known compound with the best properties relating to the invention. No lesser starting point would be appropriate. The technical problem was firstly to find out whether it was possible to make another semi-synthetic penicillin with better properties than Ampicillin and secondly to identify that better compound. Until that problem had been solved, no one piece of prior art which failed to disclose the solution was any better than any other piece of prior art that failed to disclose the solution, and none of the failed prior art was better than Ampicillin itself. Any suggestion that a reference that happened to disclose structurally similar compounds to Amoxicillin, without clearly teaching improved activity, was a better starting point than Ampicillin *only* from hindsight.

US approach to prior art

When evaluating inventive step, US patent practice, especially before the USPTO, recognises a primary reference as having the closest similarity to the claimed subject-matter, and secondary references as providing additional features.

The USPTO requires disclosure during prosecution of any prior art known to the applicant which creates a *substantial question of patentability*. Failure to comply with that requirement amounts to inequitable conduct which can render any issued patent unenforceable, and in some circumstances can involve the prosecuting attorney in allegations of professional misconduct. Inequitable conduct defences are routinely raised during litigation and are aggressively pursued. The draconian penalties for non-disclosure, coupled with the ease of adding a reference to a disclosure statement to be filed at the USPTO and filing a photocopy if the reference is other than a US patent, cause attorneys to take an expansive view of what should be disclosed. It is much less time consuming, and legally far less risky for the applicant, to add a reference to the disclosure statement than it is to make a detailed analysis of that reference and decide whether or not its disclosure is mandatory. As well as the inequitable conduce "push" there is a presumptive "pull". The examiner is obliged to study each reference in the disclosure statement and record that he has done so. There is then a presumption that the resulting issued patent is valid over each reference that the examiner has recorded that he has studied.

---

374. [1980] RPC 261, reviewed at [1979] EIPR 316, see also the corresponding decision in New Zealand [1980] 1 NZLR 192 (at first instance) and [1982] FSR 181 on appeal where the technical subject-matter was more fully analysed. It may be noted that patentability in both countries was only upheld because the claims had been restricted from the original compound *per se* claim to a claim for "A pharmaceutical composition adapted for oral administration"

However, many US practitioners are unwilling to commit themselves in advance to the identification of any particular reference that they become aware of during their pre-filing investigations as being closest prior art. The reason is that it represents a deviation from their normal practice of filing at the USPTO a list of disclosed documents without comment on their contents and leaving it to the examiner to decide which, if any, of them he or she considers pertinent. There is a fear amongst some (but not all) US attorneys that singling out any particular reference as the closest prior art, if mistaken, might itself raise inequitable conduct issues. It is submitted that the benefits of systematic technical analysis outweigh such risks, and that evaluation of technical differences based on a stated starting point is an approach that is both legitimate and beneficial.

Contents of the background section

For the reasons explained above, there is at present no consensus as between European attorneys (including those in the UK) and US attorneys about whether the background section should be confined to a generalised discussion without particular references ("the anecdotal approach") or whether the closest prior art should be identified ("the specific approach")

(a) The anecdotal approach

Many influential US attorneys, but not all US attorneys, now recommend an anecdotal approach in which the Background is of a general nature only, identifies no starting point in the prior art, and identifies no object or technical problem. The anecdotal approach now widely adopted by some large US-based corporate patentees is exemplified by US-A-6961467 (Sirivara, Intel), the introductory part of which reads as follows:

> The invention generally relates to identifying image content, and more particularly to using perceptual features of image data, e.g., an image or movie, for identifying the image data and illicit distribution thereof.
>
> Widespread availability of fast network connections has resulted in proliferation of software allowing users to share large data files encoding content, such as audio encodings (e.g., MP3 files), video encodings (e.g., Moving Picture Experts Group (MPEG), Microsoft Co.'s Video for Windows, Intel Co.'s Indeo, Apple Co.'s QuickTime, etc.), and other content and data files.
>
> Well-known content sharing application programs include the Napster program created by Shawn Fannin, as well as Macster (Napster for Macintosh computers), Gnapster, and others. Older and more traditional file-sharing application programs, include the File Transfer Protocol (FTP), Unix-to-Unix Copy (UUCP), University of Minnesota's Gopher, etc. (Please note that all marks used herein are the property of their respective owners.)
>
> Unfortunately, ease of content sharing has resulted in significant amounts of intentional and unintentional violation of intellectual property rights for shared content. This has resulted in many legal actions to shut down and ban use of content sharing application programs. Unfortunately, such actions also impede legitimate sharing.

It may be that the draftsman of the above specification had extensively researched previous solutions to the problem, and had used a closest prior art reference as the basis for difference identification and subsequent claim drafting. Or it may be that the draftsman had simply taken the inventor's disclosure at face value and drafted on the basis of what he had been told, without benefit of any investigation or analysis of the prior art. So far as the document as filed is concerned, things would look no different either way. There is a temptation to cut corners by not conducting a systematic prior art search and analysis, and a risk that the state of the art may be misunderstood, as in the *Windsurfer* patent.

(b) The specific approach

On the European view, one of the most important tasks in the Background section is to identify and discuss the closest prior art that provides a starting point for comparison with the subject-matter claimed, and possibly the earlier developments in the field of endeavour of the inventor that led up to that starting point. The selected starting point should be identified by a specific patent number, literature reference or other well-defined disclosure, so that the features that are clearly and unambiguously disclosed in that closest prior art, expressly or implicitly, can be identified.

US-A-6290464 (Negulescu *et. Al.*, BMW Rolls-Royce GmbH) provides an example of a European-originating invention where the specific approach was used. Under "Field of the invention" it mentions two references which indicate the state of the art, in the Background section, it discusses a specific starting point reference, and under "Summary of the Invention" it refers to the problems associated with the prior art and the particular solution with which the invention is concerned. The relevant portions read as follows:

> This invention relates to a blade of a turbomachine, more particularly of an axial-flow high-pressure turbine, having at least one integrated cooling air duct, which when viewed in the direction of flow of the working gas conducted by the blade, issues at the downstream back of the blade root. This invention also relates to a rotor disk of a turbomachine having several blades designed in accordance with the present invention. For related state of the art, reference is made to GB 2 057 573 A and DE 32 10 626 C2.
>
> A blade of this description may find use in the high-pressure turbine of an aircraft gas turbine engine. An optimally designed cooling system of a high-performance aircraft engine then requires for each of its generally multiple turbine stages, especially high-pressure turbine stages, an optimized, i.e. minimized, flow of cooling air of a suitably adapted inlet temperature and feed pressure. The first high-pressure turbine stage, for example, obtains its cooling air from the final stage of a multiple-stage compressor, which in aircraft engines is arranged upstream of the high-pressure turbine, while the second high-pressure turbine stage obtains its cooling air from one of the final compressor stages, and a third turbine stage, if present, obtains its cooling air from one of the central compressor stages. An engine cooling system designed along these lines needs a complex cooling air ducting network flange-mounted to the compressor and turbine casings. Said design is however impaired by its heavy weight and susceptibility to breakdowns.
>
> For cooling the turbine stages, especially high-pressure turbine stages, i.e. for cooling the associated blades and rotor disks, use can generally also be

made of the internal cooling air flow of the turbomachine/gas turbine or aircraft engine, said flow normally being delivered by a single feed source of cooling air, i.e., by the final compressor stage, but this cooling air flow lacks adequate cooling capacity especially for the final high-pressure turbine stage of the multiple-stage high-pressure turbine, considering that said cooling air flow necessarily picks up heat in its passage along the preceding cooling air ducts. Said preceding cooling air ducts normally extend through the turbine rotor disk or the roots of the blades arranged on the rotor disk, as is shown in particular in the initially cited GB 2 057 573 A.

The object underlying the present invention is to provide a remedy for the problem described above. The solution of this problem is to provide an arrangement characterized in that the cooling air duct issuing at the back of the blade root branches off from a cooling air chamber provided in the blade root from which at least one cooling air duct issuing at the gas-wetted surface of the blade is provided with cooling air, and in that the cooling air duct issuing at the back of the blade root is designed to deflect the cooling air stream it carries while providing a substantially continuous passage.

It is submitted that the specific approach is preferable for European applications and should for consistency be followed in cases sent from Europe to the US. The caution advocated by our US colleagues is sufficiently recognised by including only a relatively short factual explanation of the closest prior art and any references leading up to it, and by giving a balanced view of the prior art reference(s) including both features which are shared with the invention and features which differ and perhaps point away from it so that the Background section is not inadvertently slanted so as to make arguments for novelty and inventive step more difficult. One disadvantage of an anecdotal Background section is that it is difficult to tell from the patent specification itself (a) whether the closest known prior art in the inventor's field of endeavour has been identified, and was available for systematic comparison and (b) whether that prior art is a specific citable disclosure that was truly available to the public before the priority or filing date of the application and was not e.g. the in-house prior art of another inventor. A further disadvantage is that error may be introduced into the Background section, as the *Windsurfer* case illustrates.[375] Even more seriously, the step of systematic comparison with the closest prior art is more easily omitted, with the consequence that important detail and its significance may be overlooked, again as happened in the *Windsurfer* case. These advantages are significant, and patents that are open and informative in their discussion of the prior art should in the long run do better than those which hide behind anecdotal discussions.

We can regard the process of making an invention as going from starting position D1 within the applicant's field of endeavour as shown in the accompanying diagram to various allowable claim scopes based on Diff.1, Diff.1+Diff.2, Diff.1+Diff.3 and Diff.1+Diff.4 depending upon whether the citable prior art is D1+D2, or a combination of D1+D3, D1+D4 or D1+D5, these being various putative more relevant secondary references that might be found during search and examination. The question arises as to what should be cited in the background section to explain the process of development

---

375. See pages 230-232

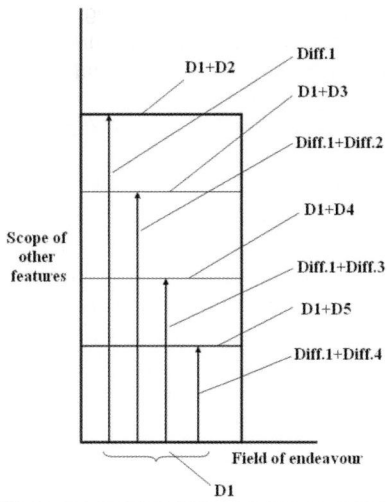

leading to the invention, and in particular whether we should cite the primary reference D1, both the primary reference D1 and the cited reference D2, or neither D1 nor D2 unless and until required to do so by the Patent Office.

The European view is that D1 is best both discussed and identified in the Background section. The question is then whether the Background section should discuss secondary references or lines of development D2-D5 which have been brought in by the inventor during the process that he followed from the starting point prior art D1 to his or her eventual invention. It is submitted that the answer is generally not, and that it is better to postpone discussion of such other references until the detailed description of preferred embodiments, where such secondary references can be presented as explaining and extending the range of alternatives that are within the ambit of the claims rather than undermining the arguments for inventive step.

(c) The generalised review approach

Generalised discussion of the prior art, including references of background interest only, such as is often found in academic theses, is usually as undesirable in a patent specification as it is in a research paper.[376] It is submitted that the legitimate US criticism of prior art discussion in the Background section is mainly applicable to lengthy and unfocused discussions of this type which in addition to making the patent document unnecessarily lengthy and expensive to translate may contain admissions that are subsequently damaging.

---

376. See page 2

Defining the invention

Coverage

The *Micklethwait* and *Daley* papers provide much fundamental guidance about the core skill of claim drafting. This paper explains and recommends systematic technical analysis based on difference identification and ranking and the use of identified differences as the basis for claim drafting. It goes on to consider European and US cases concerning post-filing claim broadening by removing claimed features, and with reference to the facts in *Improver*, the advantages of seeking functional definitions. The need for flexibility and for the inclusion of intermediate generalizations is also explained, as also is the need for coverage of all human activities flowing from the invention

After you have read this paper, you should:

1. Be aware of the advantages of systematically comparing an invention with previously identified closest prior art, identifying *all* differences from which advantages flow, and ranking the differences.

2. Routinely look for differences (ideally a single difference) that produce the most important new function or result, and which forms the basis of the main claim.

3. Be aware of the possible consequences both in Europe and in the US of including unnecessary features in claims, and the importance of routinely checking for such features.

4. Be aware of the dangers of over-structural definitions, and routinely consider alternative more functional definitions.

5. Routinely identify alternative definitions of technical field and alternative combinations of technical features for flexibility at the initial filing stage and avoidance of irrevocable commitment at that early stage to a single definition.

6. "Look up" to consider whether claims should be included to a broader whole of which the invention forms part, and "look down" to consider whether there are important components and sub-combinations that should be claimed.

7. Be aware of the advantages of, and able to use, the "distributed invention" claim format.

Identifying differences

As explained above,[377] by the time that he comes to start identifying differences and drafting claims, an attorney should have available to him both a starting point prior disclosure within the inventor's field of endeavour and details of the new embodiments created by the inventor.

The next step in structured understanding of the invention should be a detailed comparison aimed at identifying *all* differences between the inventor's embodiments and the prior art that are associated with advantageous results. The need to perform this comparison is one of the main reasons why definition of field of endeavour and identification of a suitable prior disclosure to provide a basis for comparison are such important preliminaries in the drafting process.

If it is completely and accurately carried out, the comparison will produce a set of differences that is surprisingly robust to the discovery of new and more relevant prior art. If the starting point reference used as the basis of comparison is within the inventor's field of endeavour, and a set of differences is created including every difference associated with an advantage, then if a new more relevant reference is discovered, a subset of the previously identified differences should be identifiable that will support a more restricted scope of protection. In contrast, without a prior disclosure to provide a reference point, there is no way of being certain that all the important new features will have been identified, and there is a greater risk that if unexpected new prior art comes to light, differences and advantages that would have supported a narrower but still useful scope of protection will not have been identified or adequately highlighted, and the resulting patent may not be accepted during examination or if granted may not survive a challenge.

The task of making a comparison between the inventor's embodiments and the prior art and identifying differences conveniently begins with a "brainstorming" exercise whose primary objective is to produce a comprehensive list. That step will naturally be followed by more detailed study of the differences, identifying reasons for and new functions or results associated with those differences and placing them into a hierarchy of importance. Wherever possible a single difference will be selected as the basis for defining the main independent claims at least at the initial filing stage, but sometimes it will be necessary to select a small group of related differences that collectively produce a new function or result. We should be looking for a single new function or result: more than one such new function or result as the basis for a single independent claim is a warning that the claim may be unduly restricted.[378]

The ranking step may result in the identification of two or more differences or groups of differences producing new functions or results which cannot be linked together and which merit unrelated independent claims, in which case a requirement to divide the patent application can be expected during prosecution.

---

377. At page 201.

378. See the warnings given above at pages 130-132 about "over-selling" the invention.

Defining the invention – technical features

It will be recollected that a claim should specify a set of elements, the necessary relationship between those elements, and expressly or implicitly, a new function or result that flows from selecting those elements and establishing the specified relationships between them. Use of this definition for drafting purposes calls for the following questions to be asked in sequence on the basis of the differences from the starting point prior art which have already been identified:

1. What features are to be included for defining the field of endeavour in which the invention arises?
2. What is the most important new function or result which can be relied on to justify the main independent claims?
3. What elements and relationships between those elements are both necessary and sufficient to produce the new function or result?
4. Are the selected elements and relationships present in all known or foreseeable embodiments or examples of the invention?[379]
5. Is there any element or relationship in the proposed selection that is *unnecessary* or capable of substitution by a foreseeable equivalent? For example, does the claimed subject-matter differ from the closest prior art in more than one feature?
6. Can the elements and the relationships to be included in the claim be defined by functional rather than structural language, possibly starting from means-plus-function or step-plus-function language, but where possible revising it to express each claimed element as a noun covering a genus of structures followed by a broad definition of function?[380]
7. What facts will need to be established in order to prove infringement? In particular, does the claim require features whose presence in an accused product or process would be difficult to prove, for example because of the need for difficult and expensive tests?
8. Should the specification at initial filing contain alternative claims directed to different features in order to avoid irrevocable commitment to a particular view of the invention, leaving the specification flexible up to the time of grant?

Difficulty of removing claimed features post-filing

Filing claims with unnecessary or undesired restrictions can create difficulty under European practice and under the practice of the national patent offices of the EPC contracting states. Not only should an examiner refuse to allow an amendment to remove the restriction if such an amendment is unsupported by the application as filed, but also if he mistakenly does allow such an amendment, the resulting claim is invalid[381] and can be challenged in opposition or revocation proceedings. Amendments to claim scope that would routinely be accepted without comment by

---

379. It will be recollected that at least in the US, embodiments or examples not covered by the claims are "dedicated to the public" and provide a route for designing around the patent.

380. See the paper on *Functional Claims* at page 135.

381. Art. 123(2) EPC.

the USPTO can be impossible to achieve in the EPO. Furthermore, in some instances an offending feature cannot remain in the main claims because it offends against Article 123(2) EPC and cannot be removed because it would impermissibly broaden the claims under Article 123(3) EPC, so that the only course open is for the EPO or national court to revoke the patent. The possibility that the patentee might become caught in such a trap, even where the amendment had previously been approved by an Examining Division, has been recognised by the Enlarged Appeal Board,[382] who nevertheless commented that:

> The ultimate responsibility for any amendment of a patent application (or a patent) always remains that of the applicant (or patentee).

The attitude of the national courts may be less restrictive.[383] However, at the drafting stage, our task is to write claims that will easily survive examination and subsequent hostile challenge, not to create problems that could prove expensive to litigate.

For example, in a case involving the attempted generalization of "natural cellulose fibres" to "cellulose fibres",[384] the EPO Appeal Board explained:

> In the present case, the subject-matter of claim 1 according to the main request can be seen either as a generalisation (natural cellulosic fibres to cellulose fibres in general) or omission of a feature (natural). In either case the subject-matter generated is cellulose fibres other than natural cellulose fibres, and this subject-matter is novel when compared with the original content of the application... Moreover, a future claim to cellulose fibres but disclaiming natural cellulose fibres would be anticipated by the subject-matter generated by the amendment but not by the original application.

A further example is provided by EP-B-0098070 (Secretary of State for Defence). The invention concerned a "passive-type" twisted nematic liquid crystal display in which the state of each pixel in the display could be changed by an applied electric field. It was based on the discovery that by increasing the angle of twist in the liquid crystal material of the display from $\pi/2$ to $3\pi/2$ (hence "Supertwist") the transmission/voltage characteristics became sharper and the number of lines that could be multiplexed without crosstalk could be increased. There were two ways of making the change between field-off and field-on state visible: the normal and commercially used method was to view the display in crossed polarizers, but there was an alternative method which produced a colour change by incorporating a "guest" dye into the liquid-crystal material. In their experimental work, the inventors used dye-containing liquid crystals and in the application as filed the independent claims required a dye to be present. Subsequently the applicants realised that they also needed to cover the use of crossed polarizers, and they successfully obtained claims in the UK, the US and in their European patent as granted that omitted

---

382. G 0001/93 *Mitsui Petrochemical/ Limiting feature,* Reasons at para 13.

383. Compare the current EPO approach with that of the UK Court of Appeal in *A.C. Edwards Limited v Acme Signs & Displays*[1992] RPC 131 at p. 143 and in *Texas Iron Work's patent* [2000] RPC 2007.

384. T 0194/84 *General Motors/Cellulose fibres.*

mention of the dye feature. However, the European patent was opposed, and the EPO Appeal Board held that the claim broadening was contrary to Article 123(2) EPC.[385] It is submitted that consideration of questions 4 and 5 above could have lead to the correct claim scope initially and avoidance of the problems during opposition. At the time when the claims were filed,[386] an astute draftsman should have realised that the important advance was the increase in sharpness of the voltage/transmission characteristics and that making the change of state of the display visible was known technology incidental to that advance. He should also have foreseen the need for express coverage of the crossed polarizer variant because in existing displays it was the most widely used way of making the change of state visible. The independent claims originally filed differed from known twisted nematic displays in two respects: firstly increase in twist angle and secondly a dye instead of polarizers, which is always risky (questions 7 and 8). As Mr Micklethwait observed in his paper, an over-broad claim may lead to arguments about validity, but an over-narrow claim leads to few arguments because it can be circumvented.

Similar issues can arise in the US, and the two cases discussed below both exemplify the unwillingness of US courts to enforce claims which have slipped through examination before the USPTO but which were not supported by the application as filed.

In *Gentry Gallery v Berkline Corp*,[387] the patent in issue[388] related to sectional sofas (see page 210), and the background as understood at the time of filing is explained in the introductory part of the specification as follows:

FIELD OF INVENTION
This invention relates to sofas and more particularly to sectional sofas having reclining seats incorporated into it.

BACKGROUND OF THE INVENTION
As homes become smaller and more efficiently furnished, the need for a dual purpose seating system becomes more important. For example, there is now a substantial demand for sofas having a reclining chair built into them. There is also a substantial demand for sofas having more than one reclining seat. Heretofore reclining seats have only been provided in sectional sofas at the extreme ends of the end sections, and they have been controlled by handles mounted on the end arms at the ends of the sofa. This arrangement is not usually comfortable when the occupants are watching television because one or both occupants must turn their heads to watch the same set. Furthermore, the separation of the two reclining seats at opposite ends of a sectional sofa is not comfortable or conducive to intimate conversation.

---

385. T 0319/91-3.4.2.

386. Which was soon after the EPO had started to receive applications and before the problems of claim broadening during prosecution had been fully recognised.

387. 134 F.3d 1473, 1479, 45 USPQ2d 1498, 1503 (Fed. Cir. 1998)

388. US-A-5064244

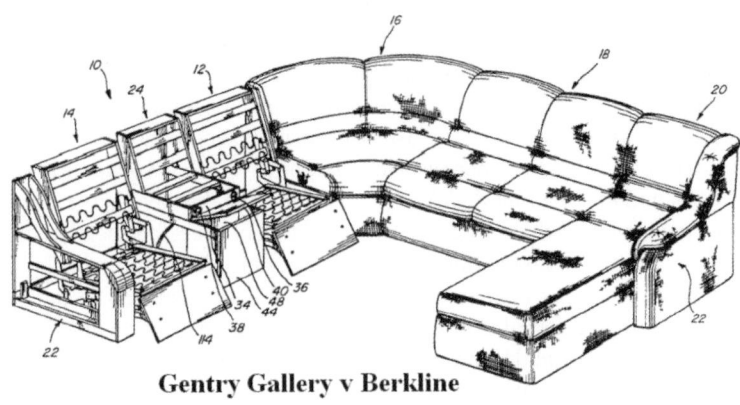

Gentry Gallery v Berkline

The Summary of the Invention section which followed contained a number of object clauses, the relevant one of which reads as follows:

> Another object of the present invention is to provide a sectional sofa segment having a pair of reclining seat sections built into it with a console positioned between them that accommodates the controls for both of the reclining seats.

The inventor's trial testimony was that *"locating the controls on the console is definitely the way we solved it [the problem of building sectional sofa with parallel recliners] on the original group [of sofas]"*. Their broadest claim as originally filed required "control means located upon the centre console to enable each of the pair of reclining seats to move separately between the reclined and upright positions."

However, Gentry subsequently became aware that competitors were locating the recliner controls outside the console. Gentry therefore endeavoured to obtain grant of a wider claim and obtained allowance of the following main claim which they averred was not limited to the features mentioned in the above object clause and covered the accused device in which the controls were not located on a console:

> A sectional sofa comprising:
> a pair of reclining seats disposed in parallel relationship with one another in a double reclining seat sofa section.
> said double reclining seat sofa section being without an arm at one end whereby a second sofa section of the sectional sofa can be placed in abutting relationship with the end of the double reclining seat sofa section without an arm so as to form a continuation thereof,
> each of said reclining seats having a backrest and seat cushion and movable between upright and reclined positions, said backrests and seat cushions of the pair of reclining sets lying in respective common planes when the seats are in the same positions,
> a *fixed console* disposed in the double reclining seat sofa section between the pair of reclining seats and with the *console* and reclining seats together comprising a unitary structure, said *console* including an armrest portion for

each of the reclining seats, said arm rests remaining fixed when the reclining
seats move from one to another of their positions, and

a pair of control means, one for each reclining seat; mounted *on the double
reclining seat sofa section* and each readily accessible to an occupant of its
respective reclining seat and when actuated causing the respective reclining
seat to move from the upright to the reclined position.

The defendants also argued that the disclosure did not support claims in which the
location of the recliner controls was other than on the console, and this argument was
accepted by the court which decided that the main claim did not comply with the
written description requirement of §112(1) and was invalid. The original disclosure
clearly identified the console as the only possible location for the controls, no
variation beyond the console was suggested and the whole purpose of the console
was to house the controls. The court's conclusion, which would not surprise a
European practitioner, was summarised as follows:

In sum, the cases on which Gentry relies do not stand for the proposition that
an applicant can broaden his claims to the extent that they are effectively
bounded only by the prior art. Rather, they make clear that claims may be no
broader than the supporting disclosure, and therefore that a narrow disclosure
will limit claim breadth. Here, [the inventor's] disclosure unambiguously limited
the location of the controls to the console. Accordingly, the district court clearly
erred in finding that he was entitled to claims in which the recliner controls are
not located on the console.

A similar failed claim broadening exercise is found in *Alloc Inc. v ITC*[389] which
provides an example where the Court of Appeal for the Federal Circuit was prepared
to read a limitation that was imported from the written description into the claims,
but which it is misleading to regard as simply an example of the narrow construction
approach as some US commentators have suggested.

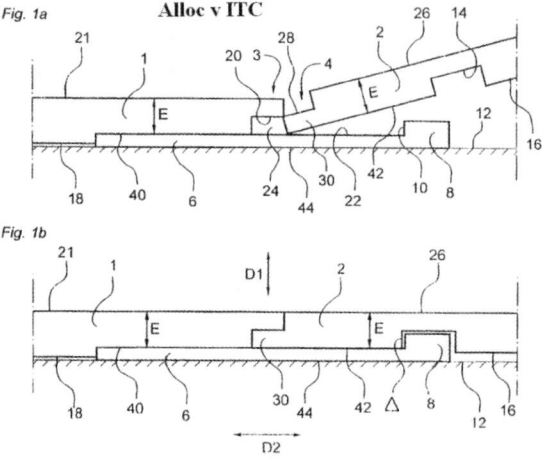

---

389. 342 F.3d 1361 (Fed. Cir. 2003)

The proceedings concerned three related patents concerning flooring, and a representative claim from one of them, with reference numerals added, reads as follows:

> A method for laying and mechanically joining rectangular building panels (1,2) in parallel rows, the method comprising the steps of:
>
> (a) placing a new one of the panels (2) adjacent to a long edge of a previously laid first one of the panels (1) in a first row and to a short edge of a previously laid second one of the panels in an adjacent second row, such that the new one of the panels is in the second row, while holding the new one of the panels (2) at an angle relative to a principal plane of the first panel, such that the new one of the panels is spaced from its final longitudinal position relative to said second panel and such that a long edge of the new panel is provided with a locking groove (4) which is placed upon and in contact with a locking strip (6) at the adjacent long edge of the first panel;
>
> (b) subsequently angling down the new one of the panels so as to accommodate a *locking element* (8) of the strip of the first panel in the locking groove (14) of the new panel, whereby the new panel and the first panel are mechanically connected with each other in a second direction with respect to the thus connected long edges, wherein the long edges, in the angled down position of the new panel, are in engagement with each other and thereby mechanically locked together in a first direction also; and
>
> (c) *displacing* the new one of the panels (2) in its longitudinal direction relative to the first panel (1) towards a final longitudinal position until a *locking element* of one of the short edges of the new one of the panels and the second panel snaps up into a locking groove of the other one of the short edges, whereby the new one of the panels and the second panel are mechanically connected with each other in both in the first direction and in the second direction with respect to the thus connected short edges.

However, the specification taught that play Δ between a locking surface 10 of locking element 8 and the locking groove 14 permitted displacement, i.e. allowed connected panels to slide relative to one another so that they could be assembled in accordance with the claimed method. Play permitted disassembly and reassembly of a previously laid floor without causing damage to the panels, whereas in prior art systems where the panels were urged tightly against one another displacement was hard to achieve and disassembly and reassembly without damage was not feasible.

The court held (with a vigorous dissent by Schall J) that the locking element and the requirement for displacement necessitated play, which was absent in the accused flooring which was therefore non-infringing.[390] Particular factors that influenced the Court are that:

1. The specification criticised prior art panels in which there was no play and disassembly and reassembly were not possible and taught that what permitted disassembly and reassembly of the panels was the existence of play

2. All the figures and embodiments disclosed in the specification required play.

---

390. Coincidentally the UK Court of Appeal recently had to consider similar factual issues in the context of a claim to Convention priority in *Unilin Beheer v Berry Floor*, [2005] FSR 56, see EP-B-1024234.

3. The claims of the PCT priority application required play[391]

4. During prosecution of the application both during international examination and during prosecution before the USPTO, the applicants relied on play to distinguish their invention from the prior art, and therefore disavowed systems without play. For example, they said in a US response:

> The claimed "play" of the present invention is important for two reasons. One, it enables the panels to slide movably with respect to each other along the direction of the joint edge, which is specifically claimed in the penultimate paragraph of claim 1. This movability allows the short ends of the panels to be placed adjacent each other when installing the floor. Second, the play further enables disassembly of the floor when required...

At the time when the decision was handed down it surprised some US commentators. However, the corresponding European patent EP-B-0698162 was granted with a main claim including the feature of play. European opposition proceedings ended with an appeal hearing in which the patent was maintained on the basis that play was the main inventive feature.[392] What the decision of the CAFC shows is that although US law does not have a direct counterpart to Article 123(2) EPC, and an applicant may obtain an advantage through the grant of a broader claim than would be allowed by the EPO, challenge in the US courts may result in a position being reached that is the same as in Europe. The scope of claim that the patentees ended with was determined by the generalizations that were included in the application as filed, and it is misleading to imply that there was some carelessly introduced language that amounted to "*clear disavowal*" of constructions not including play that might have been covered.

The lesson, for both UK and US applicants is that correct technical analysis at the time of filing is essential and that if there is an error it is better to err on the side of breadth. If all the independent claims in an application as filed contain unnecessary features, the broader claim scope may be irretrievably lost, and that careful checking of the independent claims prior to filing is essential. As previously explained, one of the best ways to check for unnecessary features is to apply the collocation test: is there a feature included in the proposed claim which does not clearly contribute to the new function or result that is the basis for the claim and/or is not defined as being connected the other features? Such a feature is usually inessential and should be deleted. It is almost as important to check the description to ensure that it does not promise that all embodiments will solve a technical problem whose solution is merely preferable, and in particular that it does not promise to solve a plurality of such problems, and does not put forward features as essential when in truth they are not.

---

391. The PCT claim required that: "*a play (Δ) exists between the locking groove (14) and a locking surface (10) on the locking element (8) that is facing the joint edges and is operative in said second mechanical connection, that the first and the second mechanical connection both allow mutual displacement of the panels (1, 2) in the direction of the joint edges (3, 4)*"

392. T1234/01 3.2.3 dated 11 March 2004. There are also eight European divisional cases, of which five have been granted with claims requiring play, one has been granted with claims not requiring play but apparently directed to a different aspect of the invention, and two are pending.

Functional rather than structural claiming

The need for caution in formulating functional definitions and the problems created by means-plus-function language devoid of all structural references have been explained in the *Functional Claims* chapter, above. The problems that can be created by wholly structural definitions are illustrated by EP-B-0101656 (Yair) which was litigated in *Improver Corp v Remington Consumer Products Ltd.*[393] The invention concerned depilatory apparatus and aimed to produce an analog to a man's electric razor for female hair removal at the roots. The solution put forward by the inventor was the use of a coiled helical spring driven by motors at opposed ends, a representative claim reading as follows:

> An electrically powered depilatory device comprising:
> a hand held portable housing;
> motor means disposed in said housing; and
> *a helical spring* comprising a plurality of adjacent windings arranged to be driven by said motor means in rotational sliding motion relative to skin bearing hair to be removed,
> said helical spring including an arcuate hair engaging portion arranged to define a convex side whereat the windings are spread apart, and a concave side corresponding thereto whereat the windings are pressed together,
> the rotational motion of the helical spring producing continuous motion of the windings from a spread apart orientation at the convex side to a pressed together orientation at the concave side and for engagement and plucking of hair from the skin of the subject,
> whereby the surface velocities of the windings relative to the skin greatly exceeds the surface velocity of the housing relative thereto.

It will be recalled that the accused device employed a cylindrical rod of elastomeric synthetic rubber which was formed with radial slits and was bent into an arc so that the slits on the convex side of the arc opened to admit hairs and the slits on the concave side closed together to grip the hair and remove it as the rod was rotated. Both the patented helical spring and the accused cylindrical rod performed the same function of gripping hair and pulling it out at its roots. The adjacent windings of the helical spring and the radial slits of the accused device opened and closed in a virtually identical manner as the spring or rod was rotated. The result in each case was to pull hair out at its roots. However, Hoffmann J (now Lord Hoffmann) refused to find infringement on the doctrine of "purposive construction" *inter alia* because he considered the slitted rod to be too different from a helical spring in terms of its mechanical performance and properties, for example, of hysteresis so that equivalence would be too much a matter of hindsight.

Our astute draftsman would be aware that the expression "helical spring" was not only a structural definition but also highly specific as to structure. A routine question would be to ask whether the inventor could think of any alternative structures that would serve. The inventor's initial answer may have been that the properties of a

---

393. [1990] FSR 181

helical spring were unique, and he could not think of anything else. He may have been so pleased with the properties of the helical spring that he was prejudiced against alternatives or he may have had difficulty as an engineer in generalizing from that structure. However, reasonable foresight should have alerted the draftsman to the danger of a structural definition and caused him to ask whether the way in which the helical spring worked could be generalised. He might then have arrived at a more general description of the main hair-removal element as a flexible member that could be formed into an arcuate shape and continuously rotated when in that shape, the member having a surface with discontinuities that were spaced apart on the convex side to receive hair and became pressed together on the concave side to entrap and pluck the hair. With that more generalised insight as to the functional characteristics of the hair removal element, the inventor might have been stimulated to think of additional embodiments that would have supported the generalization. Whether or not he could do so, it would have been worth presenting the broader generalization in the initially filed claims.

The reader will appreciate that what is said above is with hindsight not only as to the later created slitted rod variant but also as to the outcome of the infringement proceedings, and that one view of the factual matrix which accords with the decision of Hoffmann J is that all that had been invented at the time of filing was the helical spring embodiment. In the absence of alternatives disclosed in the specification, the instinct of patent office examiners may well have been to object to a broad functional definition and require restriction to the disclosed helical spring. However, our task as patent professionals is to generalise the specific embodiments of an inventor, to seek functional definitions of specific structures, to apply insight as to the fundamental way they work and to stimulate consideration of alternatives. On that view, a broader claim might have been obtained, and much litigation and cost might have been avoided.

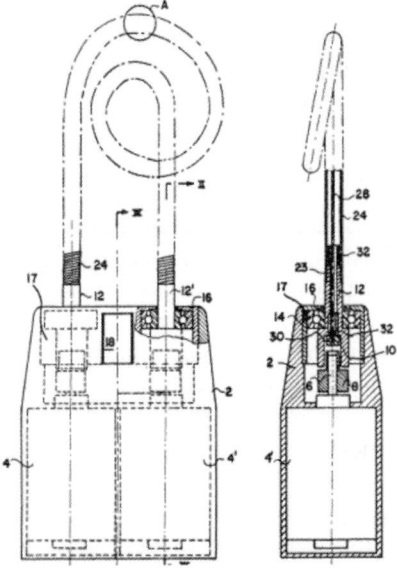

Improver v Remington

The drafting process is iterative, and reconsideration and checking at every stage is vital, as pointed out by both Micklethwait and Daley. Experience shows that it is usually quicker and more reliable to start from a definition that is largely or wholly functional and if necessary to generalise down by adding structure than it is to start from a structural definition and then try to generalise the structural language.

Flexibility on initial filing

An irrevocable commitment to a single definition of the invention at the initial filing stage or even at the end of the priority year may arise through filing an internally wholly consistent document and with statements of invention agreeing in every respect with the independent claims, so that during prosecution the only possibility for amendment is narrowing or refinement of that definition. As is apparent from the *Supertwist* example above, subsequent events may show that an alternative definition based on a different group of features is more desirable. It will therefore often be prudent to include in the application as filed several independent claims with distinct groups of features and directed to different new functions or advantages so that the application as filed is flexible. This statement applies even when the intention during prosecution is to remove that flexibility and settle on a single definition for the granted patent without incurring the expense of filing one or more divisional applications. This requirement for flexibility conflicts with the post-*Festo* advice of some US colleagues that post-filing amendment of the claims even involving mere claim cancellation is best avoided because of the risk of creating file wrapper estoppel. However, the problems created by an inflexible patent specification are likely to be more immediate and worse than any problems created by file-wrapper estoppel, and the objective of the patent draftsman should be to create claims that are literally infringed and do not need to invoke the doctrine of equivalents. In the case of an invention of known technical and commercial importance belonging to a well-funded applicant, the post-*Festo* amendment problem may be dealt with by filing the different independent claims in a portfolio of US applications.

For an example based on the facts in *Lucas v Gaedor*,[394] the invention related to a case for a battery for a motor car, lorry or other similar vehicle. There were two principal differences from the known and widely used prior art: firstly that the hard rubber which was previously used for car battery cases was replaced by polypropylene, and secondly that the wall thickness was reduced to 2.5 mm (0.1 inches) or less. The substitution of material would not in itself have imparted patentable novelty, but it would have been plausible to argue for example during prosecution of the relevant patent application that selection of a novel material in combination with selection of a reduced wall thickness gave a battery case of unexpectedly good mechanical properties and lower cost due to the reduced materials content. However, it would not necessarily have been prudent to file an initial application with a single independent claim directed to the two features in combination. More scope for manoeuvre to deal with unexpected post-filing

---

394. [1978] RPC 297

developments would have been obtained by filing a first independent claim directed to the use of polypropylene, a second independent claim directed to the use of a case of reduced thickness, and a third independent claim directed to both polypropylene and the reduced thickness.

Dependent claims and intermediate generalizations

The remaining differences and the new functions or results which flow from them can form the subject of defendable dependent claims. Such claims deserve the same attention as the main independent claims since the subject-matter of the main claims may prove to be anticipated or obvious, and it is one of the dependent claims, or even a generalization copied from the written description, that provides the basis of enforceable protection. Claims directed to features further defining the particular field of use of the invention are, as discussed above, of special importance, since further qualifying the field of endeavour of an inventor is often the best line of defence when a new and unexpectedly relevant reference comes to light.

A simple strategy for organizing the dependent claims is important for clarity and ease of checking. One school of thought is that dependent claims should be added in order of their importance, but the dependency of the resulting claim set rapidly becomes impossibly convoluted and difficult to check. A better strategy is to add claims further qualifying the features of the main claim in the order in which those features occur and then add claims to any further features. For example, if the main claim has features A, B, C, D, E, then the dependent claims should further qualify those features in the sequence A_1, A_2, A_3, B_1, B_2, B_3... E_1, E_2, E_3. Further features can be added in the sequence F, F_1, F_2, G, G_1, G_2... Claim sets that follow this pattern are likely to be more complete and less error-prone.

Often the scope of protection that an applicant or patentee wishes to achieve during prosecution or opposition is an intermediate generalization for which it is difficult to find basis in the application as filed. The applicant may seek to derive the scope that he or she requires either by generalization of something disclosed in an embodiment or example, or by deleting a feature from one of the main independent claims. Both of these approaches can give rise to difficulty, particularly in Europe.

With regard to generalizing a particular feature, the EPO Appeal Board has held that the disclosure of a document does not include equivalents of that feature. The Board first took that position in a dispute as to novelty between co-pending European applications in order to mitigate the "harsh effects" of the "whole contents" approach. The same position has since been taken in amendment cases.

The limited nature of the subject-matter that can be added through "implicit disclosure" has also been considered by the Appeal Board, which explained[395] that:
1. 'Implicit disclosure' relates solely to matter which is not explicitly mentioned, but is a clear and unambiguous consequence of what is explicitly mentioned.

---

395. T 0823/96 *PPG/Coating*.

2. Common general knowledge must be taken into account in deciding what is clearly and unambiguously implied by the explicit disclosure of a document.
3. What is rendered obvious by a document in the light of common general knowledge is a completely separate question, irrelevant to the question as to what is implicit.

A distinction has also been drawn between what is contained in a document as filed and what a skilled person would derive from it on reflection and using his own imagination.[396] It is therefore important to check so far as is possible at the time of filing that important alternative definitions of the invention are included and that and important fall-back positions are defined with sufficient generality in subsidiary claims.

Human activities and distributed inventions

When he has arrived at a workable definition of the invention, the draftsman should check for coverage of the human activities that flow from the invention, and a simple mnemonic is that he should "look up" and "look down". Looking up involves considering the wider whole of which the invention forms part and deciding whether claims should be added that reflect that wider whole. For example, the inventor may have produced a better way of making master discs for producing CDs. Looking up involves realization that this is merely a step in the better or more economic production of CD's and that it is necessary to include a claim to the use of the master discs in the production of CDs. Failure to include claims of this type, and supporting disclosure in the written description, will render the patent unenforceable against an importer of finished CDs made outside the UK using the patented master discs.[397] Looking down involves consideration of important sub-combinations and individual components which may be made and sold separately, e.g. in the case of *Windsurfer* the sail and the board.

It is important to consider the form that an invention will take when it is sold and to ensure so far as possible that there are claims that are literally infringed by the sale of the product in that form. If that precaution is not taken, the patentee may have to rely on the doctrine of induced or contributory infringement, which is more difficult to prove than literal infringement and under the laws of the UK and other EPC contracting states does not cover products supplied for export in disassembled form.

The need to include distinct claims to the individual aspects and components of a "distributed invention" has long been recognised. Marconi's UK Patent 1896/12039 directed to the use of a "coherer" as a detector of signals in a radio receiver provides an early example. The independent claims included the following:

1. The *method of transmitting signals* by means of electrical impulses to a receiver having a sensitive tube or other sensitive form of imperfect contact capable of being restored with certainty and regularity to its normal condition substantially as described.

---

396. T 0415/91 *General Motors Corporation/Deletion of feature.*
397. *Pioneer Electronics Capital Inc v Warner Music Manufacturing GmbH,* [1997] RPC 757.

12. *[The detector]* Sensitive contacts in which a column of powder or filings (or their equivalent) is divided into sections by means of metallic stops or plugs substantially as described.

15. *A receiver* consisting of a sensitive tube or other imperfect contact inserted in a circuit, one end of the sensitive tube or other imperfect contact being put to earth whilst the other end is connected to an insulated conductor.

16. The *combination* of a *transmitter* having one end of its sparking appliance or poles connected to earth, and the other to an insulated conductor, *with a receiver* as is mentioned in Claim 15.

The decision of the EPO Appeal Board in *Data Structure Product/PHILIPS*[398] is now the leading authority in Europe concerning the interpretation of claims in distributed inventions. The invention concerned pictures recorded in code that can be reproduced by a CD-1 player, and in particular with a partial read-out facility that could be used, for example, to show an enlarged representation of part of the picture. The problem with which the invention dealt was how to speed up retrieval of those parts of the track where a selected coded picture line had been recorded. Claim 1 was directed to a picture retrieval system comprising in combination a record carrier recorded with pictures according to a particular data structure and a read device arranged to retrieve pictures on the basis of that data structure. The Examining Division had no problem with the patentability of such a claim, but refused to grant a further independent claim covering "*a record carrier for use in the system of claim 1.*" The reasons given by the Examining Division were that the *for use* clause was unclear and devoid of limiting effect, and the claim as a whole was unclear because it was not possible to assess the technical merits of the invention on the basis of the record carrier alone. This decision was reversed by the Appeal Board which held that the further independent claim satisfied the requirements of Article 84 EPC because it defined an ostensibly new physical entity in functional terms. The relationship between claim 1 and claim 4 followed the standard practice for "distributed inventions" (plug and socket or bow and arrow inventions). The words "for use" explained the rationale underlying the recording format and clarified the subject-matter for which protection was sought. The Appeal Board further commented that the finding of the Oppositions Division:

...fails to take account of the special characteristics of distributed inventions which by their nature involve cooperative articles which may be "ambiguous" or even "meaningless" when considered in isolation. The effect of the for use phrase in claim 4, whereby the claim is to be interpreted with reference to the system defined in claim 1, should not be ignored when examining whether the claim meets the clarity requirement of Article 84 EPC. The line numbers, coded picture lines and addresses and synchronisations of the record carrier of claim 4 are "interpreted" in use by the reading, addressing, selecting and detection means of the read device specified in claim 1 as unambiguously as a sprocket wheel in a camera "interprets" the sprocket holes in a reel of film. It is true that the variety of possible physical implementations of the characterising features of claim 1 makes the claim very general but this simply reflects the fact that the features are specified in functional terms and that consequently the relation between the record and the reader is one of cooperative functionality. The principles governing the permissibility of functional features in claims apply equally to distributed inventions and the resulting combinational generality is not per se a symptom of a lack of clarity. In the judgment of the board, the present invention is made at a general functional level and it is therefore appropriate for it to be claimed at that level.

---

398. T 1194/97; EP-B-0500927, see also the corresponding US-A-5835674

Not only is the distributed invention approach necessary in order to achieve the full scope of protection that is necessary for many multi-part or multi-aspect inventions, but also it is often the only way of achieving protection for aspects of the invention that could otherwise not be protected. Two examples of this are given below.

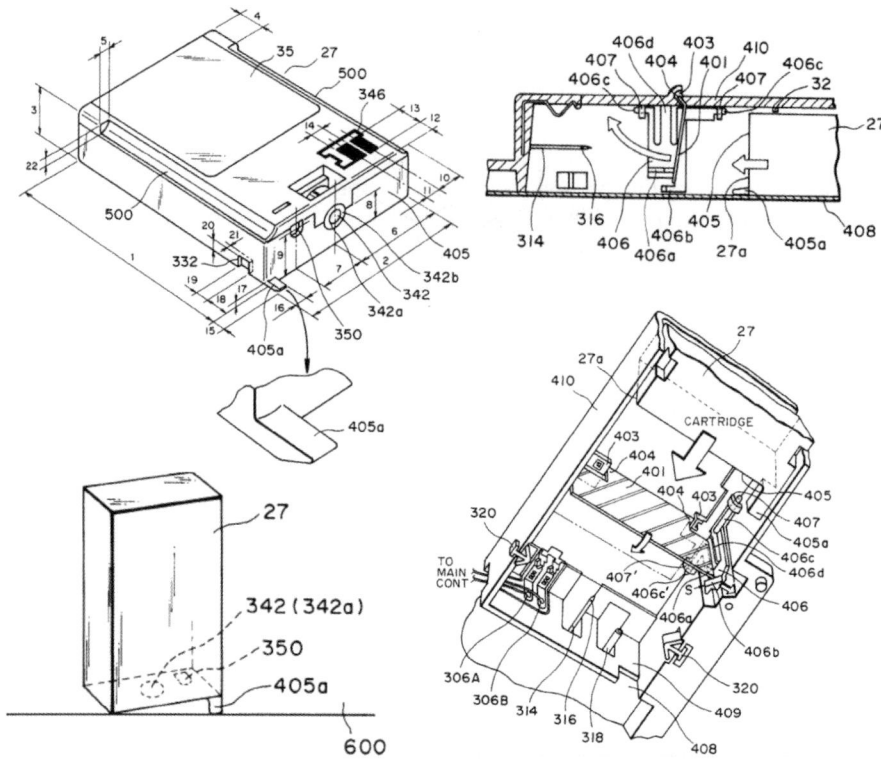

In EP-B-0478244 (Canon), applicants wished to obtain allowance to a claim to a cartridge for an ink jet printer having an ink supply port and a projection 405a, (see accompanying Figure) adjacent to the supply port. The cartridges were sold as replacements separately from the printer to which they were fitted, and one of the main objectives of the patent application was to provide coverage for such separate cartridge sales. One advantage associated with the projection 405a was that it prevented the cartridge from being stood e.g. on a valuable desktop in a stable downwardly facing attitude (see the lower left-hand sketch in the accompanying Figure). The EPO did not accept this as sufficient reason for granting a patent. However, a more significant purpose of the projection 405a was to act as a key that unlatched a protective cover 401, enabling it to pivot upwards and allow the cartridge to become fully inserted into the printer and to make contact with ink needle 314 and waste ink return line 318. The applicant's predecessor cartridge and protective cover mechanism had been disclosed in EP-A-0412459 and is shown in a further Figure. It was unlatched by pairs of projections 141 on opposite sides of the cartridge which displaced latching members 136, 137 and allowed protective cover 133 to swing upwards, but this arrangement took up more space because two projections 141 and two latching members 136, 137 were necessary and these were at the sides of the

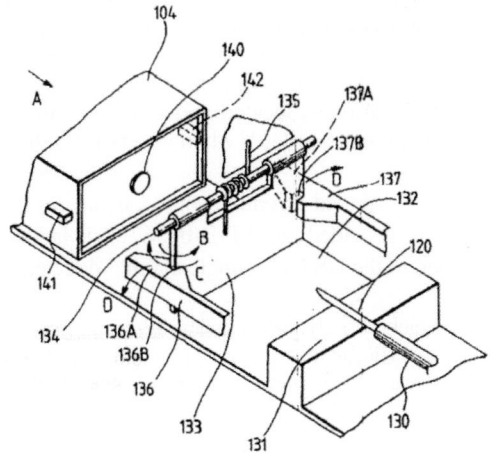

EP-B-0412459

cartridge rather than at its end face. The EPO accepted as the technical problem the devising of a more compact release mechanism for the protective cover, and granted the following claim to the combination of an ink jet printer and a cartridge for fitting into the printer:

1. An ink jet printer comprising a housing (30) having an aperture for receiving an ink cartridge, printer ink supply means (100) within said aperture couplable with the cartridge when the latter is in its operative position within the aperture to receive ink from the cartridge, a waste ink delivery port (318) provided within the aperture, said port being couplable with an inlet port (350) on said cartridge to return residual ink to said cartridge, a protective cover (401) movable between a closed position to render the ink supply means inaccessible when no cartridge is present within the aperture and an open position to permit entry of the cartridge into the aperture to the operative position, and locking means to secure said cover in its closed position releasable by said cartridge on insertion of the latter into the aperture, wherein

(a) said locking means (406, 406a, 406b) is located inside the cover (401) with respect to the direction of insertion of the cartridge; and

(b) said protective cover is shaped so as to provide a space between a peripheral edge thereof and a wall of the aperture, through which space said locking means (406, 406a, 406b) is accessible and contactable by a projection (405a) provided on the leading end of the ink cartridge, taken in the direction of insertion, to effect release of the locking means and permit the cover to be moved to its open position.

The explanation of the technical problem and allowance of the above "system" claim persuaded the EPO also to allow the following claim to the cartridge in which, as desired, the sole novel feature was the forwardly facing projection:

12. An ink cartridge for use in an ink jet printer as claimed in any one of claims 1 to 11, comprising a case (27), an ink container (340) provided in the case, an ink absorbing material (344) also provided in the case, an ink supply port (342) in one end (405) of the case for permitting supply of ink from said ink container, and ink receiving port (350) also in said one end (405) of the case for permitting residual ink to pass to the absorbing material (344) in the case, and

> a projection (405a) provided at said one end (405) which extends away from said
> one end beyond the ink supply port (342) and the ink receiving port (350) in the
> direction of entry of said cartridge into the printer, said projection having a
> transverse cross-sectional area substantially smaller than the area of said one end of
> the case, said projection (405a) being located and shaped so that it releases the
> locking mechanism of the printer cover (401) when inserted into the printer.

A further example of how the distributed invention approach may result in grant where no other approach will serve is provided by EP-B-0436717 (Maddock). The original application which was drafted in the US had a single claim[399] directed to:

> A method of treatment which comprises administering to a living being a medical
> agent and thereafter extra-corporeally removing said medical agent or metabolites,
> complexes or products thereof by passing bodily fluid over a support adapted to
> immobilise said agent.

Methods of medical treatment are excluded from patentability under the EPC. It was not possible to draft an acceptable use claim, nor was there basis for an acceptable kit of parts claim. It was argued during prosecution that it was possible to view the inventor's contribution as a distributed invention consisting of the method of treatment and the medical agent and removal materials that were collected together for use in that method. The fact that the patentee was under a disability insofar as he was statute-barred from claiming the method of treatment was not a reason for preventing him from claiming other qualifying aspects of the distributed invention. The EPO accepted this argument and allowed the following claim[400] in which patentability was grounded on the method of treatment set out in the preamble which explained and justified the relationship between the claimed components:

> A system for use in a method of therapeutic or diagnostic treatment for a living
> being in need thereof, which method comprises administering to said living being a
> medical agent to effect said therapeutic or diagnostic purpose, allowing said medical
> agent to enter the circulation system of the living being and thereafter
> extracorporally removing said medical agent or a derivative thereof from the
> circulation system of said living being before said medical agent or said derivative
> thereof would be cleared by the body under normal circumstances, said system
> comprising first and second parts to be used in sequence:
>
> the first part being a medical agent for administration to said living being in said
> method so as to be circulated by the circulation system of the living being, said
> medical agent (i) being labelled with a moiety for assisting in the therapeutic or
> diagnostic treatment and for its selective removal, and (ii) requiring artificial
> clearance after administration; and
>
> the second part being means for removing circulating medical agent or
> derivative from the blood stream of said living being, said means comprising a
> conduit for removing from the living being blood containing the medical agent or
> derivative, a unit to which the blood or a plasma stream thereof passes and which
> contains a support adapted to selectively immobilise the medical agent or
> derivative, a conduit for flow of blood from which at least a portion of the medical
> agent or derivative has been removed back into said living being ...

---

399. See WO 91/ 01749

400. See the text of the patent as granted.

A case study based on Windsurfer

Coverage

This paper considers the drafting implications of the *Windsurfer* litigation and ends with a suggested drafting checklist based on the matters discussed in this and the preceding papers.

After you have read this paper, you should:

1. Routinely check for the types of drafting error which are apparent from detailed consideration of *Windsurfer*, which are not isolated errors but occur frequently in specifications covering a wide range of technologies.

2. Be able to apply the drafting checklist on page 245, fully understanding the reasons for the various matters to be checked.

3. Routinely investigate the underlying science or engineering in any invention that you are handling in order to achieve a complete rather than a superficial understanding prior to drafting.

4. Routinely consider different possibilities for the drafting team including the addition of a litigator and/or an independent technical expert.

5. Realise that drafting and checking are iterative processes, and that you will need to update the drafting checklist so that the version that you use in your daily work reflects current legal and technical developments.

Introduction

The *Windsurfer* case provides an opportunity for showing the practical application of the principles set out in the preceding papers. Windsurfing created a new and challenging type of sailing craft and developed into a successful worldwide sport. In winds of 40 knots or more Windsurfer-type sailboards have achieved speeds of over 45 knots. The sport was awarded Olympic status in the 1984 Los Angeles Games. Under these circumstances, it seems remarkable that the UK Court of Appeal should have revoked the patent granted to the inventors of the sailing craft on which the sport was based.[401] It is therefore worthwhile to look at the way in which the specification was drafted to see whether there was anything that might have been done at the time of filing or during prosecution before the Patent Office to improve the prospects of success for the patentees in the litigation which took place some years after the patent had been granted.

---

401. *Windsurfing International Inv v Tabur Marine (Great Britain) Ltd* [1985] RPC 59

The Windsurfer invention

A patent application for the Windsurfer invention was first filed in the US in March 1968, and UK and German applications, amongst others, were filed at the end of the priority year in February-March 1969. The inventors' view of what they had achieved is set out in a lecture[402] given in April 1969 by James R. Drake, one of the Windsurfer inventors. We therefore have a record of the knowledge and opinions of the inventors as expressed to a peer group, and can assess how much of this knowledge found its way into the patent specification, how much was omitted and whether the omissions made a difference to the outcome.

Prior art known at the time of filing in *Windsurfer*

In the period 1950-1970, there was a desire for sailing craft that were faster, easier to rig and gave an improved sensation of speed. That led to a discernable trend in design towards inexpensive portable sailing craft with smaller hulls and simpler sailing rigs.

The starting point for such designs was the various types of one- and two-person sailing dinghy, see the accompanying Figure in which some of the parts of the boat and sail have been labelled to assist those unfamiliar with the terminology used in sailing. Such designs used a so-called "Bermuda" rig, which had become standard for small dinghies because of its high aerodynamic efficiency. A socket in the hull received the lower end of a mast that was held upright by stay wires. A boom was pivoted at its forward end to the mast. A generally triangular mainsail had a luff (leading edge) that fitted into a channel along the mast and a foot (lower edge) that fitted into a channel along the boom, the mast and the boom together defining the general shape of the sail. Control of the sail was by means of a wire called a "kicking strap" connected between the boom and the mast and by a rope called a "mainsheet" attached to the boom which is controlled by the user to take in or let out the sail. The boat was steered by a rudder as shown and the hull was deep enough to accommodate a user in a recumbent control position.

By the early 1970s one-man "sailboard" designs had become successful because they created a sensation of great speed. They were based on shallow board-like hulls of length about 13 ft, width about 3 ft, weight about 120 lbs and depth sufficient to accommodate a user in a recumbent control position. Their hulls were unfilled hollow structures. A freestanding mast fitted into a socket in the hull that was deep enough to hold the mast upright without stay wires. The mast carried a sail of area e.g. 75 sq. ft., at that time using an equilateral *lateen* rig (see accompanying Figure on page 225). Conventional rudder steering and mainsheet control for the sail continued to be used. James Drake, one of the Windsurfer inventors, said in his 1969 lecture[403] in relation to two commercially available boards of this type[404] that:

---

402. James R Drake, "*Windsurfing a new concept in sailing*", AIAA (American Institute of Aeronautics and Astronautics) lecture, 26 April 1969, Marina Del Ray, California Yacht Club, downloadable from www.americanwindsurfer.com/mag/back/original.html

403. James R Drake, *supra.*

404. *Sailfish/Sunfish* series then being produced by Alcourt, Inc. of Waterbury, Connecticut.

The *Sailfish/Sunfish* is, however, the best attempt so far to combine the features of speed and convenience and is the standard against which any improvements must be judged.

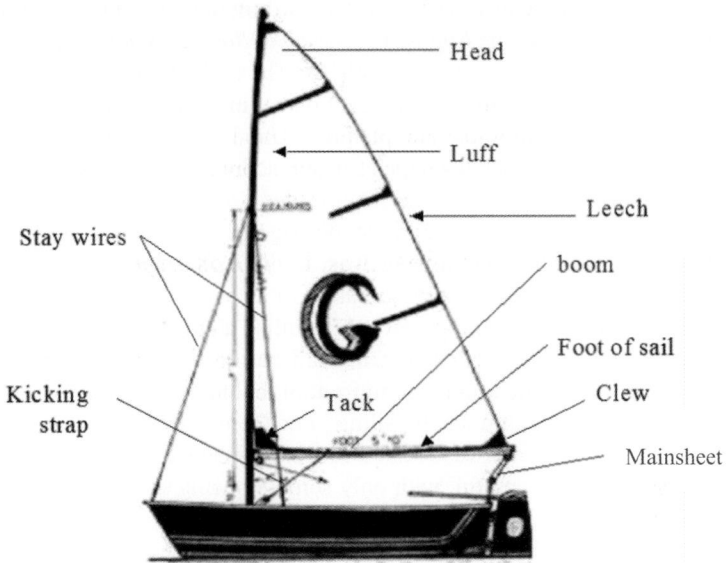

Typical sailing dinghy of the 1940's or 1950's

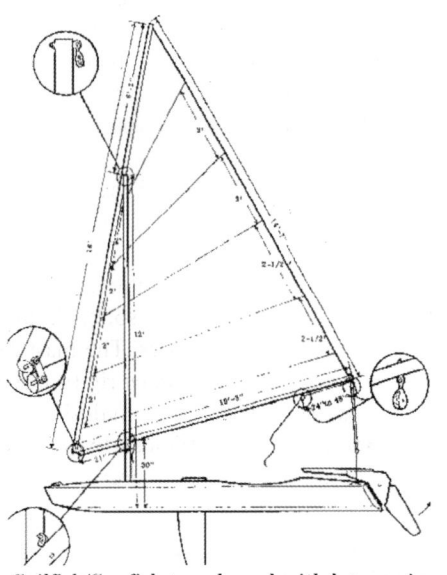

Sailfish/Sunfish type board with lateen rig

Prior art in the UK *Windsurfer* infringement proceedings

Unknown to the Windsurfer inventors and their patent attorneys the idea of a sailboard with a hand held rig had already been disclosed by an individual called Newman Darby. He started in 1964 to sell sailboards in the US of his own design and published details of them in the August 1965 issue of *Popular Science Monthly*. They had a wooden hull of length 10ft and width 3ft. The hull had the form of a double-ended "scow", which is a hull form modeled on sailing scows which were fast and generally flat-bottomed to facilitate planing. The hull supported a universally pivoted sailing rig based on a kite-shaped sail spread by a curved mast of height 11.5 ft and a single curved yard (horizontal member) of width 8.33 ft, giving a sail area of about 45 sq ft (see accompanying Figure on page 225). The kite sail was made of water-resistant polyester sailcloth. It was a type of square-rigged sail, and consequently it produced a poor approximation of an aerofoil and was less efficient than the Bermuda rig when sailing upwind.[405] Unlike a conventional sailing dinghy or sailboard and unlike the Windsurfer, the sail had to be controlled from the lee (downwind) side, so that the user stood in front of the sail. The board was steered by tilting the rig. Unusually for a small sailing craft the dagger board (labelled in the accompanying Figure below) was located in front of the sail. The Darby sailboard was not commercially successful, with only some 80 being sold in 1965-1966. In a relatively recent interview,[406] James Drake attributed this lack of commercial success to the weight of the Darby sailboard, its consequent poor hydrodynamics, and its poor sail technology. He was adamant that the Darby sailboard played no part in the subsequent development of the Windsurfer.

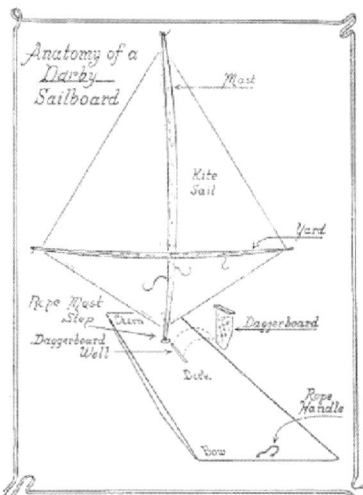

---

405. A reader of the UK Court of Appeal decision gains the impression that the Darby sailboard could be dismissed as a device of only marginally satisfactory performance. Early film of a Darby sailboard in use can be found on the Internet (e.g. using the Google search engine: availability and location of such film changes, so it is not possible to give a particular link) and shows that in fact it was manoeuvrable and performed well, although on the evidence not so well as the Windsurfer.

406. See www.americanwindsurfer.com/mag/back/7.3.4/drake.html

A second, and less well publicised, prior use of a hand-controlled sailing rig in a small sailing craft is discussed below.

The Windsurfer inventive concept

The Windsurfer was developed from sailboards, and was co-invented by James Drake and Hoyle Schweitzer. James Drake was an aeronautical engineer, worked for the RAND Corporation and in his spare time was a sailor. Hoyle Schweitzer was a computer analyst and in his spare time was a surfer. Their object was to put a sail on a surfboard and thereby to produce an uncomplicated craft that did not need a breaking wave for propulsion but maintained the speed and exhilaration of surfing. In his 1969 lecture, James Drake claimed to have originated a new concept of sailing (see Figure) in which a surfboard-like hull is controlled from a standing position using a rig based on a free-standing mast pivoted to the board.

The Windsurfer concept

Drawing by James R Drake

The lecture discussed an unsuccessful prototype called *Skate* and six successful Windsurfer prototypes. The first such prototype called *Old Yeller* is shown in perspective view in the accompanying Figure on page 228and appears in patent GB-A-1258317 (the patent in issue)[407] and the second and most successful prototype called *Big Red* is shown in the accompanying Figure (page 228) which is reproduced from the materials accompanying the 1969 James Drake lecture.

The principal features of the new design were that:
■ A different sailing skill was needed, more like surfing or skiing.
■ The prototype board (hull) and rig together weighed about 70 lbs and could be carried in two hands, one for the board and one for the rig.
■ The *Old Yeller* prototype used as its hull a "slightly enlarged" tandem (two person) surfboard 11½ ft long, 2½ ft wide and 4½ in thick. The *Big Red* prototype used as its hull a board of length 15ft and weight about 50 lbs. Its construction was as lightweight as possible, being based on 2-3 lb/ft³ plastics foam with two longitudinal stiffeners of redwood and a fibreglass covering. That constructional technique was similar to the technique then in use for making surfboards. The board had an aft fin or skeg for

---

407. See also US-A-3487800 and the successfully re-issued patent Re 31167 in which the original claims were replaced and much additional prior art cited including references describing wishbone booms and an article in *Popular Science Monthly* concerning the *Darby* sailboard. In addition to litigation in the UK, corresponding patents in Canada and Australia were also litigated and grant of the corresponding German patent was opposed.

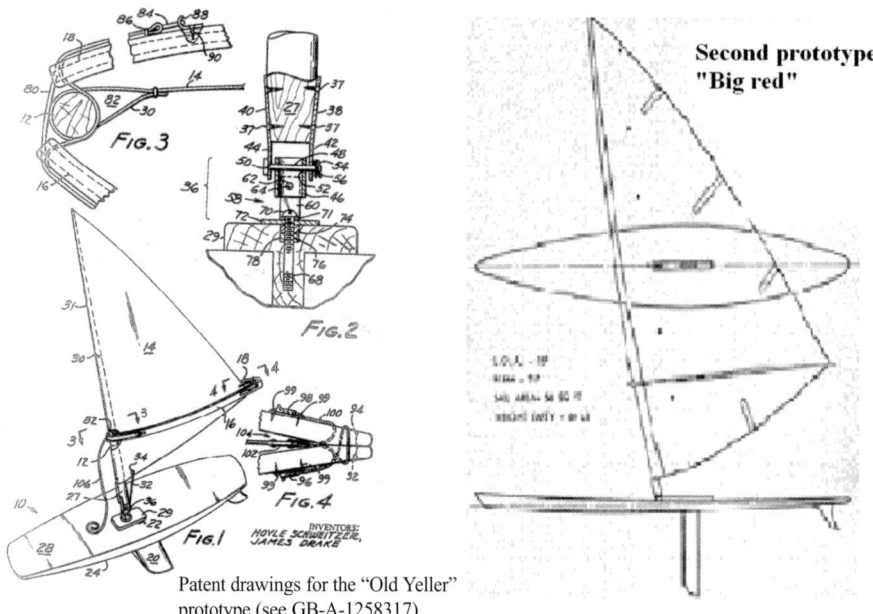

Patent drawings for the "Old Yeller"
prototype (see GB-A-1258317)

directional stability and provided buoyancy for a user of weight about 160-180 lbs. Water-resistant foam plastics was a gateway technology for both the prototypes and for the subsequent commercially produced Windsurfers.

■ The mast was attached to the board through a fully articulated stainless steel universal joint, i.e. permitting 360° mast rotation about a vertical axis and 180° about orthogonal horizontal axes, but was otherwise unsupported. Pivoting the mast in a fore and aft plane was used to steer the board, moving the mast aft steering the board towards the apparent wind, and moving it forward steering the board away from the apparent wind. No rudder was provided and none was needed. Furthermore the articulated sail assembly permitted the board to lie flat on the water when the user lost control of the rig, making recovery easier.

■ The length of the mast was 14 ft and it was of hollow fibreglass and constructed using a similar technique to that used for vaulting poles.

■ The sail was attached to the mast using a nylon sock, and it was cut from 4 oz polyester sailcloth. The sail area was about 56 sq. ft, which was about the maximum that a strong man could handle in 12-15 knot winds.

■ The sail was held taut between twin booms (also referred to as a wishbone boom) joined to the mast at chest level about 4 feet above the board so that it was easy to hold and adjust. The twin booms were of laminated wood and were curved to permit the sail to set well over its entire height. The joint between the booms and the mast was made with heavy nylon tape to prevent the development of stress concentrations on the fibreglass mast

■ An outhaul pulled the clew (aft end) of the sail towards the aft end of the booms to tension the sail. Tensioning the sail stabilised the position of the boom relative to the mast so that raising the mast automatically positioned the boom for grasping by the user. However when the outhaul was released the sail could be collapsed and the boom could be pivoted upward parallel to the mast so that the whole sailing rig could be stored in a bag.

- The combined weight of the mast, sail and twin booms was 20 lbs.
- In *Old Yeller* the dagger board and the universal joint for the mast were made as a single assembly located close to the centre of buoyancy of the board, whereas in *Big Red* the mast was located six inches forward of the centre of buoyancy, and was separate from the dagger board which was located six inches aft of the centre of buoyancy.
- The new sailboards were very fast, the *Big Red* prototype easily outracing the *Sailfish/Sunfish* sailboards.

Technical field in *Windsurfer*

The definition of technical field in the *Windsurfer* UK patent[408] suffered from two problems which discernibly made enforcement more difficult: all field-related definitions were unjustifiably broad, and there was no definition corresponding to the field of endeavour in which the inventors were working and where the invention was most likely to be put into practical use.

The main claim was directed to *a wind-propelled vehicle*, and the introduction to the specification explained that the field of art to which the invention pertained included the field of *ships, particularly sailboats and iceboats, and land vehicles with sail propulsion*. The ambit of the claim therefore included all sailing ships, including for example large offshore keelboats for which the invention had no foreseeable utility. Unfortunately for the patentees, the "wishbone rig" of *Windsurfer* had been used in some offshore keelboats. No example was given in the *Windsurfer* decision, but the author has found an example in the ocean-going yacht "Sintra" built in 1959, a photograph of which appears below on page 230. The wishbone boom or rig can be seen controlling the upper sail on the forward mast. If there had been a claim limiting the hull to the single-person sailboards that were the true field of endeavour of the inventors, then the argument would have been available that transfer of the wishbone rig from offshore keelboats to the new field of single-person sailboards for which that rig was novel contributed to inventive step. However, since there was no such claim, there was no basis on which the court could find that selecting a wishbone rig contributed to inventive step.

Equally significantly, there was no claim to the use of a surfboard hull. This omission is surprising given the objective of the inventors to produce a watercraft which combined the thrills of sailing and surfing. During the later stages of the infringement proceedings, *Windsurfer* asked permission to limit their claims to the combination of a hand-held rig with a surfboard hull. However, the Court of Appeal refused permission to make this amendment on the ground that

> ...no-one, from first to last, advanced or considered the specialised qualities of a surfboard as an inventive concept

and it was too late to raise this new issue after the trial and appeal had taken place and the patent had been held to be invalid.

---

408. GB-A-1258317

Although this issue was never explored during the litigation, the written description of the Windsurfer patent included no ice-craft or land vehicle embodiments, and there is nothing to suggest that the inventors had considered how to apply their hand-held sailing rig to such vehicles. The only risk from loss of control and collapse of the rig used for a watercraft is that of an unintentional swim. On land, the inevitable loss of control of a vehicle with a collapsible rig traveling at speed

"Sintra" ocean-going yacht - wishbone rig and Windsurfer-like sail on foremast

would involve a fall onto hard ground and consequential risk of injury. Although land yachts influenced by Windsurfer have been constructed, they do not work like a Windsurfer because they have a fixed recumbent control position and a rig that is stayed to prevent unexpected collapse. Extending the field of the invention into these speculative areas arguably created little additional protection whilst opening the way for prolonged and expensive debate about non-enablement and lack of utility. If the initiative to extend the field to, for example, a land yacht came from the inventors, the prudent attorney response would have been: "*OK, but we must disclose a workable embodiment. Can you let me have a drawing of what you have in mind?*"

The Background section in the Windsurfer patent

If we consider the *Windsurfer* invention using the EPO approach,[409] the closest prior art within the field of endeavour of the inventors, based on what was known to the inventors at the time of filing, was prior *Sailfish/Sunfish* sailboards. The twin split boom or wishbone boom was derived from the neighbouring field of offshore keelboats although its use was not widespread. The hull was derived from the more distant field of surfboards. The universal joint came from the yet more distant field of mechanical engineering and had not (so far as the inventors were then aware) been used to connect a mast to a hull of a sailing vessel. The EPO would not have regarded a surfboard as the appropriate starting point for considering inventive step because it was not in the field of the invention, although it might have accepted a surfboard as a plausible secondary reference.

Since the inventors knew nothing of the *Darby* sailboard and considered that the *Sailfish/Sunfish* sailboards set the standard against which improvements should be judged, it would have been logical to explain this fact in the Background section of the patent. It would then have been helpful to include in the patent diagrammatic plan and side views of these boards to facilitate comparison with the new surfboard-based

---

409. It should be noted that we are considering this patent with hindsight: at the time the patent was drafted the EPC had not yet come into effect and many of the developments of UK and US law discussed in this paper had not taken place.

From Sailfish/Sunfish to Windsurfer

sailing craft that had been invented, to describe the significant features of the hull and rig that differed from the newly invented surfboard-based sailing craft, and to include a reference to either a review of *Sailfish/Sunfish* in a yachting journal or to an advertisement if no such review could be found. That would have defined the inventor's view of the objectively prevailing state of the art and provided a definite starting point from which the process of development of their invention was considered to have started. It was good practice to do so in the late 1960s, and as discussed above continues to be good practice under the EPC.[410] The inventors could then have further explained that rigidly securing the sail and mast to a board-like hull prevented the feel and enjoyment of a surfboard from being obtained and that the skills needed were only those required to sail a conventional light sailing craft.

Instead, the Background section of the Windsurfer patent was of the anecdotal type[411] and contained a statement that sail propulsion had been suggested *for such watercraft as surfboards and landcraft such as sleds i.e. generally any small craft.* This was a clear admission that the *idea* of creating a sail-propelled surfboard was known to the public, so that novelty and inventive character could be found only in the implementation of that idea.[412] If the statement were true, it was important to find out

---

410. T 24/81 *Metal refining/BASF*

411. See page 200

412. Proving that the *idea* of producing the claimed invention is known or obvious is a major step towards proving invalidity. In *Texas Iron Works' Patent* [2000] RPC 207, the defining moment was when the technical expert giving evidence on behalf of the patentees admitted that the idea of making the claimed invention was obvious, since this then became an undisputed fact. The task of proving lack of inventive step then required evaluating the various difficulties in implementation that he had identified and showing that each of them was either non-existent or easily overcome by a skilled person. The patent was revoked by the Patents County Court for lack of inventive step, and that decision was affirmed by the Court of Appeal.

413 At this stage, of course, a reference to the earlier *Darby* board would have been difficult to find because Darby's article appeared in a general interest scientific magazine and not in a specialised yachting magazine.

when and how the idea had come into the public domain,[413] whether others had tried to reduce the idea to practice, and if so what constructions of board and rig they had proposed. Such disclosures would have been closer prior art than *Sailfish/Sunfish* and would have been the starting point for evaluating novelty and inventive step. However, since Drake in his 1969 lecture[414] said that the inventors had pioneered the concept of applying a sail to a surfboard, it is unlikely that the admission was intentional.

One probable explanation is that the inventors had mentioned the idea of using a kite to propel a surfboard. That idea of kitesurfing predates Windsurfing, although its successful reduction to practice followed that of Windsurfing, and the sport did not become popular until the 1990s. In the later developed sport of kitesurfing, a traction kite is flown about 25-30 metres above the water, is held by the kitesurfer and steered by two or four control lines attached to a control bar. Problems that may have delayed the development of the sport include the design of kites that could tack against the wind and could be re-launched from the water, and control systems that enabled the power of the kite to be controlled dynamically on the water. A kite differs from a sailing rig because the kite is separate from the board and is not controlled by a mast and booms.

Another possibility is that the statement might have been made in relation to the unsuccessful *Skate* prototype, but that prototype was not prior art because it was unpublished. It should only been mentioned in the background section accompanied by a clear explanation of what was being discussed, which was an unpublished earlier proposal.

A further possibility is that the attorneys who drafted the application were confusing the board-like hull of *Sailfish/Sunfish* with a surfboard and equated a sail on a *Sailfish/Sunfish* hull with a sail on a surfboard. However, it is unlikely that any surfer would have accepted the *Sailfish/Sunfish* hull as a surfboard because it was too deep and heavy and was recessed to define a recumbent control position that is not used when surfing.

The background section of the *Windsurfer* patent aptly illustrates the point[415] that generalised statements of prior art not based on specific identified disclosures can be misleading and dangerous.

Differences in *Windsurfer*

Like many inventions in the mechanical arts, the Windsurfer is deceptively simple, and it is easy to take for granted features that merit detailed investigation and explanation. If *Sailfish/Sunfish* is taken as the closest prior art known to the inventors, then the following differences are apparent simply on inspection, negative differences being potentially as important as positive differences:

Hull:
● *Surfboard* replaces conventional dinghy hull.

---

414. *Supra*
415. See the discussion at pages 200 to 203.

- Smooth top – no recess defining a control position.
- No rudder.
- No mast socket.

Sailing rig:
- Universal joint pivots mast to hull.
- Boom positioned higher along mast for control from a standing position.
- *Wishbone boom replaces single boom.*
- Sail is positioned by grasping the boom – no sheets (ropes) for controlling the sail.
- *Single pocket at leading edge of sail fits onto mast.*
- *Pocket is cut-away for attachment of wishbone boom to mast.*
- Lower edge of sail not attached to boom.
- Sail extends below boom to adjacent the mast foot.
- *Sail shape differs from both Sailfish/Sunfish and from a Bermuda rig.*

In *Windsurfer*, the differences which most closely agree with the initial perception by the inventors of what they had achieved are the unsupported pivoted mast and re-positioning the booms along the mast so that they can be grasped from a standing control position. A subset of the above differences which remains novel over the Darby disclosure is shown in italics. The word *surfboard* is italicised because there is believed to be a significant difference between the *Windsurfer* board and the *Darby* board, although that difference is subtle and debatable.

The *Windsurfer* claims

The Windsurfer patent was granted in the UK with only seven claims. To highlight relevant issues, the main claim and some of the subsidiary claims have been combined into the composite claim which appears below, features derived from the subsidiary claims being shown in italics, and features selected for discussion being shown in bold type:

> A [**wind-propelled vehicle**] *watercraft* comprising
>   **body means** *having an attached leeboard*,
>   an unstayed spar connected to said body means through a joint which will provide **universal-type movement** of the spar in the absence of support thereof by a user of the vehicle,
>   a **sail** attached along one edge thereof to the spar *and having a lower edge extending outwardly from the spar, the sail being substantially the sole means for changing the direction of travel of the watercraft,*
>   a pair of **arcuate** booms, first ends of the booms being connected together and laterally connected on the spar, second ends of the booms being connected together, and
>   means on the booms connected to the sail such that the sail is held taut between the booms.

Initial attention was focused on the unsupported pivoted mast that was held upright by a user to sail the board. Embodiments of the pivot could have either a single axis, two axes or three axes. On the premise that it is best to start with the minimum difference from the known prior art, in this case the *Sailfish/Sunfish* sailboards, it would have been logical at the initial filing stage to ask whether the claims should cover pivoting about a single axis. One starting point statement of invention could then have been based on a board having a sailing rig including firstly an unsupported mast pivotally attachable to the board for movement about at least one axis and secondly at least one hand control member positioned along a mast of said sailing rig for grasping by a standing user for holding the mast upright and positioning the sail. The US versions of the *Windsurfer* patent preserve the broadest definition of the invention as originally filed, and refer to "wind propulsion means *pivotally* associated with the body means and adapted to receive wind for motive power." The word *pivotally* in the above statement covers all three possibilities for the number of pivot axes. From this definition, it would have been possible to reconstruct a technical problem, treating the *Sailfish/Sunfish* sailboards as closest known prior art, as that of providing a sailboard whose control demands new skills and that provided a greater sensation of speed and excitement.

The inventors might have objected to such a broad statements of invention based on their experience with their unsatisfactory *Skate* prototype in which the mast and sail were pivoted only for movement in a fore and aft plane. In that prototype, heeling movements of the sail were transmitted to the board and made it impossible for the user to stand on the board, so that *Skate* was never sailed. However, the patent attorney could have replied that Skate used a surfboard hull and was therefore of low roll stability. If the inventors intended to cover other sailing craft, their heavier and deeper hulls might provide sufficient roll stability for control from a standing position. Part of the task of the patent attorney is to seek protection covering versions of the invention that use only some features of the preferred embodiment, thereby sacrificing some but not all of the benefits obtainable. Limiting the claims to multi-axis pivoting at the initial filing stage would have been unwise because of the risk that a third party would find a way of making single-axis pivoting practical.

In the disclosed embodiment pivoting the mast in the fore and aft plane appeared to be the most important because it facilitated steering. Providing an additional axis for pivoting the mast in a plane transversely of the hull prevented heeling forces on the sail from being transmitted via the mast to the hull which though advantageous was arguably less critical. Permitting the mast to rotate about its axis relative to the hull becomes advantageous where the sail is attached to the mast by a sock and is stiffened by battens so that the actions of pulling the sail in or letting the sail out tend to rotate the mast. In the prototypes where the booms are pivoted to the mast and the sail is wholly of flexible cloth the mast rotation feature may be a non-critical refinement. One useful subsidiary claim could therefore have specified that the sailing rig was pivotally attachable to the board for movement in at least a plane aligned with the fore and aft direction of the board, with the supporting advantage that the hand control means could be used to steer the board towards or away from

---

416. This definition would have covered the Bermuda rig and all other fore and aft rigs. A question that the patent attorney might routinely have put to the inventors was whether moving the rig fore and aft was the *only* way of steering the sailboard by means of the rig, or whether other steering movements were possible e.g. moving the rig transversely of the board or by shifting the user's weight relatively to the board. Darby's kite rig when tacking was steered by moving the mast obliquely and when running was steered by moving the mast from side to side.

the apparent wind by manual adjustment of the mast position in said fore-and aft plane.[416] Further subsidiary claims could have introduced the second and third pivot axes, with their associated advantages being explained in the description.

Structural v Functional claiming in *Windsurfer* – arcuate booms

The use of the word A*rcuate* for the shape of the booms provides an example of a structural definition where a functional definition would have been more effective. It suffers from the further problem of being a geometrical term and, as explained above, such terms have been a recurrent source of difficulty during enforcement proceedings.

The meaning of *arcuate* became critical in the UK infringement proceedings because it provided the only available distinction from another prior sailing craft[417] that had been found by the defendants. It used a split boom formed from straight pieces of wood that became curved to some extent when the craft was being sailed. The only purposes disclosed in the patent for the *arcuate* booms were to provide a grip for the user and to hold the sail taut. Straight booms achieved these purposes equally effectively. The UK Court of Appeal refused to take notice of the fact that the booms were shaped and curved so that the sail would take up an aerofoil shape because such a requirement was neither discussed in the specific description nor a feature of any dependent claim, and the fact that the feature might be discerned by inspection of the drawing was not persuasive.

As we have seen, structural claims often suffer from the problem that they are narrow and easily circumvented, especially when they introduce a geometrical feature. In the

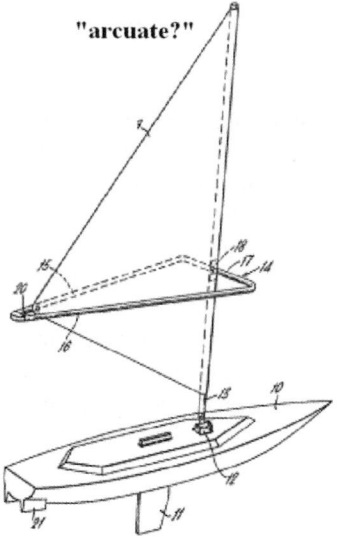

---

417. Sailed by an individual called Peter Chilvers, then 12 years old, during 1958 at Hayling Island, on the south cost of the UK. The hull of the Chilvers sailing craft is not described in the judgment, but it seems to have been a conventional dinghy hull originally steered by a rudder. It will be recalled that the Windsurfer patent had no claim that distinguished a surfboard hull from such a conventional dinghy hull.

case of the *Windsurfer* patent, it was foreseeable that third parties might design a split boom arrangement in which the booms were spaced apart between their ends to give the sail sufficient space to take up its natural aerofoil shape, but that were not *arcuate*. An example appears in the accompanying Figure on page 235 which is taken from a third party patent[418] that formed part of the Windsurfer licensing package considered by the EU Commission.[419] If an unauthorised third party had adopted such a triangular boom structure, there would have been no literal adoption of the *arcuate* claim language, and proof of infringement on the basis of a widened "purposive construction" of that language would have been difficult and even if successful could have required prolonged and expensive argument in court.[420]

The general desirability of using functional language has to be considered, however, in the light of particular problems that arise in the US,[421] and a noun or noun phrase recognizable by those skilled in the art as covering a genus of structures together with a definition of the function to be performed by such structure may be preferable to the familiar means-plus-function format.

Direct or contributory infringement?

The claims of the UK *Windsurfer* patent provide an example where forethought as to the form in which the invention would be distributed to customers was apparently lacking. For practical reasons, the sailing rig of a small boat is dismantled and stowed when the boat is not being sailed, and *Windsurfer* users follow this practice. In the prototype shown in the patent, the sailing rig can be detached from the board, the boom can be detached from the mast, and the sail can be detached from both the mast and the boom. However, the main claim included the words *connected, attached* and *held taut* which can only refer to the sailing craft when fully rigged and ready for use. The point passed without comment in the UK because the Court of Appeal did not need to discuss infringement in its opinion, but in proceedings for infringement of the corresponding patent in Canada,[422] the Federal Court of Appeals held for the above reason that there had only been induced infringement. Expression of the relationships between the parts in terms of conditional words (for example *connectable*) or purposive words (for example *for connection*) coupled with a statement in the description that the invention included the sailing craft both when dismantled for storage and assembled for use could have avoided this problem.

An assembled Windsurfer and its components can be regarded as a *distributed invention* where both the assembly and the individual novel components may be patentable provided that the appropriate claim format is used.

---

418. GB-A-1551426

419. Proceedings before the European Commission and the European Court are discussed below.

420. "Arcuate" is an example of a £100,000 word, such words possibly being stretchable to give the required coverage, but only following prolonged and costly argument in Court.

421. See the paper on *Functional Claims* beginning at page 135.

422. *Windsurfing International Inc v Trilantic Corporation* (1985) 8 CPR (3d) 241 (FCA); 63 WR 218.

In *Windsurfer,* it would have been most advantageous to claim:

- The assembly of the board and rig.
- A sailing rig for use in the assembly of claim 1 and having [defined novel rig features] (arguably patentable over both *Sailfish/Sunfish* and *Darby*).
- A sail for use in the assembly of claim 1 and having [defined novel sail features] (arguably also patentable over both *Sailfish/Sunfish* and *Darby*).
- A board for use in the assembly of board and rig and having [defined novel board features] (arguably patentable over *Sailfish/Sunfish*; more difficult to distinguish effectively over *Darby*).

Selection of the drawings

The granted patent has only a single sheet of drawings, and they provide scant details of either the new sailing craft or the way in which it is operated. In particular:

- A drawing like that of the *Baja Board* showing a person sailing the new board would have increased the impact of the patent and made it possible to see at a glance why the design features of the sailing rig were selected and what their purpose was. In particular the reasons for the unusual sail shape, the selected height of the booms and the flat top surface of the sailboard would have been apparent by inspection.
- A drawing showing the components of the Windsurfer prototype in disassembled state would have supported claims covering the board in disassembled form.
- The diagrammatic perspective view of the hull was inadequate, and there should have been at least a plan and a perspective view, and at least one sectional view. If there were significant changes in hull profile along its length or internal construction (for example to react load from the mast and centreboard) then additional views were needed showing how the section and internal construction changed with position.
- A plan would have been preferable showing the actual shapes of the split booms instead of the fragmentary views in the patent.
- When filing in the UK and in other countries outside the US, drawings of the *Big Red* prototype which had been the most successful and included significant changes compared to the *Old Yeller* prototype should have been included. It is dangerous to omit description of improvements made during the priority year because, although these may seem minor at the time when updating the specification is being considered, subsequent events may demonstrate their importance

Written description – comprehension

Complete comprehension of the detailed embodiments of the invention, and the significance of all the technical features in them, is essential for effective specification drafting. However, that comprehension is facilitated within a structured program of investigation after the identification of a starting point which provides a basis of comparison.

For example, at the time when the Windsurfer was invented what did the skilled person have to do to adapt a Bermuda rig for use with a sailboard having an unstayed hand-controlled rig? As previously explained, designers do not start from first principles, but take an existing design and modify it for the new requirements that it has to meet. Of the various rigs for a small sailing craft, the Bermuda rig was the most efficient and by far the most popular and it would have provided the most logical starting point. In such a rig, the main sail had the general form of a right angle triangle with its two shorter sides forming the luff and the foot of the sail respectively attached along the mast and the boom and with its hypotenuse forming the leech. The problems that confronted the inventors were how to provide for effective hand control of the mast and rig, how to facilitate that control from a standing position, and how to achieve good power while keeping the centre of effort and hence the heeling moment of the sail relatively low.

The solution adopted for the Windsurfer prototypes was to provide a sail in the form of a right angle or scalene triangle with its longest side forming the luff and attached along the mast, and with its two shorter sides forming the leech and the foot and with the clew located at the junction between them. The sail was controlled by a wishbone boom attached to the mast at its forward end between the tack and the head of the sail at a position corresponding to chest height and attached at its aft end to the clew. This arrangement had two practical advantages. Firstly the region of the sail that extended below the booms provided power with only slight increase in the heeling moment. Secondly it provided protection against uncontrolled upward movement of the booms caused e.g. by strong wind forces on the sail. Upward movement of the booms can only take place if the lower region of the sail stretches. That region is resistant to stretching because the tack is attached to the mast and its clew is attached to the booms by an outhaul which is tensioned by the user when the boat is rigged for sailing. The booms therefore assume a relatively stable position relative to the mast, which facilitates control of the rig and avoids the need for a kicking strap. Although the Lateen sail of *Sailfish/Sunfish* has a different shape to a Bermuda sail, from the standpoint of this discussion it suffers from the same unbalanced forces as

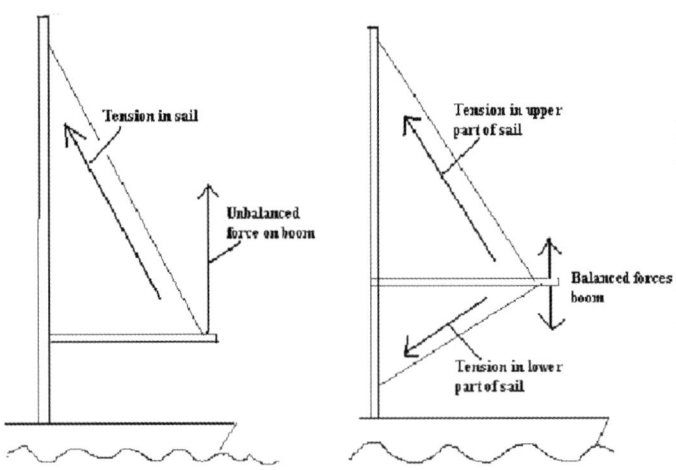

**Bermuda rig (sail is right-angle triangle)
and Windsurfer rig (sail is scalene triangle) showing
how vertical force on the boom differs**

a Bermuda rig and it would therefore have provided an equally unpromising starting point for a completely hand-held sailing rig.

The contribution of the sail shape and in particular of that part of the sail which extended below the booms was recognised both in Windsurfer's granted German patent and in their reissued US patent.[423] However, in the UK patent sail shape features were not claimed and their advantages were not described so that they could be of no help to the patentees in their UK infringement proceedings.

The patent attorney might reasonably have taken the view that it was inappropriate to specify that the sail had to be strictly triangular.[424] He could have distinguished the Windsurfer sail shape from a conventional Bermuda sail shape by specifying that the luff of the sail was longer than the leech or the foot, that the foot was rearwardly and upwardly inclined, and that the booms were attached at their forward ends to the mast at a spacing above the foot and at their aft ends adjacent where the leech joins the foot.

Additional claims could have referred to the pocket formed along the luff of the sail, and the forward-facing cut-out partway along the pocket to allow the booms to be attached to the mast. These features have remained in Windsurfers from the initial prototypes to the present day, but neither of them was claimed or remarked on as contributing ingeniously to the development of a practical rig.

If an explanation of the problems that the inventors had faced and the reasons for the selections that they had made had been included in the specification together with appropriate claims, the UK courts might not have been so easily persuaded that the Windsurfer rig was a simple step from Darby's kite rig, because the evidence on this point gives a strong impression of impermissible hindsight.[425] It should be noted that the German Patent Office decided that the rig was patentable following third-party oppositions based on the *Darby* disclosure.

---

423. See the corresponding US Re 031167 at column 3 lines 48-52 and claim 20.

424. Modern Windsurfers do not use strictly triangular sails. Their masts are no longer straight but are formed with strong rearward curvature. The sails are more nearly four-sided with the fourth side being defined by a short horizontal region at the head of the sail leading from the mast head to the leech. Furthermore, Windsurfer sails are now no longer formed of sailcloth but of a plastics sheet or film. However the family descent from the original triangular sail of the Windsurfer prototypes is clearly apparent.

425. The only expert witnesses in the UK proceedings who had read the *Darby* article at the time when it was published (a Mr Ellison) said in his evidence that the obvious thing to do to improve performance was to fold Darby's sail in two and wrap it round the mast, holding the sail taut by a boom on either side, see the Court of Appeal judgment at page 70. Mr Ellison was arguably trivializing the difficulties that a designer would in reality have faced, and his knowledge of the answer enabled him to propose a superficially simple but unrealistic route to the solution. A designer wishing to improve Darby's kite rig would not naturally have adopted as his starting point an unconventional rig of predictably poor performance, but instead would have started with the familiar and efficient Bermuda rig or the lateen rig of *Sailfish/Sunfish*. He would immediately have realised that it was not self-evident how to adapt that rig for a surfboard hull. The more you understand about the forces in the Windsurfer rig, and the way in which control is achieved, the cleverer the rig design of the Windsurfer appears.

Written description – definitions

As discussed above, following the decisions of the US courts in *Markman* and *Festo*, best practice nowadays is to include in the specific description definitions of the various terms used in the claims. The *Windsurfer* case demonstrates the wisdom of this practice for the UK and Europe also.

For example what is the meaning of *surfboard,* which appears in the description and should have been the subject of an independent claim? What is the ambit of the term, and does it cover the hull of the *Sailfish/Sunfish* sailcraft known to the inventors at the time of filing? If not, why not?

To answer these questions one would need to study existing surfboards, identify their distinctive constructional and hydrodynamic characteristics, and consider which of those characteristics had been incorporated unchanged into the *Windsurfer* prototypes and which had been modified. Following US practice, a description of the particular surfboard hulls that had been made and tested by the inventors should have been followed by a discussion of known or foreseeable equivalents. Without such a definition, the UK courts were unwilling to attach any importance to the belated attempt of the patentees to limit their claims to a California surfboard hull. That was also the opinion of the German Patent Office, which after being notified about references disclosing wishbone rigs and about the *Darby* sailboard allowed a claim to the rig but refused a claim to the rig/board combination on the ground that the board contributed nothing novel.

If the *Windsurfer* prototype boards existing at the time of US or international filing had been described in detail, patent offices and courts could not have treated their novelty, at least over the *Sailfish/Sunfish* sailboards, so dismissively. For example, the *Windsurfer* prototype boards were shallower than and less than half the weight of *Sailfish/Sunfish* sailboards, and it would have been easy to specify permitted depth and weight ranges that would have covered most boards likely to be useful in *Windsurfing* but were different from the *Sailfish/Sunfish* boards. Implicit in the above discussion is density, which could also have been discussed with advantage because it was important in surfboard design, where there had been a quest from the 1940s onwards for low-density materials to give better performance and maneuverability. First to be used was balsa wood and subsequently sheathed structures based on a foam plastics core. Such constructions were not conventional for sailing craft hulls. The completely closed board structure with a smooth uninterrupted top surface formed without a recess defining a recumbent control position and the absence of fittings for supporting a rudder are further differences that could have been specified.

Starting from the *Sailfish/Sunfish* sailboards, it is arguable that it was not obvious to reduce the weight and thickness of the hull, to form a closed structure with a smooth top surface and to omit provision for rudder steering without awareness of the *Windsurfer* concept. The *Windsurfer* prototype boards also differed from surfboards because they had a central aperture for a centreboard that was required to enable the board to be sailed upwind. What would have been the motivation for a skilled person to form a centreboard opening through a surfboard (but not to provide for steering by means of a tiller) unless he was aware of the *Windsurfer* concept? It is submitted that there was scope for adding useful dependent claims directed to board design features and thereby further distinguish over the *Sailfish/Sunfish* prior art. The hydrodynamic properties of a surfboard are different from those of the *Darby* board which was designed for slower lake sailing with a less efficient rig. It should have been possible to introduce claims to the planing aspects of the *Windsurfer* which had, for example, flat aft butt planes (vertical sections parallel to the centreline of the board) and a sharp-edged tailfor that purpose.

The absence of detailed information about the hull (and corresponding claims) had significant adverse consequences for Windsurfer's licensing programme in Europe. Windsurfer had a policy of granting licenses to manufacture boards only on condition that they were supplied together with rigs. The EU Commission objected to this policy on the ground that a patent should not be used to restrict competition in the boards which were not covered by the claims of the German patent, and their objection was upheld on appeal to the EU Court.[426] The same view about the separate novelty of the board and other components was taken in proceedings for infringement of the corresponding Canadian patent,[427] where the Federal Court of Appeals said:

> No one has ever alleged in this case infringement by the components of the invention. They are acknowledged to be old. The invention is the combination of the old components or elements...

Whenever a product based on a new combination of components is developed, the starting position of an attorney should be that the individual components are likely to be novel, and that although they may resemble similar components in existing products, they will have been modified for use in the new combination. The attorney should therefore seek out such modifications and ensure that his findings are described in the specification and claimed appropriately. If the attorney does not include the necessary information in the specification, then a patent office or court has no alternative but to reach an adverse conclusion about the novelty of the components, as happened in Canada in *Windsurfer*.

In the present case, at least one prototype had been designed and made before the original US application was filed and additional prototypes had been made before the UK and other foreign applications were filed. There was no reason to suppress constructional and dimensional information, which turned out to be more important than had been appreciated at the time of filing and could have supported patentability. For example, the sail area of the *Windsurfer* prototypes was greater than that of the kite sail of the *Darby* sailboard, the height of the mast was greater which tended to increase the

---

426. The patent in question was the equivalent DE-B-1914602; see 83/400/EEC: *Commission Decision of 11 July 1983 relating to a proceeding under Article 85 of the EEC Treaty (IV/29.395 – Windsurfing International)*, Official Journal L 229, 20/08/1983 pp. 0001-0021 which explains the technical problem identified by the German Patent Office for the above patent and gives the text for the main claim in its final form; for the appeal see *Windsurfing International Inc. v Commission of the European Communities, Agreements prohibited by Article 85 of the EEC Treaty, Case 193/83*, [1986] ECR 611. Both of these decisions are available on the Internet.

427. *Windsurfing International Inc v Trilantic Corporation, supra.*

heeling moment, and the rig was of greater aerodynamic efficiency, implying greater control forces. There was room for argument whether it was obvious from the *Darby* publication that these changes to a more powerful rig were possible, but that argument became available only if the relevant figures had been provided in the specification, and the fact that the prototypes had out-raced the best previously known sailboards had been reported. The prototypes can be regarded as experiments that gave favourable results but went unreported, to the disadvantage of the patentees.

Where adoption of a particular feature involves choices amongst alternatives, reasons for the selection should be given and the associated advantages should be identified. For example, the specification states that the booms were located about 4ft above the board when the mast was upright, but the reason for the distance selected was not explained. It becomes immediately apparent if a drawing like the *BAJA BOARD* Figure (page 227) showing a standing user is included. However, the visual image would have needed to be reinforced by a written explanation that the boom height had been selected for comfortable and convenient control from a standing position, and that a height range of, for example, from 3 to 4.5 ft would be convenient for most adult users, with about 4 ft being preferred.

Written description – enablement

There may be arguments that the disclosure was insufficient, both from the standpoint of the new sailing craft as a whole and from the standpoint of the very limited board disclosure. One addressee of the specification would be a potential boat builder with skills in aerodynamics and hydrodynamics. However, was it legitimate to disregard skilled amateur boat builders with ordinary practical skills of the kind who routinely built sailing craft from plans and descriptions in magazines? There was a striking lack of detailed information and directions about sizes, sail area, board construction, materials and the like. Why should the information in the specification be less than that which would enable an amateur boat builder to make a workable sailboard straightforwardly from the disclosure in the specification or which the inventor James Drake included in his 1969 lecture, very shortly after the end of the priority year? Patents are often concerned with the protection of general principles, but it does not follow that all information as regards dimensions and proportions or ranges of them should be omitted. For example, how is the skilled person to know from the information in the *Windsurfer* patent how big the board should be and what is the range of practical possibilities? Is this something he should be left to work out for himself?

If this had been a European patent, a patent attorney acting for a potential opponent should have considered making an objection of insufficiency based on (a) undue experimentation and (b) non-availablilty of a suitable board. At the priority date of the patent, surfboards for use with fore-and aft-rigged sails were not available for purchase because the product was new, the patent did not contain a reference providing detailed instructions about how such boards should be made, there was no specific starting point disclosed for the design of a suitable board, and no established methodology for adapting a surfboard to accept a sailing rig and dagger board. The design problems of surfboards had received considerable attention but surfboards for use with sails were new and their design problems had not been addressed. Under the jurisprudence of the EPO Appeal Boards, any deficiency in disclosure can only be remedied by reference to the common general knowledge of the skilled person at the priority or application date, and the body of qualifying information that is available to remedy a deficiency in disclosure is therefore relatively small.[428] An argument concerning non-enablement would not have been certain of success, but it was clearly feasible.

Conclusions

It will be apparent that if a patent is to be of any value, it has to be written with at least a full understanding of the technical background known to the inventor(s) and a full technical understanding of the further developments that the inventors have contributed. Shortcuts in ascertaining the technical facts produce specifications with critical details omitted and either an unenforceable patent or a disproportionate expenditure of effort and cost in remedying the deficiency. Judges have the recurring characteristic that they treat ill-prepared documents dismissively and patent specifications are no exception, as the recent US Supreme Court decision in *Festo*[429] demonstrates. Unfortunately, a recurring characteristic of inventors is shortage of funds at the time when patent specifications have to be written, but if they impose undue budgetary constraints on their attorneys they put their rights at risk.

Consideration should be given, in important cases, to the composition of the drafting team which is responsible for preparing the specification. At a minimum the team consists of the patent attorney drafting the specification and the inventor(s). Consideration should be given to supplementing the team by the addition of (a) an independent expert in the field who can provide additional technical information and provide an independent view of the disclosure, and (b) a trial lawyer (in the UK a barrister) who can review the description and claims from the standpoint of his day-to-day experience of litigation and first-hand knowledge of issues that concern judges. Such a team was created by Guglielmo Marconi for his wireless telegraphy patent mentioned above after his UK provisional application had been filed and while a complete specification was being prepared, the trial lawyer who advised him being John Fletcher-Moulton QC (as he then was, afterwards Lord Moulton), who had relevant expertise in his own right being also a Fellow of the Royal Society[430] by virtue of his electrical research. At a more humble level, a team of the same type was brought together during the prosecution of the patent in issue in *A.C. Edwards v Acme Signs*[431] and arrived at claim wording which successfully overcame serious objections as to added subject-matter and lack of inventive step, and which was subsequently held valid and infringed.

---

428. T 0171/84 Redox Catalyst/AIR PRODUCTS.

429. See the discussion at page 133-134

430. See Dott. Anna Guagnini, *At the roots of patents – The role of patent agents and scientific advisers in paving the way to Guglielmo Marconi's technological achievement*, down-loadable from the Internet.

431. [1990] RPC 621 (HC) and [1992] RPC 131 (CA).

In summary, technical understanding is facilitated by the structured approach suggested above, in which:
- The field of the invention is identified.
- A single starting point within that field and providing the closest known prior art is identified.
- The invention is compared systematically with that closest known prior art to identify *all* differences from which advantages flow, and to identify the advantage or advantages associated with each such difference.
- Main independent claims are drafted where possible in terms of a single advantageous difference expressed in functional terms (or in structural language defining a genus of functionally-related structures).
- Dependent claims are drafted covering the remaining advantageous differences and possibly additionally more specific field-related features.
- Distributed invention aspects are considered and appropriate components, methods, etc are independently claimed as such.
- Definitions are obtained for all terms used in the claims, including appropriate equivalents or alternatives and including literature references describing appropriate components, starting materials and procedures.
- Descriptions are obtained in full detail for specific practical embodiments, avoiding mere "high-level" or "hand-waving" description or black boxes unaccompanied by supporting detail.

Characteristics of effective patent attorneys which have been highlighted by the present study include:
- Enquiring and persistent minds that prompt them to insist on knowing, for example, what are the significant differences between a sailboat hull and a surfboard (which at first sight look quite similar) and to investigate the history of surfboard and sailing craft development until answers are forthcoming.
- Powers of observation that enable them to focus on differences between the invention and the prior art and to notice, for example, that the triangular Windsurfer sail is attached to the mast along its longest edge, whereas a conventional Bermuda sail is attached along one of the shorter edges, and then to ask whether this difference might be significant.
- Analytical skills that provide a structured law-based framework within which the description and claims can be written. The technical problem approach of the EPO goes far towards providing this framework, and its development by the EPO Appeal Boards is arguably the most valuable contribution to the development of patent practice over the last two decades.
- A realistic and practical approach, identifying the interests of the applicant that need to be protected. For example, in *Windsurfer*, the highest priority was to protect the invention for surfboards from whence it originated, and it was foreseeable that the licensing program would need to cover individual components. Defining an invention by a set of claims is not a mere academic exercise between a patent examiner and an attorney, but is a real-world task that requires the claims as granted to be legally and commercially effective. Safeguarding the commercial interests of clients is, of course, the major purpose of our existence as an independent profession.

PATENT DRAFTING CHECKLIST

BACKGROUND/STARTING POINT

- Field of the invention
- Closest prior art/inventor's actual starting point
- Ancillary art in other fields?

DEFINING THE INVENTION

- One key difference preferably defined functionally
- Other differences
- Benefits associated with the differences
- Elements claimed by generic structural noun + function
- All embodiments covered?
- Human activities
  - Product
  - Method for making product
  - Method for using product
  - Distributed inventions (claims to components; "look down")
  - Component inventions (claims to system; "look up")

SUPPORTING THE INVENTION

- Examples
- Drawings
  - Show all claimed elements
  - Show movements and alternative positions of movable parts
  - Show invention in use

SPECIFIC DESCRIPTION

- Definition of terms used in claims (US Markman practice)
- Description of embodiments
  - Starting materials
  - Identifiable structure for *each* claimed element
  - Equivalents for each claimed element
  - Method of assembling/producing the invention
  - Results achieved
  - Description of uses

CHEMICAL DRAFTING SKILLS

Empirical research inventions – allowable generic claim scope

In science there is only physics; all the rest is stamp collecting.[432]

Results! Why, man I have gotten a lot of results. I know several thousand things that won't work.[433]

We have learned from experience that truth will out. Other experimenters will repeat your experiment and find out whether you were wrong or right. Nature's phenomena will agree or they will disagree with your theory. And although you may gain some temporary fame and excitement, you will not gain a good reputation as a scientist if you haven't tried to be very careful in this kind of work. And it's this type of integrity, this kind of care not to fool yourself that is missing to a large extent in much of the research in cargo cult science.[434]

Introduction

This discussion is with particular, but not exclusive, reference to practice in the pharmaceutical industry for claiming new chemical entities, and in particular to the feasibility of defining a genus of compounds that validly covers compounds that have not yet been made and tested.

In the early days of the pharmaceutical industry claims were to single compounds. The well-known Felix Hoffmann US patent No 644077 granted in 1900 for aspirin provides an example. Another researcher had previously described acetyl salicylic acid, but Hoffmann demonstrated that the compound that the earlier researcher had made did not possess the correct properties. Hoffmann had developed a new process that gave *"the real acetyl salicylic acid"* which *"exhibits therapeutical properties"* and claimed:

As a new article of manufacture the acetylsalicylic acid having the formula being

---

432. Attributed to Ernest Rutherford. Notwithstanding his preference for systematic over descriptive knowledge, the lives of most readers will have been saved at least once by the descriptive knowledge embodied in a pharmaceutical product.

433. Attributed to Thomas A. Edison.

434. Richard P Feynman, "Cargo Cult Science", see footnote 10 on page 2.

when crystallised from dry chloroform in the shape of white glittering needles, easily soluble in benzene, alcohol and glacial acetic acid, difficultly soluble in cold water, being split by hot water into acetic acid and salicylic acid, melting at about 135°C, substantially as hereinbefore described.

Compounds isolated from nature and produced synthetically could also be claimed. An example is provided by US patent 3880888 (Firmenich S.A.) which reports the isolation of the compound 3,4,7-trimethyl-2-oxo-1,6-dioxa-spiro[4.5]dec-3-ene from an essential oil derived by distillation of Burley tobacco. The compound is said to provide a mild herbal or woody note to the tobacco, and is claimed as a composition of matter consisting essentially of a compound of the formula.

As is well known, the pharmaceutical industry was an offshoot from the dyestuff industry. From the beginning of the 20th century onwards, the practice developed within that industry of claiming classes of dyestuffs generically by means of structural formulae. US-A-1744172 provides an example of so-called Markush practice as it had developed by the mid 1920s. The patentees had claimed a novel class of azo dyes which had the benefit of producing durable colours on cotton and other vegetable fibres, and which are defined in claim 2 of the patent (with slight editing) as follows:

As new products azo dyestuffs having most probably the general formula:

wherein Y stands for alkyl, oxyalkyl, oxyaryl or halogen; X represents either the sulfone group SO_2 or the carbonyl group CO, and R_1 represents ... alkyl, aryl, aralkyl ... which are in the dry state reddish to dark coloured powders, soluble in concentrated sulphuric acid with from blue to dark violet colours ... and which when produced on vegetable fibres yield reddish shades of excellent fastness to kier boiling.

The patentability of the compounds of this genus flows from the link between the chemical structure and the newly discovered and valuable properties possessed by the compounds of that structure. That formulation is consistent with the question put forward by Sir Stafford Cripps K.C. in UK proceedings between *Sharp & Doehme v Boots*[435] which concerned the manufacture of certain alkyl-substituted resorcinols which were known as antiseptics (at that time chemical product claims were not allowed in the UK). Published papers had already disclosed that the C_1-C_4 members of the class had been made and that antiseptic activity increased as the number of carbon atoms in the alkyl chain increased. The patentees averred that because drug research was empirical, the skilled person knew in advance neither that the higher alkyl resorcinols could be produced by the claimed method nor what their antiseptic properties would be. The compound that proved to be of therapeutic value was n-hexyl resorcinol which is of formula:

HO — O —

The defendants replied that because therapeutic activity increased in the known compounds from C_1 to C_4, it was obvious to make the higher members of the series. Sir Stafford Cripps argued that the question concerning inventive step that the court had to decide was based on whether there was an obvious link between structure and value, and was as follows:

Was it for practical purposes obvious
- to any skilled chemist
- in the state of chemical knowledge existing at the date of the patent, which consisted of
  - the chemical literature available, a selection of which appeared in the Particulars of Objections, and
  - his general chemical knowledge,
- that he could make **valuable** therapeutic agents
- by making the **higher alkyl resorcinols**? (Paragraphing and emphasis added).

The same link between structure and value is implicit in the requirement for utility in US law, as is apparent, for example, from the following passage from *Brenner v Mason*[436] which calls for the product to be useful, i.e. to have a "*specific benefit*":

Until the process claim has been reduced to production of a product shown to be useful, the metes and bounds of that monopoly are not capable of precise delineation. It may engross a vast, unknown, and perhaps unknowable area. Such a patent may confer power to block off whole areas of scientific development, without compensating benefit to the public. The basic quid pro quo contemplated by the Constitution and the Congress for granting a patent monopoly is the benefit derived by the public from an invention with substantial utility. Unless and until a process is refined and developed to this point – where specific benefit exists in currently available form – there is insufficient justification for permitting an applicant to engross what may prove to be a broad field.

435. (1928) 45 RPC 153
436. 383 U.S. 519 (1966)

In the azo dyestuff case referred to above, it is clearly credible that the whole class of compounds would dye cotton with the indicated combination of colour and resistance to boiling. However, the credibility of similar Markush claims for pharmaceuticals or agrochemicals is open to question since human, animal and living plant cells are more complex than cotton fibres.

Generic claims to the results of empirical research

Finding pharmaceutically active compounds has been at least until recently a task of empirical research of the kind pioneered by Thomas Alva Edison, and the rules applicable to patents of this category have been known at least since the decision of the US Supreme Court in the *Incandescent Lamp case*[437] which concerned a third party patent which was alleged to be infringed by the electric lamps being made and sold by Edison licensees. The third party patent purported to monopolise all carbonised fibrous or textile materials for use as filaments for electric lamps, as is apparent from the following main claim:

> An incandescing conductor for an electric lamp, of carbonized fibrous or textile material, and of an arch or horseshoe shape, substantially as hereinbefore set forth.

The evidence adduced in the case showed that the researches carried out by the third party could not support such a broad monopoly and that the field was unpredictable. The factual background and the reasoning of the court will be apparent from the following passages from the Opinion:

> Is the complainant entitled to a monopoly of all fibrous and textile materials for incandescent conductors? If the patentees had discovered in fibrous and textile substances *a quality common to them all*, or to them generally, as distinguishing them from other materials, such as minerals, etc., and such quality or characteristic adapted them peculiarly to incandescent conductors, such claim might not be too broad. If, for instance, minerals or porcelains had always been used for a particular purpose, and a person should take out a patent for a similar article of wood, and woods generally were adapted to that purpose, the claim might not be too broad, though defendant used wood of a different kind from that of the patentee. But if woods generally were not adapted to the purpose, and yet the patentee had discovered a wood possessing certain qualities, which gave it a peculiar fitness for such purpose, it would not constitute an infringement for another to discover and use a different kind of wood, which was found to contain similar or superior qualities.
>
> The present case is an apt illustration of this principle. Sawyer and Man supposed they had discovered in carbonized paper the best material for an incandescent conductor. Instead of confining themselves to carbonized paper, as they might properly have done, and in fact did in their third claim, they made a broad claim for every fibrous or textile material, when in fact an examination of over 6,000 vegetable growths showed that none of them possessed the peculiar qualities that fitted them for that purpose. Was everybody, then, precluded by this

---

437. *Consolidated Electric Light Co v. McKeesport Light Co*, 159 U.S. 465 (1895)

broad claim from making further investigation? We think not.

The injustice of so holding is manifest in view of the experiments made, and continued for several months, by Mr. Edison and his assistants, among the different species of vegetable growth, for the purpose of ascertaining the one best adapted to an incandescent conductor. Of these he found suitable for his purpose only about three species of bamboo, one species of cane from the valley of the Amazon (impossible to be procured in quantities on account of the climate), and one or two species of fibers from the agave family. Of the special bamboo, the walls of which have a thickness of about 3/8 of an inch, he used only about 20/1000 of an inch in thickness. In this portion of the bamboo the fibers are more nearly parallel, the cell walls are apparently smallest, and the pithy matter between the fibers is at its minimum. It seems that carbon filaments cannot be made of wood, that is exogenous vegetable growth, because the fibers are not parallel, and the longitudinal fibers are intercepted by radial fibers. The cells composing the fibers are all so large that the resulting carbon is very porous and friable. Lamps made of this material proved of no commercial value. After trying as many as 30 or 40 different woods of exogenous growth, he gave them up as hopeless. But finally, while experimenting with a bamboo strip which formed the edge of a palm-leaf fan, cut into filaments, he obtained surprising results. After microscopic examination of the material, he dispatched a man to Japan to make arrangements for securing the bamboo in quantities....

... how would it be possible for a person to know what fibrous or textile material was adapted to the purpose of an incandescent conductor, except by the most careful and painstaking experimentation? If, as before observed, there were **some** *general quality*, running through the whole fibrous and textile kingdom, which distinguished it from every other, and gave it a peculiar fitness for the particular purpose, the man who discovered such quality might justly be entitled to a patent; but that is not the case here. An examination of materials of this class carried on for months revealed nothing that seemed to be adapted to the purpose; and even the carbonized paper and wood carbons specified in the patent, experiments with which first suggested their incorporation therein, were found to be so inferior to the bamboo, afterwards discovered by Edison, that the complainant was forced to abandon its patent in that particular, and take up with the material discovered by its rival. *Under these circumstances, to hold that one who had discovered that a certain fibrous or textile material answered the required purpose should obtain the right to exclude everybody from the whole domain of fibrous and textile materials, and thereby shut out any further efforts to discover a better specimen of that class than the patentee had employed, would be an unwarranted extension of his monopoly, and operate rather to discourage than to promote invention.*

The views of the US Supreme Court coincide with those of the English judges. In the case of claims to newly discovered compounds, the basic principle is as set out by the House of Lords in *May & Baker v Boots*[438] which explains that generic claims are permissible where there is a rational basis for them, and sets out the following principles for research in an empirical art:

---

438. 67 RPC 23 at 50

(i) in a field where progress is by empirical discovery, an invention must be in respect of a substance which has actually been produced, since there cannot be an empirical discovery in respect of a bare formula;

(ii) each new compound is a separate invention since its worth is a new discovery; but

(iii) where the chemist has found some law or principle by which he can predict therapeutic effect in advance so that each of a group of new products will be of value, the art will have lost its empirical nature, at least to some extent (i.e. a Markush claim may be allowable).

The factual situation in *May & Baker* is of interest. The invention claimed in the patent in issue GB-A-533495 covered sulfathiazole (M & B 760) and sulfamethylthiazole, the first of which was the most important of the *sulfa* antibacterials[439] and is of the formula indicated below:

M & B 760

The specification did not have specific claims directed to the two exemplified active compounds. It only had generic claims to benzene sulfonamido thiazole derivatives, the genus of compounds claimed being described in words rather than by a structural formula. The description explained that the NH_2 group could be substituted amino (e.g. alkylamino, N-acyl-N-alkylamino or aralkylamno) and that the benzene ring could have alkyl substituents. The thiazole ring could also be substituted. The resulting genus covered tens of millions of compounds, and although it covered compounds additional to the two compounds exemplified that had been found to be active, it admittedly also covered compounds that were inactive. The patentees therefore proposed to replace their generic claim by a claim to the two exemplified compounds, arguing that it was apparent on the face of the specification that they were drawing an inference from their specific data and should not be penalised if that inference proved unfounded. In a split (3:2) judgment the House of Lords rejected this approach and said:[440]

> The argument and the construction of the specification implied in it are open to grave objections. They set aside the plain categorical statements of the specification that the invention consists in the manufacture of new benzene-sulphonamido-thiazole derivatives, and that the new benzene-sulphonamido-thiazoles have especially favourable therapeutic properties. These general statements are no longer to be accepted as statements of fact, and they are to be regarded rather as a scientific hypothesis. It seems to have been forgotten

---

439. Dr. A.W. White recalls "M&B 693" as a commercial product which was sulfapyridine. A Google search shows that M&B 693 was a life-saving drug in the late 1930s and was much used during World War II until penicillin became available. M&B 693 had the generic name of sulphanilamide and/or sulphpyridine, whereas the infringement case discussed here concerned a compound having a thiazyl ring, rather than a pyridine one.

440. Lord Normand at p. 38

that they were the basis of a patent grant just because they were treated as statements of fact, and that they were put into the specification and followed by the commensurate claims for the purpose of obtaining a monopoly in the large field covered by the claims ... Let it be here recalled that the Appellants have acquiesced in the finding of Jenkins J that on a proper construction of the specification there is an assertion that every substance capable of being produced by the described methods from the prescribed materials was of the especially therapeutic value, and that they have obtained from the same learned judge a finding that they believed what they asserted, that is they committed themselves to this statement as a true generalization from their experimental data. Having so committed themselves they cannot now draw back and say that they are committed only to the truth of their assertions about two specific substances and to an unproved scientific hypothesis.

The generic claim was therefore invalid, and in the absence of specific claims to the two exemplified compounds or an "omnibus claim" directed to the individual examples, the patent was held to be unenforceable.

The same principles were followed by the UK House of Lords in *Biogen v Medeva*: [441]

Thus if the patentee has hit upon a new product which has a beneficial effect but cannot demonstrate that there is a common principle by which that effect will be shared by other products of the same class, he will be entitled to a patent for that product but not for the class, even though some may subsequently turn out to have the same beneficial effect..... On the other hand, if he has disclosed a beneficial property which is common to the class, he will be entitled to a patent for all products of that class (assuming them to be new) even though he has not himself made more than one or two of them.

In the EPO, although technical analysis is conducted within the formal framework of problem/solution analysis, the outcome principally determined by whether the claimed subject-matter leads to a new effect, some new function or advantage that cannot be predicted from the teachings of the prior art references considered collectively.[442] Szabo made that clear, for the chemical field at least,[443] when he said that:

The practice of the Board of Appeal (Chemistry) has been relying on an effect-centreed problem and solution approach to the question of inventive step.

This observation is supported by the decision in the well-known case of *Agrevo/Triazoles*[444], which concerned a class of herbicidal triazole sulphonamides.

---

441. [1997] RPC 1 at page 49 lines 1 to 9.

442. The existence of an unexpected new effect may be a *necessary* condition for patentability but it is not a *sufficient* condition. If the prior art when considered collectively suggests some other advantageous new effect, then arguments concerning mere *"bonus effect"* or *"one-way street"* become relevant, and inventive step may be denied.

443. G.S.A. Szabo, *"The Problem and Solution Approach to the Inventive Step"*, [1986] 10 EIPR 293-303.

444. T 0939/92,

The dispute was whether the whole class of compounds had to be herbicidal in order to establish patentability, or whether it was enough for the applicants to show that:
(a) some of the claimed compounds were herbicides; and
(b) the cited art did not teach the skilled person to make *any* compound within the class.

The origin of the objection was that the genus of compounds claimed included open-ended definitions that covered very large substituents and the Examining Division considered that it was not plausible that the claimed compounds had utility for all possible substituents. The applicants argued that the Board need only consider whether the skilled person *would* make the claimed compounds starting from the prior art teachings – i.e. the relevant question was what the public would do, not what the inventor had achieved. The Board rejected the applicant's argument in uncompromising terms, and based its opinion on the legal principle that the extent of the patent monopoly should correspond to, and be justified by, the technical contribution to the art that is contained in the specification. It went on to say that mere structural ingenuity was not sufficient. If the result that the skilled person was seeking to achieve was simply obtaining further chemical compounds, then all known chemical compounds were equally suitable as starting points and all known methods of transformation might be used, so that the selection of particular compounds to be made was a mere arbitrary choice. For that reason

> ...the selection of such compounds, in order to be patentable, must not be arbitrary but must be justified by a hitherto unknown **technical effect** which is caused by those **structural features** which distinguish the claimed compounds from the numerous other such compounds ... It follows directly from these considerations that a technical effect which justifies the selection of the claimed compounds must be one which can fairly assumed to be produced by **substantially all** the claimed compounds.

Single change in a genus of molecules of known structure-activity relationships

The UK decision in *Olin Mathieson v Biorex*[445] provides an example of a generic definition in the pharmaceutical field that was not successfully challenged. The tranquiliser chlorpromazine (Largactil) had been patented in 1950 and provided a breakthrough in the treatment of mental illness. It was of formula:

---

445. [1970] RPC 157

The discovery of chlorpromazine stimulated structure-activity investigations aimed at the production of compounds with improved properties. The patentees had discovered *inter alia* the drugs trifluopromazine and fluphenazine, which were based on a ring CF_3 substitution and were of formulae:

Trifluopromazine

Fluphenazine

The patent in issue GB-A-857547 (which had been divided from GB-A-857546 claiming a wider genus) covered a genus of compounds of the formula:

wherein A is a lower alkylene radical and B is a basic nitrogen-containing radical with fewer than 12 carbon atoms.[446] The compounds were said to be antihistaminic, anti-emetic and tranquilising agents and to be useful for the treatment of psychotic states, the compound trifluopromazine being disclosed as more potent than chlorpromazine. The defendants proposed to manufacture a compound called trifluoperazine (Stelazine) that was covered by the generic claims of the patent in issue but had not been exemplified or specifically disclosed. It was of formula:

Trifluoperazine

---

446. By modern standards the supporting disclosure of the patent is sparse. The introduction does not discuss the prior art, and the presentation of the invention is almost exclusively chemistry-oriented with only a brief value statement. Although comparative activity of the claimed compounds relative to chlorpromazine is discussed, no procedure is disclosed for measuring activity, and animal models for the indicated diseases are not mentioned. Dosages are related to that for chlorpromazine adjusted for relative activity. Pharmaceutical compositions are neither disclosed not claimed, which is a surprising omission given the advantages of such field-specific or medical indication-specific claims if the patent becomes the subject of litigation.

An initial allegation of non-enablement was not maintained, and the argument centred on whether the disclosure supported the broad generic scope of the independent claims. The Court's decision to uphold the generic claims was based primarily on the facts that:

1. the side chains covered by the patent in issue had been disclosed in earlier patents concerning phenothiazines and had been shown to be active,
2. there was no reason to suppose that change of the ring substituent from Cl to CF_3 would affect the range of side chains that was compatible with activity,
3. for any given side chain the CF_3 substituent in the 2-position gave the highest activity, and
4. all the CF_3-substituted phenothiazl compounds that the plaintiffs had made and tested were therapeutically active.

A further instance where the same principles were adopted arises in *Chiron v Murex*[447] which concerned the sale of test kits for the hepatitis C retrovirus. The patentees had isolated from an infected chimpanzee called Rodney a polynucleotide that contained the instructions for making the antigenic determinant of the virus i.e. the site on the viral particle to which antibodies of the immune system attached themselves. They had then determined the sequence of that sample. These were the critical steps in identifying the cause of HCV infections and in harnessing the HCV antibody:antigen reaction to produce diagnostic test kits. The patent claimed inter alia:

> A polypeptide in substantially isolated form comprising a contiguous sequence of at least ten amino acids encoded by the genome of Hepatitis C virus (HCV) and comprising an antigenic determinant, wherein HCV is characterised by:
> (i) a positive stranded RNA genome;
> (ii) said genome comprising an open reading frame (ORF) encoding a polyprotein; and
> (iii) said polyprotein comprising an amino acid sequence having at least 40% homology to the 859 amino acid sequence in Figure 14.

The defendants alleged that the claim did not relate to a new class of chemicals because the members would be different chemically or biologically from one another, and because there was not prescribed a formula that linked them. The patentees replied that the link was their discovery of the virus and the presence of the antigenic determinants of the virus to which HCV antibodies would bind. The Court held that the facts differed from those in *Biogen* and stated:

> We prefer the submissions for Chiron. We will take claim 1 as the paradigm. There is nothing in that claim as a matter of language or in the specification as a whole to differentiate between one polypeptide falling within the claim and any of the millions of others. At the other end of the scale, there is no doubt that it was the finding and sequencing of the Rodney virus genome which was of the greatest importance for this discovery and analysis enabled the antigenic determinants to be found in the protein expressed by the sequence. In view of the fact that an antigenic determinant can only be defined by reference to the antibody which

---

447. [1996] FSR 153

binds to it, and the further fact that the immune response of an individual produces a whole range of antibodies to any given virus it is not possible to define antigenic determinants by reference to any common chemical formula. Thus the invention is the chemical comprising at least 10 amino acids in which there is an antigenic determinant to which an antibody to HCV will bind. In our view, both in substance and in form, this is a single invention properly defined by the common denominator of the existence of an antigenic determinant of HCV, notwithstanding that the resultant polypeptides will have divergent characteristics in other respects. The invention of one is the invention of all of them because that which is common to all is of the essence of the discovery and that which distinguishes one from the other is irrelevant to that discovery.

A recently litigated Markush claim in the pharmaceutical industry – You may be in trouble if you Markush!

Monsanto et al v Merck[448] concerned infringement of a patent covering non-steroidal anti-inflammatory drugs. Pumfrey J at first instance handed down a 78-page opinion on 4 February 2000.

By way of background, US-A-3743656 (Brown) had previously disclosed a class of diaryl heterocyclic compounds said to be anti-inflammatory agents and of the formula:

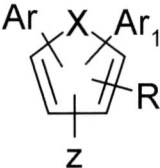

in which:
    the heteroatom X could be O, S or –NH-;
    Z could be hydrogen;
    Ar and Ar$_1$ could be phenyl or substituted phenyl in which the substituents could be F or CH$_3$SO$_2$; and
    R represented an alkyl group.

Amongst the specific disclosures in the Brown specification was a sub-class of compounds of the formula:

in which X and R have the meanings given above.

---

448. [2000] RPC 709 (HC), see *Pharmacia v. Merck* [2002] RPC 775, and [2002] IP&T 828 (CA).

DuPont had been working on diaryl heterocyclic compounds from 1979/80 onwards, and had published in 1989 details of a compound called DuP 697 that was said to combine good anti-inflammatory characteristics with low gastric irritancy.

F

S Br

DuP 697

CH_3SO_2

The properties of that compound had been described in a slide shown at a prostaglandin conference as follows:
- Active as an anti-inflammatory, antipyretic and in models of inflammatory pain.
- Selective inhibition of cyclooxegenase (COX) in cellular and enzymatic assays.
- Lack of platelet activity and safety profile may reflect in vivo results of selective CO inhibition.
- May be a useful tool to understand role of COX 1 and COX 2.

Despite its promise, DuP 697 was never commercialised because it turned out to be eliminated only very slowly from the body.

Soon after the prostaglandin conference the claimants had started work on developing diaryl heterocyclic anti-inflammatories using DuP 697 as lead compound. The object of their work was to discover another compound that was not only effective but also novel and hence patentable. The claimants found that:
- For cyclooxegenase activity the aromatic rings had to be located in adjacent positions on the heterocyclic ring.
- A CH_3SO_2 group in the p-position had to be present to inhibit the COX 2.
- The F atom on the other ring was not essential.

Their EP-B-679157 claimed a group of compounds said to exhibit anti-inflammatory or analgesic activity without causing erosion of the lining of the stomach because they selectively inhibit COX 2 (which produces inflammation) without substantial inhibition of COX 1 (which controls gastric secretion). The claimed compounds were therefore alleged to open up the possibility of an effective treatment for arthritis with reduced harmful side effects. They were of the formula:

Y

X

R^2 R^3

in which:

R[1] and R[2] represent aryl or heteroaryl which may be optionally substituted with a specified range of substituents, provided that one of them is substituted with methylsulfonyl (CH_3SO_2) or sulfamyl (NH_2SO_2);

X is hydrogen or is selected from a long list of possible substituents, including, amongst others, hydroxy (OH) and halogen (includes Br); and

Y is selected from S, O and – NR^1 – in which R^1 is selected from hydrogen and alkyl.

The specification mentioned by name more than 140 compounds, of which 15 had been exemplified as being made (the remainder presumably being prophetic), all 15 had been tested *in vitro* for activity (IC_{50} against COX I and COX II) and five had been tested *in vivo* for anti-oedema or analgesia. No structure/activity relationship was disclosed except what could be gleaned from the claims. Unfortunately for the claimants, the most promising compound that they had identified within the class claimed in their patent was dropped because of poor bio-availability.

Merck had started work later than the claimants, but had succeeded in finding a compound MK 966 that was commercially exploitable, and that was of formula set out below:

CH$_3$SO$_2$ MK-966 (rofecoxib; Vioxx)   CH$_3$SO$_2$ (Enol - minor component)

The claimants had not made MK-966 and had no specific claim in their patent directed to that product. They therefore had the more difficult task of establishing that one of the broad generic claims in their patent was valid and covered MK-966.

In defence to the infringement proceedings, Merck adduced experimental evidence that a number of the compounds covered by the patent did not have the claimed properties, including the materials of Examples 1, 2, 5, 11 and 15 of the patent in issue, three of which were held at the trial not to demonstrate any anti-inflammatory effect. One further compound that the defendants tested, referred to as Compound 68, had been listed in the patent as preferred. It had the formula:

Compound 68

NH_2SO_2 OMe

Despite being "preferred", Compound 68 proved to have all the undesirable features that the claimants aimed to overcome: it was selective for COX 1 and not COX 2, and it was a gastric irritant. The evidence included photographs of the gastric lesions that it caused. The claimants replied that the compounds made and tested by the defendants were not representative but had been carefully selected.

The Patents Court found that the patent was not valid and not infringed. The major conclusions of Pumfrey J are summarised below:

☐ The invention with which the patent in issue was concerned was a class of compounds predicted to have anti-inflammatory activity and fewer or less drastic side effects owing to COX 2 specificity.

☐ A claim is invalid for insufficiency if it covers subject-matter that owes nothing to the invention disclosed. For a claim to a class of compounds to be valid, it must be possible to make a well-founded prediction that they have a common property that unites them as a class.

> If compounds having the features of the claim may or may not possess the qualities which the patent says unify the class, it cannot be said that the claim represents a true class at all. It is just a generalised description of a large number of chemical compounds. Such a claim is not analogous to a claim to a new principle, since the patentee has given no information, such as a structure/activity relationship, which enables the reader of the specification to draw any conclusions as to the properties of any particular compound without further experiment. All he has done is to describe the scope of the claim with *spurious precision*.[449]

☐ The onus was on the claimants to show that the defendants' test compounds were exceptional, and they had not done so, nor was there any substance in the defendants' criticisms of their experimental technique. The experimental evidence showed that the properties of compounds within the claimed class were unpredictable, and that there were a substantial number of compounds that did not exhibit either COX 2 specificity or diminished side effects. The most distinctive feature of the claimed compounds was the 3,4-disubstitution rather than the 2,3-disubstitution of DuP 697, but this did not give success on its own, and it was not possible to identify features that did. Accordingly the patent was invalid for insufficient disclosure.

The above decision was affirmed on appeal to the Court of Appeal[450] where Aldous LJ said:

> The patent in this case claims a class of compounds. There is no technical contribution in a list of compounds which a skilled person would know how to make at the priority date. The 20-year monopoly was granted because of the disclosure in the specification that the class of compounds claimed had the

---

449. The following earlier UK decisions were referred to on the issue of sufficiency: *British United Shoe v Simon Collier (1910) 27 RPC 567, May & Baker v Boots (supra), Olin Mathieson v Biorex (supra) and Biogen v Medeva (supra)*.

450. *Pharmacia v. Merck*, [2002] RPC 775; [2002] IP&T 828.

quality disclosed in the specification. The invention or technical contribution justifying the monopoly claimed can only be that quality. I have already decided that the judge was right when he held that the specification would be read by the skilled person as disclosing that the claimed class of compounds had anti-inflammatory and/or analgesic effect with fewer and less drastic side-effects, the reduction in side-effects being due to Cox II selectivity. It is that disclosure which is the technical contribution and invention ...

I agree with the judge. He could have gone further and pointed out that the claims covered an enormous number of compounds and that upon his findings many hundreds if not thousands did not have the quality of the class. For example, the list of possible substitutions for X is extremely large and a very large number would be inactive because they are too large. As pointed out by Professor Baker, many of that group can be bigger than the rest of the molecule. The term "aryl" is unbounded and the term "aryl" introduces groups which are at least as large as the rest of the molecule itself.

In parallel proceedings before the EPO, EP-B-0679157 was revoked on the ground that all the requests (sets of amended claims) submitted by the patentees related to intermediate generalizations that were not supported by the application as filed and hence contravened article 123(2) EPC.[451]

American Home Products and Professor Sir Roy Calne v Novartis[452] – you may be in trouble if you don't Markush!

Rapamycin is a macrolide. It was known prior to Professor Calne's invention as an antifungal antibiotic and was known to have the formula:

Rapamycin

Chemical formula: $C_{51}H_{79}NO_{13}$

---

451. See T 0812/00 Thiophenes/Searle et al dated 26 February 2002.
452. [2000] RPC 547

Professor Calne's contribution was to discover that rapamycin could also be used as an immunosuppressant. The patent in issue was EP-B-0401747,[453] and its main claim read:

> Use of rapamycin for the preparation of a medicament for inhibiting organ or tissue transplant rejection in a mammal in need thereof.

There was, however, a broadening statement in the description,[454] which read:

> The present invention includes the use of natural and synthetic rapamycin, genetically engineered rapamycin, and all derivatives and prodrugs of rapamycin, such as described in ... US Patent Nos. 3929992, 3993749, 4316885 and 4650803.

The defendants' compound had been made by replacing the OH group on the ring of the side chain with a 2-hydroxyethyl group. Proceedings had by agreement covered only issues concerning infringement and sufficiency of disclosure, leaving other issues such as novelty and inventive step to be considered later if so required. The questions before the court were whether:
- The claim covered the defendants' compound, which was not rapamycin but instead was 40-O-(2-hydroxyethyl)-rapamycin.
- The patent was bad for insufficiency if the claim did so. Possible grounds of insufficiency were that the claim covered a class of compounds whose scope was impossible to determine, and that in order to discover rapamycin derivatives within the scope of the claim a skilled person would have to embark on a prolonged and unduly burdensome research program.
- There was a distinction between ordinary claims and "second medical use" claims.

Laddie J handed down an opinion of the Patents Court on 6 December 1999.[455] He held that the claims covered the defendants' derivative and rejected the arguments concerning insufficiency, i.e. because of the fundamental nature of Professor Calne's discovery it was legitimate for his patent to "reach-through" to other structurally similar compounds discovered by subsequent empirical research. His opinion in favour of an affirmative finding of infringement made the following points:

☐ The word *"rapamycin"* used in the claims meant a single known chemical and did not mean *"rapamycin and derivatives of rapamycin which exhibit rapamycin-like immunosuppressant activity."*

---

453. Some indication of the significance of its contribution can be gauged from the fact that his equivalent US Patent 5100899 at the time of writing has 121 forward references according to the Delphion database. Rapamycin has been found to have a novel mechanism of immunosuppression to prevent rejection of organ transplants. Treatments conventionally used, such as cyclosporin and FK506 are effective in ensuring the short-term survival of the transplant, but the organ is rejected in the long term. It gives rise to a reduced incidence of acute rejection episodes, lower GFR at one year post-treatment and appears to cause fewer side effects than the standard anti-rejection treatments. It is now marketed under the tradename 'Rapamune' by Wyeth. A visit to the Novartis website has not shown that the rival 2-hydroxyethyl compound has yet matured into a product.

454. The title of the patent included a reference to "derivatives" although the specification itself was silent about these. However, it is not apparent that anyone seriously argued that this reference in the title should influence the construction of the claims which only mentioned "rapamycin".

455. [2000] RPC 547

☐ There was a distinction between the meaning of the words used in a claim and the meaning of the patent. In the present case, as in *Kastner v Rizla*,[456] the inventor had not made it clear that his intention was only to seek limited protection, but instead there were factors e.g. the statement about derivatives and prodrugs that showed that the intention was to cover more than rapamycin. If the specification were limited to a single compound, it would be virtually valueless because: *"It would have disclosed to the art the novel seam of interrelated molecules but have claimed only one of them."* Any reasonable addressee would have been surprised at such a limitation. Instead, the patent covered those derivatives of rapamycin that produced the same type of inhibition of organ rejection as did rapamycin itself.

☐ Because there was no sure way of predicting which derivatives would be effective, the inventor should not be forced into a choice between accepting narrow protection and putting forward a wider claim with neatly defined boundaries but where the appearance of certainty was an illusion and the claim was in truth a calculated gamble. *"Where the technology makes prediction impossible it cannot be right that the law requires it."*

☐ (after reviewing *Biogen v Medeva*[457] and *Genentech I/Polypeptide expression*[458]). There is nothing wrong in principle in the patent covering both rapamycin and derivatives that work in the same way. *"Sufficiency requires the monopoly to match the contribution. The fact that here, as in most if not all other pharmaceutical cases, there is no way of predicting with accuracy which derivative molecules will possess new and improved properties does not mean that a monopoly which covers all rapamycin derivatives which work extends beyond Professor Calne's contribution. On the contrary, although his discovery of the effectiveness of rapamycin was, no doubt, empirical, once that discovery had been made, it made available to the art the opening through which a new class of immunosuppressants could be found. The discovery of other molecules which achieve the same or better results is no longer empirical. The addressee of the patent can work in a logical and predictable way from the one molecule disclosed in the patent to the similar molecules, which are derived from it. Unlike the examples given in Biogen, this patent is not attempting to cover all new immunosuppressants. It is directed only to those molecules which can be reached as a result of rapamycin having shown the way."*

☐ The research necessary to find further derivatives did not impose an undue burden because the required iterative work was standard and expected for finding good candidates in the pharmaceutical industry, and the time and money required was only an indication that the research in this field was slow and expensive.[459]

---

456. [1995] RPC 585

457. [1997] RPC 1

458. T 0292/85; [1989] OJ EPO 275

459. *Valensi v British Radio Corporation* [1973] RPC 7, *Mentor v Hollister* [1993] RPC 7, T 0032/85 *Gist-Brocades/Biomass* [1986] 5 EPOR 267 and T 0226/85 *Unilever/Stable bleaches* [1989] 1 EPOR 18 considered. Note that during the appeal stage during the *Viagra* litigation in the UK, Pfizer successfully submitted in relation to a generic claim to inhibitors of the PDE 5 enzyme: "Once you

However many derivatives had been disclosed in the patent, it could still be argued that the same process of synthesis and testing would be required to find further derivatives. If the only safe course were to limit the patent to the molecules that had actually been tried and tested, that would make patents for pharmaceuticals more or less valueless.

☐ The second medical use form of claim should make no difference to the outcome..

> If Professor Calne had happened to find his novel use for rapamycin before it had been found to have fungicidal properties, his claims would not have needed to be in second use form. However, the invention would have been exactly the same and the requirement for sufficiency would have been exactly the same.

The Court of Appeal[460] agreed with the High Court that "rapamycin" when used in the claims referred to the single known molecule and did not also refer to derivatives that also inhibited organ rejection. Aldous LJ based his conclusion on a linguistic analysis of the specification, which showed that a distinction was made between rapamycin and its derivatives, and on the fact that the specification did not disclose a single derivative of rapamycin that had been shown to work.

He went on to find on the basis of the "Protocol questions"[461] that the defendant's compound was not a variant falling within claim 1 of the patent in issue. The defendant's compound did not satisfy the test imposed by the second Protocol question, which in the interests of third parties required for an affirmative answer that the variant should be obviously or clearly immaterial. In the present case, although the defendant's compound might have been a good candidate to try, it was not obvious that it would work as an immunosuppressant and in order to find that out you would have had to make and test the compound, which required research. The inventor had only discovered and described the second medical use of rapamycin, and it was left to others to find out which derivatives, if any, worked. Furthermore, it was unfair to the patentee to construe his claim in a way that was not intended. To ignore a limitation could render a patent invalid contrary to the wishes of the patentee. In answer to the third Protocol question, the skilled person would have understood that strict compliance with the primary meaning was essential because:
- the specification "rapamycin" was used to denote the molecule itself, and it would be surprising if a different nomenclature was used in the claims;
- the inventor's discovery had been defined in relation to rapamycin itself;

---

know what you are looking for, you can get it and screening does not involve inventive effort or undue labour.", see Lilly Icos v Pfizer [2001] FSR 201 (HC), [2002] IP&T 244 and BL C/2/02 (CA), downloadable from *www.courtservice.gov.uk/judgmentsfiles/j507/Lilly_Icos_v_Pfizer.htm*.

460. [2001] RPC 159

461. These were formerly called the *Catnic* questions, see the discussion above at page 102, and as then formulated were: (1) Does the variant have a material effect upon the way that the invention worked? (2) Would it have been obvious to a skilled person that the variant would not have a material effect on the way the invention worked? (3) Would the skilled person have understood from the language of the claim that the patentee intended that strict compliance with the primary meaning was an essential requirement of the invention?

- if the patentee had intended to cover derivatives, he could easily have done so; and
- a claim covering rapamycin and rapamycin-like derivatives would not have been allowed by the EPO as it would have lacked support and been speculative. The broadening passage relied on by the claimants contained an unqualified reference to *all* derivatives and prodrugs of rapamycin whereas the EPO would not have permitted *all* derivatives to be claimed.[462] Furthermore a test or standard was needed by which a skilled person could decide whether or not a particular derivative had a rapamycin-like effect and the specification did not disclose any such test.

If claim 1 had the broader scope for which the patentees had argued, then Aldous LJ concluded that the specification would be insufficient. The requirements for sufficiency were (a) that the claim should be enabled over its whole scope[463] and (b) the skilled person should not be required to carry out research to ascertain how the invention is to be performed[464] (though he could be required to use appropriate skill and tenacity). In this case, if the patent had covered derivatives of rapamycin, it would have needed to teach how to perform the invention with such derivatives. The specification did not do so because although it told the skilled man where to start, it left him to ascertain by research which derivatives work, the number of derivatives was vast and the task of ascertaining those which would satisfy the functional part of the claim was correspondingly burdensome. A claim covering derivatives would cover all molecules that would work while leaving it uncertain which ones did and how many of them there were. Such a claim did not reflect a class with a unifying characteristic but was a claim to a number of compounds with the number and identity being left to the skilled person to find out.

It was not true that a patent covering only a second medical use for rapamycin would be virtually valueless. The patent protected that use and the long and expensive work needed to obtain regulatory approval. Anyone who wished to market a derivative would have to make the derivative and carry out the long and expensive work to get the derivative on the market. The patent system should not be used to enable a person to cover more than he had described in sufficient detail to amount to an enabling disclosure, and in this case it would stifle research aimed at finding a derivative of rapamycin that was a better immunosuppressant than rapamycin itself. In support of the latter proposition Aldous LJ quoted as apt a passage from the *Biogen* case in which Lord Hoffmann discusses the work of Samuel Morse and the Wright Brothers and concludes that:

> ...It is inevitable in a young science, like electricity in the early nineteenth century or flying at the turn of the last century or recombinant DNA technology in the 1970s that dramatically new things will be done for the first time. The technical contribution in such cases deserved to be recognised. But care is needed not to stifle further research and healthy competition by allowing the

---

462. Aldous LJ does not give a reference in support of the proposition that it is objectionable in claims to chemical compounds to cover all possible substituents, but presumably he had in mind the well-known EPO Appeal Board decision in *T 00939/92 AGREVO/triazoles*

463. *Biogen Inc v Medeva Plc* [1977] RPC 1

464. *Mentor Corporation v Hollister* [1993] RPC 7

first person who has found a way of achieving an obviously desirable goal to monopolise every other way of doing so...

The defendants' compound contained up to 0.8% of rapamycin and the patentees argued that this was sufficient to establish infringement. Aldous LJ rejected this argument on the ground that the medicament had to be essentially rapamycin and there had been no discovery that medicaments containing only 0.8% rapamycin had any therapeutic effect. Accordingly the Court of Appeal, reversing Laddie J, found that the patent was valid but not infringed.

Conclusions

In an empirical research field, and in particular in the pharmaceutical field, it is difficult for a pioneering inventor to formulate a generic claim that is both wide and scientifically supportable because there are no established structure/activity relationships that can be used as a basis for rational prediction. The difficulties are illustrated by the *Rapamycin* case where Professor Calne had researched the prior art concerning rapamycin derivatives, but that prior art was relatively sparse and potential sites for modification and the range of permissible changes at those sites were only beginning to be investigated. It was only *after* Professor Calne's invention that significant numbers of patents disclosing structure/activity investigations for compounds within the rapamycin family started to appear. Similarly in the *Monsanto* case, although pharmaceutically active disubstituted thiophenes were known, the COX-2 target was relatively new and there was no body of knowledge concerning previous selective inhibitors of COX-2 on the basis of which valid predictions could be made. A reader of the specification would be struck by the limited information as to activity supported by reports of actual tests, and might view the claim scope as driven more by insight as to what was chemically available than insight as to biological effectiveness. This situation may be contrasted with that in *Olin Mathieson v Biorex* where a specific change was being made at a particular position within a well-explored family of compounds, and an existing body of knowledge of structure/activity relationships in parts of the molecule that were not subject to change provided basis for a claim of useful generic scope that nevertheless survived the challenge of litigation.

Two drafting points emerge. Firstly, as shown by the *Agrevo* and *Monsanto* decisions discussed above, when dealing with inventions concerning biologically active compounds, including open-ended substituent definitions e.g. *alkyl* or *aryl* in a generic claim is risky and should be backed-up by other claims with more specific generalisations in which the maximum number of carbon atoms is specified or e.g. an overall range of molecular weights is specified. Secondly, if the invention involves a specific change at a location in a known family of molecules, then it may be to the applicant's advantage to discuss in detail the results achieved in structure/activity relationships at other locations within the molecules described in the prior art because this helps to show that in these aspects the genus claimed is not an irrational prediction but builds on previous successful experimental work, as in *Olin Mathieson* above.

Where, during the course of development, a particular compound becomes a likely drug candidate or receives regulatory approval, there are strong arguments in favour of filing a divisional application directed to that particular compound and/or its pharmaceutical use. The patent directed to the candidate compound or new drug is thereby freed, at least partly, from the problems that will inevitably arise from the wider generic claims and enforcement will be more straightforward. In the US, a concise patent directed to a single compound which has been incorporated into a valuable new drug will readily be understood by members of a jury (it will be recollected that in the US, jury trials in infringement proceedings are commonplace). If the jury is confronted with a ten-page Markush claim, their bewilderment could rapidly be shifted by an astute defendant to distaste, especially if there are allegations that some of the claimed compounds are inactive and that the Markush prediction lacked scientific basis. Up to now, there have been relatively few instances where Markush predictions have been seriously challenged: that climate may owe more to custom and practice within the pharmaceutical industry than it does to the underlying science. It may change given the rise of generic manufacturers in rapidly industrializing countries such as India and China where experimental work can be carried out inexpensively, and given the availability of molecular modelling software which nowadays permits *in silico* identification of compounds which (a) do not conform to an expected pharmacophore, or (b) from *in silico* docking investigations will not be expected to bind in a required way to the enzyme or cell membrane protein on which activity is based.

There is no fully satisfactory way of claiming generic pharmaceutical inventions. The Markush approach has at least 80 years of use, but the validity of Markush claims if challenged by a resolute and well-resourced opponent or defendant should not be taken for granted. No judge is likely to treat a generic claim sympathetically following demonstrated inactivity within the genus. Over-broad claims should be avoided, and participation not just from chemists but also from biologists and molecular modellers can be helpful. Furthermore, it is important to claim the disclosed compounds individually as well as within the genus because the claims to the individual compounds *may* be the only valid claims.

Can "reach-through" claims be enforced?

The US Court decisions in
University of Rochester v G.D. Searle & Co., Inc et al.

Non-steroidal aspirin-like drugs act by inhibiting prostaglandin synthesis, but suffer from side effects, in particular gastrointestinal bleeding which has been responsible for some 16,000 deaths annually in the US consequent on their long-term use. It is now known that aspirin inhibits the action of two closely related enzymes, one of which called COX-1 is responsible for gastrointestinal protection and the other of which called COX-2 releases substances responsible for pain and inflammation.

There is room for controversy about who should be acknowledged as the discoverer of COX-2 and its structure and physiological role. In the US, Professor Philip Neederman in St Louis has been credited with having first hypothesised that there are two COX enzymes. Professor Daniel Simmons of Brigham Young University, Utah claims to have discovered COX-2 in 1989 and published his team's findings in April 1991.[465] However, Dr Donald A. Young at the University of Rochester (the team involved in the present dispute) claimed to have built on the work of the Simmons team and to have described in successive US patent applications dating back to 22 September 1992:
* That there are two COX (PGHS) genes, one of which was constitutively expressed and is called COX-1 and the other of which is responsive to regulatory control and is called COX-2.
* That COX-2 is a unique isoform of cyclooxygenase which in contrast to COX-1 is dramatically up-regulated by growth factors, tissue injury and proinflammatory cytokines, and plays a major role in peripheral inflammation.
* The cDNA and predicted amino acid sequence of COX-2.

Based on these discoveries the Rochester team produced cell lines stably expressing COX-2, which could be used to provide a simple *in vitro* screen for new drugs that would inhibit inflammation and which were predicted to be free from side effects.

Compounds that acted as COX-2 inhibitors were in existence as of September 1992 although they had, according to the University of Rochester, not been specifically disclosed for human use.[466] For example, EP-A-0317332 (Taisho Pharma) described

---

465. Xie *et al.*, Proc. Nat'l. Acad. Sci. US, 1991, 2692-2696 (April 1991), see also the deposited sequence at AAA58433.

466. The early development of COX-2 inhibitors is extensively discussed in the UK case *Monsanto v Merck* [2000] RPC 709 (HC), *Pharmacia v Merck* [2002] RPC 775 and also at [2002] IP&T 828. [2000] (CA) which concerns *inter alia* non-enablement of a patent claiming a Markush group of compounds, some of whose members had been experimentally demonstrated not to be selective COX-2 inhibitors as alleged in the specification.

and claimed sulfonanilide compounds that showed anti-inflammatory, antipyretic and analgesic effects combined with a decrease in gastrointestinal side effects. Amongst these was a compound NS-398 which has been widely used in experimental work e.g. in the rat, but which has not been developed for clinical use. The activity of this compound was acknowledged by the Rochester team in their US patent 6048850 (the patent in issue) which states:

> The fact that induced cyclooxygenase activity is blocked by NS-398, a specific inhibitor of PGHS-2, confirms that induction of PGHS-2 is responsible for increased prostaglandin production in cytokine-treated astrocytes.

The Rochester inventors did not consider that what they had invented was merely a research tool, and they wished to "reach through" to claim the clinically useful compounds that resulted from their discoveries. The main claim of their patent read:

> A method for selectively inhibiting PGHS-2 [COX-2] activity *in a human host*, comprising administering a non-steroidal compound that selectively inhibits activity of the PGHS-2 gene in a human host in need of such treatment.

The patent was granted on 11 April 2000, and legal proceedings against Searle and Pfizer were started on that day. On the following day the University of Rochester announced in a press release that they had been awarded a pioneering patent for the use of the entire class of COX-2 inhibitors that included the blockbuster drugs Celebrex and Vioxx, and that over the 17-year life of the patent the royalty payments could yield the University billions of dollars, making it the most lucrative pharmaceutical patent in history.

The hopes of the University received a potentially fatal setback following an application by the defendants for summary judgment on the grounds of lack of written description and non-enablement because the patent disclosed no selective COX-2 inhibitor and finding such compounds required further empirical research.

In its opinion,[467] the US District Court accepted the defendant's arguments. It explained that although the University may have laid the groundwork for the later invention of COX-2 inhibitors, they had not taken the last critical step of isolating such a compound or developing a process by which a skilled person would be directly lead to such a compound, and that even if the inventors were reasonably certain that the necessary compound existed and could eventually be found, there was no showing in the patent that they knew this to be a fact. The Court summarised its conclusions as regards written description[468] in the following passage:

---

467. US District Court, Western District of New York, 00-CV-616L, Larimer J, 5 March 2003, 249. F. Supp. 2d 216 (W.D.N.Y. 2003), for the appeal decision see 358 F 3d 916 (Fed Cir., 2004)

468. For the written description requirement in biotechnology patents see: *Regents of the University of California v Eli Lilly & Co.*, 119 F.3d 1559, 1568 (Fed. Cir. 1997), *cert. denied*, 523 U.S. 1089 (1998); *Fiers*, 984 F.2d at 1171; *Enzo Biochem, Inc. v Gen-Probe Inc.*, 285 F.3d 1013 (Fed. Cir. 2002), rehearing 296 F.3d 1316. Cases found non-persuasive because the patent specification contained enough information to lead a skilled person to the claimed compound included *Union Oil Co. v Atlantic Richfield Co.*, 208 F.3d 989 (Fed. Cir. 2000), *cert. denied*, 531 US 1183 (2001); *In re Herscher*, 591 F.2nd 693 (C.C.P.A. 1979), and *In re Edwards*, 568 F.2d 1349 (C.C.P.A 1978).

In effect, then, the '850 patent claims a method that cannot be practiced until one discovers a compound that was not in the possession of, or known to, the inventors themselves. Putting the claimed method into practice awaited someone actually discovering a necessary component of the invention. In some ways, this is reminiscent of the search for the so-called "philosopher's stone," eagerly sought after by medieval alchemists, which supposedly would transmute lead into gold. While the Court does not mean to suggest that the inventors' significant work in this field is on a par with alchemy, the fact remains that without the compound called for in the patent, the inventors could no more be said to have possessed the *complete* invention claimed by the '850 patent than the alchemists possessed a method of turning base metals into gold.

The Court's interest, if not fascination, with the history of the philosopher's stone is further demonstrated by the following footnoted passage:

A patent for the philosopher's stone was actually issued during the reign of Edward III. "The invention we now regard as a superstition, but the application was referred by the King to a commission, which reported favourably upon it, and the patent issued apparently upon what we now regard as sound doctrine, that the invention was new and useful." [*McKeever v United States*, 14 Ct.Cl. 396 (1878)] It is not apparent whether the patentee claimed actually to possess the stone, or whether he simply described it in terms of its function, in the hope that he would be entitled to royalties should it ever be discovered.

The Court further held that the patent was non-enabling because it provided little guidance about selecting a particular compound or narrowing the range of candidates, with the result that a suitable compound could not be found without undue experimentation. Although the need for trial and error experimentation was not *per se* decisive, there had to be reasonable detail to enable members of the public to understand and carry out the invention and tossing out the mere germ of an idea was not enough.[469] Searle had started a screening programme in August 1992, and by May 1993 had screened some 600 compounds and identified a number of selective COX-2 inhibitors, but the Court held that this merely demonstrated that considerable research was necessary to turn the claimed invention into reality. Although not cited in the judgment, a significant paper by Kunin *et al*[470] foreshadowed the conclusion reached by the Court and expresses a firm view at a senior level within the USPTO that reach-through claims should not be allowed.

---

469. See, *inter alia*: *W.L. Gore & Associates, Inc. v Garlock, Inc.*, 721 F.2d 1540, 1557 (Fed. Cir. 1983); *Genentech, Inc. v Novo Nordisk A/S*, 108 F.3d 1361, 1365 (Fed. Cir.), *cert. denied*, 522 U.S. 963 (1997); *In re Wands*, 858 F.2d 731, 736-40 (Fed. Cir. 1988); *Enzo Biochem, Inc. v Calgene, Inc.* ("*Calgene*"), 188 F.3d 1362, 1371 (Fed. Cir. 1999); *Amgen, Inc. v Chugai Pharm. Co., Ltd.*, 927 F.2d 1200, 1213 (Fed. Cir.).

470. Stephen G. Kunin, Deputy Commissioner for Patent Examination Policy at the USPTO, Mark Nagumo, Administrative Patent Judge in the Board of Patent Appeals and Interferences, Brian Stanton, Technology Centre 1600 Practice Specialist, Linda S. Therkorn, Patent Examination Policy Advisor, Office of the Deputy Commissioner for Patent Examination Policy, Stephen Walsh, Associate Solicitor, Office of General Counsel at the USPTO, *American University Law Review*, **51**, 609-638, 2002. The article can be downloaded from www.wcl.american.edu/journal/lawrv/51/Kunin.pdf.

The decision of the District Court was subsequently affirmed on appeal to the Federal Circuit. However, the discovery and structure determination of COX-2 were scientific breakthroughs, not alchemy. The prediction that useful inhibitors would follow quickly upon the discovery of the enzyme proved true. It could reasonably have been argued that subsequent events demonstrated the incorrectness of the Court's view concerning non-enablement. The commercially successful[471] compounds *Celebrex* and *Vioxx* appeared in the late 1990s, which, in the timescale of the pharmaceutical industry, was rapid and it is therefore disingenuous to say that the necessary skills were lacking There was the further argument that the written description requirement should not be applied so strictly that the reward for discovering COX-2 inhibitors went in its entirety to the discoverers of the active compounds and was not shared with the academic scientists whose breakthrough in identifying the relevant target enabled those compounds to be discovered.[472] Such arguments did not appeal to the CAFC. The case was not taken up by the Supreme Court[473] so that the decision that the patent is invalid is now final. However, the question is still on the table whether a less onerous view should be taken as to what patent law should demand of researchers in academic institutions.

---

471. As of the time when this paper was written.

472. Review of CAFC decisions by the Supreme Court is rare. However, there is an argument that the Court should review this question if it arises in a subsequent case (possibly with a better fact pattern) because the question whether and in what circumstances reach-through claims are allowable affects the balance of risks and rewards as between academic and industrial research over an important range of technologies.

473. Originally published at (1981-82) 11 CIPA 424.

SUCCESSFUL INVENTIONS

Workmate

By Ronald P. Hickman (inventor)
and Michael J. Roos (patent agent)

Introduction (by Michael Roos, 'MR')

This paper[474] [originally written in 1982 and reprinted in the *CIPA Journal* in January 2005] is offered with some hesitation since the transactions of the Institute are replete with academic dissertations, and the authors admit that their contribution might be regarded, by comparison, as somewhat lightweight, but perhaps this is not entirely out of place in this summer of centenary celebrations. Nevertheless, it is hoped that some of the practical aspects of a remarkable success story will be of interest and, if nothing else, the paper outlines an example of where an individual inventor can still succeed, and that in this age of high technology there are still simple but important inventions to be made.

The story also illustrates that the patent system, it is hoped with justification, has successfully provided the inventor and his licensees with wide protection for a product which is now marketed throughout the world at a sales rate measured in millions of units a year.[475]

Some historical landmarks

1968: An offer of a WORKMATE licence by **Ron Hickman** to Stanley Tools was rejected because in their view the potential of the product 'could be measured in dozens rather than in hundreds'. Ron Hickman commenced manufacture himself.

1972: Black & Decker took licences.

1976/77: Mr Justice Graham in his High Court judgment said:

> The conception, design and marketing of the WORKMATE has been a success story of which Mr Hickman is, in my judgment, entitled to be proud... The unsolicited praise received in respect of the WORKMATE from members of many sections of the community who have used it, is, in my experience of these cases, wholly unique.

Lord Justice Goff in his Court of Appeal judgment said:

> Some of the main features which make WORKMATE the brilliant invention it is admitted to be... Mr Hickman arrived at the WORKMATE by an independent and highly ingenious and skilled inventive process... He (Mr Hickman) made his invention entirely independently which was a great feat...

---

474. For the UK decision, see *Hickman v Andrews* [1983] RPC 147 (this reproducing both the Patents Court and the CA decisions).

475. Tibor Gold's figures, on page 278.

1981: Ten millionth WORKMATE sold.

[Tibor Gold.: I am reliably informed that the 2005 figure of total sales comfortably exceeds 65+ million!]

Early days... (by Ron Hickman, 'RH')

It is never easy, long after the event, to analyse clearly and precisely how the various aspects of any invention come about, but in the case of WORKMATE I believe that there were a host of 'chance' or 'luck' elements. There were also certain 'special needs' which forced me in certain directions, various acts of 'innovation' and, not least, certain cases of 'surprise result', all of which contributed to the making of this particular invention or series of inventions over a span of many years.

It is interesting to reflect that I was not, to use the patent term, 'a person skilled in the art'. It was true that I was practical and perhaps had experience in aesthetic design, but it seems extremely unlikely, if I had in fact been a skilled designer in workbenches, or sawhorses, or vices, that the end result would ever have been achieved. It must be borne in mind that I was not briefed by the head of a research team to 'go and design a portable workbench'.

It may even be asked whether the very concept of producing a portable workbench which could be used around the home, in the garden, or carried readily in the boot of a car, was not in itself the first innovative act, but clearly that concept was not in itself patentable.

The very fact that I lacked any basic engineering training, and had no experience of design in any of the allied fields, may well have contributed to my success, because I could be quite uninhibited in my approach and was perhaps more free than most to take a 'lateral thinking' type of approach to innovation as advocated by Dr Edward de Bono.

There is little doubt that the invention of WORKMATE arose from the fact that I was, and still am, an ardent do-it-yourself enthusiast. I wanted to be able to do simple woodworking jobs in a home which had no workshop, and early efforts had included the damaging of a chair during sawing, which was perhaps one of the first chance occurrences leading me into making my first workbase (see picture 1 on page 279).

This first workbase had a top formed by two second-hand heavy beams each of which was fixed firmly to a sturdy sub-structure which included a platform enabling me to stand in front of the top and to utilise my weight to stabilise the whole unit, in contrast to the common problem which occurs when trying to work on a lightweight support such as a chair or sawhorse.

The choice of the two fixed beams was also a piece of luck since, if a single solid one-piece top had been the only thing available to me at that time, the spacing of these two old beams would not have occurred and, as will be seen later, the idea of moving one of these beams in the manner of a vice would probably never have arisen. At this stage, however, a vice facility was obtained by fixing a heavy 'Record' vice to the left hand end of the front beam, and this workbase, although very heavy, proved very much more useful than had been expected.

Picture 1: First workbase

It was reasonably portable and it provided a worktop which was many times larger than an ordinary sawhorse but much smaller than a conventional workbench, and yet it could support quite large workpieces such as hardboard panels. The gap between the beams was found useful for sawing, drilling, and knocking out nails, etc, and the unit as a whole gave the user an ability to walk all round it which is not usually possible with a fixed workbench.

Nevertheless, it had unsatisfactory features. For example, the vice had guides and a screw thread which extended under the gap between the beams, and these were sometimes fouled during the use of the gap for sawing. Also, although the positioning of the vice at the left-hand end was ideal for planing for a right-handed person, the same right-handed person really required a vice at the right-hand end when sawing. I found that the vice I had adopted was extremely heavy, and whilst satisfactory for fixed workbenches, was not really suitable for the portable concept. In hindsight this also led me onward, since, because no-one made a small, light, quick-release vice which would do the job on a portable workbench, I was unsatisfied with the product at this stage.

I was nevertheless convinced that my experience with the first workbase showed that a product of this kind would be extremely useful and might have commercial potential, particularly if it could be made lighter. This led me to the production of a similar prototype having a knock-down sub-structure which I recognised as potentially useful for marketing, but which I later realised would be of no use to the user when trying to store the assembled unit at home.

I had long felt that it would be very desirable to have a folding base, but had not seen how to achieve this with any rigidity. Also the addition of more complex structure such as a folding base would inevitably add additional expense and might contribute to difficulties in marketing a product which was already in danger of being perceived as a rather over-expensive substitute for a sawhorse.

At this time I was beginning to think of approaching a potential licensee such as Black & Decker, but I was very conscious of the fact that at that time, Black & Decker's products were centred around fractional horsepower electric motors and I could foresee difficulty in interesting them in an entirely non-electric product.

I therefore started to think of sophisticated ways of mounting on to the unit powered tools such as saws, drill stands, and Black & Decker's amateur lathe. The idea of using G-Clamps did not attract me, but I then thought of the idea of providing each power tool with a protruding bar or peg on its base which would pass into the sawing slit of my workbase, and somehow be retained there by a sliding bolt or clamping pad. This idea of clamping pads attracted me, and I began to think of how these pads could also be used to clamp workpieces in the gap, but these were only seen as an ancillary to the wood-working vice secured to the front.

It was at this stage that the idea of the giant vice-top of the workbench came about. The various ideas and conflicting factors and needs were constantly in my mind. At one time I would try and look at the problem 'in the round', then again I would focus on the details, and then I would try to look at the project as a whole, to see if that brought out any ideas.

It was during this rather long drawn-out process that I was suddenly and forcibly struck by the visual resemblance between the open jaws of a woodworking vice and the two spaced beams which formed my work top, but which, of course, were both still stationary at this time. I realised that if I could only make one of the beams form a movable vice-jaw I would have a giant full-length vice which would, in a stroke, overcome many of the problems of cost and weight which I have been experiencing. Also, the vice would suit right and left-handed people and would overcome the problem of the wood-working vice at the left-hand end being inappropriate for sawing for a right-handed person. I could also increase the jaw width which would give a very large area for gripping long planks.

Closer analysis, however, pointed to many problems or drawbacks. At this stage I had only thought of trying to develop a vice-operating mechanism that would use a single screw positioned centrally, but this would involve the screw extending at all times under the middle of the sawing slit, rendering the sawing slit virtually useless. Even more worrying was the feeling that any system of guide-rods which I tried to adopt from traditional vice structures would almost certainly run badly and perhaps jam up. I knew very well that it was a basic requirement of modern vices that the jaws should be constrained to remain as parallel as possible in plan view and in side view. These basic requirements for a long time led me to try to devise methods of guiding the movable beam so that it would always remain parallel to the front beam, but I found that one simply could not make such a very wide jaw run on guides of any practical dimensions without some jamming occurring. The idea of trying to solve the problem of seizure of the guides by using two screws, one at each end, instead of a single central one, then occurred to me as a possible solution. However, when I thought of using the two screws I instinctively knew that it would be very difficult to operate a pair of screws in perfect synchronism and, anyway, it would need two hands to wind the handles, leaving no hand free to position the workpiece in the vice.

The next major step involved going diametrically away from conventional notions of having accurate parallel guidance in plan view, so that if I could achieve true independent operability of each screw it would leave a hand free to position the work piece. However, the angling of the beam in plan view had to be achieved somehow without losing the guidance which would maintain the jaw face vertical in order to give effective clamping. Eventually, I produced a design in which the clamping screws each carried a nut which was connected to the underside of the moving beam by a special connection which permitted angling of the beam in plan with respect to each of the screws, about vertical axes. At the same time I provided effective guidance against lifting or tilting of the moving beam and included a restriction against excessive lateral movement of the beam so that there was just sufficient clearance to enable the beam to move in an angular manner in plan, yet without making the whole construction sloppy.

I nevertheless had other worries about the giant vice-top idea. For example, would a moving work surface ever be acceptable? With an ordinary vice, one does not provide a working surface on the vice itself, but relies on the workbench to provide the work surface, but here I was endeavouring to combine half of the work surface of the bench with one of the vice beams, which would be totally unconventional.

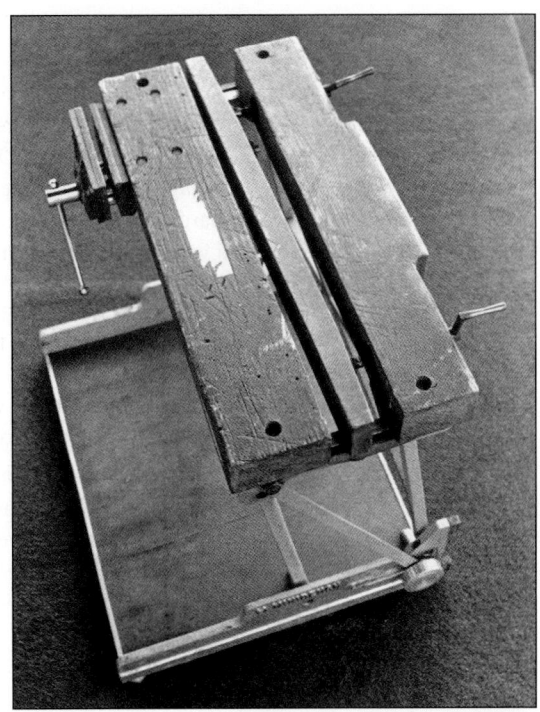

Picture 2: Third prototype

Also, until now, I had relied on the two fixed beams to provide a rigid top to the unit which contributed significantly to its overall strength and stability. The idea of making the worktop solely from two beams forming a giant vice would, I thought, jeopardise this stability and therefore this scheme was abandoned at this stage. The third prototype (shown above in picture 2), maintained the early idea of two fixed beams. The spacing between the beams was, however, increased and a third beam was introduced between them to act as a vice beam. It also had the angling mechanism referred to above.

This prototype also included my so-called 'folding box structure' which comprised a pair of folding frames which together with the two fixed beams, the base and end braces, formed a locked three dimensional parallelogram. I experimented with this third prototype at home for some time whilst continuing to consider improvements, which, in particular, would simplify the top structure and lighten the unit as a whole to make it more portable and cheaper and simpler to manufacture.

Eventually, I reverted to the two-bar idea and found that its early drawbacks could be overcome and that, in fact, the moving of half of the work surface was not in practice a significant worry. I developed further the mechanism which allowed independent operation of the two screws and the resulting design (shown on page 282 in picture 3), was found to work perfectly and I was happy, finally, to discard the 'RECORD' vice. This structure formed the basis of my early patent protection, and as will be seen, after abortive attempts at obtaining licensees, was put into production by me.

Early scepticism

By 1968 when I had reached the design shown in picture 3, I was convinced that the product would have great practical utility. I therefore approached various British manufacturers including Stanley, Record, Black & Decker, Burgess, Polycell, Salmens and Marples. In most cases I managed to obtain interviews at a fairly senior level and made a. full presentation of the hardware I then had available, and demonstrated the jobs it could do. In all cases the idea was rejected, in many instances the reason being given that it had no potential.

First production

As a result of these failures to find licensees I decided to produce the bench myself. The manufacture of the parts was contracted out but the assembly and marketing were done by a small team I recruited for the purpose. The original WORKMATE (shown below in picture 3), first appeared in 1968 and within four years sales had increased to 14,000 units a year, mainly by mail order.

Picture 3: MK I WORKMATE

The success of the product prompted me into developing the Mk II version shown in picture 4. This design, which had further features, including alternative heights, and a system of swivelling pegs in the vice beams for clamping awkward shapes, had just been completed when I was approached for a licence in UK and Europe by Walter Goldsmith, then General Manager of Black & Decker in the UK.

The licence to Black & Decker

Black & Decker decided to manufacture the Mk II design of picture 4, virtually in the form I had developed, and tooling for this purpose was installed in their factory at Spenymoor. The first market launch was in 1972 and was an immediate success. For several years demand outstripped supply and production lines for supplying the European market were set up in Eire, Spain, Germany and Italy.

Picture 4: MK II WORKMATE

Later, under a further licence covering America and the rest of the world, production also started in Canada, the US, Mexico, Brazil and Japan.

Licensing considerations (MR)

The licensing arrangements with Black & Decker have been governed by three agreements covering different territories, initially two for the UK and Europe, and later, a third for America and the rest of the world. Certain specific aspects of the licences may be of interest.

The Royalty

The royalty was settled at a flat rate of 3% of NSV. Bearing in mind that, at the time of the negotiations, WORKMATE was already showing signs of being a revolutionary product, and that significant patent protection was likely to be obtained on many aspects of the product as a whole, I advised Ron Hickman that the 3% figure was too low. This is a view I still hold, although I admit that the financial return produced by the 3% royalty has been considerable.

The UK and European agreements provided that the royalty percentage of 3% was split into two tranches of 1.5%. One of these tranches was payable for know-how and copyright, and was unaffected by the patent position. The second tranche of 1.5% was subject to a quite complex formula which required the inventor to achieve and maintain four defined levels of patent protection in various groups of countries in order to maintain portions of the 1.5% royalty. This rather unusual stipulation actually defined, in patent claim terms, the scope of protection which had to be achieved, providing a considerable burden upon the authors during the prosecution of some of the early patent applications in Europe.

In the agreement covering America and the rest of the world, the same 3% royalty applies, but this is tied completely to patents and is paid as long as patent protection is in force either in the country where the product is manufactured or where it is sold.

Minimum Royalties

The three agreements with Black & Decker all included substantial advance royalty and minimum royalty terms.

Option to purchase after five years

The UK and European (but not the American) agreements included an option permitting Black & Decker to take an assignment of all rights under the agreements for a lump sum based on a factor multiplied by the best year's royalties. This option was exercised in 1977 by Black & Decker and accordingly they now own the original UK and European patents outright.

Policing infringements

During the subsistence of the UK and European agreements the inventor maintained the right, and indeed was obliged, to sue infringers, the cost of (and any profit from) the litigation being shared between the licensee and licensor. This left the inventor in a position of being able to administer patent litigation himself, as for example occurred in the UK. Most importantly, because of this, the inventor was in a position himself to defend the inevitable counterclaim of invalidity. This right of the inventor to defend his own patents and hence to keep secure his royalty position was a significant advantage but nevertheless an extremely expensive burden.

When it came to negotiating the licence for America and the rest of the world, the inventor passed the initial right to sue, and hence the control of the litigation, to the licensee. In the event this has proved perfectly satisfactory, and for example during the course of extremely expensive litigation in the US against Sears Roebuck, the licensee and inventor have, as joint plaintiffs, put forward a forthright defence to attacks on the validity of the patents. Nevertheless the situation in the US has highlighted the fact that, in some cases, it may be dangerous for a patentee to relinquish his right to sue infringers and thereby lose control of the defence of the patents on which royalties depend.

Some problems for the patent agent

Having faith

The scepticism met by the inventor in trying to interest industry in the basic proposals of WORKMATE, was initially shared by myself, the patent agent, when first approached for advice. Was there really a likelihood of the public being interested in purchasing the product, and what chance was there of significant commercial sales, or of competition which would warrant expenditure on patents? How often are patent agents told by an inventor that he has a world beater! How easy it is to be polite and, whilst doing a perfectly adequate job for the client, being unable to develop sufficient faith in the idea to advise the client that he should afford an exceptional financial involvement that would allow the patent agent to apply more than an average amount of his time to the drafting and prosecution of a range of British cases, let alone wide foreign filings.

In the case of WORKMATE, there is little doubt that, although Ron Hickman's finances were considerably limited in the early days, he was perhaps better placed financially than many individual inventors. Accordingly, well before licences had been accepted, and royalties received, he was in a position to allow me to be involved much more than would be usual, and to incur very considerable expense in prosecuting British and foreign filings. The credit for this rests entirely with the inventor in having the tenacity to instil in me sufficient faith in the product to enable me to take a continuing active and deep interest.

The flexibility of pending patent applications

The UK

In the UK, the 1949 Act provided an ideal system for allowing the final moulding of an inventor's protection to be left flexible for several years. A period of up to 15 months between provisional and final filings, and a further two years nine months (previously three years nine months) for obtaining acceptance, plus the ability to divide freely and voluntarily at any time up to acceptance, gave Ron Hickman a tremendous ability to develop and expand his protection, particularly as the importance of the invention became more and more apparent.

It is interesting that the 1977 Act theoretically increases this overall period to four and a half years from priority, but the flexibility is not really the same because of the time limits now set for reply to substantive examination reports. To some extent the filing of divisionals is a way of keeping options open, but even here the freedom is not the same as under the 1949 Act.

The US

The US system is perhaps the most flexible in the world and allows the extensive filing of divisional and continuation applications with the result that patents may be granted many years after filing and nevertheless run from the date of grant. Caution naturally has to be exercised in utilising this remarkable flexibility to an undue extent, and practitioners are no doubt aware of the need to offer voluntarily a 'terminal disclaimer' if the protection afforded by a later divisional or continuation is really based on the same invention as that of the earlier case.

Other countries

Prosecution flexibility is available in many other countries although in the case of WORKMATE, particular problems have been experienced in Germany, Japan, Australia and Sweden while attempting to file divisional applications at a late date, and in some cases after the acceptance of the original application.

The approach to claiming WORKMATE

From the beginning, Ron Hickman maintained hopes of licensing the production of WORKMATE. As has been seen, early efforts at seeking licensees were entirely unsuccessful, and the inventor turned to manufacturing and marketing the product himself for several years, but even during this time it was well recognised that, if the potential of the product was to be fully exploited, it required a capital investment, and a world-wide marketing organisation, well beyond the means of the inventor.

These factors had a considerable effect on the drafting of patent claims. Firstly it was essential to secure realistic protection on the product which would satisfy a potential licensee that worthwhile sustainable patents were available for the price of the royalty. On the other hand, it was tempting to be content with fairly limited claims in order to secure at least some protection on the product. Despite this, from the beginning, efforts were always made to draft claims which were as wide as possible and as a result it will be found that many WORKMATE patents obtained in different parts of the world have broad claims and this is certainly the case of one of the basic British patent No. 1267032, which was successfully litigated through to the Court of Appeal where its validity was upheld. This patent had a main claim in the following terms:

> A workbench including a pair of elongate vice members disposed in side by side relationship and having their upper surfaces lying in substantially the same horizontal plane to form a working surface, the members being supported from below by a supporting structure and means being provided to prevent movement of each member upwardly away from the supporting structure, at least one of the vice members being capable of movement towards and away from the other vice member, the said movement being caused by actuation of either one or both of a pair of spaced, independently-operable, vice operating devices which are operatively coupled to at least one of the members by means which enables the gap between the vice members at one end thereof to be greater than the gap at the other end thereof.

Wherever possible, however, independent claims have also been included of a more limited nature with the intention of securing the royalty position for the Inventor, and at the same time providing the licensee with detailed but not unduly restricted protection on the specific product to prevent exact copying. In the event, where litigation has taken place, the broad claims have been held valid and resort to narrower claims has not usually been required.

The portfolio principle

During the prosecution of the patent applications on WORKMATE, efforts have been made in most major countries to protect different combinations of features often by filing divisional applications. For example, in the UK there are ten patents, and in the US, nine patents on the Mk I and Mk II benches shown respectively in pictures 3 and 4. This has provided a significant umbrella of protection over the whole product, hopefully making it extremely difficult to copy in any significant respect – a major advantage to the licensee.

A further advantage, this time to the inventor, of this so called 'portfolio principle' has been the ability in infringement proceedings to limit an attack against a competitor to one or two patents at most out of the portfolio, leaving other patents on the product not vulnerable to validity attack by way of counterclaim. For example, in two cases of litigation, the inventor and/or Black & Decker have been able to proceed under one patent only against quite small competition, even though one or more other patents might have been relevant, in the knowledge that, should the litigated patent fall in the proceedings, other patents would survive and hopefully deter major competition. In other words, some powder was always kept dry. These non-litigated patents have also maintained a secure royalty position for the inventor on the specific workbenches marketed by the licensee.

Taxation (RH)

The taxation of world-wide licensing royalties occurs essentially at two levels. Initially, in the form of withholding taxes, in the various countries in which the licensee operates and subsequently, in the form of income taxes, in the country in which the licensor is based.

This basic position is extensively complicated by the existence or otherwise of tax treaties between the various countries involved and the exchange control regulations, if any, within each country. Naturally, the tax posture of the licensor is also critical and, in the context of the UK tax laws of the early 1970s, I was fortunate to have retained my South African domicile-of-origin.

As a result of this foreign domicile, although the total tax burden in the early years was considerable, I did enjoy an important advantage by comparison with UK residents without foreign domicile: I was not liable to UK Income Tax on foreign income unless it was remitted to the UK.

In 1973, a Guernsey Company, controlled from Sark, was formed to help administer the funding of new development projects and the growing patent portfolio.

Despite the continuing failure to license the ex-European WORKMATE Patents (e.g. North and South America, Japan, Australia, etc.), I continued to believe that WORKMATE would eventually be a world-wide success and these patents were also transferred to the new company. Later, therefore, when these patents were also licensed to Black & Decker, the principal Licensor was the Guernsey Company.

One of the disadvantages of a Channel Islands base arises from the Islands non-membership of the Paris Convention. This led to the formation, in 1976-77, of three Irish Companies, solely for the purpose of acting as nominee agents for patent filing in a Convention country.

In 1976/77, the increasing tax burden contributed to a decision to move the entire development activity outside the UK. After looking at several alternatives, Jersey was selected despite having, in fact, the least favourable tax treatment of patent royalties of all the countries considered.

In 1979/80, a new Dutch subsidiary company was formed with several objects. Firstly it was able to take advantage of Holland's membership of the Paris Convention so that further patent filings on ideas emanating from my Jersey design and development company could be filed in the name of the Dutch Company. Also we were able to simplify our corporate structure and, most significantly, take advantage of many of Holland's taxation treaties.

Although my foreign domicile was an unplanned advantage probably not open to many, it is nevertheless clear that the taxation of world-wide patent royalties is both extremely complex and subject to constant change and, therefore, professional, specialised advice is, despite its cost, strongly recommended. Also it is always easier and cheaper to create a tax-efficient structure while the commercial values involved are low rather than when they are high.

The educational process (MR)

The scepticism with which WORKMATE was viewed by potential licensees in early stages, due mainly to a failure to recognise WORKMATE as an entirely new product in its own right, has already been highlighted earlier in this paper, but it was found that the same scepticism was prevalent, not only with patent office examiners throughout the world, but also with local patent agents and counsel. The danger of this scepticism was recognised at an early date by the authors and it was agreed that, wherever possible, a full-scale educational process should be mounted to give local patent agents or Counsel, or both, a full understanding of the product and its advantages so that they in turn would have the confidence to persuade examiners, and eventually courts, that the product contained a variety of patentable features which together gave it its uniqueness.

As a consequence of this realisation that an educational process was required, the prototypes, and/or production units of WORKMATE have been transported around the world (in fact, around the world many times) and shown to local patent agents and counsel and/or examiners not only in the UK, but also in Australia, France, Italy, Germany, Sweden, Japan, Canada, South Africa, Argentina and the US. Usually at least one, but often both, of the authors have been present at these interviews. It has always been apparent that where the examiners have been shown actual hardware it has generated immediate practical interest in the product and one lesson which has clearly been learnt from this experience is that a client should be pressed wherever possible to get samples of his product into the hands of local counsel to enable them fully to understand the invention in three dimensions and also to enable them to show it in turn to the examiner.

At an early stage in this educational process it was decided that a series of six films should be professionally made which would show the history and development of WORKMATE from its early prototype days through to production. In addition, each film would deal specifically with one aspect of the workbench on which patent protection was being sought. This aspect would be shown in a practical environment such as the home, workshop or building site. These films were to be introduced to patent agents, Counsel, and examiners in various countries and perhaps be used in any potential litigation in support of the patents.

The films were produced in colour with soundtracks in English, German and Japanese versions and have also been placed on individual cassettes for use in portable projectors which have the capability of either being used on a desk top with an integral screen, or being converted for projection onto a larger screen or wall. This film project took many months to complete and involved professional scriptwriters and film producers and significant involvement of both authors. Whether the considerable cost of this project, which was over £50,000, [at 1982 prices] was justified will probably never be known, but it is another indication of the determination of the inventor to leave no stone unturned, at very considerable expense to himself, to ensure that the very best patent protection could be obtained wherever possible. It will probably come as no surprise that the overall cost to Ron Hickman and his companies, excluding management time, of the filing and prosecution, and the litigation of his patents has already exceeded one million pounds.

The use of demonstration models (RH)

Soon after I commenced manufacture myself of the early Mark I WORKMATE (shown in picture 3 on page 282), I established a small development workshop and was able to produce the early prototypes for the Mark II design (shown in picture 4 on page 283), and also the many other prototypes for other projects outside the WORKMATE field. During the course of the prosecution of the many patent applications on WORKMATE throughout the world, and in the course of litigation, full-size models of all the most significant pieces of prior art were also made for close analysis to determine their relevance and, in particular, any hidden drawbacks.

Secondary considerations or 'sub-tests' in assessing obviousness (MR)

The so-called 'secondary considerations' looked at by patent offices and courts in various countries in assessing inventiveness became of significant importance in the case of WORKMATE. One test which is often applied is whether the invention solves a technical problem which others have been working on unsuccessfully. It might be difficult in the case of WORKMATE to say that there were serious technical difficulties or problems in arriving at the basic concept of the structure as a whole. It may perhaps be easier to argue that a technical prejudice may have existed, exampled by the scepticism of industry which could not recognise the latent potential of the product. At that stage, manufacturers tended to see the market in conventional terms as being satisfied by three standard, well-developed, products, namely fixed workbenches, vices for application to workbenches, and simple portable sawhorses, very often manufactured by a carpenter for use on a building site and readily discarded when worn out. Those offered licences at this stage tended to see WORKMATE merely as an inadequate workbench, or an oversized vice, or an over-complicated sawhorse, and failed to recognise it as a new and unique product in its own right.

Again, it might be difficult to argue that there was a long-felt need unless one argues that it was an unseen need, but the sales of over ten million units within ten years, and current sales of several million units a year, suggest that there has been a substantial need for a long time. Whilst we have had to be cautious in arguing that commercial success is a significant sub-test by itself, initial scepticism and the subsequent success of the product have jointly proved to be of significant advantage in pleading the validity of the patents in various countries and when answering arguments that the combination of features was obvious.

Another sub-test which is often applied is that of 'imitation'. As will be outlined in the next section of this paper, there has been significant competition all over the world and three examples are shown in pictures 5, 6 and 7. Surprisingly, the competitive products have often not been truly portable workbenches, but the giant vice-top feature has been adopted in virtually every case, and this fact has been argued in support of the validity of the patents.

Competition (MR)

Infringement proceedings under WORKMATE patents, and in one or two instances under unfair competition laws, have stopped the sale of competitive workbench products twice in the US, once in Canada, three times in the UK (on one occasion with actions against ten defendants), once in South Africa, twice in France, three times in Germany, twice in Japan, once in Italy and once in Denmark. In only two countries, namely UK and the US, have the infringement proceedings resulted in full trials, both going to appeal.

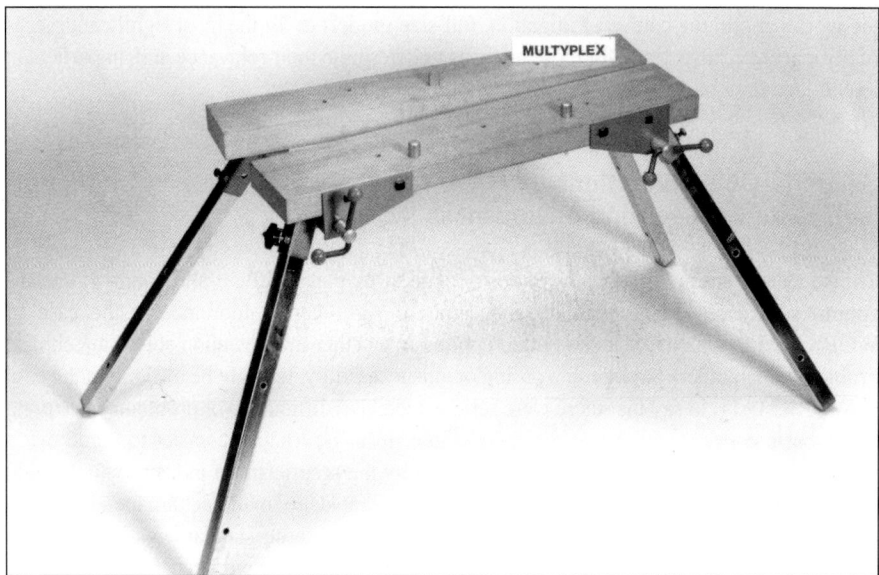

Picture 5: Andrews UK infringement

Litigation in the UK

In the UK, proceedings were commenced in 1974, reaching the Court of Appeal in 1977, where the unanimous judgment of Lord Justice Buckley, Lord Justice Goff and Sir David Cairns was in favour of the inventor, both on infringement and validity aspects. The British proceedings perhaps did not result in any striking legal judgments but one aspect of the case which may be of interest to Fellows is that the validity of Claim 1 of the WORKMATE patent in suit, as set out above, depended entirely, in both the Court of first instance, and in the Court of Appeal, on the meaning of the term 'workbench' at the beginning of the claim.

Picture 6: Kinzo Japanese infringement

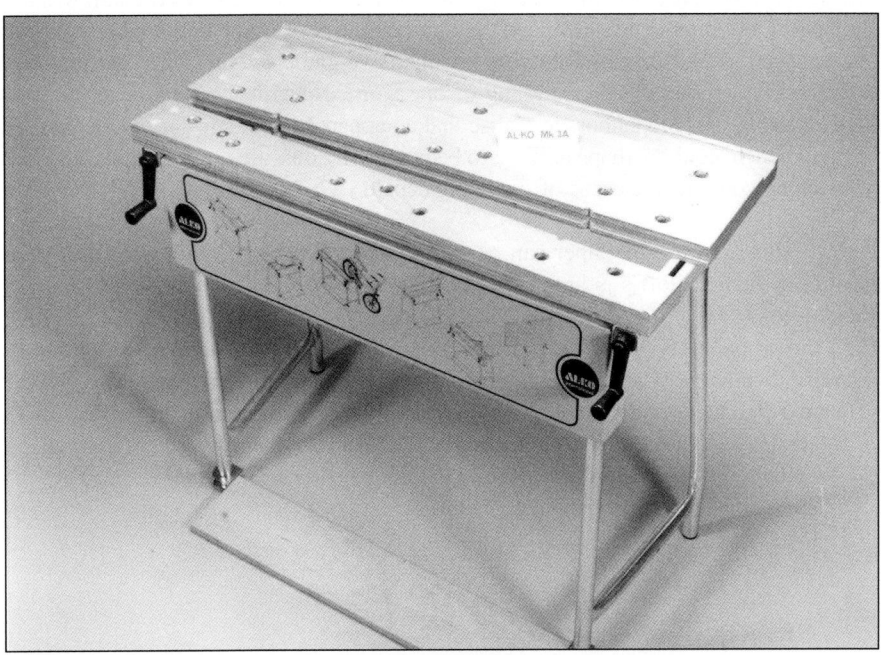

Picture 7: 'ALKO' UK and German competitor

This claim had been drafted in the belief that all significant prior art available world wide was now known from the results of international searches and the searches by examiners in most major examining countries. This is always an unwise assumption and proved to be the case in the British litigation. The defendant presented a new piece of prior art which exercised the minds of the Judges for many days. This came from the book-binding trade and was a small book-binder's press – see picture 8.

Picture 8: 'Russell' book binding press

It comprised two wooden beams each about 18-inches long and was operated in the manner of a clamp by two wooden screws. This so-called 'Russell' press was held by both courts to have all the structural integers of the claim above, but did not satisfy the term 'workbench' at the beginning of the claim. The Court of Appeal upheld Mr Justice Graham's view that the 'Russell' press was not a workbench. In the view of the Court of Appeal, it was far too small to be regarded as a workbench so that the claim was not anticipated and both courts also held that the obviousness attack failed. There may be other instances in patent cases, but they are unknown to the authors, where the question of anticipation turned on the meaning of one word. Nevertheless, it was at the time rather alarming for the authors to realise that an apparently straight-forward term such as 'workbench' could perhaps turn out to be potentially obscure or ambiguous, and that its meaning could be the cause of such long debate.

Perhaps this item on the paper can be summarised best by the following quotation from Lord Justice Goff's judgment in the Court of Appeal:

> It should be observed that the learned Judge (Mr Justice Graham) said that the word 'workbench' is of such generality that you do not get anywhere by consulting various dictionaries, with which we agree, but that the Court of Appeal would know what a workbench is. Mr Justice Graham added: 'You would get a fairly quick answer I should say.' We think that is right and for our part we feel no difficulty in interpreting it.

Litigation in the US

The authors believe that there may be few British patentees and British patent agents who have been involved in full scale litigation to appeal in the US. The authors' experiences perhaps go well beyond the scope of this paper, but a few of the significant aspects may be of interest.

US judges rarely have a technical education, and probably no professional experience in IP prior to elevation to the Judiciary. Also, it is such a contrast with the practice of the UK, where nearly all patent cases are heard in London, to realise that in the US a patent case may come up in any part of the country before a Federal Court Judge who deals with a whole spectrum of legal work and who may have handled few, if any, patent cases. For example, in the WORKMATE litigation in Baltimore in 1981, the judge twice adjourned the hearing to give sentence in drug cases.

It is well recognised practice in the US to assess a client's chances of success, be he patentee or defendant, before any particular judge, and to look at the record of the relevant Appellate Court before commencing proceedings. Whilst the ability of a patentee to commence proceedings in a District of his choice may in some instances be limited, a choice is often present, and such a choice is taken on the basis that the Court of First Instance which is chosen, and the relevant Appellate Court, are perhaps more favourably inclined to patentees than other choices.

As in the case of WORKMATE, this can give rise to intricate manoeuvres at an early stage, commonly called forum-shopping, where the defendant attempts to get the case heard in a District of his choice. The authors' experience involved a separate Declaratory Judgment action started by the defendant in a different District, and also attempts by the defendant to shift the action started by the patentee to a District of the defendant's choice. These initial proceedings in themselves involved significant effort and expense for both parties. For example, evidence was filed by the defendant, endeavouring to show that the court of his choice was better positioned as regards the residence of the two parties, and the distances to be travelled by them in attending depositions and the main trial. These arguments of the defendant were supported by evidence of the comparative distances which Ron Hickman would have to travel from the Channel Islands to the two courts in question, and the defendants exhibited airline and ship timetables to show the different travel times for the inventor between the two courts and, as they put it, 'Downtown Sark'!

These extensive manoeuvres prior to the main action indicated that it could be dangerous to threaten an infringer prior to commencing litigation, since it would give the infringer the opportunity to be the first to commence litigation with a Declaratory Judgment action in a court of his choice. This might well give him an advantage in the forum-shopping exercise to argue that his choice of court should prevail.

At an early stage in the litigation against Sears Roebuck in the US it was decided by Black & Decker that the action, which was heard in the District Court in Baltimore, should be tried by jury. This is not an uncommon practice even with patent cases in the US but it was a unique experience for the authors.

The future

Whilst it might have been tempting for Ron Hickman to relax and enjoy the financial security resulting from the success of WORKMATE, he is in fact still actively involved in the design and development of new ideas, with a team of designers and supporting staff in Jersey. This team, apart from developing ideas of its own, also welcomes ideas from outside inventors. Further successes have included the HANDYJACK Step-Stool, and two exercise machines, the PACER and the ROWER, now marketed by Black & Decker.

Summary

The close co-operation achieved by the two authors, and advisors all over the world, during the 14 years since the original filing of the first British provisional specification has been a most rewarding experience, not simply in financial terms for the inventor, but in the sense that the patent system has been used to the full to extract from it a monopoly for the inventor's designs which, at least at the time of drafting this paper, has withstood virtually all attacks.

These years of effort have been particularly satisfying for myself, the patent agent, since there has been an intense involvement in world-wide patent prosecution, and litigation in many countries, which perhaps relatively few members of the profession have experienced. These years have seen the developing story of an individual's invention struggling to gain acceptance, but eventually reaching a position when the product is today a household word in very many countries.

In the course of his live presentation, Mr Hickman also referred to one aspect of the story, not mentioned in the paper, but which had dominated the efforts to obtain and sustain the patent protection all over the world. This concerned the great variety of prior art which had been brought forward, not only by patent office examiners, but by competitors in attacking the patents either during infringement proceedings or during oppositions, particularly in Germany. In the WORKMATE prior art files there are now hundreds of documents, including examples of material where attempts have been made to mosaic huge factory machines, weighing up two tons or more for clamping engines, with small two-inch jewellers vices. In one German Appeal, the *Bundespatentgericht* refused a basic WORKMATE application, relating to the collapsibility aspect, in the light of art as diverse as beer garden chairs and a hydraulically operated machine, about ten or 12-feet high, which was used for extracting turbine rotors from jet aircraft. Mr Hickman felt that it was extraordinary that the theoretical designer, at the date of the patent, and working in the workbench or sawhorse field, should be presumed to have at his elbow knowledge of, and seek inspiration from, such remote and diverse art.

More encouragingly, despite an attack based on dozens of prior documents, after a very full hearing, during which the court had been presented with a huge array of hardware including all the WORKMATE prototypes, many production models, and competitive benches, as well as the WORKMATE films, to support the 'sub-test' arguments referred to the paper, success had been achieved with two other basic

WORKMATE patent applications, dating from 1969, one directed to the angularity feature of the worktop and the other directed, with claims in very broad terms, to the giant twin-beam worktop-vice idea.

At the end of the authors' commentaries, Mr Hickman said how greatly he had appreciated working with Mr Roos over the years. It was important for any inventor to have the support of his patent agent but in this case, not only had Mr Roos given him good professional advice, but he had also been forthcoming with criticisms much of which turned out to be of great value in the decision making process. There had been fruitful cooperation over many years.

Postscript

By a remarkable coincidence on the same day as the authors were presenting their paper to the Institute, the United States Court of Appeals, Fourth Circuit, delivered its judgment in the WORKMATE litigation against Sears which is referred to elsewhere in the paper. The judgment was in favour of Ron Hickman and his licensees Black & Decker, upholding the validity of both the patents in suit. The Appellate Court held that the jury was correctly instructed by the Judge in the Court of First Instance that use size and proportion may be considered in deciding what is analogous art and the Court also disagreed with the view of Sears that the WORKMATE workbench must be declared obvious as a matter of law.

One other extract from the judgment which may be of interest was as follows:

> It is apparent from the record that the WORKMATE, unlike any of the proposed prior art, is a combination workbench and vice ideal for use by amateur woodworkers and weekend handymen. Also unlike any of the proposed prior art, its vice mechanism is designed to allow secure clamping of irregular shaped objects through angulation of the vise jaws. Its usefulness in clamping a wide variety of workpieces of different shapes and sizes was demonstrated at trial. None of the proposed prior art is appropriate for performing even a small percentage of these functions.
>
> These facts alone would very likely have been sufficient to sustain the jury verdict. However, further evidence of the validity of the WORKMATE workbench can be found in its tremendous commercial success... In this case, the 'indicia of non-obviousness' is particularly strong. Since production began on the WORKMATE in 1968, over 10,000,000 units have been sold worldwide. Over 3,500,000 have been sold in the United States alone, constituting a sales volume of approximately $162,000,000. Certainly such commercial success, virtually unparalleled in the industry, makes it highly unlikely that the WORKMATE is a device which would 'have been obvious... to a person having ordinary skill in the art' when patented in 1971.

EPILOGUE – Ron Hickman OBE
with his wife Helen outside Buckingham Palace after his investiture

The Anywayup Cup

This is the story of a successful individual inventor, how she came to make her invention, what the reaction of the industry initially was, and how she triumphed in the marketplace and in the UK High Court.

Mrs Mandy Haberman has a degree in graphic design from St Martin's School of Art and subsequently worked in the field of adult literacy. In 1982, she had a baby who suffered from severe feeding problems and could not suck from a bottle. She was dissatisfied with the equipment that was available to deal with the problem, and developed a special feeding bottle called the *Haberman Feeder* which is the subject of UK Patent 2169210 and is now marketed worldwide.

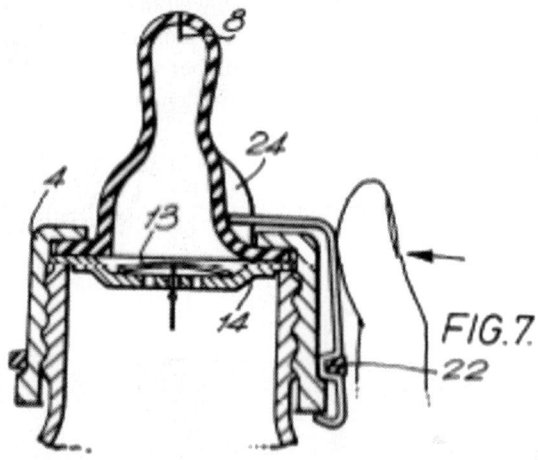

FIG. 7.

She went on to make a second invention relating to trainer cups which is the subject-matter of the present dispute. When infants no longer need a feeding bottle, but before they have learned to use an ordinary cup, they use a feeder cup which has a container closed by a lid and has a spout through which the child can suck the liquid contents into his or her mouth. The lumen of the spout is permanently open, and all the products available in the 1970s and 1980s leaked to some degree. By the early 1990s although the idea of making a leak-proof trainer cup was known to manufacturers, nobody had come up with a design that was completely satisfactory. The products that were available fell into the following main categories:
- cups that simply leaked;
- cups with lids that could be rotated between ON and OFF states by the parent, but which could leak when ON and required parental intervention to turn them OFF;
- cups with snap-on leak-resistant covers, again demanding parental intervention; and
- cups with complicated multi-part mechanical valves that were expensive to make and difficult to clean.

The evidence was that although numerous efforts had been made to design a truly leak-proof trainer cup, no existing design worked well, and that the solutions that had been suggested or put into production were complicated.

In the summer of 1990, Mandy Haberman visited the home of another parent and watched that parent's child drinking from a trainer cup. Her friend was desperately trying to get the milk into the baby and prevent the milk from getting onto the floor. As a result, Mandy decided that she could design a better product, and in particular a trainer cup that would not leak, even if it was:
- turned upside-down and shaken vigorously for ten seconds, or
- left upside down overnight.

Her idea was simply to combine a rubber slit valve that was well known for feeding bottle teats with the spout of a trainer cup. When the child wanted a drink, his or her suction would open the valve, and at other times the valve would close. Mandy built a prototype with a slit valve that worked so well that it could be left upside down for weeks on end without spilling any of its contents. In 1992, she filed a patent application to protect her idea of using a rubber slit valve to control the flow of milk through the spout of a trainer cup, and it was granted as patent GB-B-2266045.

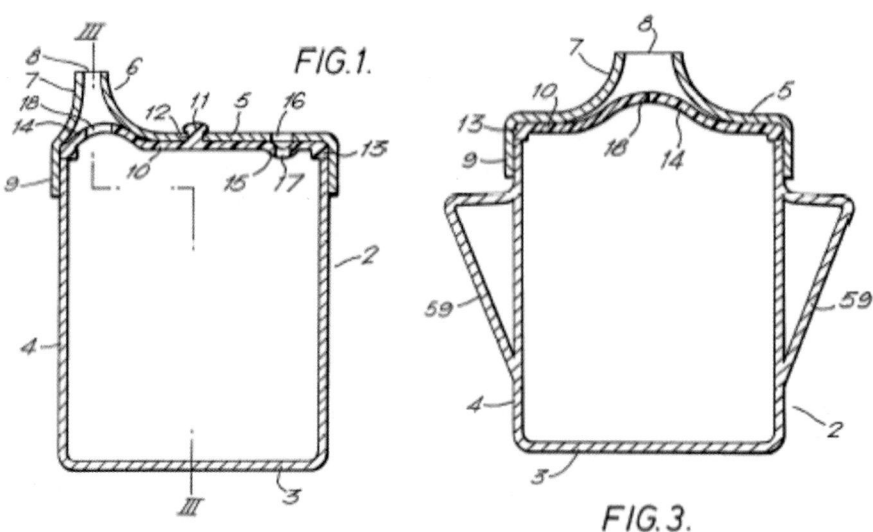

FIG.1.

FIG.3.

Claim 1 of her patent, with bullet points added to make the specified features easier to identify, read as follows:

> A drinking vessel suitable for use as a trainer cup or the like, comprising:
> - an open-mouthed generally cup-shaped container; and
> - a lid for the open mouth of said cup-shaped container,
> - the lid having a mouthpiece associated therewith;
> - the vessel being provided with valve means comprising a self-closing slit valve adapted to prevent flow of liquid from the interior of the container

through the mouthpiece unless a predetermined level of suction is applied to the mouthpiece, and to enable a user to draw liquid through the mouthpiece by the sole application of suction thereto;

- the configuration of the valve means being such that said slit valve is adapted to open upon no more than a predetermined difference of pressure, greater within the vessel than outside, being present across the said valve.

Once she had finalised her prototype, she offered it for licence to 18 companies, mostly British, concerned with the manufacture of products for infants, but they declined to take a licence. Amongst the companies approached were the defendants in the present infringement proceedings, Jackel International Limited. Did they all make a mistake? Of course they did, as subsequent events were to show – a mistake that was smaller in scale, but was similar in kind to that made by record producers who turned down a then unknown pop group called *"The Beatles"* or the publishers who turned down a book by the then unknown author J.K. Rowling concerning a character called "Harry Potter". A strategic product planner responsible for developing a range of trainer cups, knowing the limitations of existing designs, and knowing that the trade was looking for a leak-proof product, should have taken Mandy's prototype very seriously.

Subsequently, Mandy found support from a company in Wales called V & A Marketing limited. At the time V & A was a very small company employing only five people. The judgment records the following milestones along the road to commercial development.

- V & A first went to the market with a version of the trainer cup that was less than glamorous, being described in the judgment as *"dull"* and having *"unconsidered aesthetics"*. They decided to launch the product at a trade exhibition, but selected the wrong one, an exhibition for organisers of nursery schools and creches, not for trade buyers of baby products. They learned of their mistake only a few days before the exhibition opened, and because they had already incurred costs they decided to go ahead. To quote from the judgment:

> The evidence was that the response was overwhelming. The plaintiffs' stand was besieged by would-be customers. Advance orders for £10,000 worth of cups were taken. The plaintiffs also found the correct fair to attend, the Baby & Toddler Fair, and took space there. Once again the product was a success. According to Mr Victor Davies, a director of the second plaintiff, the response was very impressive. Although at the time of these two fairs in the Autumn of 1995 the plaintiffs were not in production and therefore had nothing to sell, a total of 8000 advance orders were taken.

- UK sales began in March 1996 and by 1998 had reached 2 million cups, achieved on the basis of an advertising expenditure of £2100 and expenditure at exhibitions of £15,000, sales being achieved almost entirely by word of mouth and by recommendation from mother to mother. Exceptionally for a new product from a small and unknown source, V & A succeeded in having their product accepted by major supermarket chains such as Safeways and Tesco's within a few months from launch. Their tactics are described in the judgment:

> Mr Llwelyn-Jones decided to send a cup, filled with a highly coloured fruit drink, Ribena, to the buyer at Tesco's in a box without internal packing so that the cup rolled about inside the box. He sent the box by post. Inside he enclosed a letter in which he said that if the contents had leaked he had shot himself in the foot. Apparently the contents did not leak...

During a follow-up interview, Tesco's buyer took only ten minutes to decide to buy the Anywayup Cup.
- In August 1996, a US company called *The First Years Incorporated* approached Mandy for a licence, and they are now her exclusive US licensee, selling trainer cups under the name *Tumble Mates*.
- The Anywayup Cup is now sold through Cow & Gate and through MAPA GmbH.

Once the Anywayup Cup had become established on the market, Jackel decided to market a similar product, taking the view that Mandy's patent was invalid for lack of inventive step. To paraphrase another Mandy (Rice-Davies: famous in 1963 for her involvement in the *Profumo* affair): *Well they would say that, wouldn't they?* Fundamentally Jackel's case was that nothing that Mandy had done was outside the range of normal workshop variation that was available to skilled people, and that she had merely solved a known problem with simple and readily-available expedients, namely a well-known slit valve applied to a well known form of drinking cup. They referred to a number of prior patent specifications, including in particular US-A-5079013 Figs. 1 and 2 which disclosed a trainer cup in which liquid flow through the drinking spout was controlled by a spring-loaded valve. Mandy and V & A denied Jackel's allegations and pointed to the commercial success that they had achieved.

The opinion of Mr Justice Laddie is of legal interest because of the way in which he sought to decide between the evidence of experts in the field employed by the opposing parties, both of whom put forward reasonably held but conflicting opinions. It could be difficult to resolve the conflict created by such evidence because:

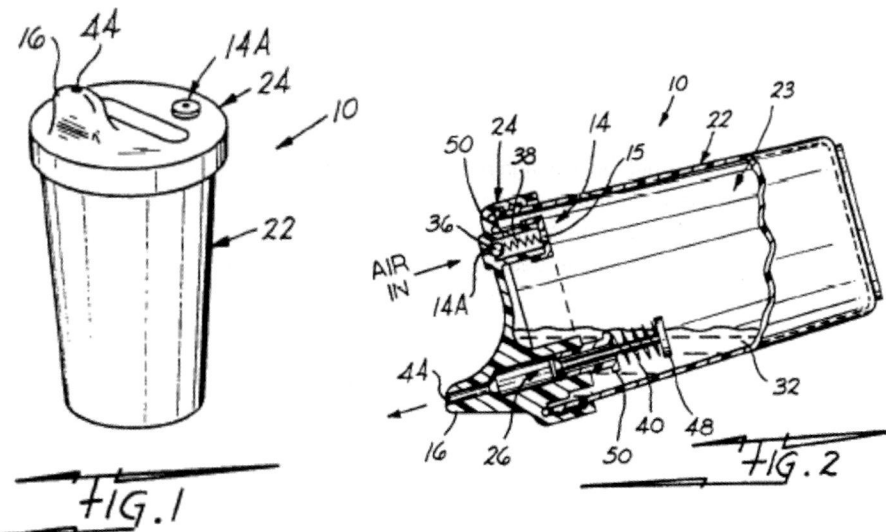

...A problem with evidence from an expert is that he addresses the prior art and the patented development from his own unique standpoint. An expert with the relevant expertise who thinks that the development would have been obvious at the priority date may be right or he may just have greater insight than the notional uninventive man in the art. Likewise an expert who thinks that the development is inventive may be right or may have a more constricted insight...

Laddie J accepted that the defendants had put forward a strong case of lack of inventive step, but went on to conclude that the key question was:

Does it reflect what an ordinary man in the art, steeped in the folklore, perceptions and prejudices of the trade would have done?

He then went on to produce a systematic list of the matters that were of value in determining whether an invention was obvious or not:

(a) What was the problem that the patented development addressed?

(b) How long had that problem existed?

(c) How significant was the problem seen to be?

(d) How widely known was the problem and how many were likely to be seeking a solution?

(e) What prior art would have been likely to be known to all or most of those who would have been expected to be involved in finding a solution?

(f) What other solutions were put forward in the period leading up to the patentee's development?

(g) Were there factors that would have held back the exploitation of the solution, even if it was technically obvious?

(h) How well has the patentee's development been received? Once the product or process was commercialised was it a commercial success?

(i) Was all or much of the commercial success due to the technical merit of the development – i.e. because it solves the problem?

In the present case, there was no dispute about the problem that Mandy's patent sought to solve, nor was it disputed that the problem had existed for a long time. The evidence established that numerous solutions to the problem had been put forward, but that they were all complicated.

These efforts should be set against the simplicity of what Mrs. Haberman suggested. All the raw materials were readily available. The simplest of valves, used frequently in the same trade, could be used to make a product which had all the virtues which anyone designing a product would wish to achieve. The advantages of such a design would have been immediately apparent, once it was thought of. There was nothing holding anyone back...

... On the evidence before me, I accept that the Anywayup cup has been far more successful than the plaintiffs could reasonably have hoped. I also accept that this was almost entirely due to the inclusion within it of the simple slit valve.

...Mrs. Haberman has taken a very small and simple step, but it appears to me to be a step which any one of the many people in the trade could have taken at any time over at least the preceding ten years or more. In view of the obvious benefits which would flow from it, I have come to the conclusion that had it really been obvious to those in the art it would have been found by others earlier, and possibly much earlier. It was there under their very noses. As it was it fell to a comparative outsider to see it. It is not obvious...

Based on the above findings Mandy's patent was held to be valid and infringed.[476] Although the decision of Laddie J was appealed, the parties reached a settlement and his decision is now definitive, at least so far as the UK is concerned. The decision is of legal interest because of what it says about the evaluation of evidence as to obviousness, as well as being an encouragement to private inventors and those working in the small business sector.

What, then, are the lessons that a private individual or small business can derive from Mandy's experience? I suggest that they are as follows:

● An inventor is likely to make a worthwhile invention in a technical field in which he or she has worked or has special experience. Mandy had become alerted to the way in which infants drink and to the deficiencies in existing equipment for them because of the problems that she had encountered with her own child. It is no coincidence that she made two significant inventions in that field.

● Having a good idea is not enough – the inventor has to have the determination and commitment to see the idea through to development and possibly even into production. Ron Hickman, the inventor of the Workmate, met with initial rejection when he had no more than a prototype to offer and was only successful in obtaining a licensee after he had started to manufacture the Workmate and had established a small business that industry could recognise as worthwhile expanding. Similarly, Mandy persevered with her product, got it to the attention of the relevant public, and even after it had become successful was on a stand at the *Tomorrow's World* exhibition personally explaining and selling her invention to interested members of the public.

● In order to obtain a sensible decision concerning a product to be licensed, it is vital to make contact at the appropriate level with somebody who can take a strategic view of new product development, who is sufficiently senior not to be influenced by *"not invented here"* and who has a sufficiently broad viewpoint to appreciate what the invention can do for the potential licensee.

● If the product has been launched and proves successful, the cost of a patent or trade mark infringement action should simply be written into the budget. Hopefully the invention will have a quiet life, in which case the budget earmarked for legal expenses simply becomes part of the profit.

---

476. *Haberman v Jackel International* [1999] FSR 683.

Biographical notes

Paul Cole is a practising UK and European patent attorney, a UK and Community trade mark attorney and a CIPA authorized intellectual property litigator. He read chemistry at University College, Oxford and has an LL.M in advanced litigation from Nottingham Trent University. He has served as an examiner in patent drafting for CIPA and was a member of the committee that successfully negotiated with the UK government for High Court litigation rights for patent attorneys. He has been a member of the CIPA education committee and is currently a member of the litigation and publication committees. He lectures on patent law and practice at UK universities and at conferences organized by CIPA, the American Intellectual Property Law Association and the Japan Intellectual Property Association.

He founded and edited *Intellectual Property Decisions* and has contributed numerous articles to the *CIPA Journal*, *BNA's World Intellectual Property Review*, *European Intellectual Property Review* and *Intellectual Property Quarterly*. He is a past and present contributor to the *CIPA Guide to the Patents Acts*.

Michael Roos after service with the Royal Artillery (1949-1951) joined Kilburn & Strode as a technical assistant to Eric Micklethwait. He passed CIPA finals in 1959 and won the Gill prize. He served as a partner in the firm until his retirement in 1986, being extensively involved in litigation on behalf of Hoover and then on behalf of Ron Hickman.

Eric Micklethwait (*CIPA* July/August/September 1986 page 475 obituary by Michael Roos) As was recorded in the May issue of *CIPA*, Eric Micklethwait passed away on 21 May 1986. He was 79, and died in hospital in Abergavenny, following a heart attack the previous day.

Eric was one of four brothers, each of whom had a notable career, and of whom only Sir Robert Micklethwait survives. Their father, St. John Micklethwait, was Recorder of Reading for 27 years. Eric went to school at Clifton College, and read Mathematics and Mechanical Sciences at Corpus Christi College, Cambridge, from 1925-1928. During the General Strike in 1926 many students were recruited to man various public utilities. Eric, being a very practical engineer, enlisted with others from the Cambridge Engineering School, to provide the maintenance team for the trams of Hull. He used to recall that the trams were driven by Oxford undergraduates, and hence needed much maintenance!

Eric's entry into the profession was as an articled pupil with Boult, Wade & Tennant, and he passed the Institute Qualifying Examination in 1933. Shortly afterwards he joined Kilburn & Strode and became a partner in 1937, retiring from the firm in 1981.

The, Transactions of the Institute record his wide interest in all matters touching the profession, and in 1946 he wrote his famous paper entitled "Brushing Up Our

Drafting" (Institute Transactions Vol. LXV, p.71). This is still regarded very highly and is quoted as essential reading for entrants to the profession.

During the Second World War, Eric joined the School of Tank Technology at the Military College of Science. He became an expert on tank design and, as well as teaching at the school, he was the author of various manuals on the subject. His lectures of that era are still regarded with such high esteem that, in more recent years, he was invited to make a formal presentation of his lecture notes to the Museum of the Tank Regiment.

From his early days in the profession, Eric showed that he was a clear thinker, and he had a remarkable ability when working with his clients, of being able quickly to ferret out the real inventive step from a mass of unpromising material. He also had the ability to express himself with clarity and precision.

He was an excellent teacher, insisting on high standards of drafting in his pupils, for which they are, to this day, most grateful. He was never impatient with them, nor hurtful with his comments, for example when' handing back a feeble draft to be done again. His clients also appreciated his qualities, and, even though his recommendations may sometimes have seemed unwelcome, they were usually right.

A strong supporter of the Institute, he was elected to the Council in 1938, and became President in 1956. He served on most of the Council's committees, several of which he chaired with considerable distinction. Whenever Eric spoke at the Institute, whether at formal meetings, or in Council or committee, he immediately commanded attention. Even if members disagreed with him on an issue, they were left in no doubt as to the reasons for the views he held. An example was the proposal to merge CIPA and ITMA which he strongly, and successfully, opposed.

Eric's often used, and perhaps classic, phrase "I have no strong views" belied quite firm, and at times somewhat rebellious, opinions. He was never afraid to attack "sacred cows" where he felt strongly that change was required. Nevertheless, he was greatly respected, and it was this regard, coupled with gratitude for a virtual lifetime of remarkable service to the Institute, which led to the bestowal on Eric in 1982 of Honorary Membership. In 1958, Eric was a member of the official UK delegation to the Diplomatic Conference in Lisbon for the revision of the Paris Convention.

The intense international activity in the patent field in the later period of Eric's working life required all the skill of both himself and other experienced members of the Institute in order to guide the government as the movement towards the European and Community Patent Conventions developed.

One example of Eric's "strong views" was his almost passionate dislike of the Germanic "two-part" claim, which he felt provided an unnecessary restraint on good claim drafting. It was this strong opinion which assisted in the eventual inclusion in the European Rules of the words "wherever appropriate", thus providing for the omission of the characterising clause in some circumstances.

Eric also developed an interest and expertise in Plant Variety Rights, both in the UK and internationally.

Eric's interests outside the profession included membership of the Worshipful Company of Salters.

Whilst he was not a motoring fanatic, he liked large and venerable cars, and, at one time or another, he owned a Bean, a Bentley, in which he toured the Continent with Freddy Leistikow, a rare boat-decked Delage and several old Rolls-Royces, one of which the author of this obituary had the pleasure of borrowing for his honeymoon, 30 years ago.

Michael J. Daley (*CIPA* March 1997 p. 233, written by Tom Tribe) Michael Daley died at the age of only 60 on 21 January after a brave fight against cancer.

He was educated at Repton, did two years national service during which time he learnt the Russian language, went to Cambridge to study Natural Sciences, but decided to stay for only one year. He entered the patent profession in 1957. After his father died in 1961 his brother ran the family textile business in Nottingham with help from Michael, and this commercial experience proved invaluable later on in his professional career.

In common with many of his contemporaries, his first few years in the profession were spent in a variety of locations. He started at Sanderson & Co in 1957, where he met Joy his wife to be. He then moved on to Forrester Ketley & Co with whom he stayed from 1959 to 1964 and where he started a lifelong friendship with Chris Howden. After that he had a short spell with Philips Electrical from 1964 to 1965 – during which time he qualified and became a Fellow of the Institute – and then with A.A. Thornton & Co. from 1966 to 1967 before finally joining F.J. Cleveland & Company in mid-1967. He became a full partner there in 1972.

In his early years in the profession he was an energetic member of the Institute, being an active member and lecturer at the Informals, and later he put this same energy into the UNION of European Practitioners in Industrial Property.

He became President of the British Group of UNION in 1980 after having served for a number of years as Honorary Secretary. He was also active as a British Representative on the Executive Committee of the main body of UNION, serving as Secretary-General for a number of years and also taking the Chair of several specialist committees.

He was very knowledgeable and interested in the law of industrial designs and served on various international committees relating to the development of law in this area. In particular he served on the Institute Committee which made recommendations to Parliament prior to the introduction of the 1988 Act.

Within FJ Cleveland his early commercial experience was invaluable to the running of the practice and he played a central role from the time he became a partner until he retired from the partnership in 1994.

Almost from the moment he joined the partnership, Michael took an active interest in the running of the firm's records and renewals section. He completely re-organised the records system at the time of the 1977 Act with a view to introducing a computerised records system in the early 1980s.

Michael was also a firm believer in continuing professional education, and he started a series of weekly lunchtime educational meetings for the technical staff (partners and TAs) at FJ Cleveland. These meetings soon became an institution within the company and his lively interest in IP law in general served to awaken the awareness of his colleagues to some of the more recondite aspects of law and practice as it affects our profession.

Both through his activities with UNION and in furthering the business of FJ Cleveland, Michael developed a wide circle of professional friends and associates. Since the announcement of his death large numbers of letters have been received by Joy and by the firm from many parts of the world which have included warm tributes, and this is a measure of his international standing.

He had many interests outside the patent profession. In his early years, he was an enthusiastic hill-walker, rock climber and cyclist. Michael was keenly interested in old and unusual books, he was a knowledgeable and hands-on expert in relation to clocks of which he had a fine collection and indeed he had an impressive regulator clock in his home which he had constructed himself; and he was actively involved in his local branch of the National Association of Decorative and Fine Arts. He enjoyed music, particularly opera, and was something of an expert in wines having visited many wine-producing areas with his local wine society.

After his retirement, Michael undertook an active consultancy with FJ Cleveland and found that wonderful balance between business and pleasure that others find so difficult to achieve.